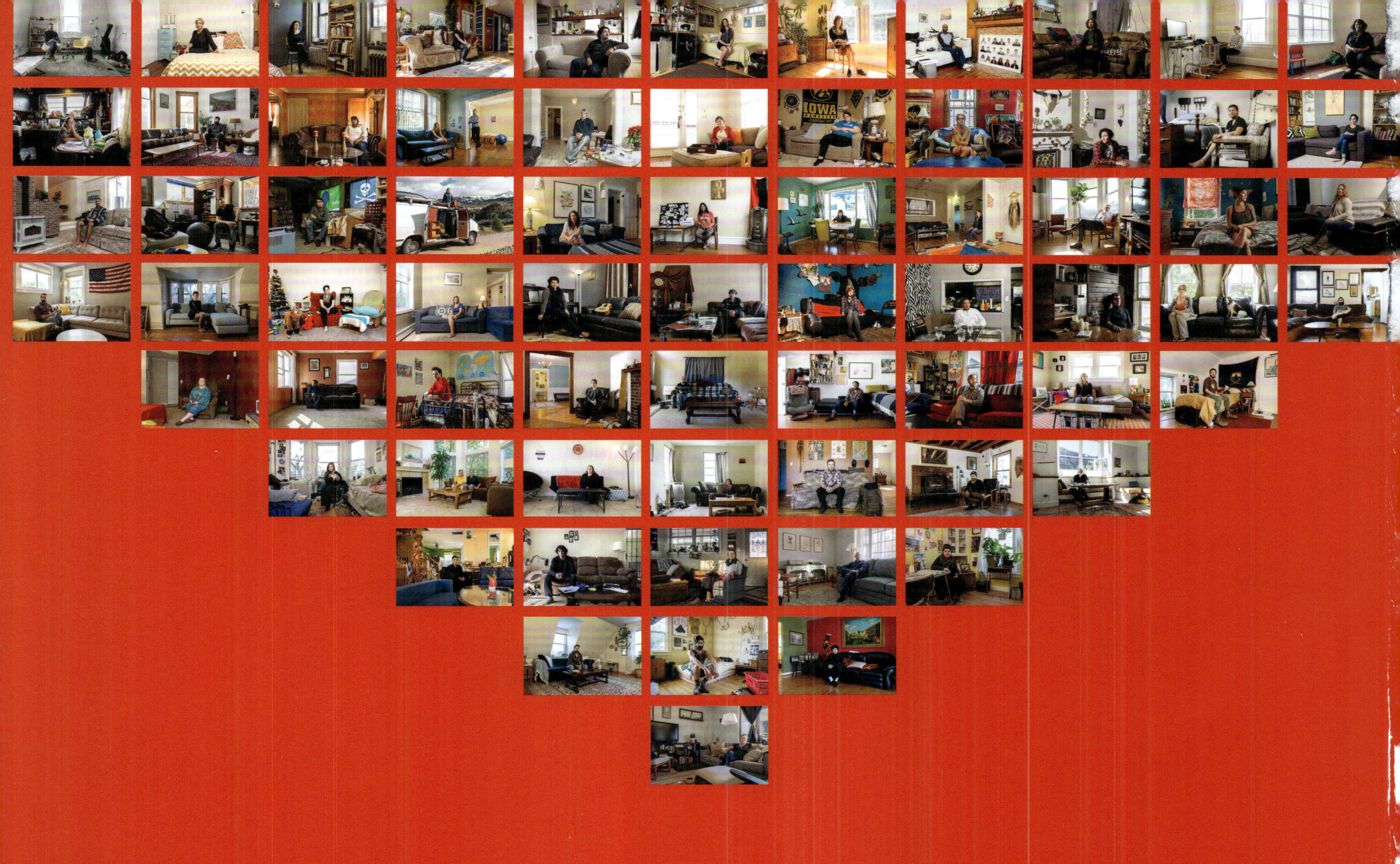

THE DEBT PROJECT
99 PORTRAITS ACROSS AMERICA
BRITTANY M. POWELL WITH A FOREWORD BY ASTRA TAYLOR

GRAPHIC ARTS BOOKS

Library of Congress Cataloging-in-Publication Data

Names: Powell, Brittany M, author.
Title: The debt project : 99 portraits across America / Brittany M Powell ;
    with a foreword by Astra Taylor.
Description: Berkeley : West Margin Press, 2020. | Summary: "The Debt Project
    is a photo series of 99 portraits and handwritten stories of debt across
    the US"—Provided by publisher.
Identifiers: LCCN 2020016450 (print) | LCCN 2020016451 (ebook) |
    ISBN 9781513264332 (hardback) | ISBN 9781513264349 (ebook)
Subjects: LCSH: Debt—United States. | Debt—United States—Pictorial works.
Classification: LCC HG181 .P665 2020 (print) | LCC HG181 (ebook) | DDC 332.7/43092273—dc23
LC record available at https://lccn.loc.gov/2020016450
LC ebook record available at https://lccn.loc.gov/2020016451

Proudly distributed by Ingram Publisher Services.

Printed in China
5 4 3 2 1

Graphic Arts Books
is an imprint of

WEST
MARGIN
PRESS
WestMarginPress.com

WEST MARGIN PRESS
Publishing Director: Jennifer Newens
Marketing Manager: Angela Zbornik
Project Specialist: Gabrielle Maudiere
Editor: Olivia Ngai
Design & Production: Rachel Lopez Metzger

This book is dedicated to my son, Waylon Pcwell Zuaro, who I hope will one day live in a world where equality is the default, instead of the goal.

FOREWORD

It is always hard to see an absence. What does lack look like? How do you represent the existence of debt, of accounts past due, in a world obsessed with affluence and plenty? Brittany Powell's powerful series *The Debt Project* offers a compelling and moving visual response to these urgent questions.

As a writer, filmmaker, and organizer, I have been working in various media to make the crisis of indebtedness both visible and actionable, and to transform it from a source of individual shame and anxiety into an opportunity for shared indignation and solidarity. After all, being broke is something we are socialized not to discuss, even though most people are in arrears. We need to break this silence and be honest about the financial burdens we all carry. That is the only way to expose and transform the complex system of debt and credit that dictates the terms and conditions under which so many of us live.

Debt is a paradoxical thing. Every balance owed is someone else's asset, a source of interest and income for lenders positioned to profit. Those assets are a key way a handful of vast fortunes grow. In 2019, three billionaires held more wealth together than half of the country's population combined. But the math isn't that surprising. The same year it was reported that the average

American dies with a negative balance of over $60,000 hanging over them. When you add up the balances of millions of people who are worth less than nothing, even zero proves impossible to reach.

It is time for a moral accounting. Who actually owes what to whom? What debts are just and which are unjust? These questions took on a new urgency when the coronavirus pandemic crashed the global economy in early 2020. The outbreak precipitated a dual crisis, a medical one and a financial one. As people across the country were ordered to "shelter in place" for the physical health of their communities, countless jobs disappeared almost overnight.

These images help explain why the economic devastation was so fast and furious for so many people, for they offer a window into the period just before coronavirus appeared on the scene. Since debtors by definition have no savings, a loss of income means falling deeper into a debt trap or spiraling into default. Contrary to the myth of the profligate spender, the vast majority of people borrow money to make ends meet. Hundreds of millions of regular working Americans pay for housing, medical care, and schooling with credit. They barely manage to hold on by a thread, and in early

2020 that delicate thread snapped in two.

Most borrowers are not in debt because they live beyond their means; they are in debt because they are denied the means to live. That was as true last year as it is today. In countries that have universal health care, medical debt is unheard of; in the United States, medical debt is the leading cause of bankruptcy and the prospect of accruing medical debt discourages people from seeking the treatment they need. If we had tuition-free public college available to all, educational debt would virtually disappear. If workers were paid fairly for their labor, predatory payday lenders and many credit card companies would be forced out of business. Instead, decades of flatlining wages and the deregulation of the financial sector have fueled the explosion of consumer debt.

The Debt Project reveals the human faces and stories behind the numbers and statistics. What does debt look like? It is not just a number on a past-due notice. Debt looks like a human being. It looks like a mother taking out a title loan on her car, a child denied nourishment because her parents owe the school "lunch debt," a senior citizen having their tax returns garnished to settle a judgment, a patient jailed because they can't pay their hospital bill.

Debt looks like me in 2008, the year I defaulted on my student loans because I couldn't pay my monthly balance and rent at the same time, especially not in the midst of an economic crisis. And yet, instead of being offered a lifeline, my loan servicer punished with an even higher principal and pushed deeper into a financial hole while destroying my credit. What if, back then, I had encountered *The Debt Project*? I could have seen that my circumstances, which felt so humiliating and desperate, were hardly unique.

Fortunately, I eventually found others in the same boat. Around the time Powell started her project, a revolt began to brew. The Debt Collective, a union for debtors I cofounded, was born of the Occupy Wall Street movement that also inspired Powell's decision to feature 99 portraits. (It was Occupy, after all, that popularized the idea of the 99%.) The Debt Collective is a union of sorts. We aim to help debtors come together and wield their financial obligations as leverage. In 2015 we launched a strike, with hundreds of people refusing to pay their student loans. Since then, we have won over $1.5 billion of debt abolition for tens of thousands of borrowers, and put the proposal for a student loan jubilee—the mass cancellation of all student debt—on the national agenda.

I see Powell's work as part of this insurgency. She uses her camera to challenge preconceptions. The subjects featured in this book have a grace and dignity. They are in their homes, sometimes looking into the lens but often gazing toward the distance. They do not appear guilty or repentant, but honest, sympathetic, and unashamed. This is vital, because for centuries debtors were regarded as criminals who could be locked away and denied their basic democratic rights. Debtors, it was believed, deserved to be punished, a dehumanizing attitude that lingers on today.

And yet, debtors are fighting back. They are finding each other and recognizing, as The Debt Collective's motto insists, that they are "not a loan." My hope is that this alliance of debtors will grow, and that they will be not only dignified but defiant. Our economic system is an abomination. Why should people be forced into debt because they want to learn, or because they had bad luck and got laid off, or became ill, or because they need shelter or food to eat? Why should debtors dutifully make payments when profiteers deny all of us the public services and protections people need to weather a pandemic, a depression, or whatever the next disaster might be?

Forget debt forgiveness—we must demand justice. In order to make that demand together, more debtors must come out of the shadows. I hope Powell's powerful and empowering photographs will give more people the courage to do so.

Astra Taylor
March 2020

INTRODUCTION

> Like air, [debt is] all around us, but we never think about it unless something goes wrong with the supply. Certainly it's a thing we've come to feel is indispensable to our collective buoyancy. In good times we float around on it as if on a helium-filled balloon; we rise higher and higher, and the balloon gets bigger and bigger, until—poof!—some killjoy sticks a pin into it and we sink. But what is the nature of that pin?
> —Margaret Atwood, *Payback: Debt and the Shadow Side of Wealth*

I started *The Debt Project* in 2013, just months after concluding the process of filing for bankruptcy in San Francisco court. Coincidentally, I completed this work seven years later—exactly the amount of time it took for the bankruptcy to be removed from my credit report and financial record. And unfortunately, I am writing this introduction in March 2020, as the COVID-19 asteroid hits the US economy.

In 2012, after several years of struggling with a significant income loss from my photography business after the 2008 economic decline, my personal and business debt had skyrocketed. I had essentially gained in debt what I had lost in income. I was struggling—cobbling together freelance photography assignments, teaching surfing lessons on the weekends, and barely making my rent and bills.

I had a résumé I felt good about. I'd spent two years working on a project for National Geographic—a dream job—but I also had undergraduate loans from college, lived in one of America's most expensive cities, and

just couldn't ever quite make ends meet. I was always inches away from a disaster, putting car repairs and pet vet bills on a credit card, or charging necessities and gasoline because I had to pay my rent or make payments on my debt. I lived in an apartment with three roommates, bought groceries with food stamps, and got my health care through Medi-Cal. I didn't understand that many others around me were struggling with debt too, because we didn't talk about it. I thought the problem was me. Looking back, I was working as hard as anyone.

The difficult decision to file for bankruptcy sparked my interest in investigating the role that debt plays in how we relate to one another socially and financially in our culture. I was surprised that once I filed, I no longer felt ashamed about my experience, and I wanted to talk to others about theirs. There was something incredible about the weight that disappeared overnight. I felt like I could breathe again, like I could finally learn to live within my means.

The theme of debt is a loaded one—it

exploits issues of identity, morality, class, politics, and shame. The topic of debt is stigmatized, a social epidemic that is publicly enforced but privately experienced. From that position, it wields great power. Debt is in many ways an abstract form without material weight or structure, yet with heavy physicality and burden in a person's everyday life.

I began *The Debt Project* by asking subjects to sit for a portrait and an interview in their homes, surrounded by their belongings, and to handwrite the amount of debt they have and the story behind how their debt accumulated. These "stories of debt" are an important part of the project. They are meant to serve as a document and testimony that is a personal, measured representation of the abstracted form that debt takes and its invisible role in our lives. They are also a way for subjects to tell their individual stories— their own feelings about their situation or the debt system at large.

I wanted to photograph 99 people in total, across America, in widespread diverse geographic areas, in order to recontextualize a nebulous, often shamed experience. I wanted to help people feel less alone in their situation and put a face to the average, everyday experience most of us have with debt.

I chose the number 99 in reference to the political slogan "We are the 99%," coined by the Occupy Wall Street movement. The slogan directly refers to the income and wealth inequality in the United States, where the wealth is concentrated among the top 1% of citizens.

At first I met my subjects through word of mouth. I'd spoken in detail with a few people about our shared experiences, and they wanted to participate. There seems to be no shortage of people in debt, but far fewer who are willing and comfortable discussing it. This is less an obstacle than it was initially in the time since I began the project.

I wanted to break that silence. Eighty out of 99 pictures in *The Debt Project* are of strangers I connected with through the internet across 17 states. To actually sit with someone you've just met and discuss your finances for an hour is a significant experience for most people. As the project grew, I primarily used Craigslist.org to find subjects. I posted an ad, usually in the gigs or part-time work section, seeking people in debt for a photo project. I paid people anywhere from $25 to 50 for their time, depending on my available resources for the project.

The Debt Project took far longer than I ever imagined it would, but upon completion, the project includes a diverse representation of the average American's economic reality for almost a decade. What I found were stories that were both unique and average about debt, told by subjects as young as

19 and as old as 74. Some of my subjects were still paying their own student loan debt while now paying for their children's college tuition. There are stories of people who couldn't afford health insurance and now carry astronomical medical debt as a result of being uninsured. There are stories of people who tried to do the right thing, and were penalized for it. What unites them all is the failed system that continues to exist.

The politics surrounding debt have changed since 2013 when I began the project. Before the COVID-19 pandemic, as we entered the 2020 election year, people had already begun discussing it more openly. Two Democratic presidential candidates addressed student loan debt specifically as part of their respective platforms. It seems widely acknowledged that an alternative strategy based on a campaign of mutual support and collective refusal, plus a social practice of deshaming, is long overdue.

As I write this in mid-March, with the federal government weighing a trillion-dollar emergency injection of stimulus to the economy, I honestly have no idea what the economic and financial picture will be for America's 99% when this book comes out— if it does. The projections of unemployment are staggering. I know the amount of debt will be crushing.

We are all in this together. We always were, but it took a global event of this magnitude to make it clear. I hope that when we rise from the ashes of the COVID-19 pandemic, we leave the stigma of debt behind. These images can be a record of the time before.

Brittany Powell
March 2020

THE DEBT PROJECT
99 PORTRAITS ACROSS AMERICA

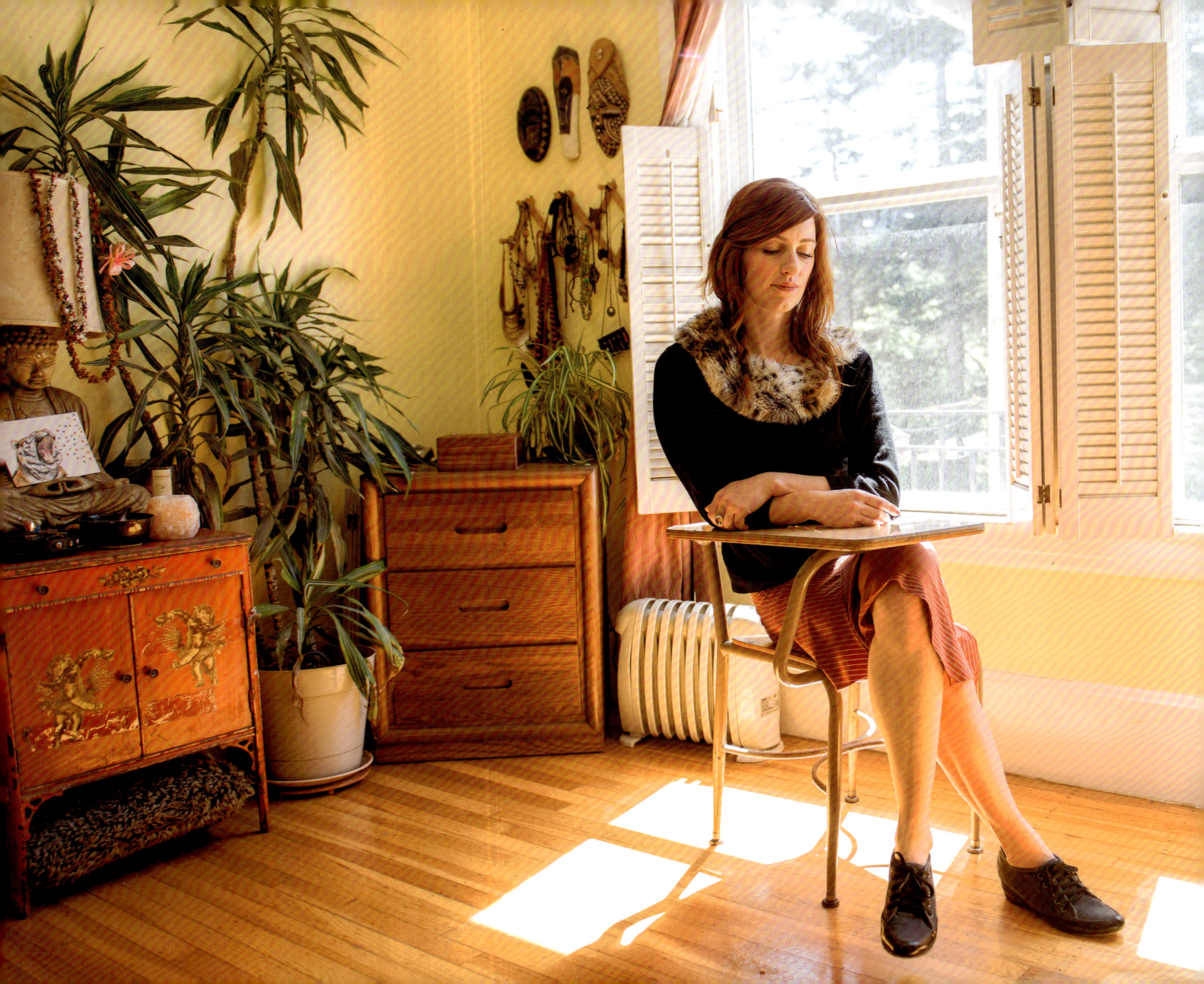

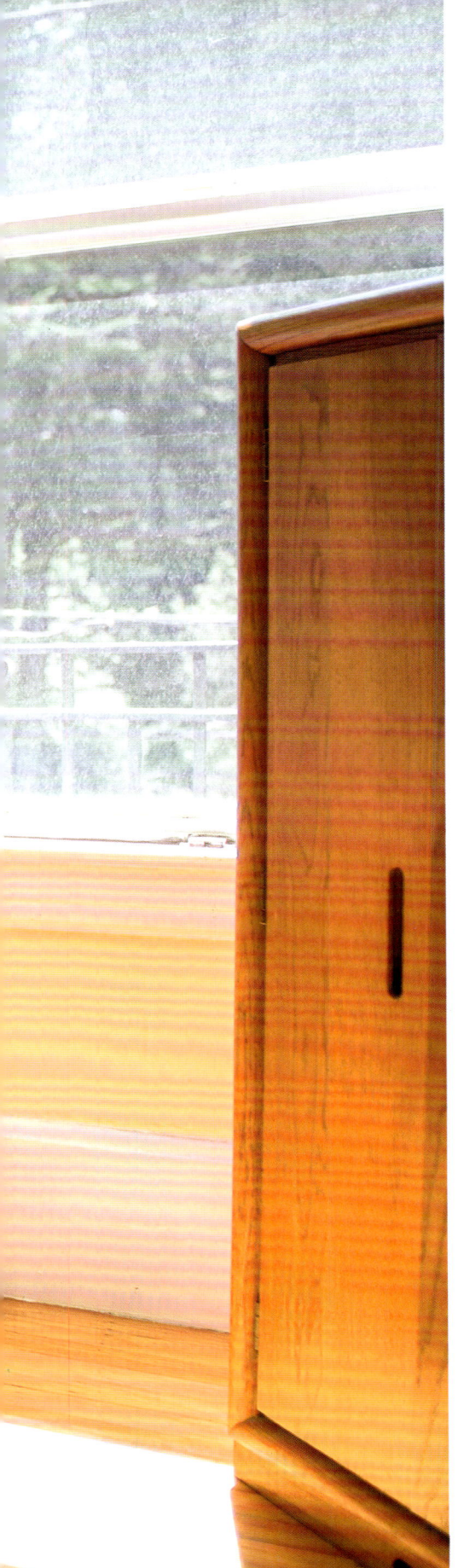

Danielle Brandon
Hair stylist
$ 12,324.00

In my early 20s i got a credit card to "build credit". They some how gave me a $6,000 limit. At the time i never had money to pay bills & eat. so i decided to buy a little new clothes. Why not? soon that avalanched until i could not pay off my dept at the end of the month. Dental bills, car repair, plane tickets at times groceries & gas were put on the card. No matter how i try to chip away i can never seem to get out from under it. even though i live a frugal life.

Debt Portrait #1, San Francisco, CA 2013

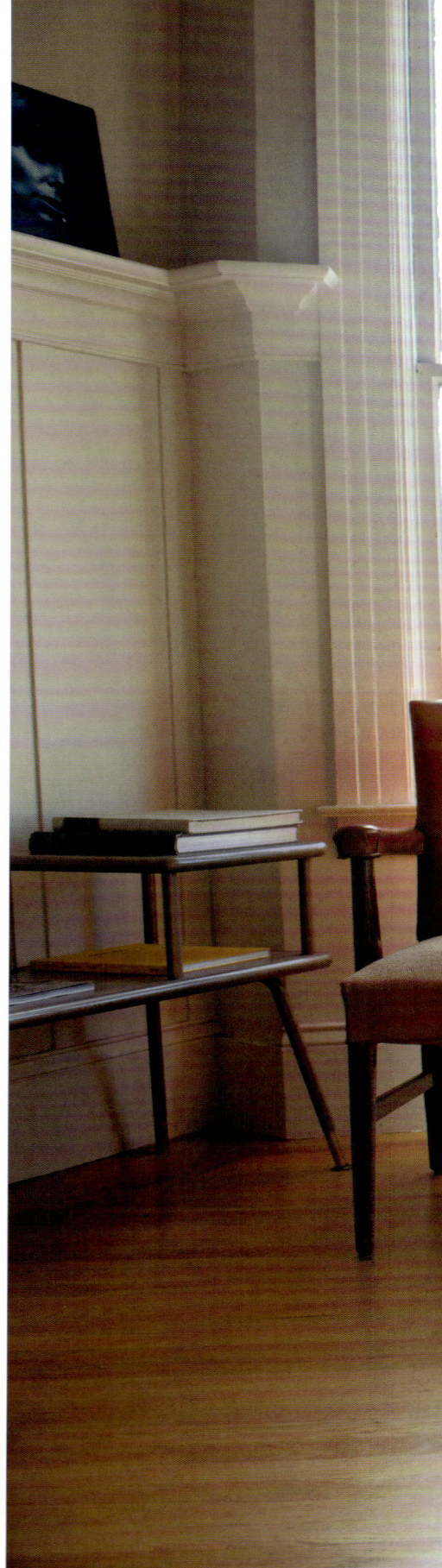

JAMES M. THOMAS

GRADUATE STUDENT / WRITER

24,500

I've been in and out of graduate school since 2003, with brief stints of full-time work in between degrees.

Although I have (had!) a small amount of savings, it was never commensurate with my decisions to ~~❖~~ attend an expensive school, ~~❖~~ cover the difference between income (fellowships, etc) and monthly expenses, or ~~❖~~ support my desires to live in expensive cities (New York, San Francisco).

Debt Portrait #2, San Francisco, CA 2013

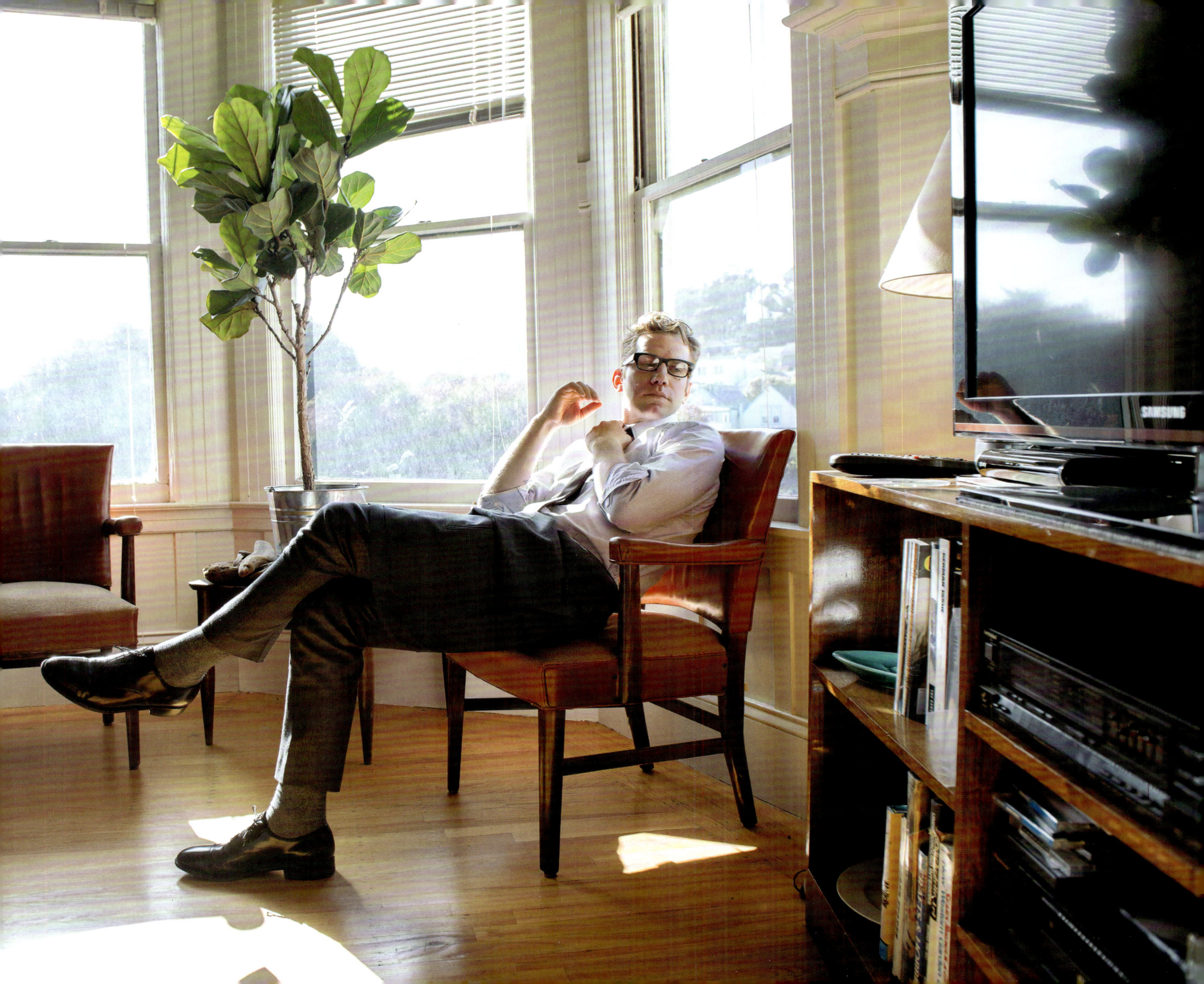

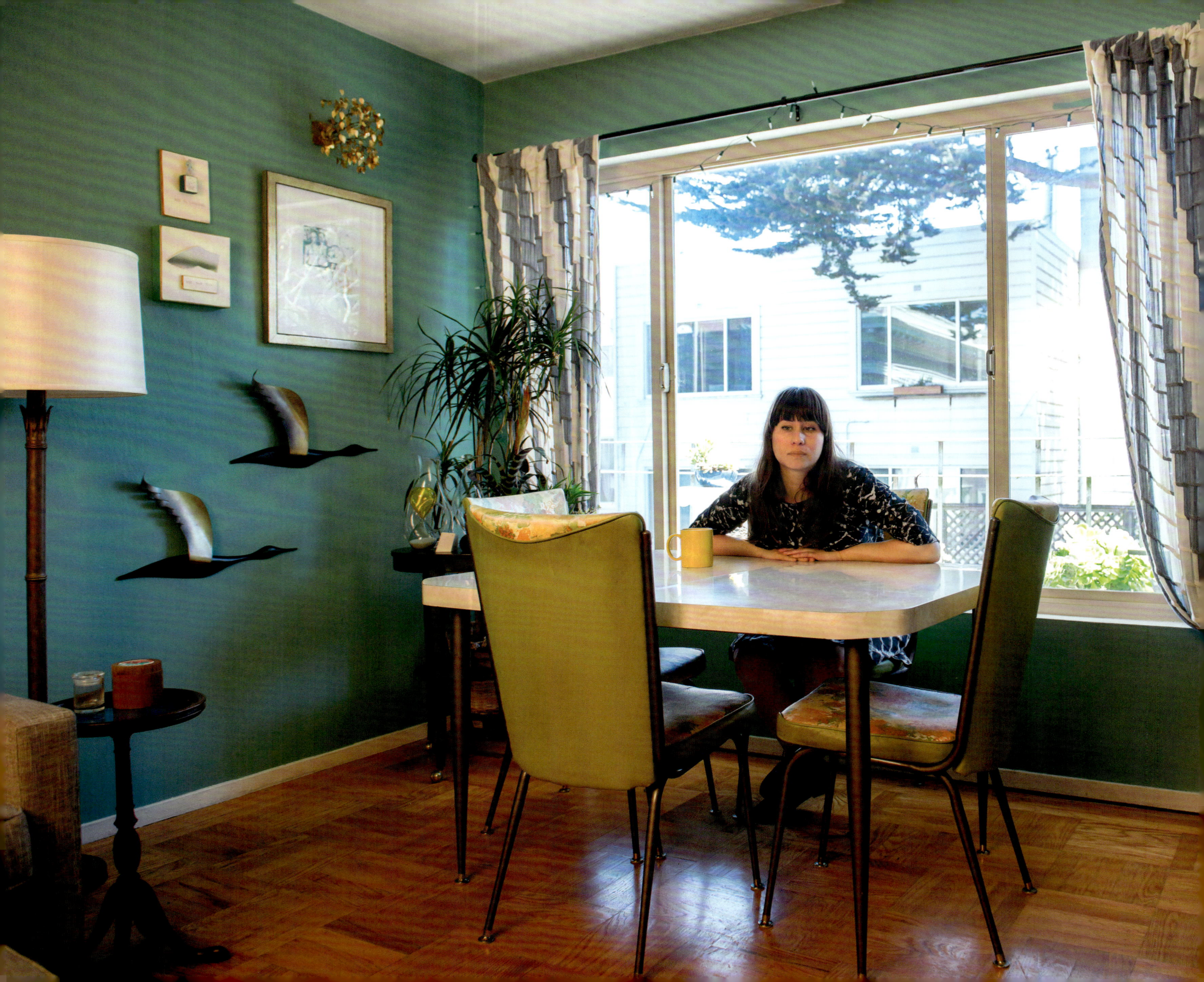

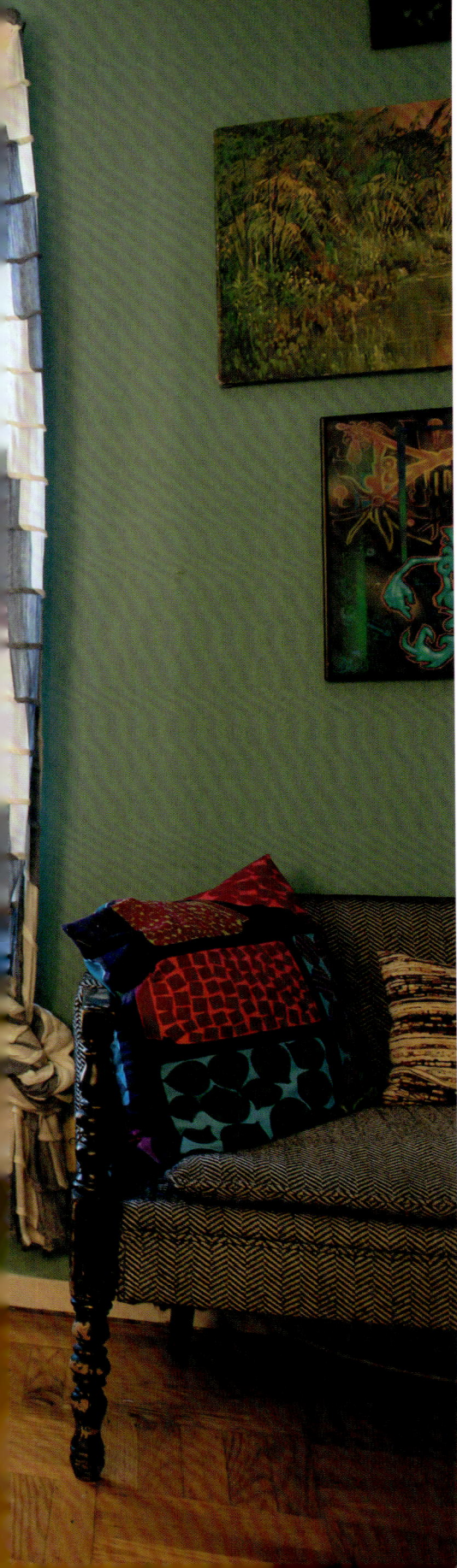

SHAREEN JALLAD
MASSAGE THERAPIST
$10,120.98

I was given a high credit line after
receiving Life Insurance money.
While greiving and not working
I accumulated over $20k in debt
on frivolous spending

Debt Portrait #3, San Francisco, CA 2013

TAYLOR NAIRN

SURVEYER AND DATA MANAGER FOR A
LONG-TERM SHORELINE MONITORING PROJECT

$ 59,636.27

STUDENT LOANS AND BEING NAIVE ABOUT
FINANCES - ALSO THE FACT THAT WE LIVE
IN A CULTURE THAT VALUES DEBT AND
MONEY MORE THAN EDUCATION AND THE
NEXT GENERATION.

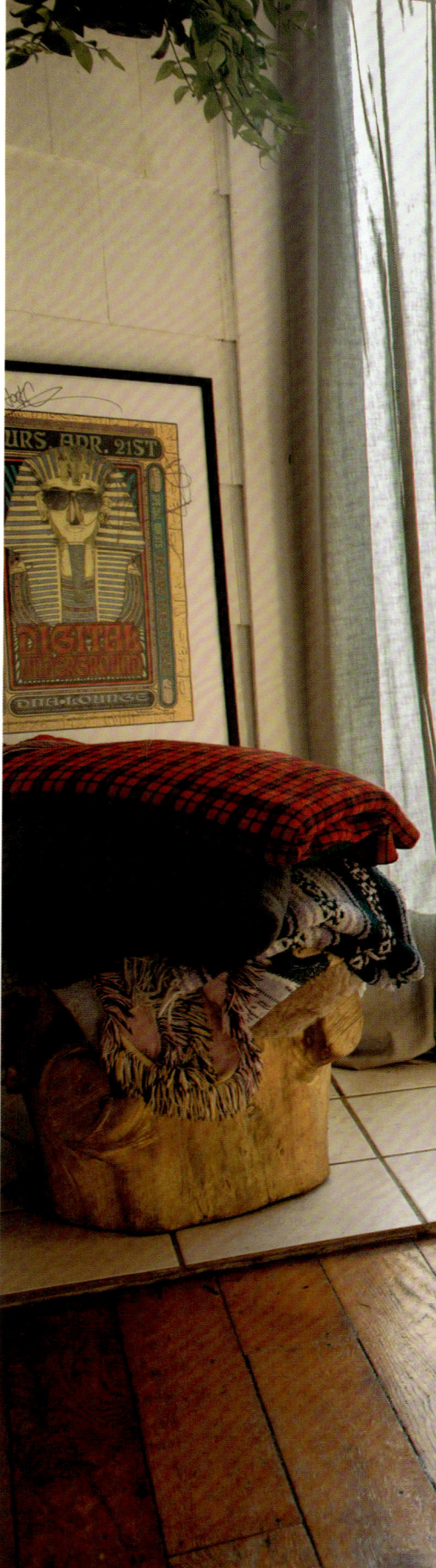

Debt Portrait #4, San Francisco, CA 2013

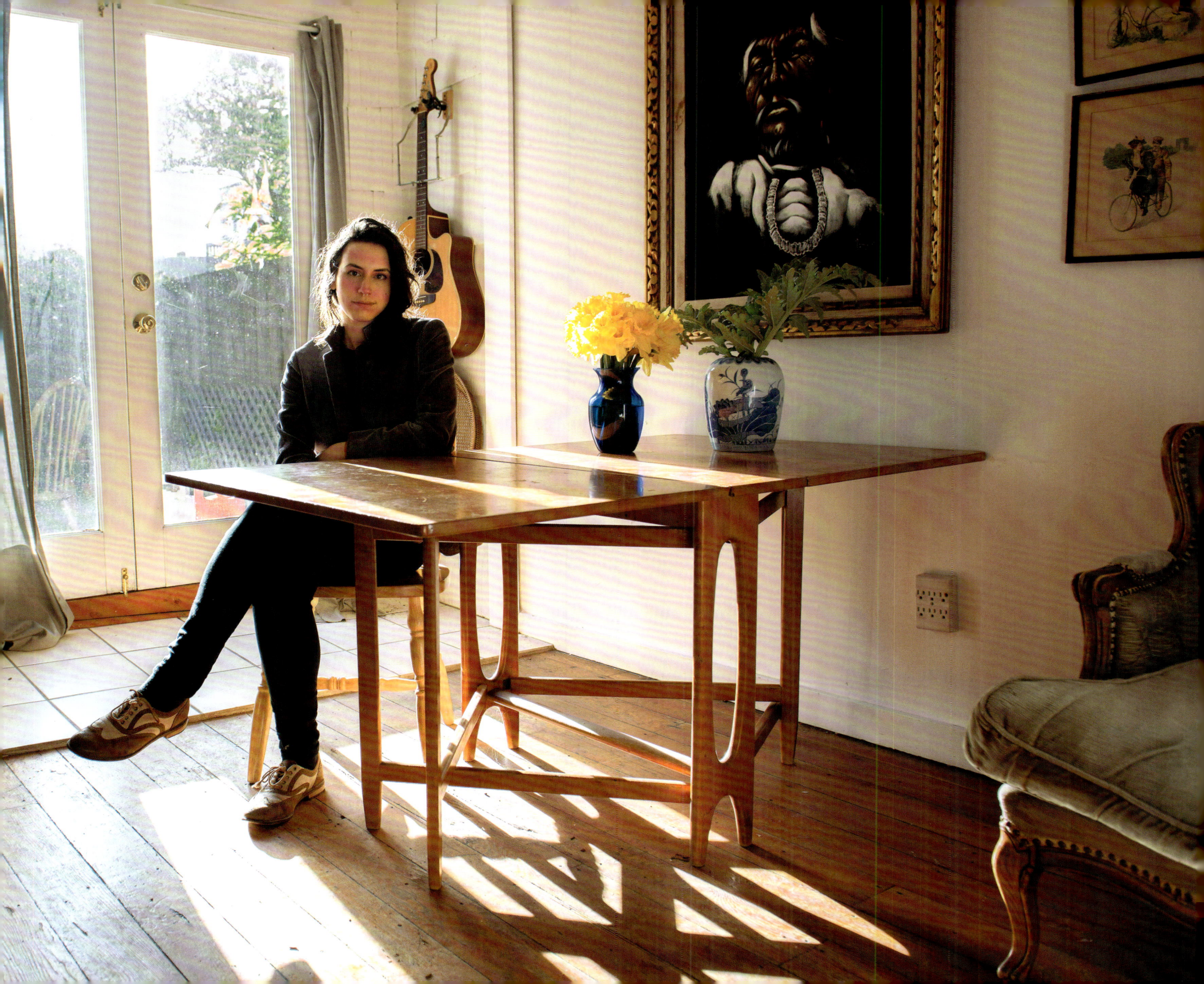

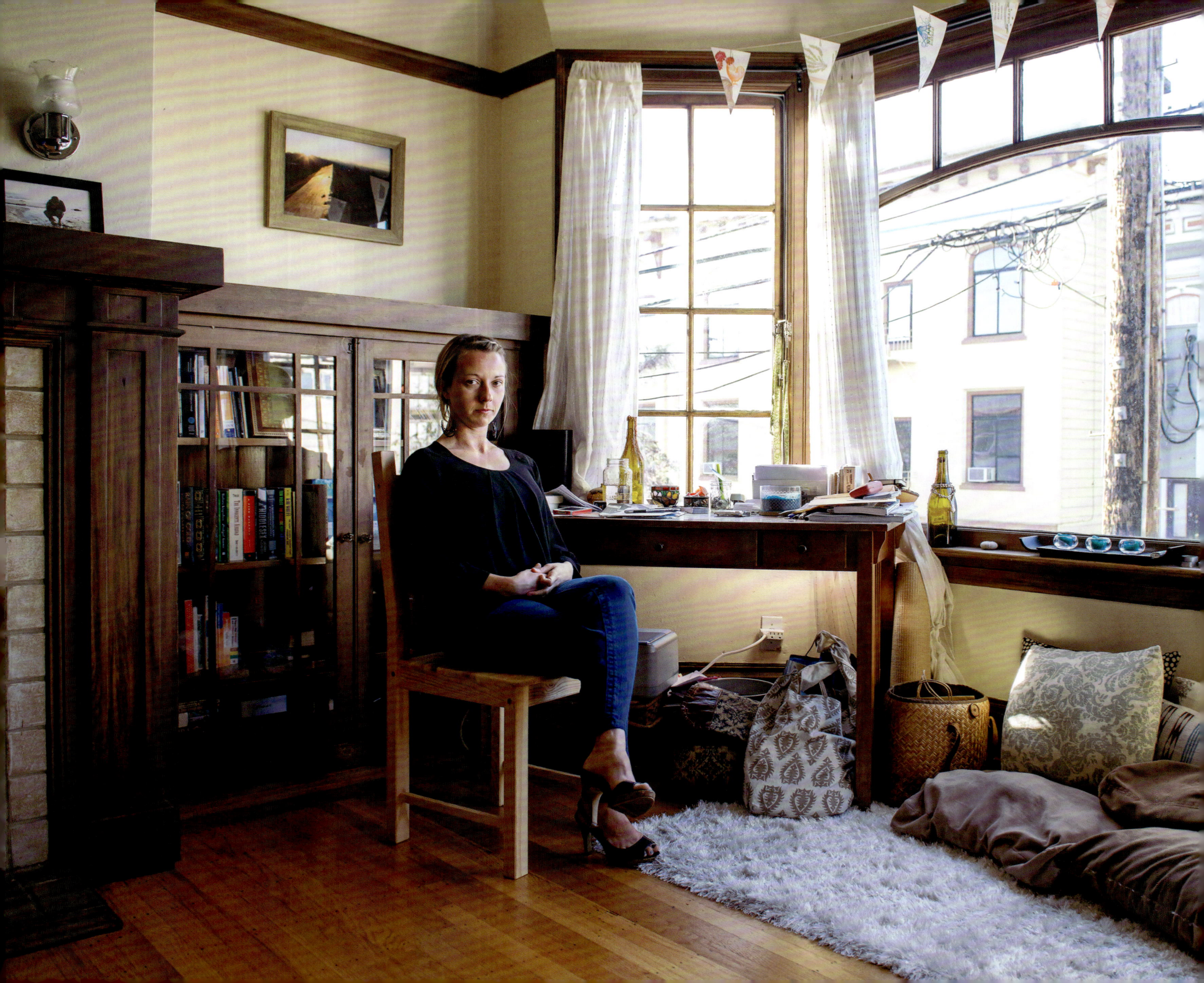

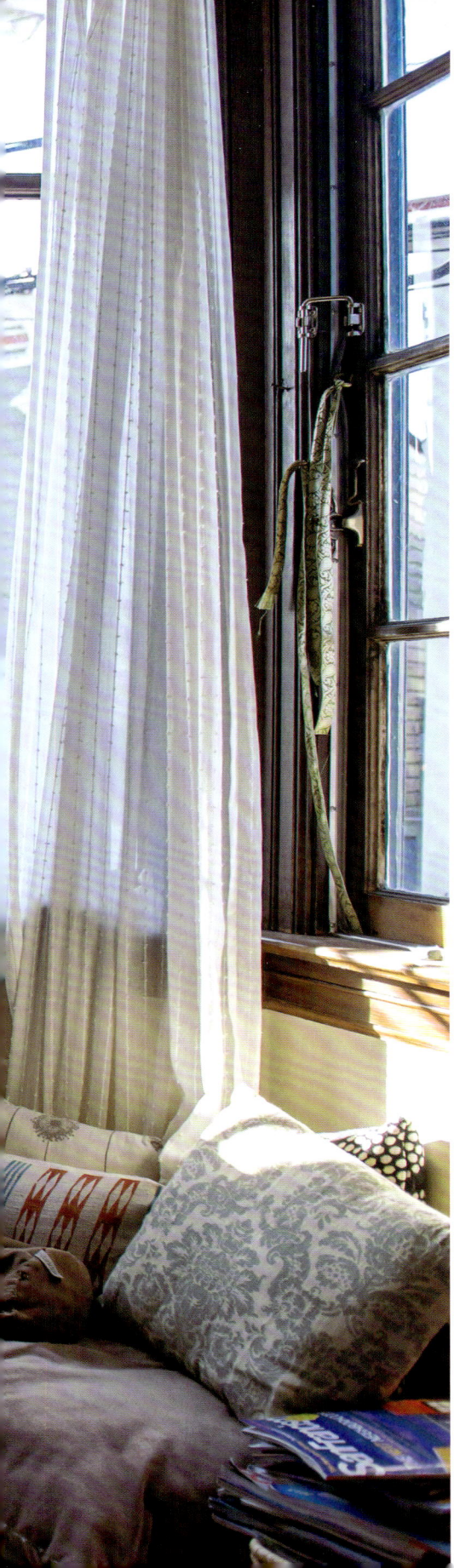

Serena Renner

$ 7,473.26

I first started accumulating debt to travel after a study abroad trip to Spain. While it scared me a little, I thought the benefit outweighed the cost. Since then, my debt has increased due to moving around the state of California and pursuing a journalism career — While taking care of life expenses (rent a car) along the way. Taking on some debt has ultimately helped me achieve independence from my parents and launch a career. But now I want to pay it off!

KEVIN

Graduate Student → Assistant Professor
of Economics

43,000

I acquired most of my debt
(35 K) while in graduate school
pursuing a Ph.D. in Economics

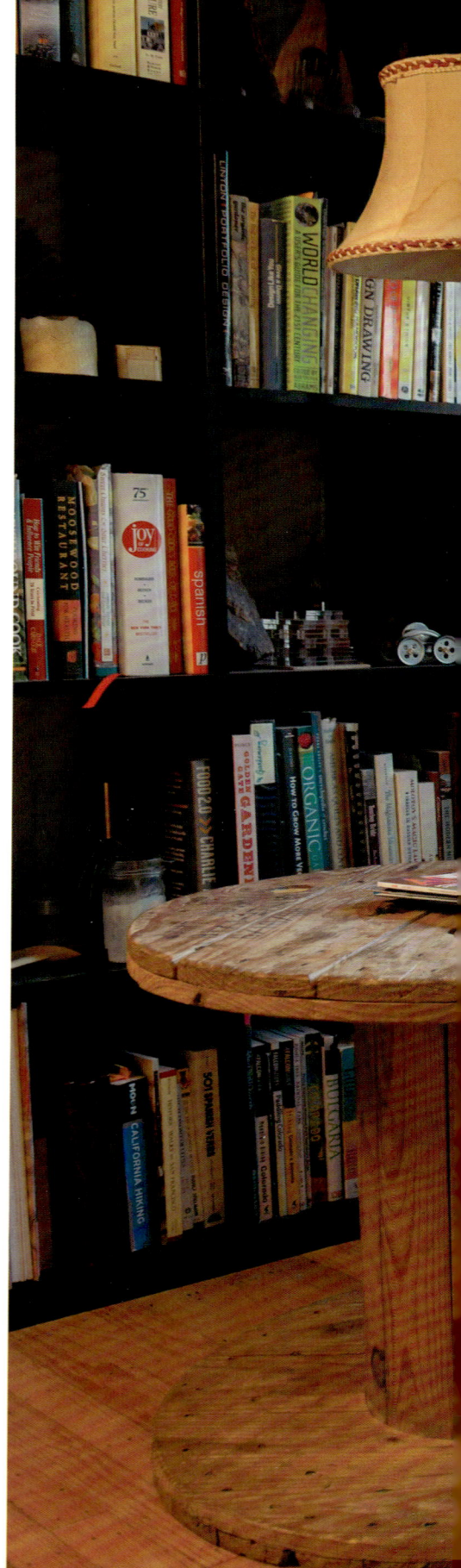

Debt Portrait #6, San Francisco, CA 2013

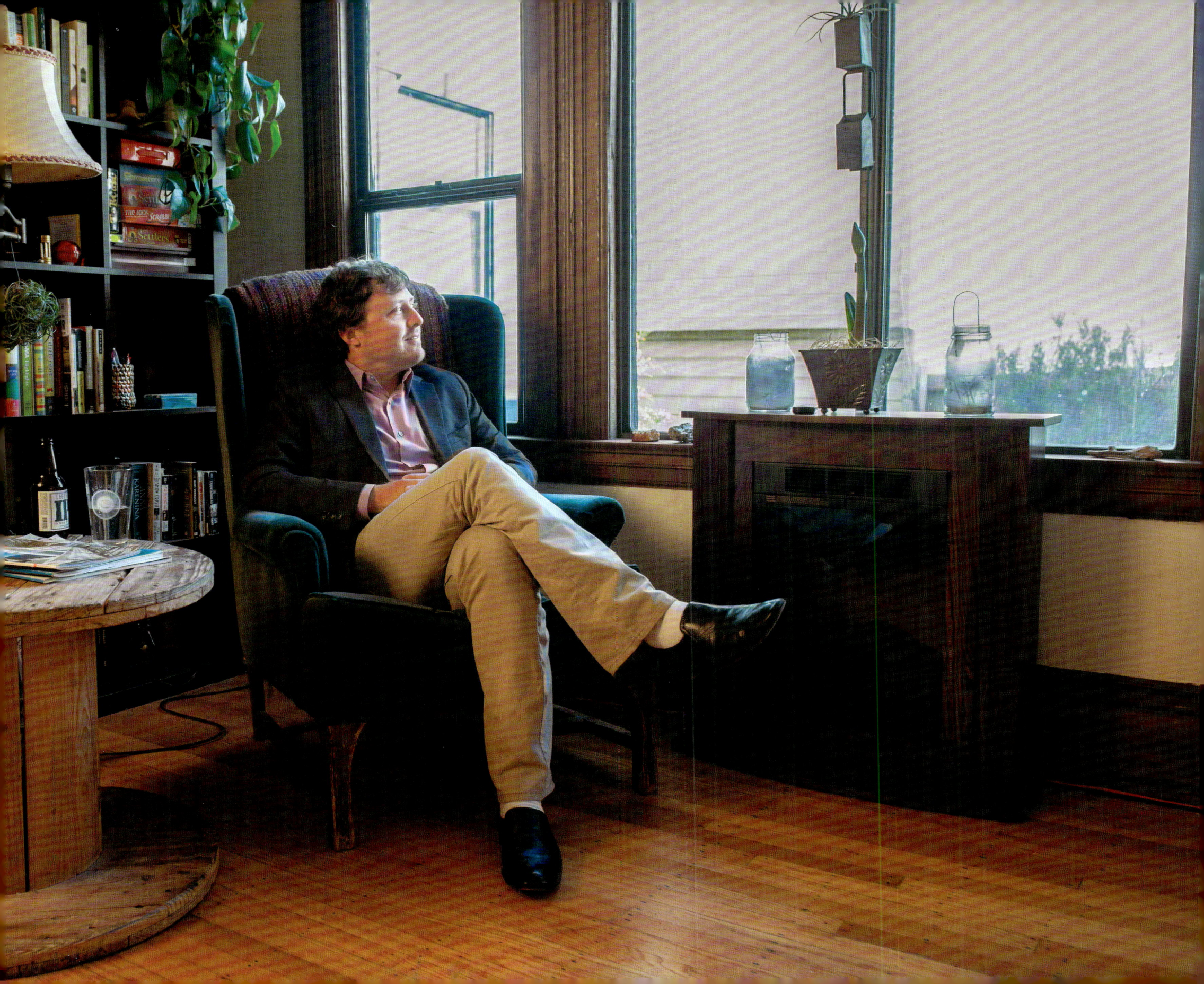

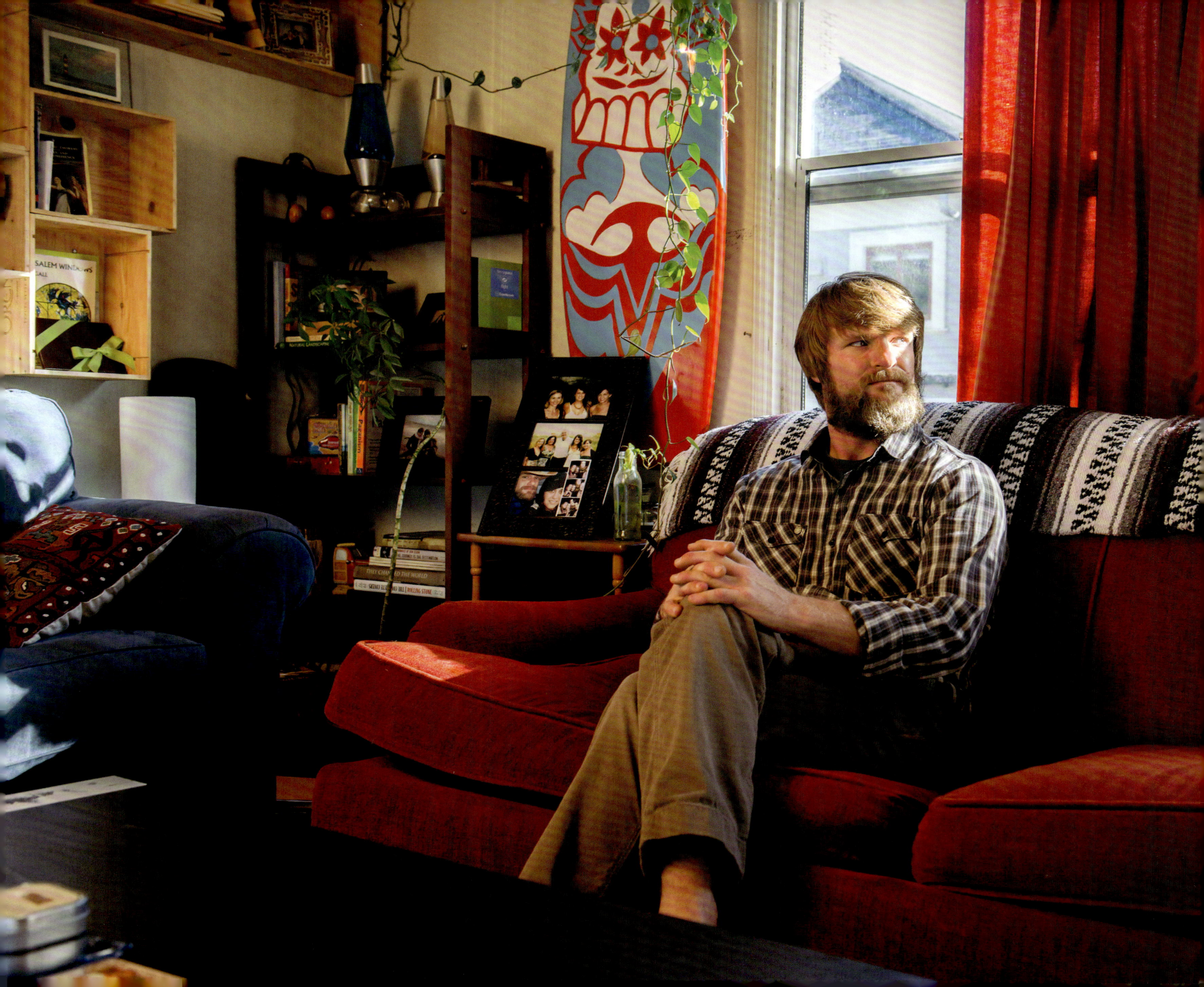

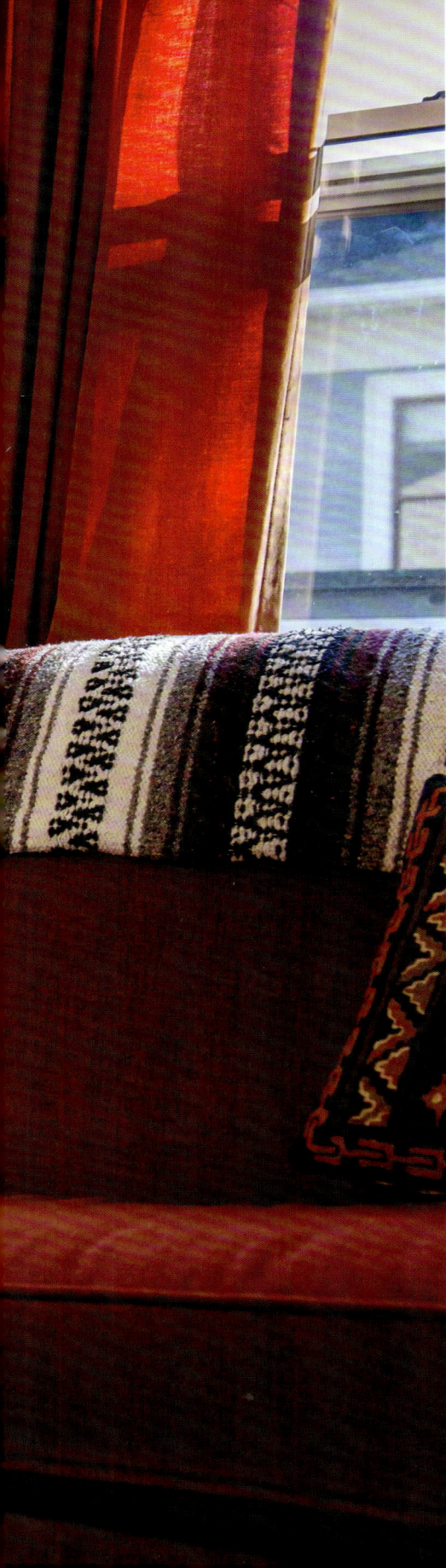

James Riggs Davison III (J.R.)

Electrical Contractor

- Business/Consumer Debt => $39,318.²⁶   Total
- Back Taxes   => $13,017.³⁷ $52,335.⁶³

I bought a truck & moved to California where work was scarce. Then decided to go back to school to finish a degree. After Graduation, I decided to start my own business & take on more loans needed for equipment & slow times. Within 2ⁿᵈ year of business had to buy new truck due to an accident. By 3ʳᵈ year of business was making triple payments on most loans so as to pay off quickly... then the economy tanked & my triple payments were barely a single payment due to most lenders Ramping their interest Rates to cover "Losses"...

Debt Portrait #7, Oakland, CA 2013

MIKE

ARCHITECTURAL DESIGNER

$160,800

MASTERS DEGREE (4) YEARS
REAL ESTATE DEAL
UNEMPLOYMENT

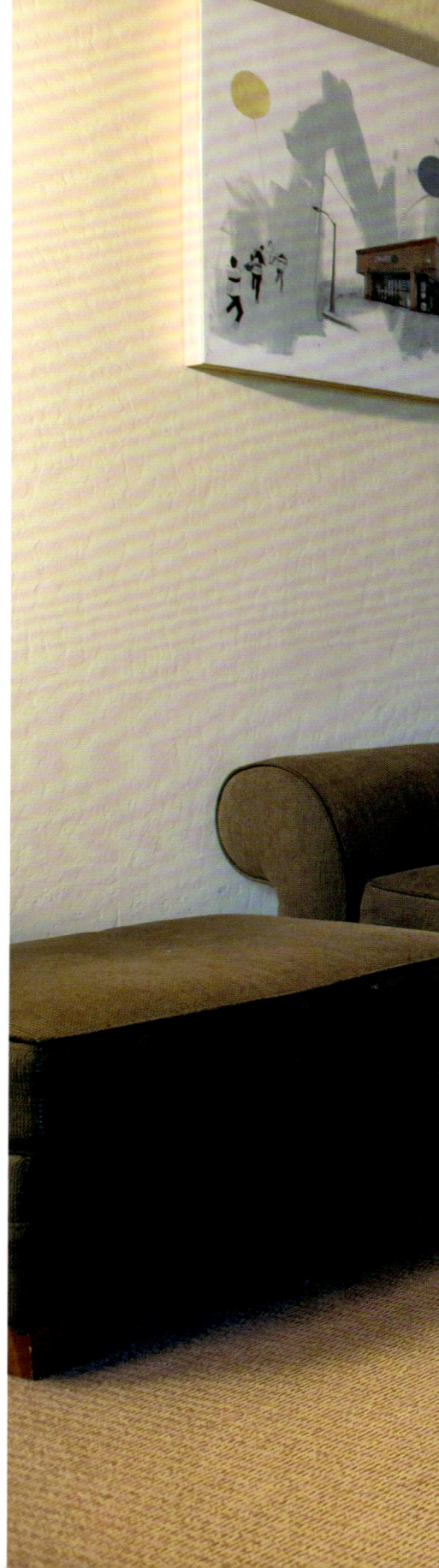

Debt Portrait #8, Oakland, CA 2013

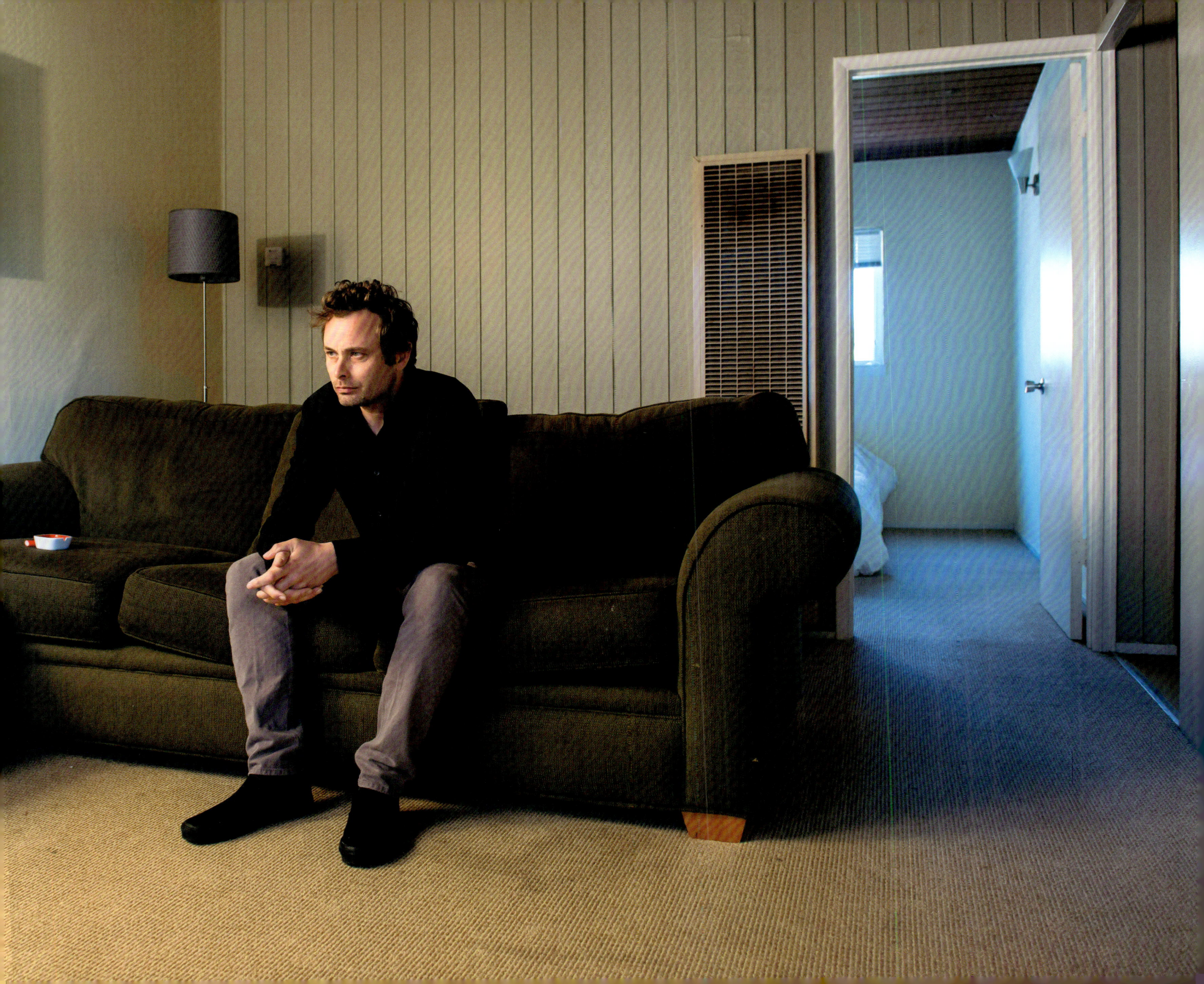

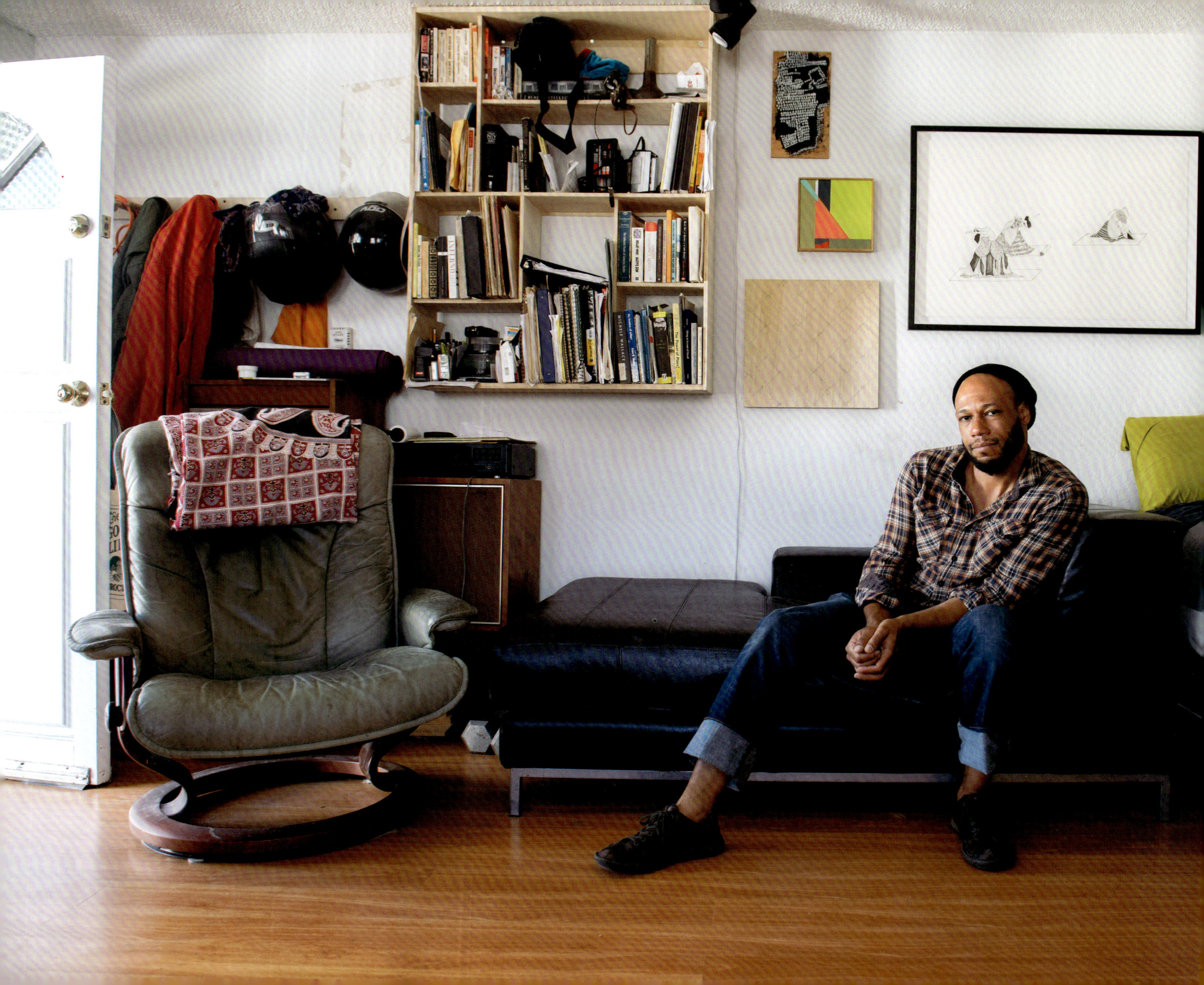

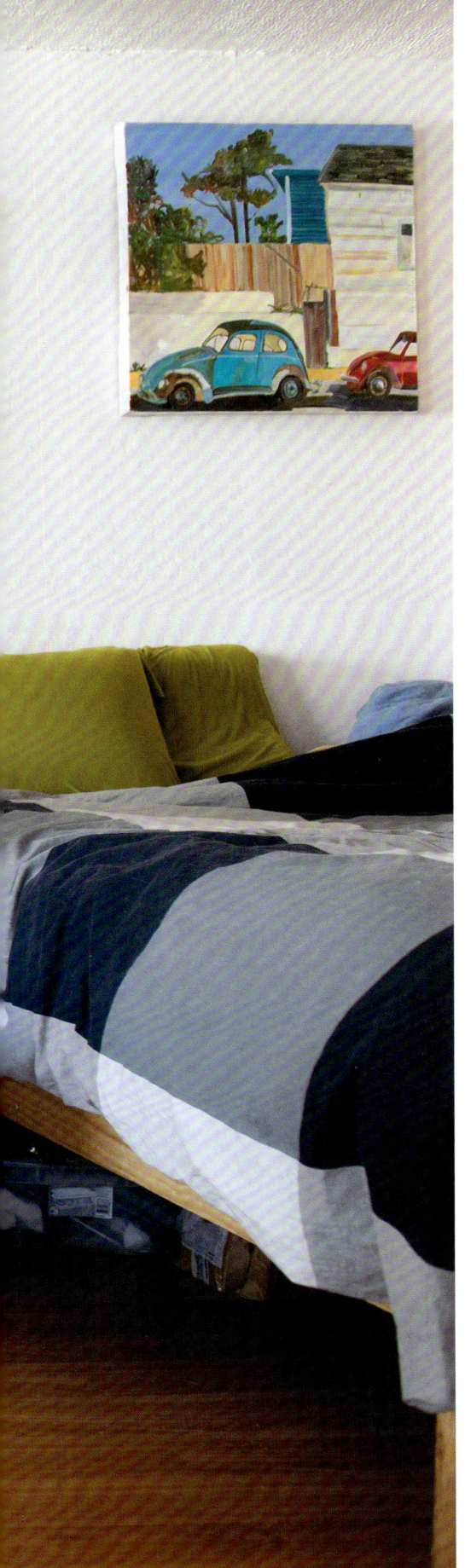

Nathan Watson

Artist, Teacher, Director of Public Glass

37,000

When I finished graduate school, the jobs I was getting didn't cover my expenses for the first year. I was spending to create opportunities and trying to stay in a city that was expensive, but could support my skill set. Along the way car expenses, rent, food, medical bills have been momentary set backs.

Debt Portrait #9, San Francisco, CA 2013

Martin Olive
Executive Director - Vapor Room Cooperative
$930,716.54

I was audited by the IRS for opening a medical cannabis dispensary in 2004 & 2005. The IRS applied an obscure IRS provision - 280E which disallowed me from deducting cannabis "cost of goods" as a standard business deduction. Subsequently, I am forced to pay the full income tax plus interest & penalties. Added to that huge tax burden, I suffered a brain aneurysm & had surgery plus 10 days in ICU without health coverage!

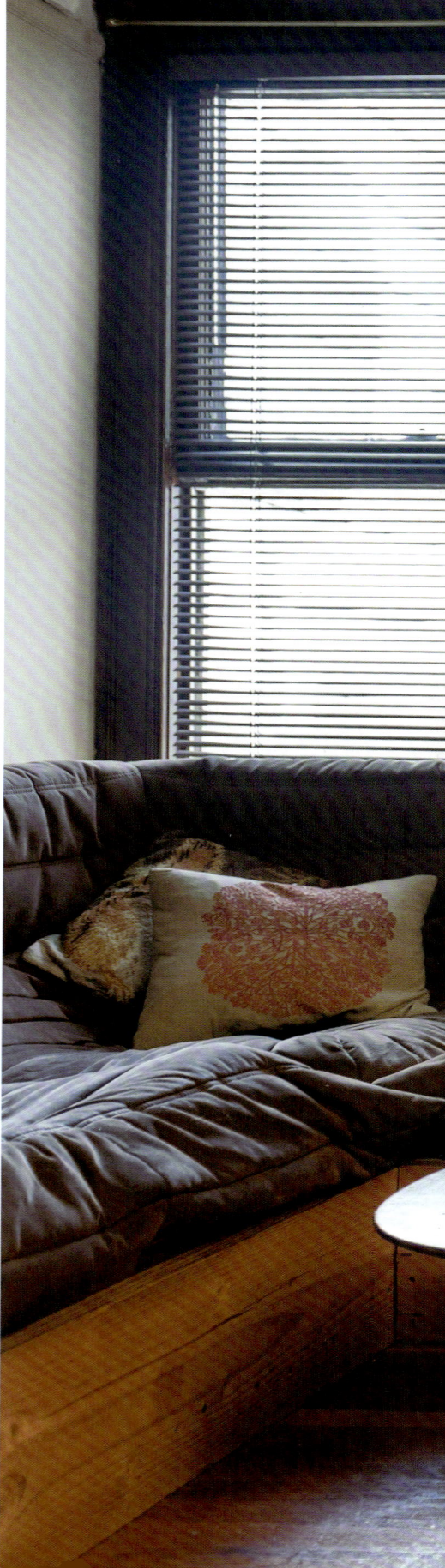

Debt Portrait #10, San Francisco, CA 2013

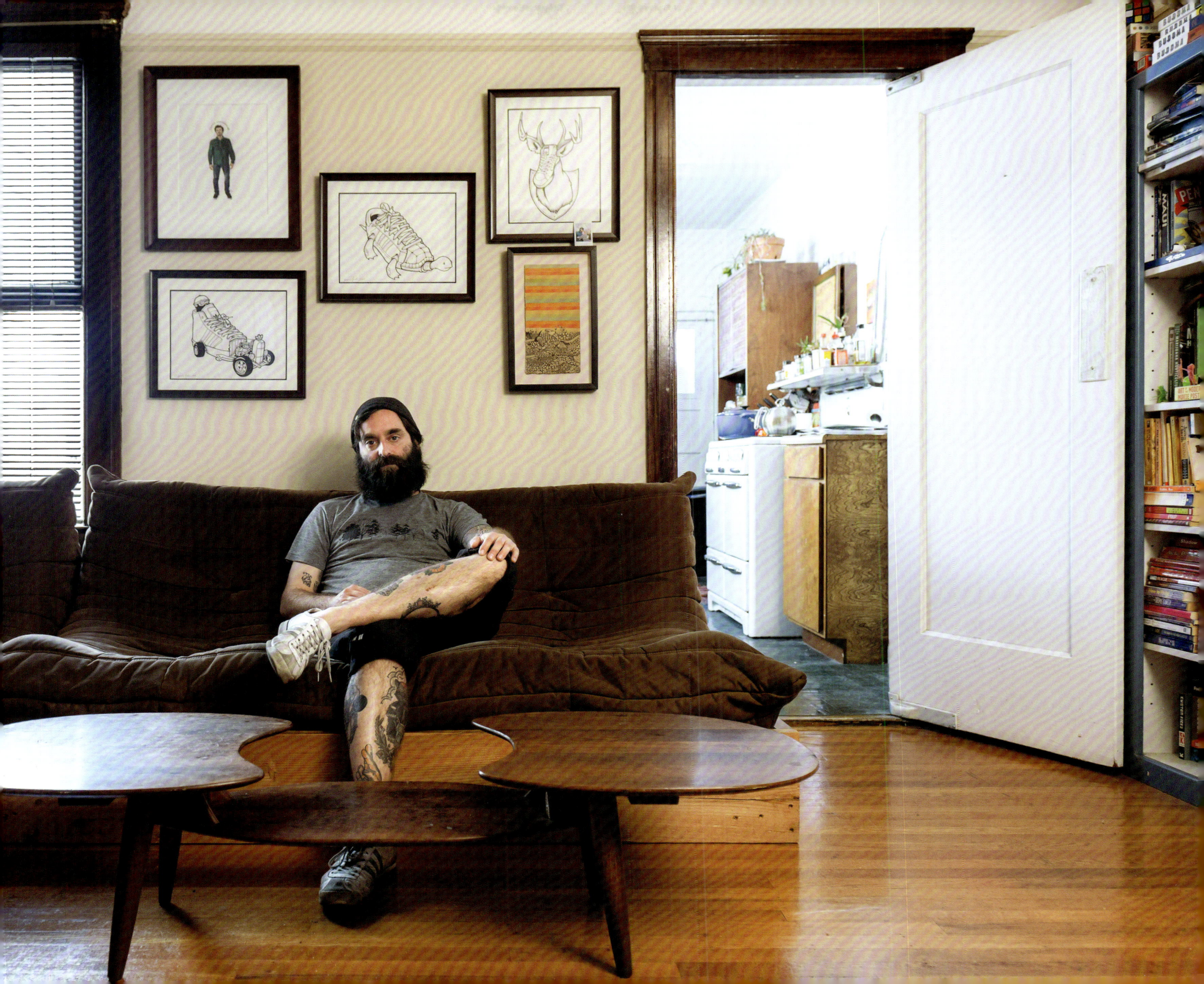

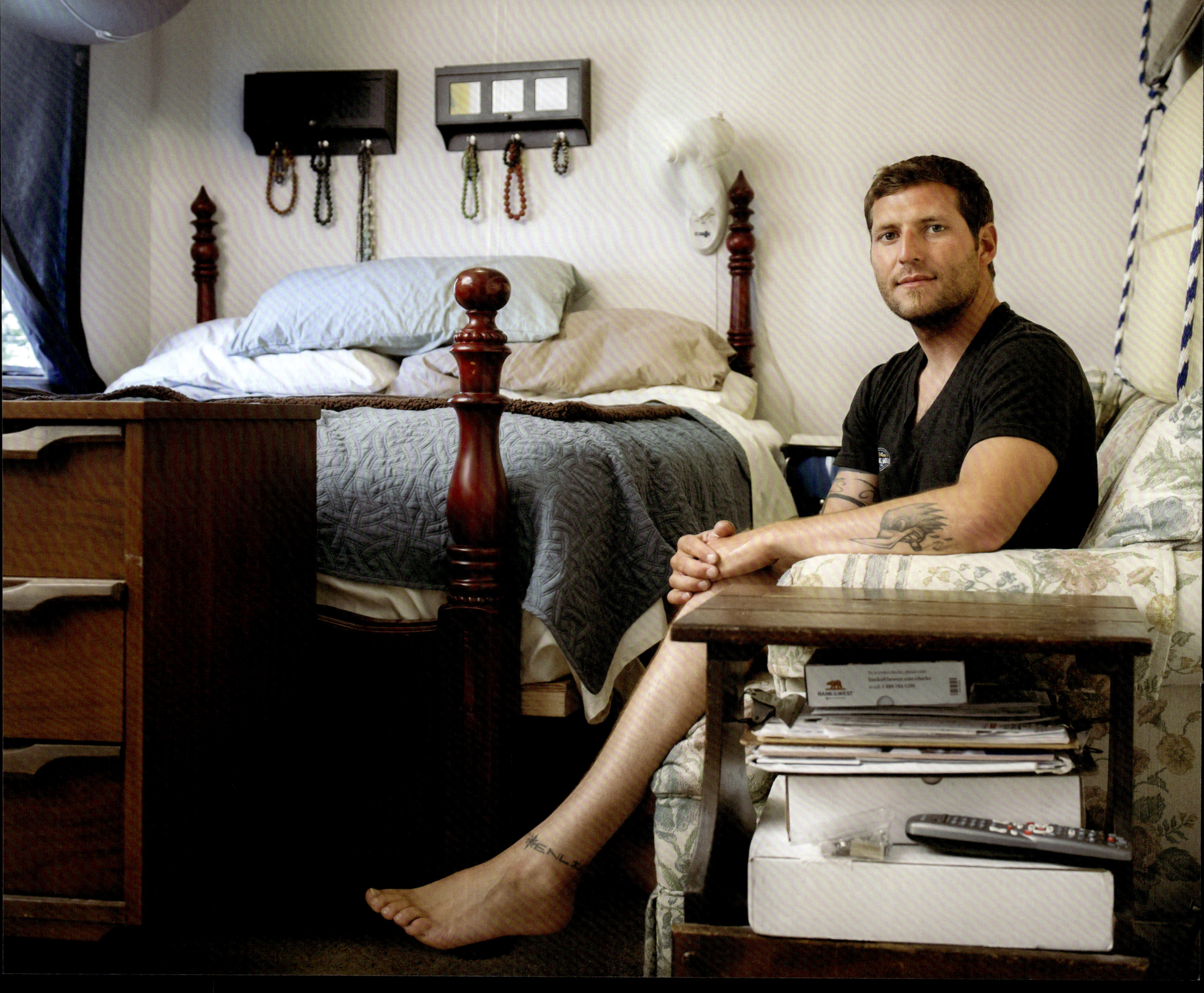

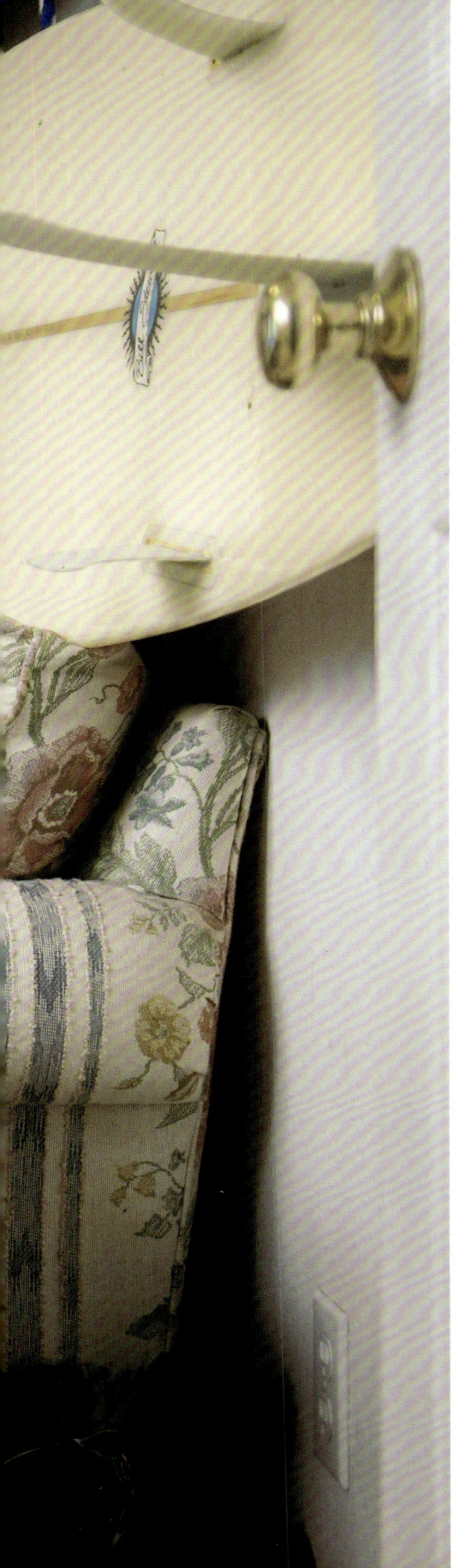

J.D. Bates

Surf Instructor, Food Server, Entrapanner

$30,000⁰⁰

I was working for a startup, and they could only afford to pay me very little so I racked up ~~dp~~ debt on credit cards to pay for everyday life stuff. Then, the business went under, the recession hit, I moved, couldn't find a good job, and I've been under ever since...

Debt Portrait #11, Hayward, CA 2013

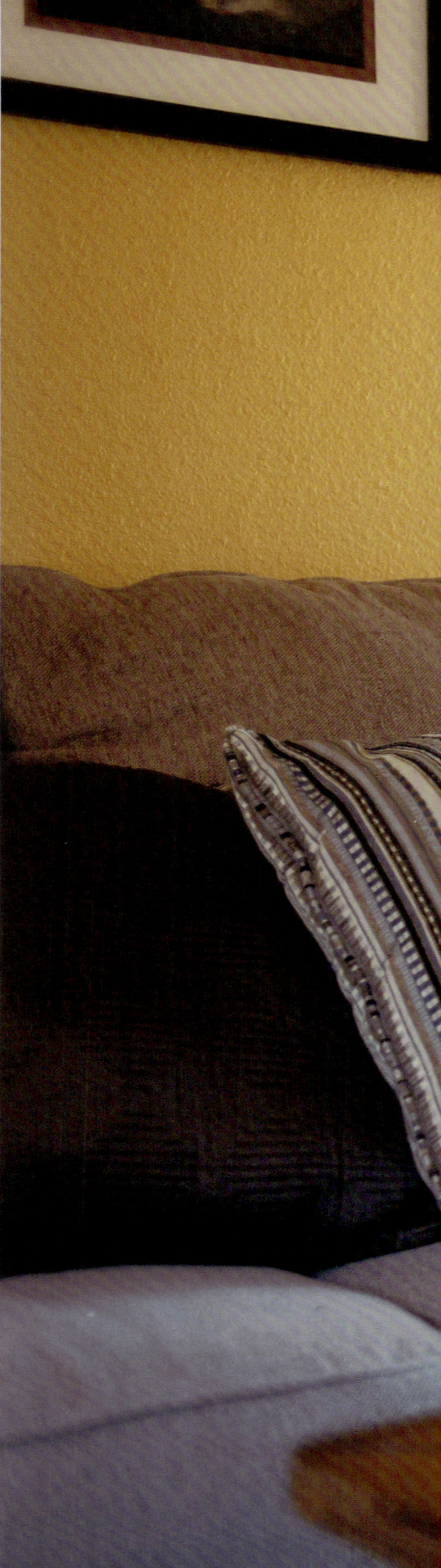

Morris LeGrande
Musician

$150,000

Bad mortgage, job loss in 2005.

Debt Portrait #12, Richmond, CA 2013

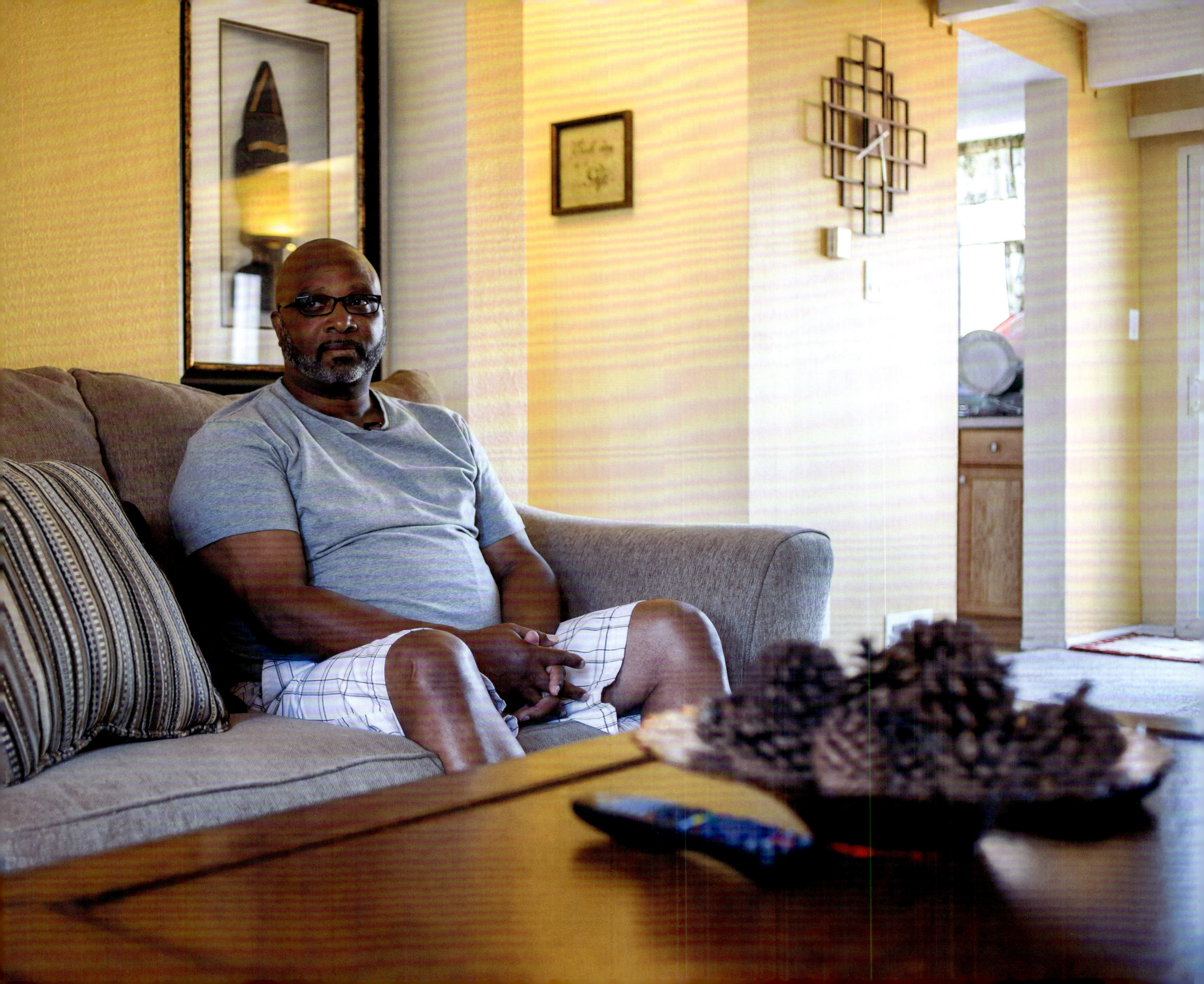

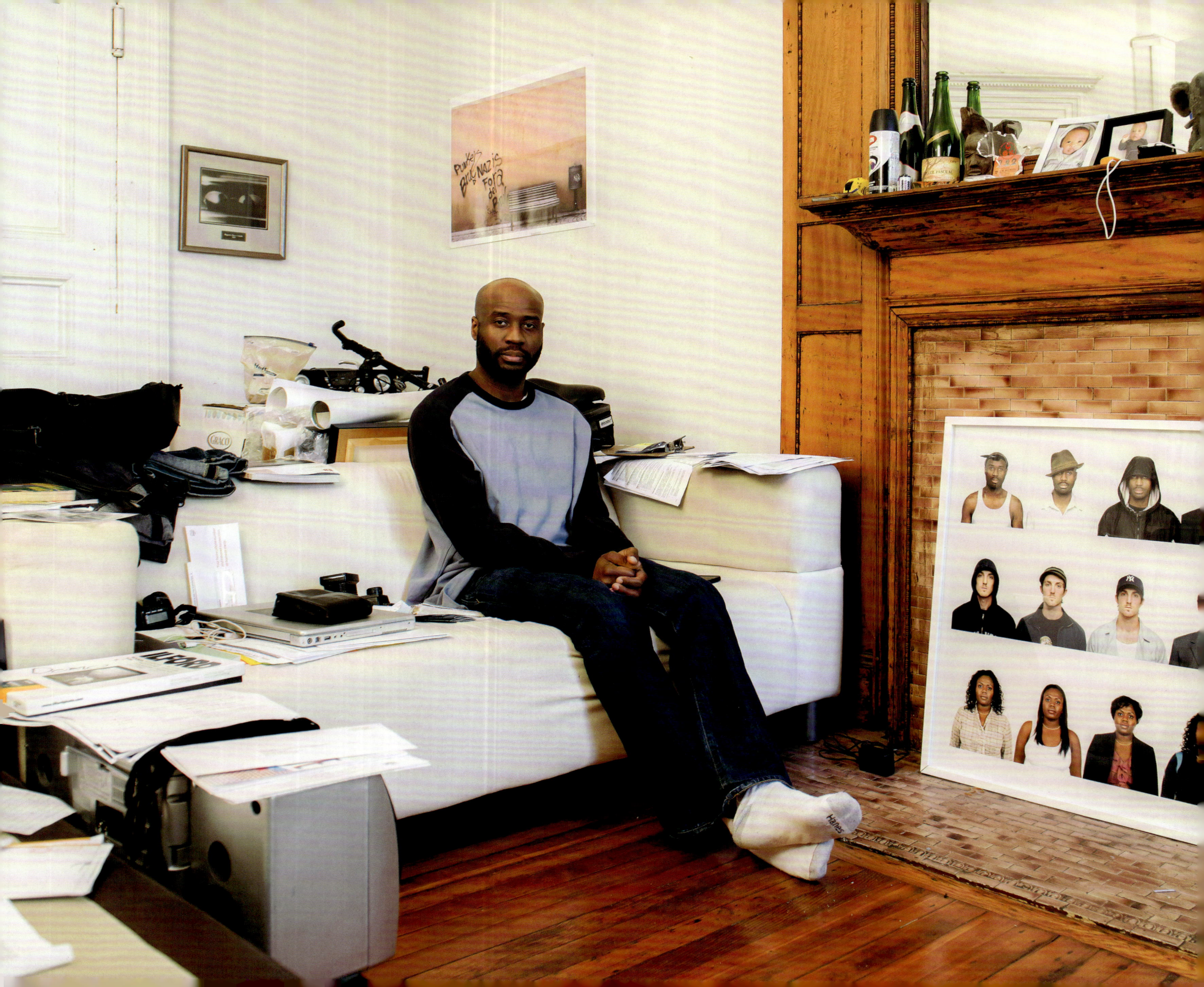

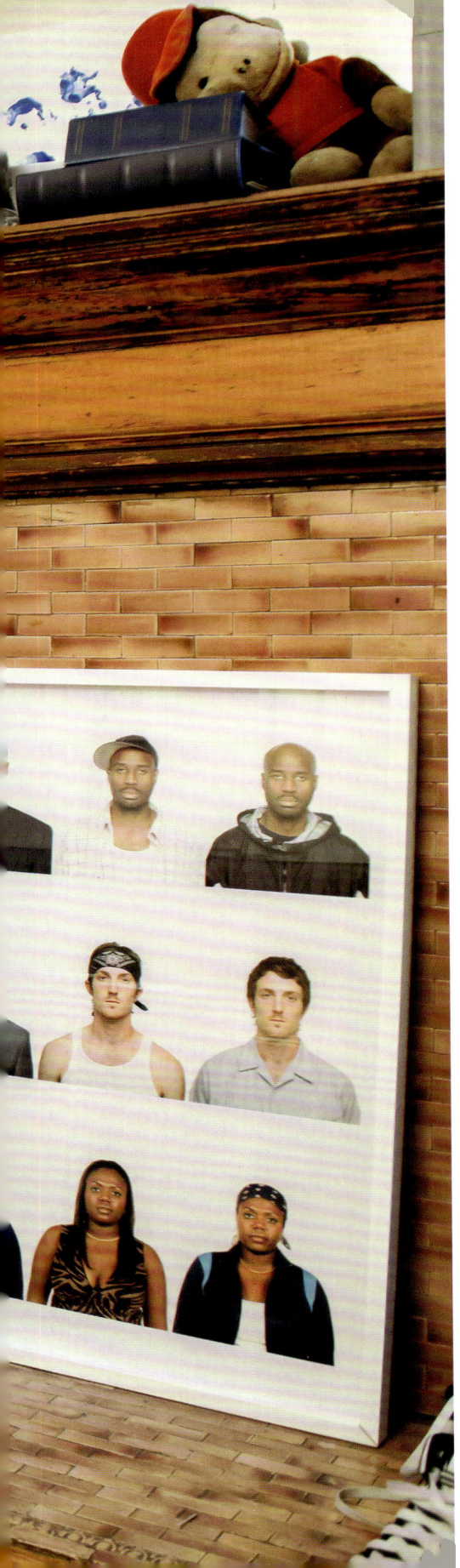

Bayeté Ross Smith

Photographer, Multi Media Artist
Professor, Visual Artist, Educator

"When you are in creative professions and work as an entrepreneur you must wear many hats"

Approximately 91K from Student Loans

Debt Portrait #13, Harlem, NY 2013

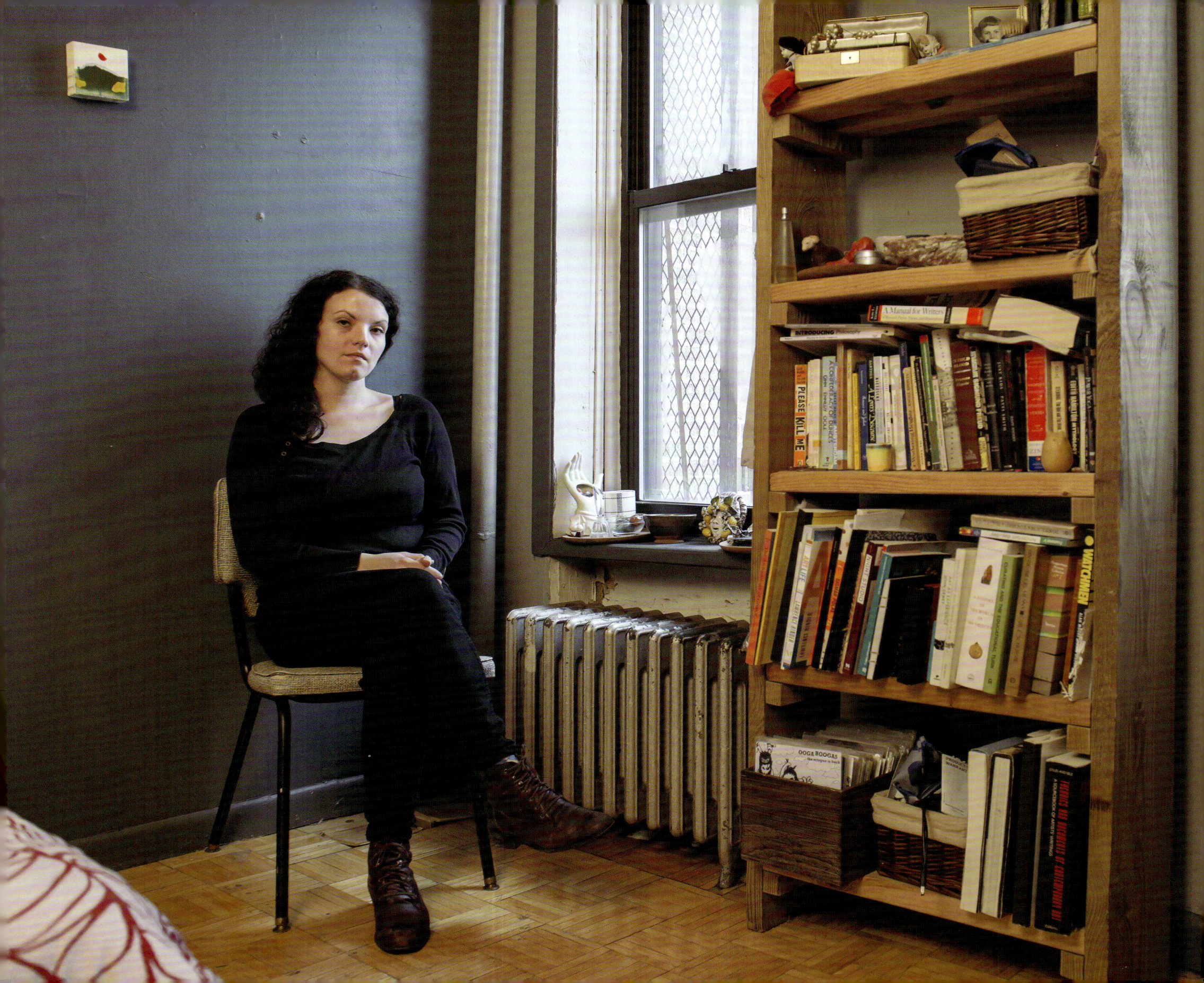

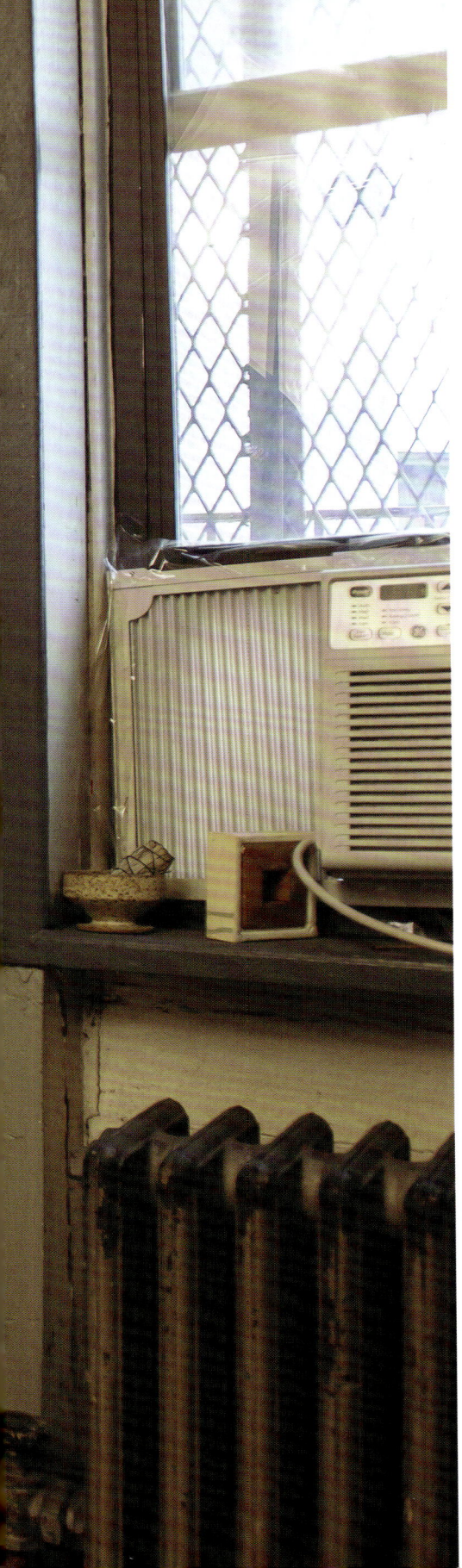

kelsey knutson
artist, executive assistant

$110,000   student loans
$3,000   credit cards

transitioning into a professional
in the arts- I realized I had
to have a graduate degree.
As the economy worsened I saw
entry-level positions turn into
unpaid internships. It's taken
almost a year and half to find
a full time job in my field...
and still can't make ends meet.

Debt Portrait #14, Brooklyn, NY 2013

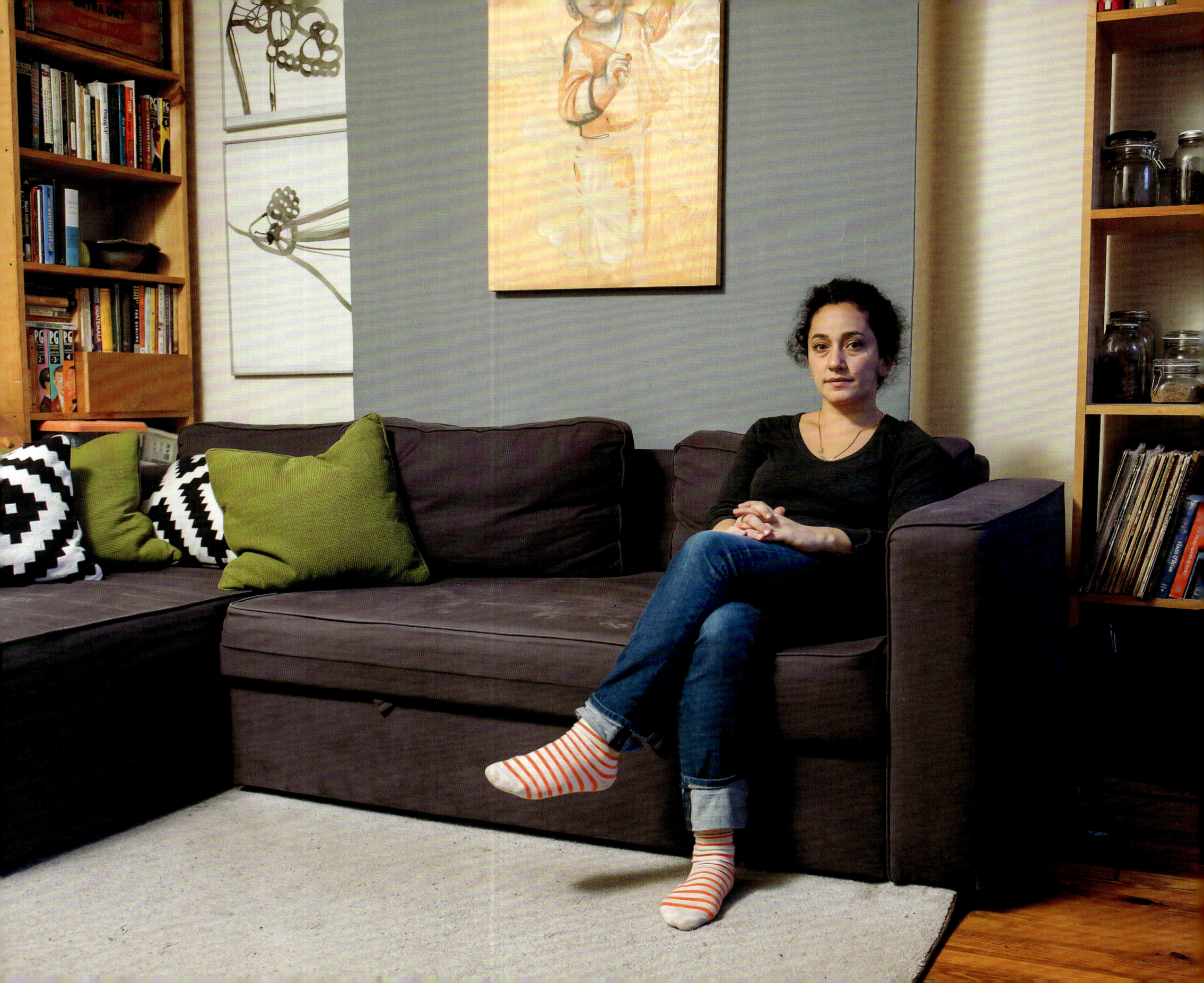

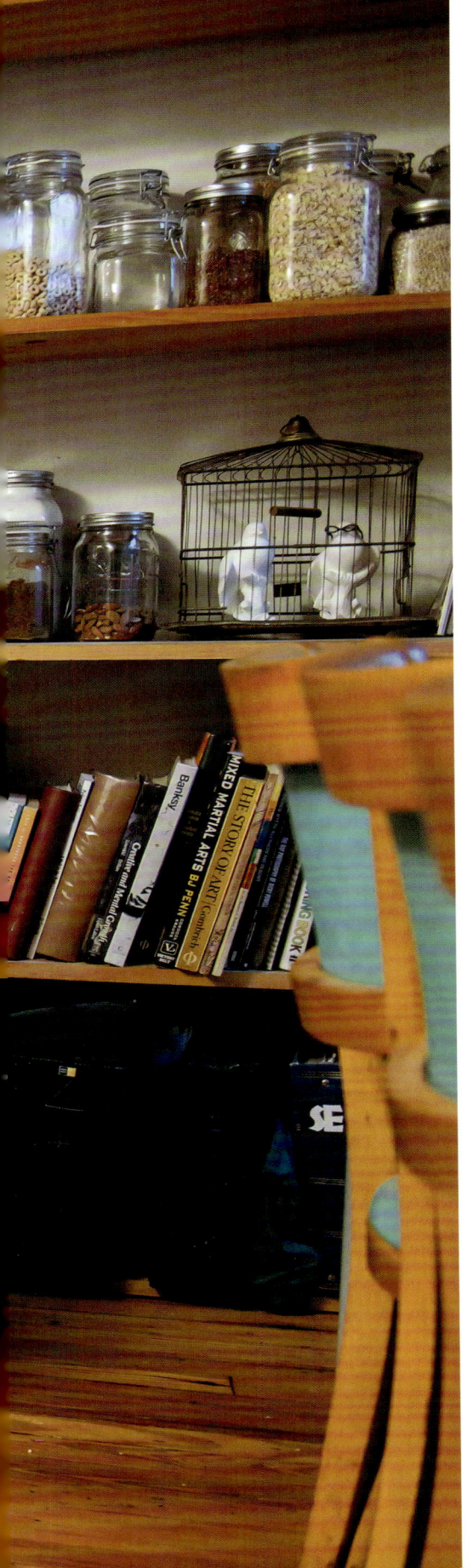

Naomi Cohen Thompson
art therapist, artist, mother of 2

approx $75,000

mostly school debt from
2008 art therapy graduate
degree — some consumer debt
from living expenses etc while I
was in school.

Debt Portrait #15, Brooklyn, NY 2013

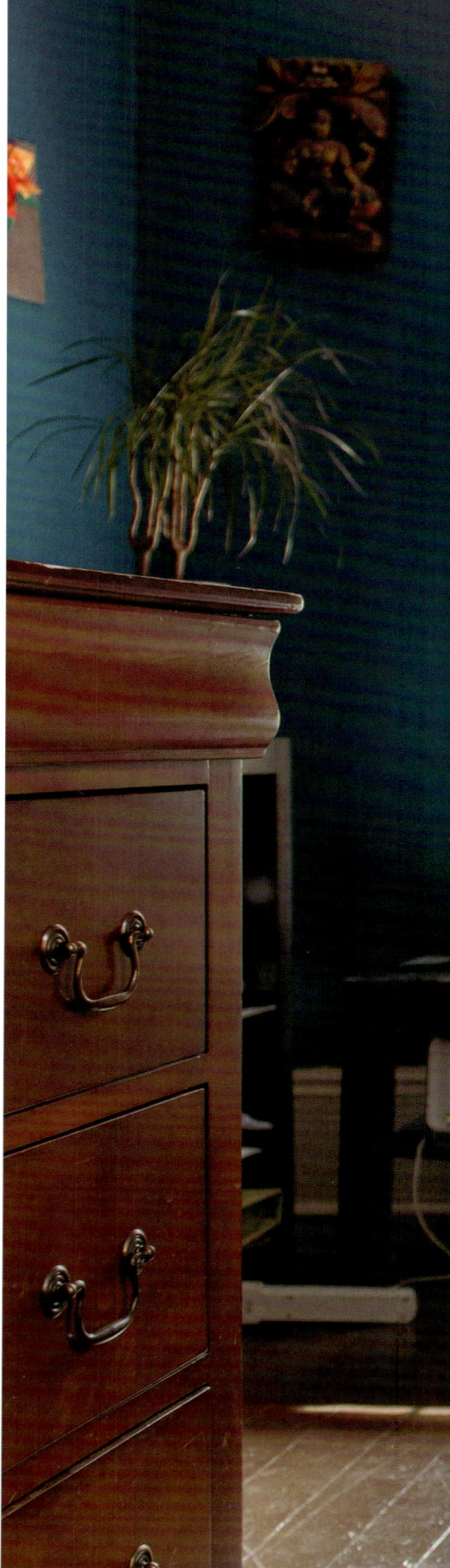

Juliet Maisel
teacher / server

$100,000 DEBT

I have accumulated that debt from
my bachelor's at University of Kansas
my Montessori teacher training,
and my master's in Education
from Loyola College of Maryland.

Debt Portrait #16, Portland, OR 2014

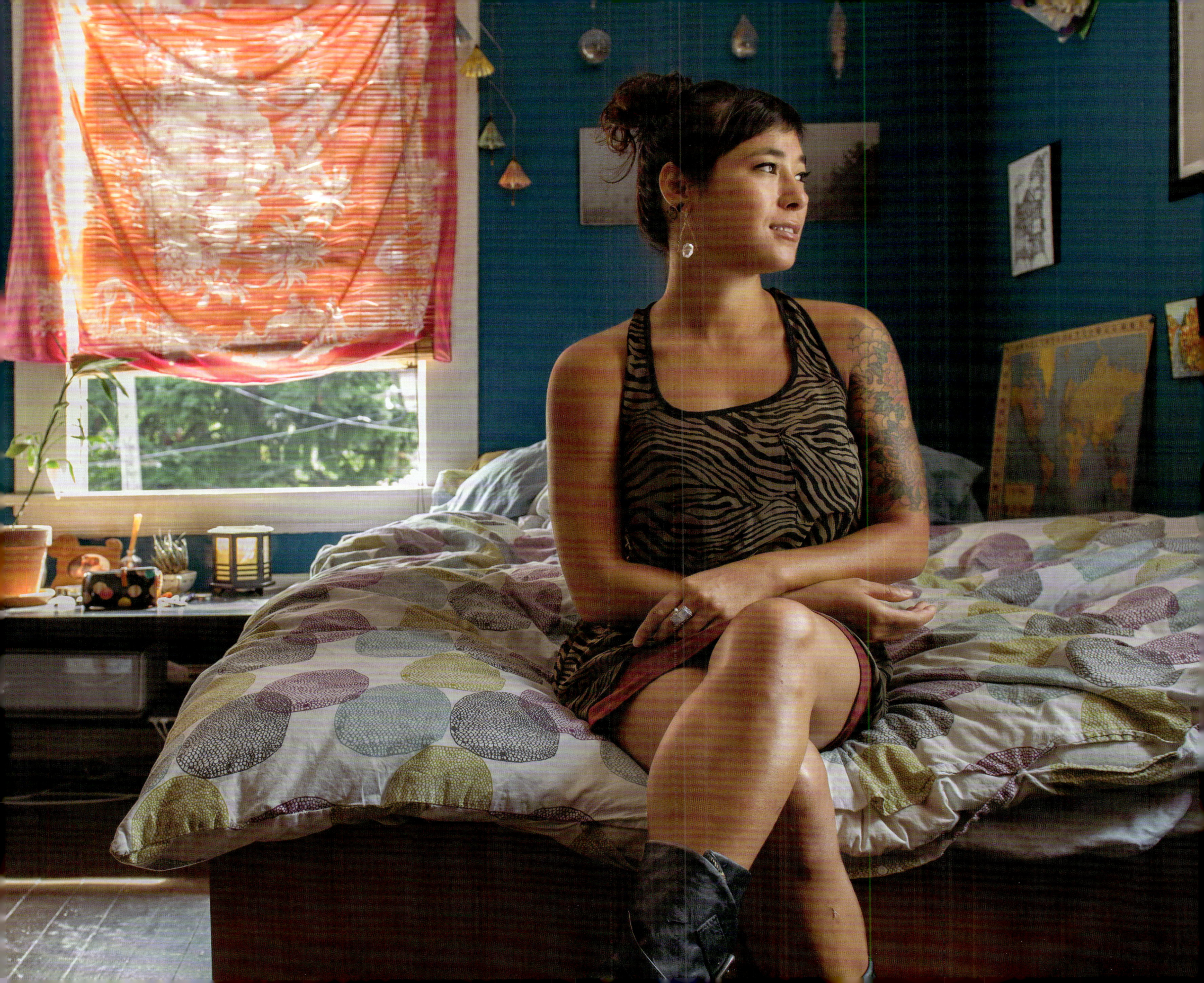

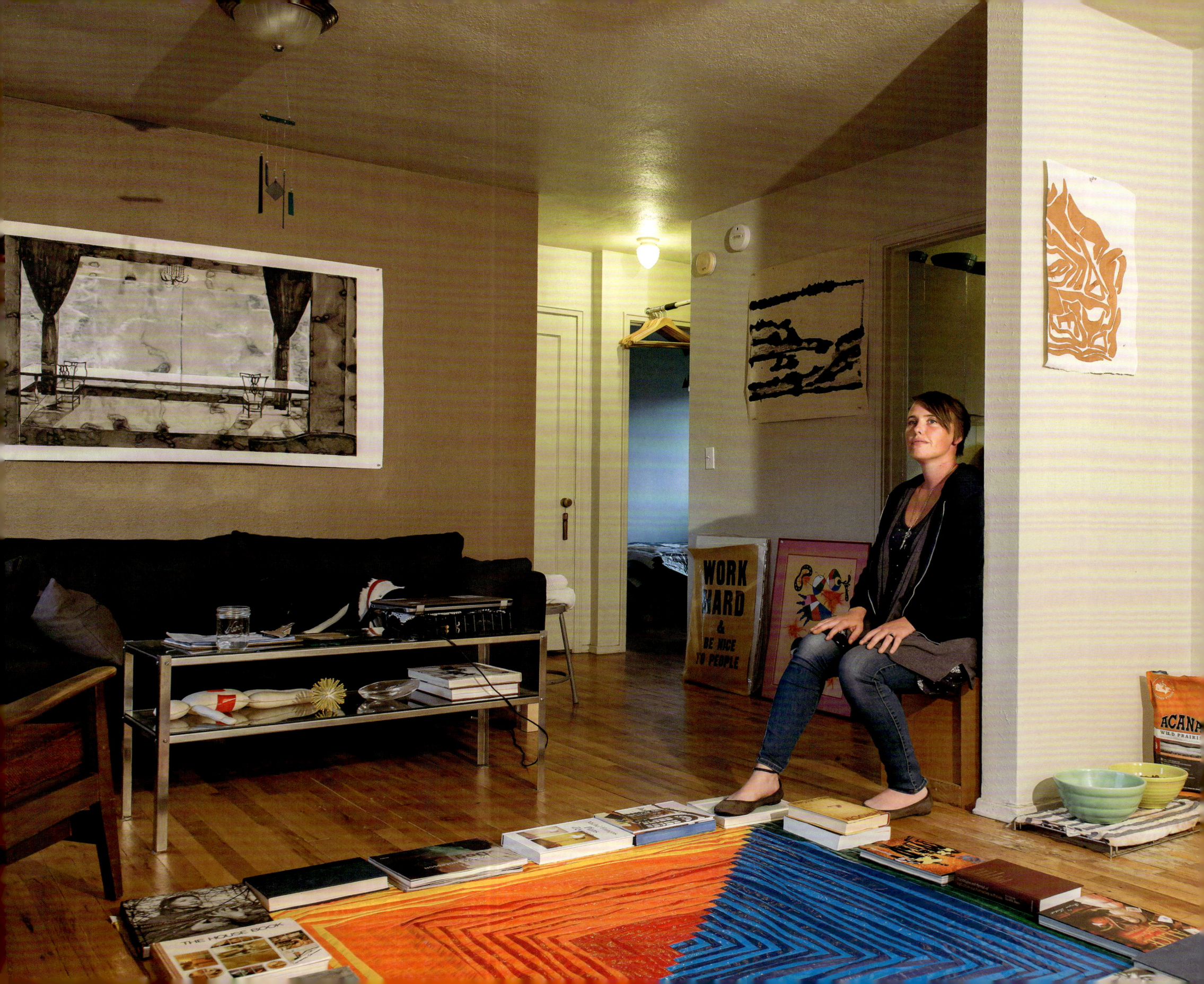

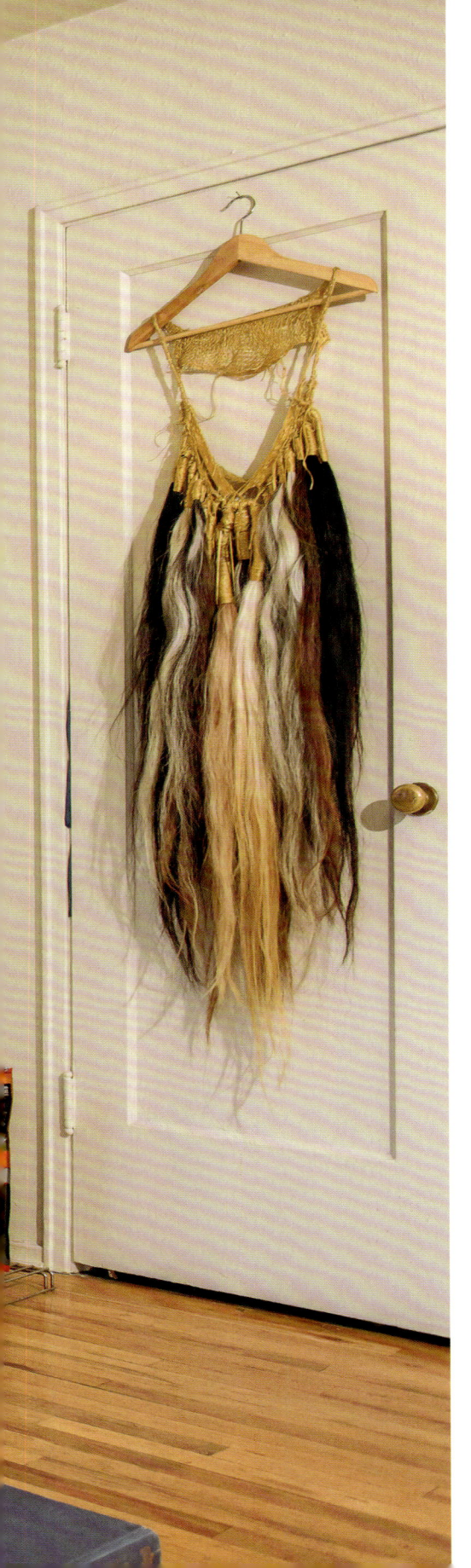

WYNDE DYER
ARTIST/CAB DRIVER

$ 150,000 +/—

My mom took out credit cards in my
name. From 1988-1998 she incurred
"A mortgage worth of debt" (according
to my bankruptcy attorney) on my SSI,
Mostly to feul her compulsive shopping
and hoarding habits. I have no
credit debt, just about $3000-$5000
owed to various banks and cell phone
companies and other evil corporations
who hit me with erroneas charges.
But I was an idiot and took out the
maximum student loans available to
me, even though I had a graduate
teaching assistantship w/a stipend
and tuition remission. I have
defaulted, and interest has risen.
I owed about $139,000 last
time I opened a bill several
years ago. so it goes

Debt Portrait #17, Portland, OR 2014

Maia Laperle
Artist / Teacher
$14,500
I'm in debt from student loans
and making not very much money.
I'm not making any payments
on it right now. I went to
school for Fine Arts.

Aaron Call
Tutor / Artist
$74,000
I'm in a lot of debt from student
loans for a BA in Psychology & a
Master in Education. I place a lot
of value in what I got in exchange
for the debt but it doesn't feel
like a fair trade.

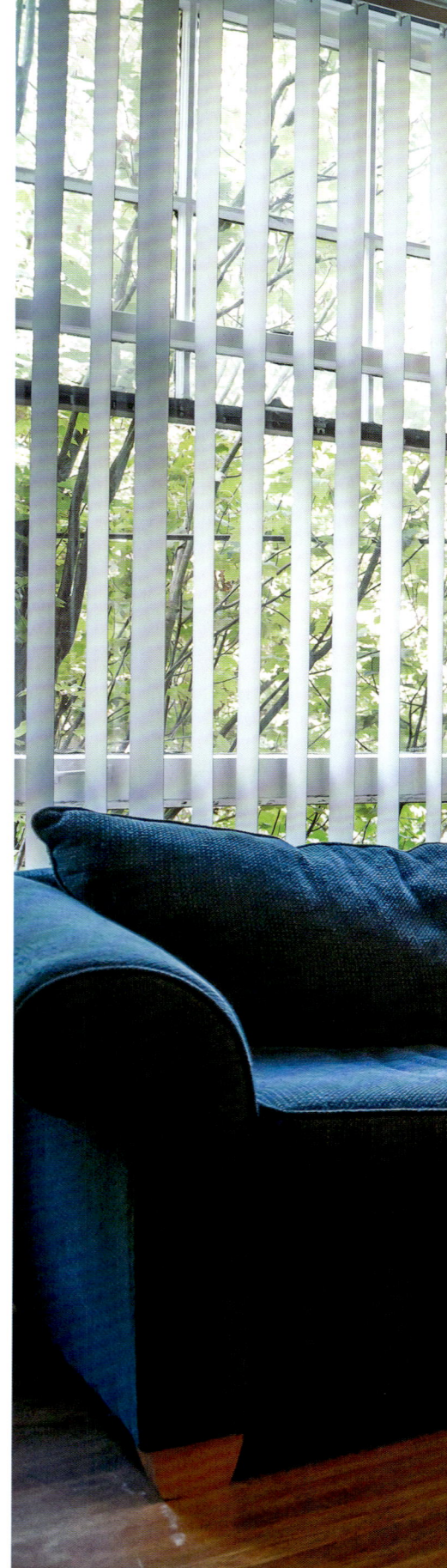

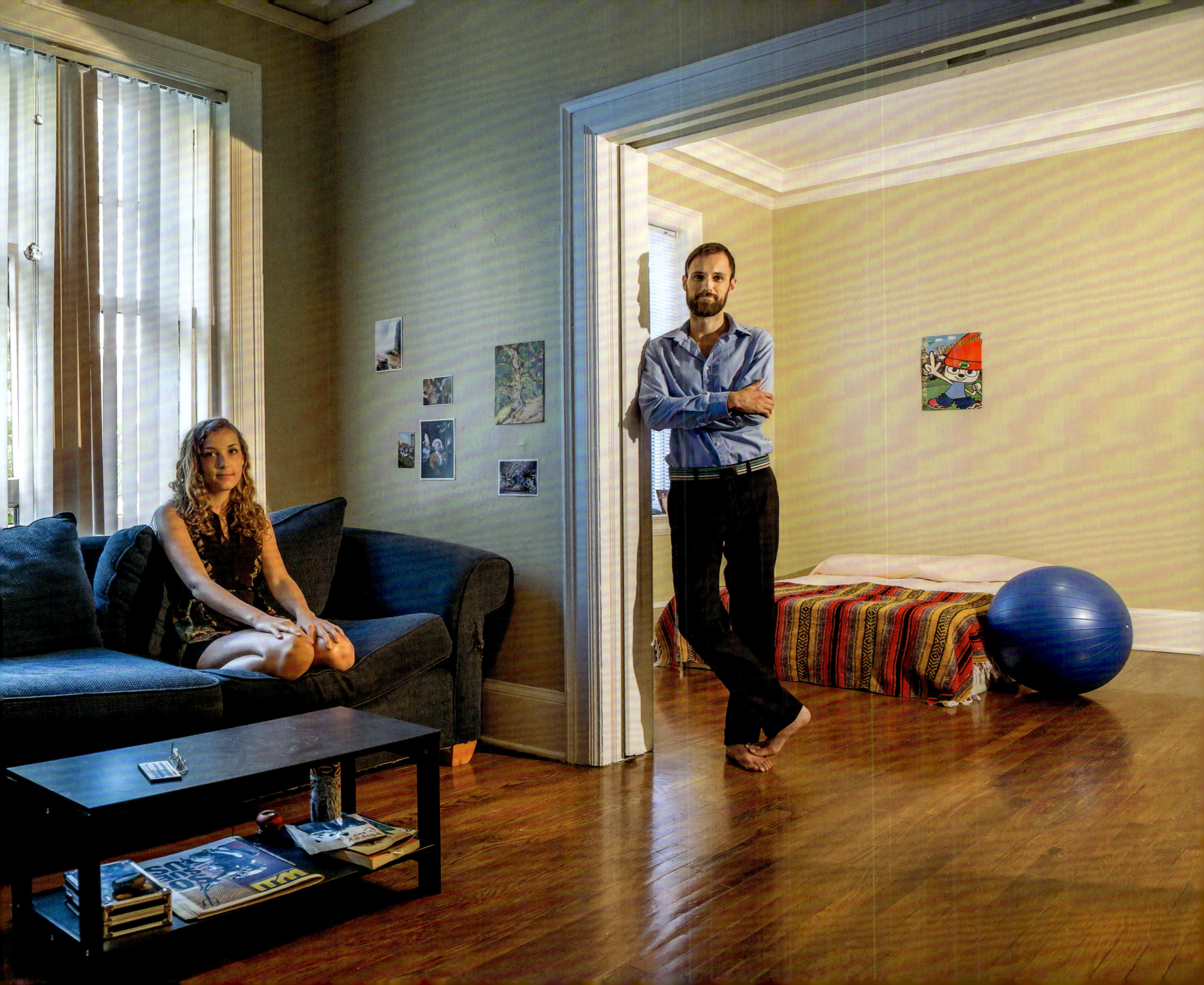

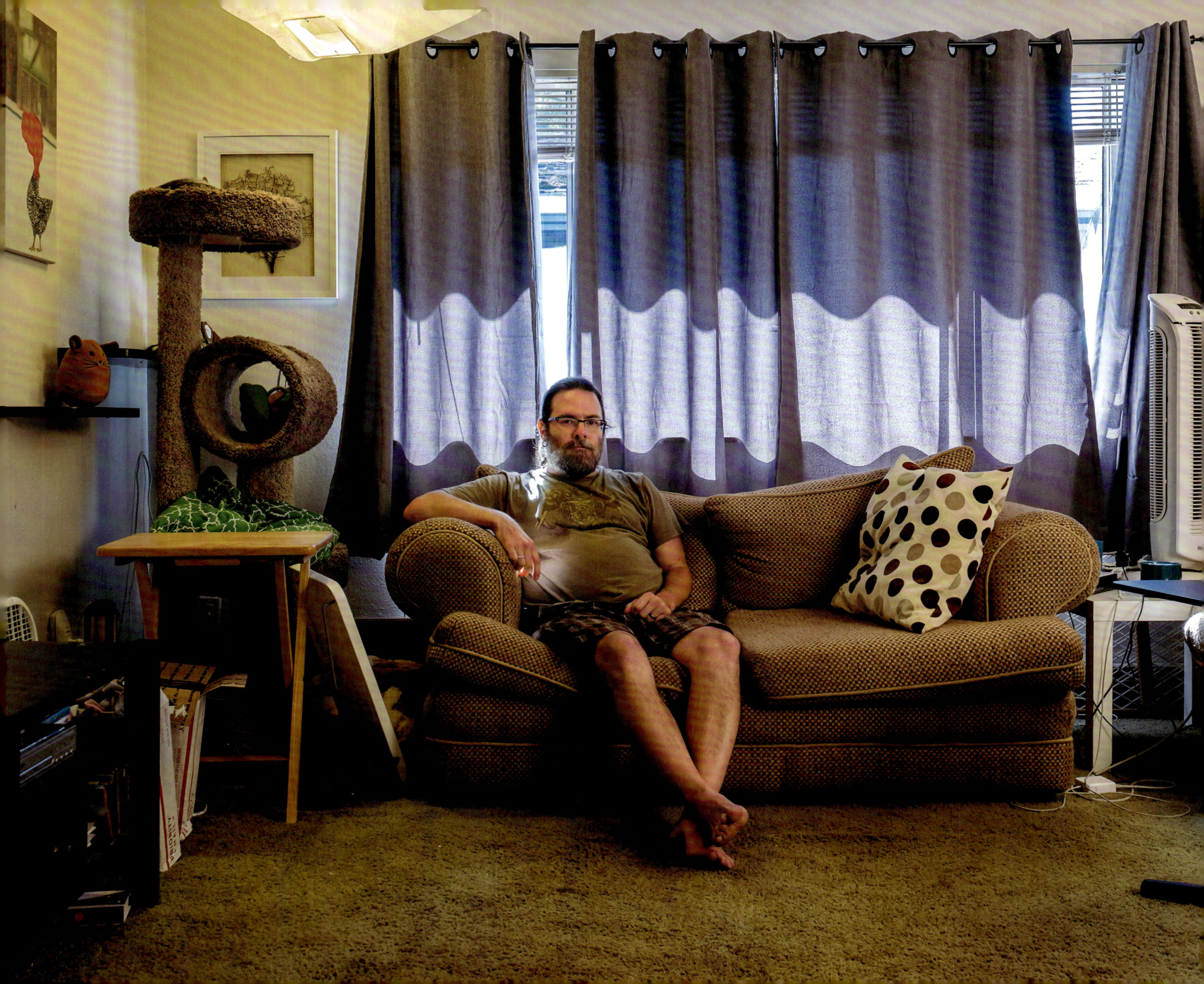

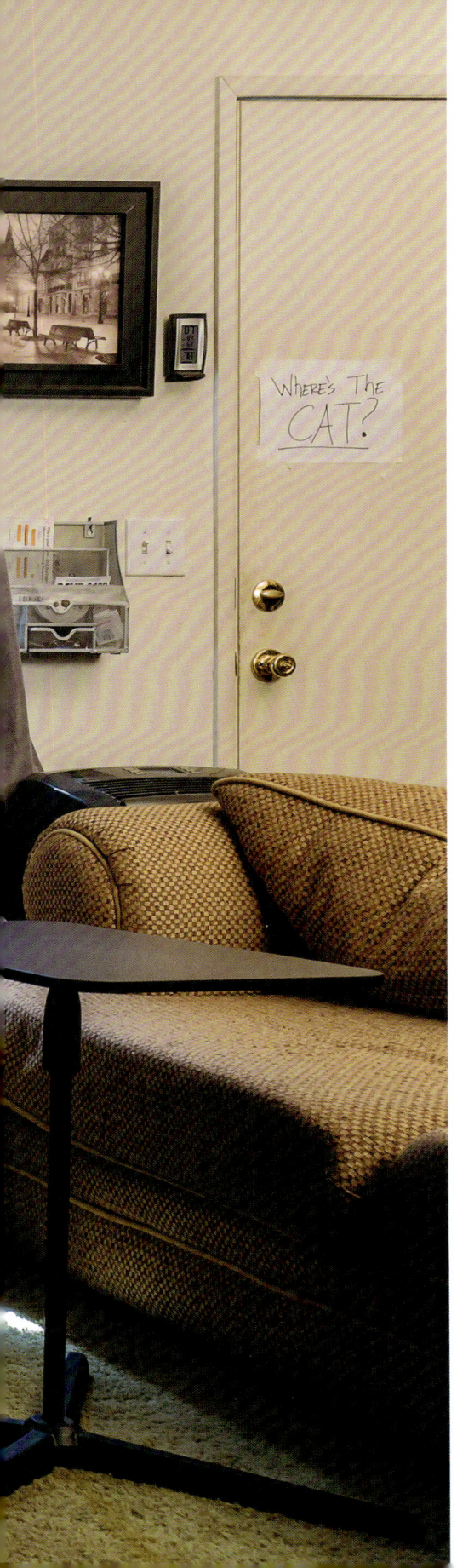

Sean Scott
Unemployed/student
$20,000

Most of my debt is student loans
and credit cards. I ran
up all my cards after my divorce
nine years ago and it's been
hard to catch up since then.
I've also been out of work
off and on over the years.

Debt Portrait #19, Portland, OR 2014

JEREMY E. MILLS
35 YRS.
Unemployed

I am currently in debt for $30,000 in student loans. I grew up in Boise, ID. where I attended college for a degree in Railroading Operations. I am scheduled to begin repayment of my loans next month, but have no current plans on how to pay them.

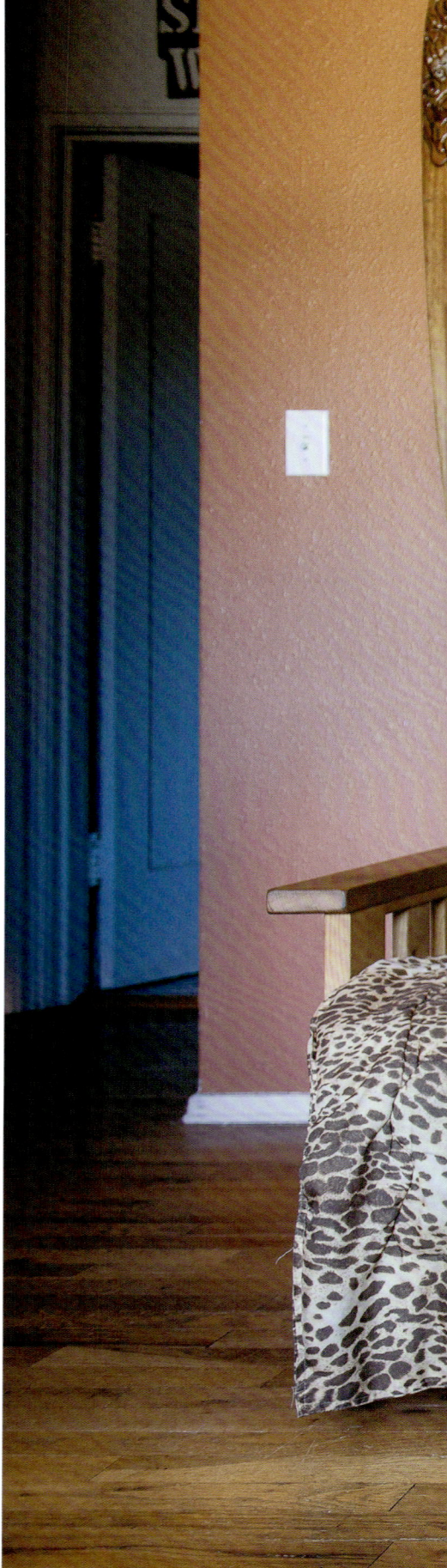

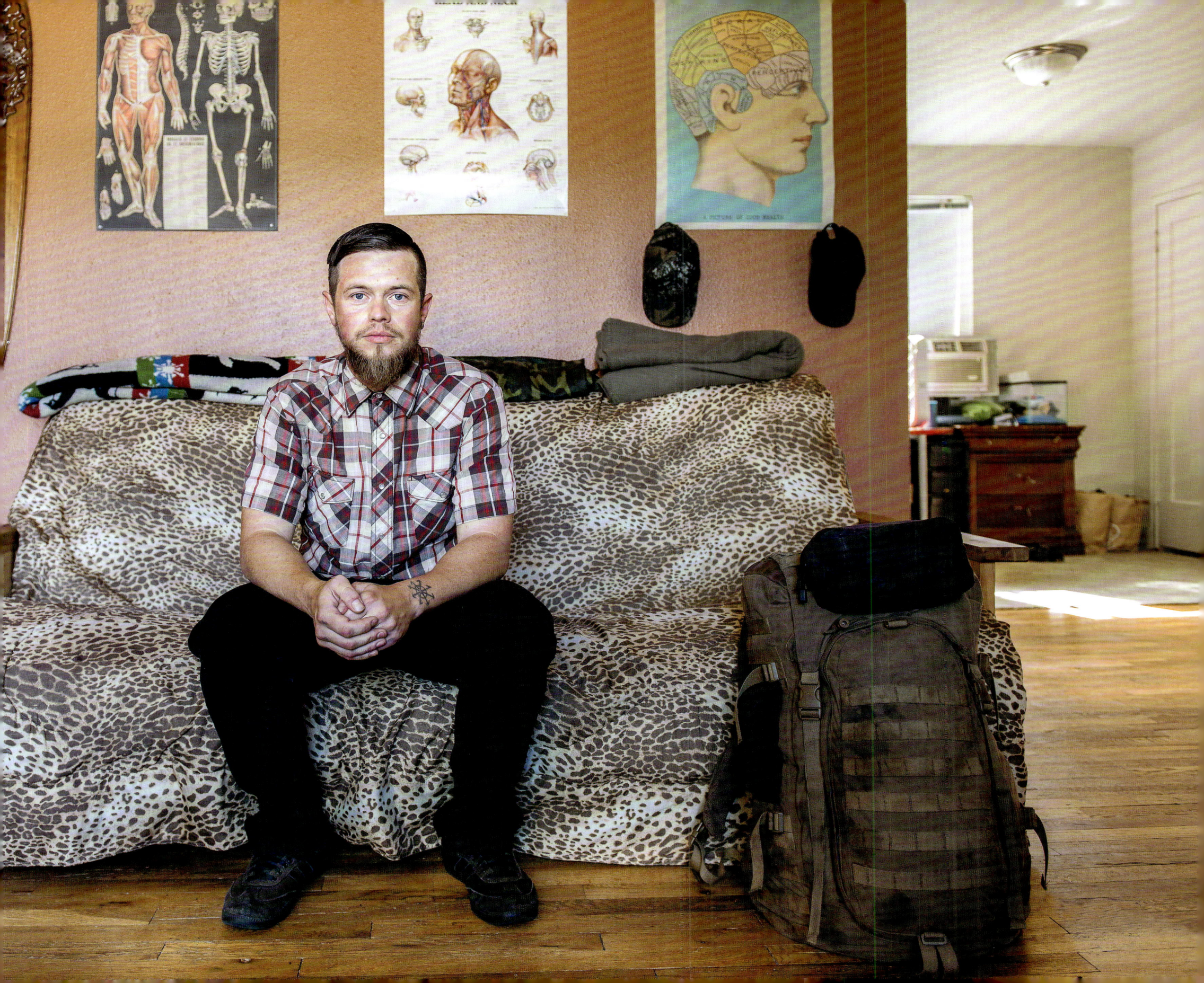

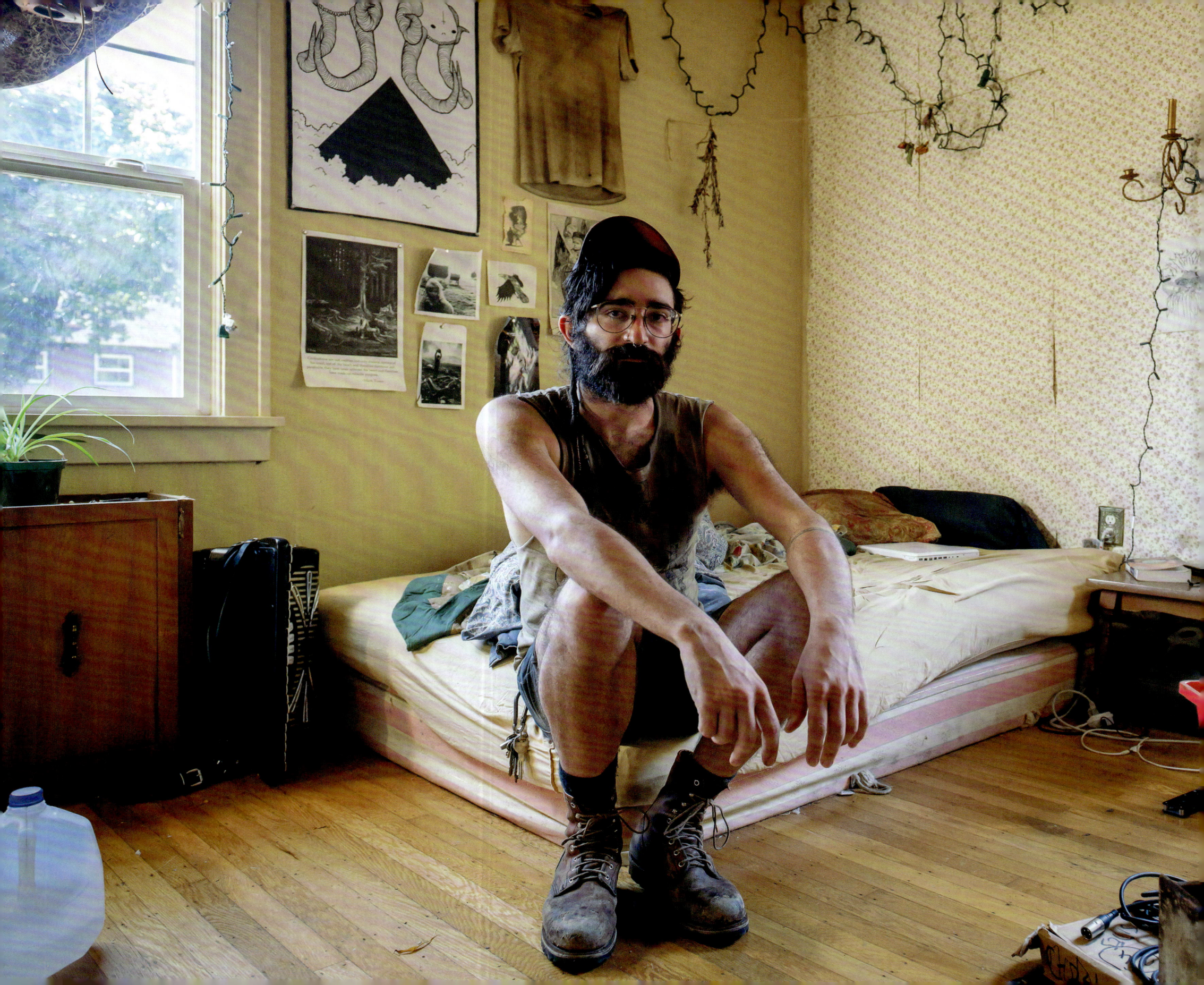

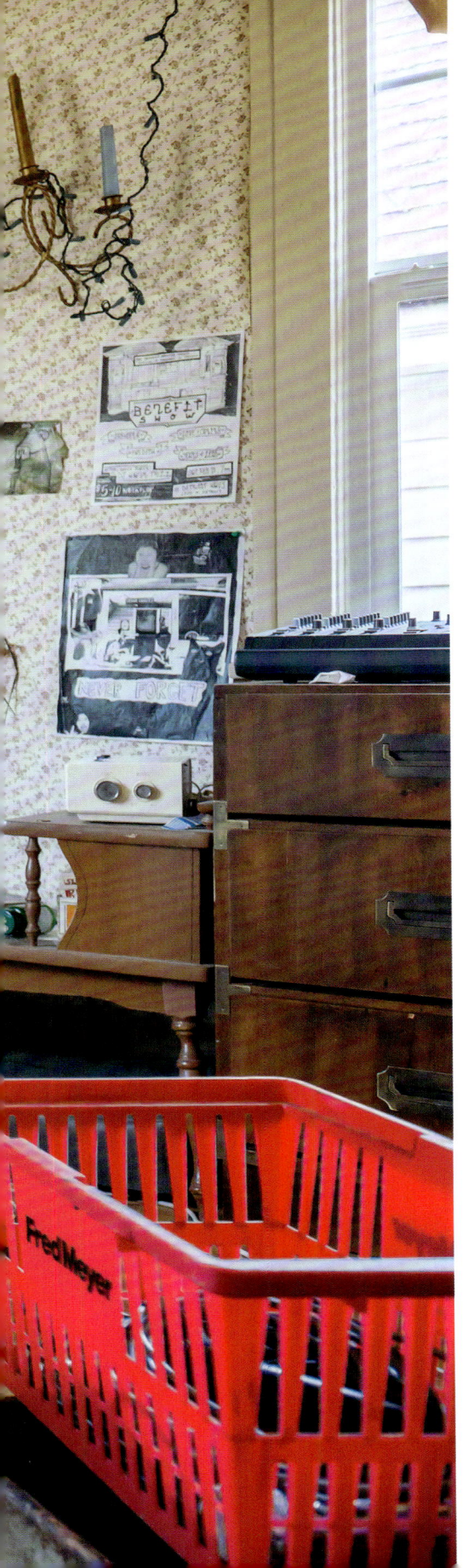

AUGUST GOLDEN
27 yrs old
NON PROFIT CARE PROVIDER

I AM CURRENTLY IN DEBT FOR ABOUT $30,000 FROM A CREDIT CARD USED TO PAY FOR COLLEGE IN CALIFORNIA. I HAVE BEEN PAYING THIS OFF SLOWLY AND LIKELY will CONTINUE TO FOR A LONG TIME. OR MAYBE I'll DECLARE BANKRUPSY

Debt Portrait #21, Portland, OR 2014

Craig

I am currently in debt over 50 k My life is so Stressful Due to my Debt I find that Bankrupsy may be my only choice but I'm not confortable with that. Never thought I'm my life that I wald be in this much Debt for So long, it never ends. And I wish it would

Over 50 K

JOHN Y
50 YEARS OLD
BUSINESS OWNER

AFTER BUILDING ABOUT $30,000 IN DEBT I FILED FOR BANKRUPTCY. THIS WAS A VERY SHAMEFUL THING FOR ME. I BELIEVE THERE SHOULD BE MORE EDUCATION ON THE DEBT SITUATION IN OUR SOCIETY.

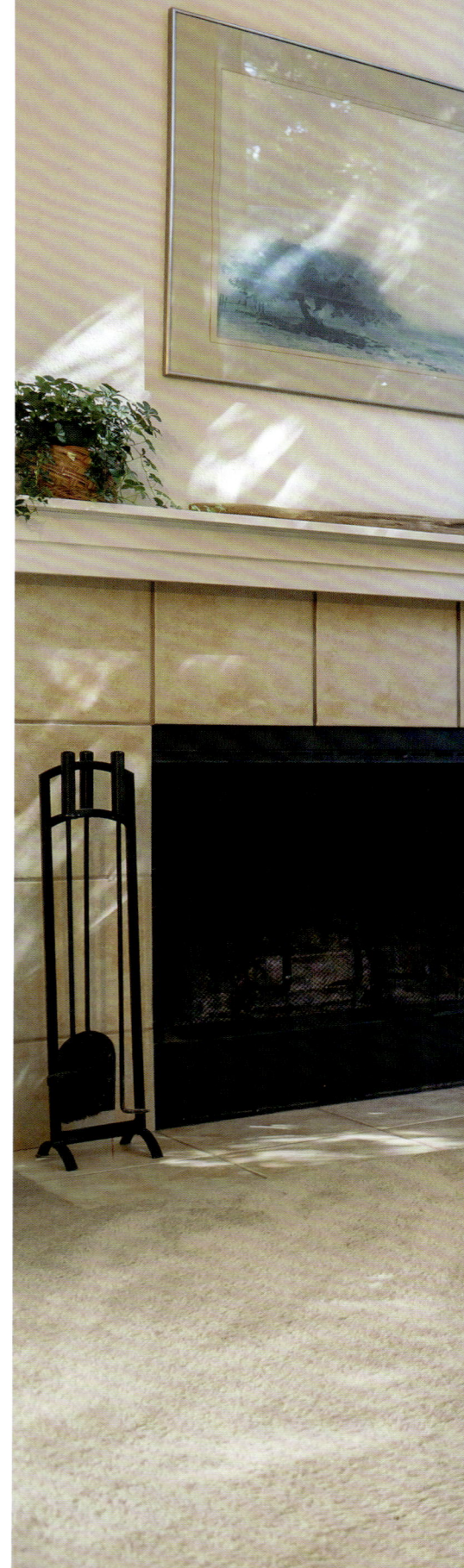

Debt Portrait #22, Beaverton, OR 2014

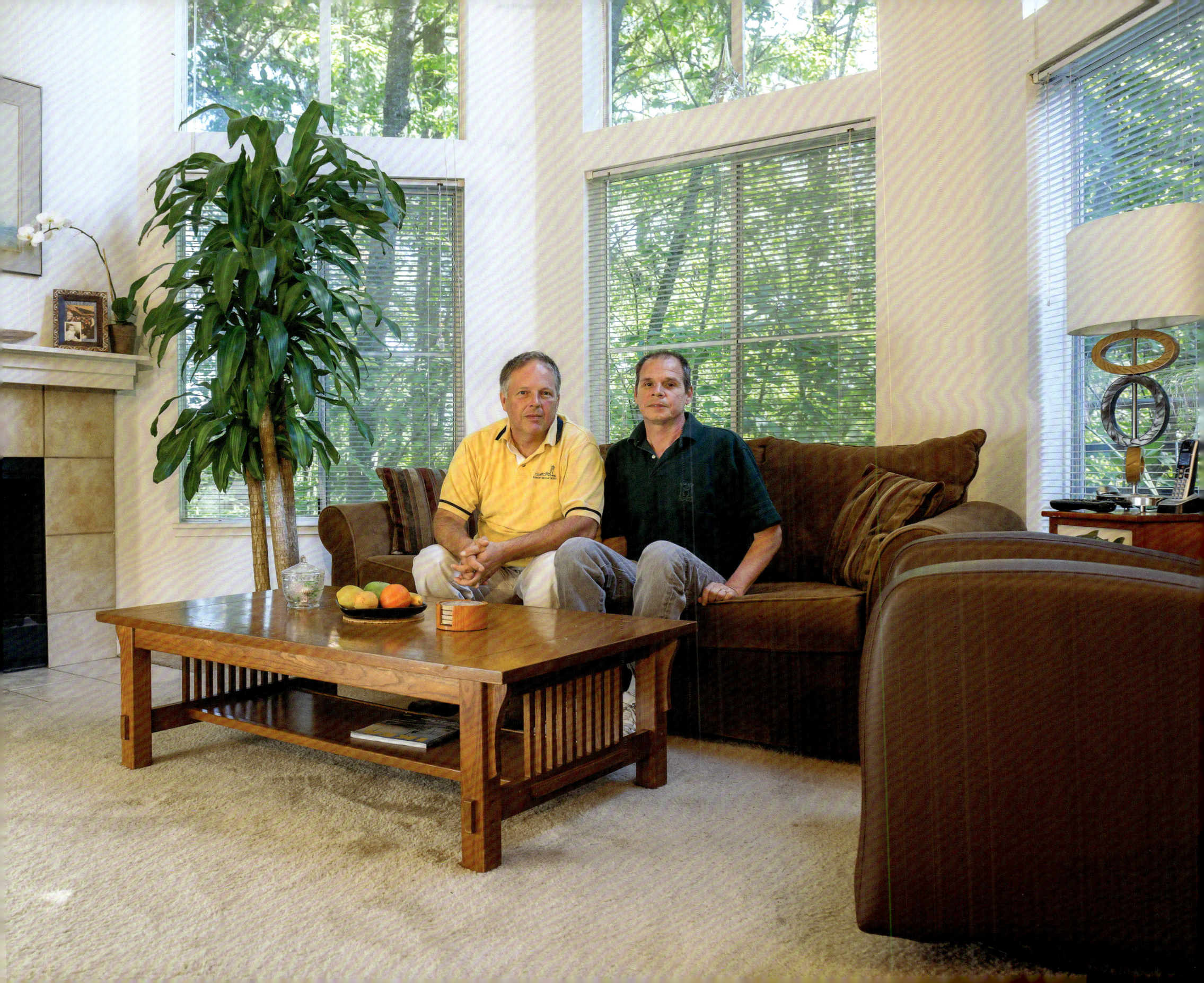

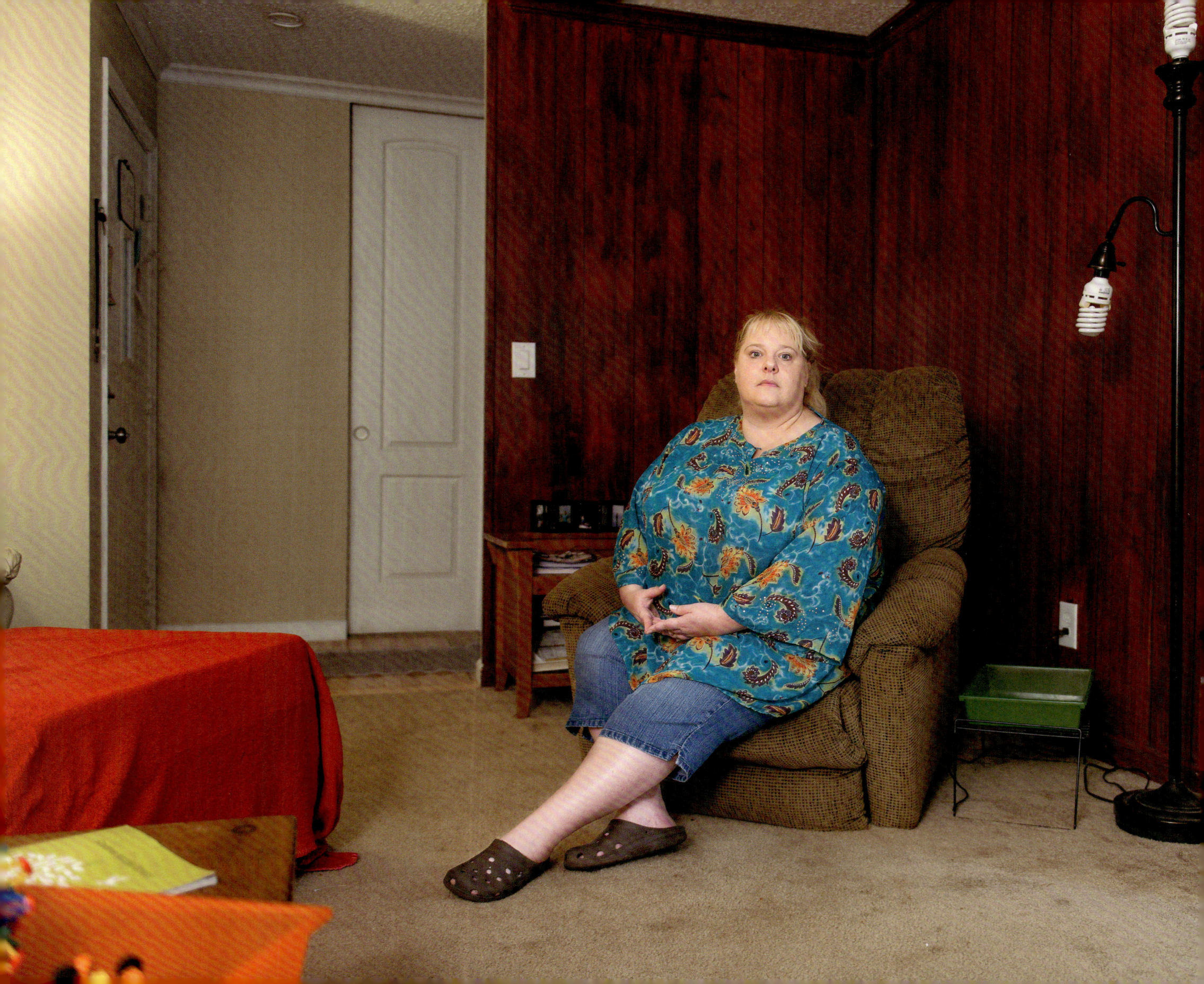

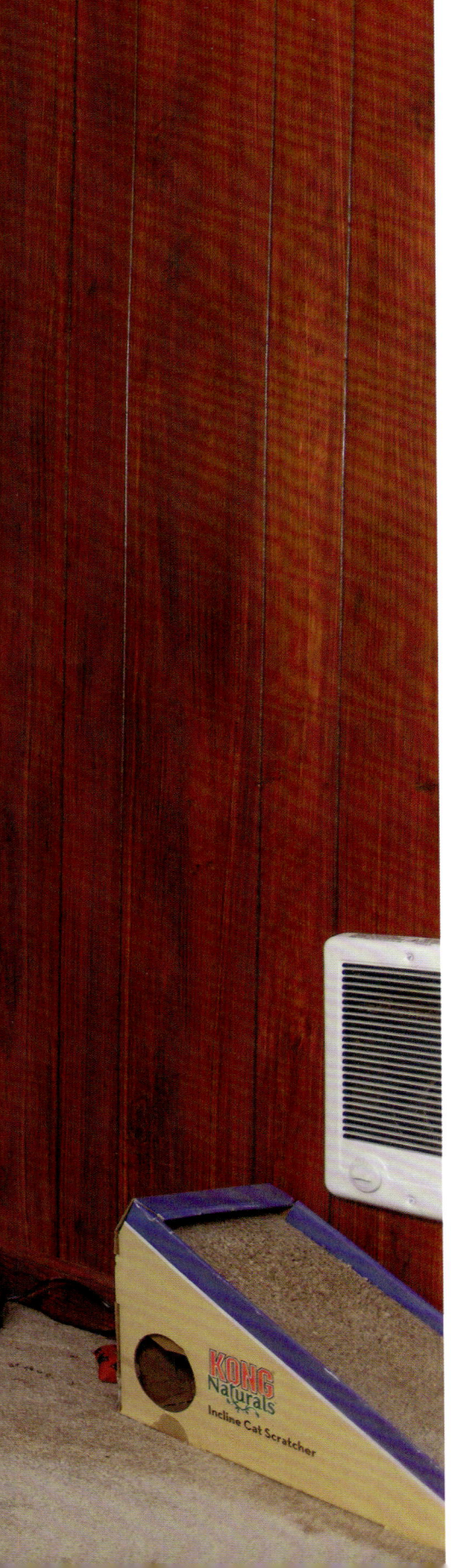

Grace Ragland $75,000!

Family Support Worker

    I began my history of debt when I started college. I was never taught how to handle money so I spent all my earnings. Going full time to college I needed the extra money from student loans so I used the remainder to live off of-pay car loan, ect.

    When my ex-husband got incarcerated and left me as sole supporter of the family, I wasn't able to pay any on previous debts. I kept building debt even though I worked 2-3 jobs 7 days a week for 7 years. My health took a toll and I now have 1 Ft. job and my kids are older. Starting to see the light at the end-thanks to some help from family and lots of prayer! It affects every part of my life and I wish I had been taught to prioritize handling money.

Debt Portrait #23, Oregon City, OR 2014

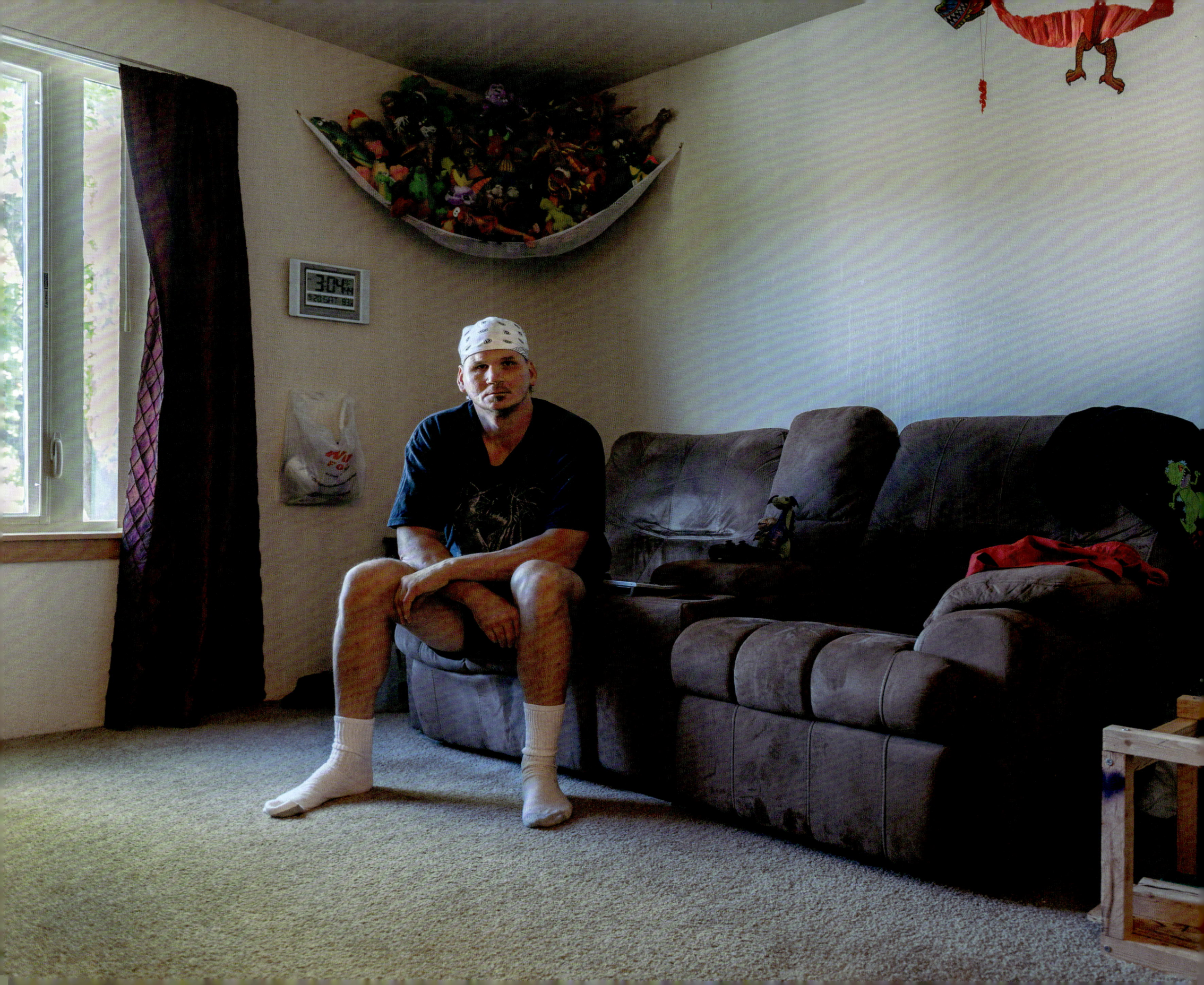

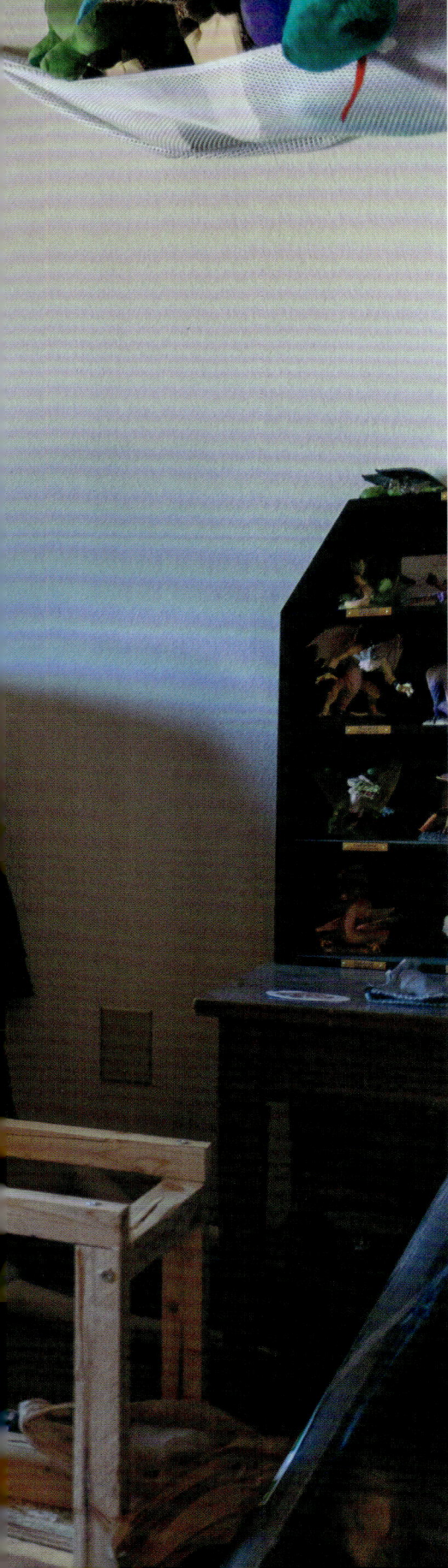

Dragon
41
Disability

I have 6000 in debt through
on point and clackamas federal credit
union and Sears and Aarons
when I make my payments to the
two credit unions i Just pull the money
right back out again because I need
it for food because I was kicked
off of the food card program for a
reason I really do not understand. I try
to find odd jobs to do to make some
money from craigslist and friends of
mine I also eat my dinners at the senior
center which I also help out at from
time to time life right now is pretty
stress full.

Debt Portrait #24, Happy Valley, OR 2014

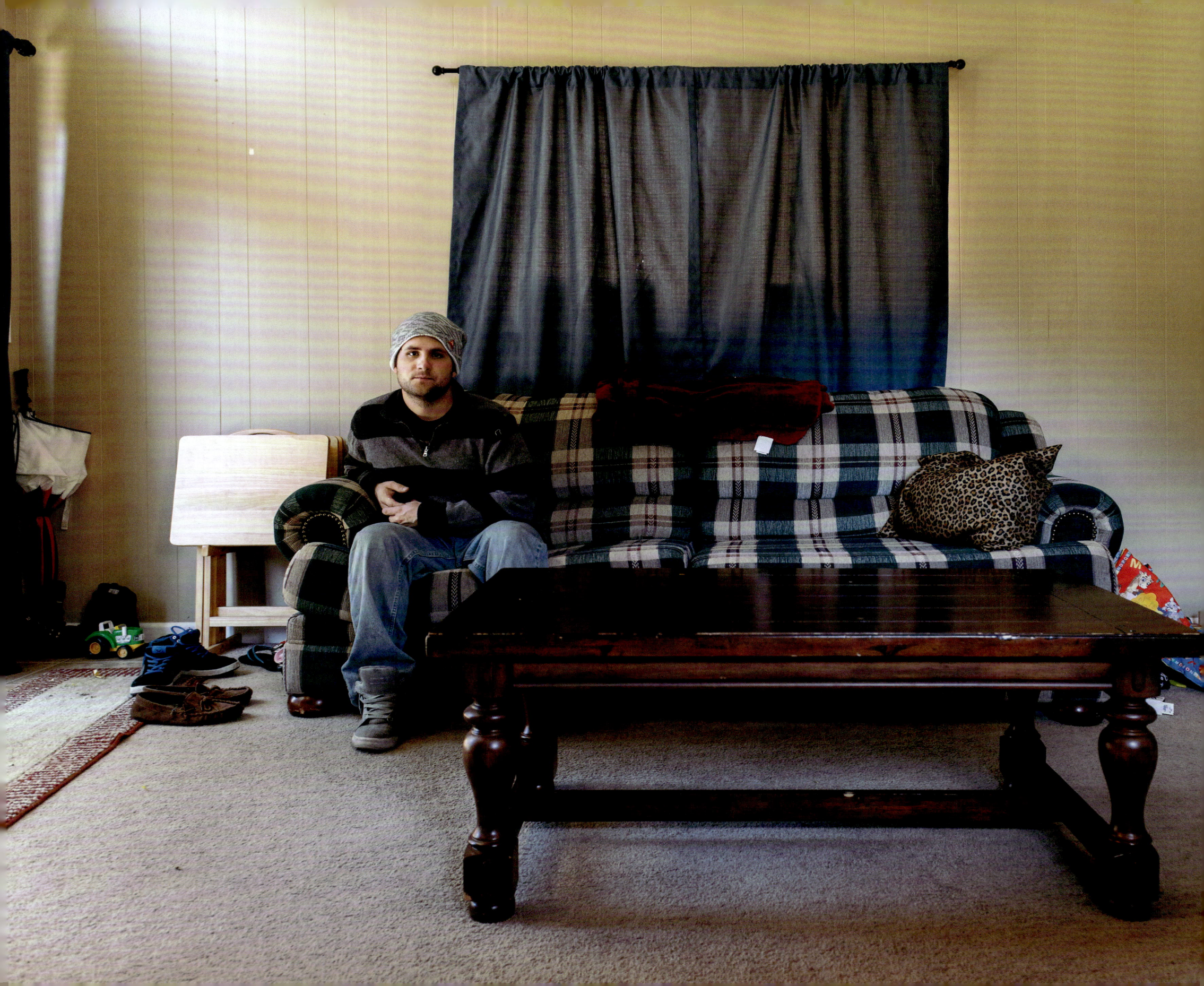

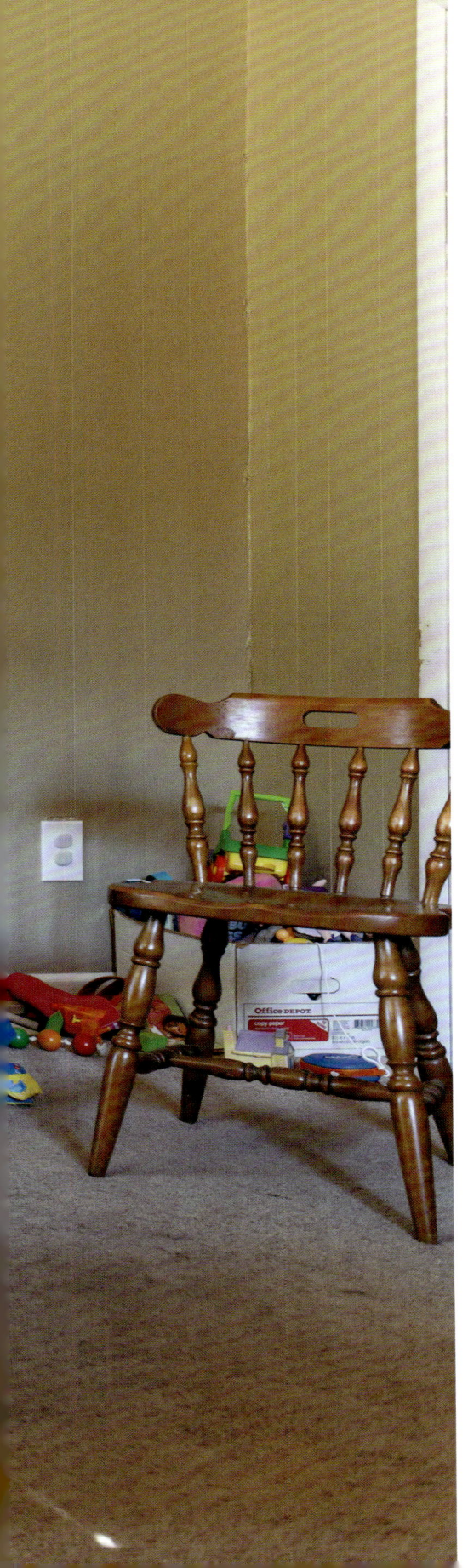

Tyler Katchever, Age 27
Painter/Handyman

$6,000 in Debt

* Student loans were required before I was
even able to get a stable career.

* Credit cards for "Emergencies" became a way to
spend money when I had not been paid yet...

Debt Portrait #25, Detroit, MI 2014

Mario Garnes, 28 yrs
Tattoo Artist / Biker
$40,000+ in debt

I graduated from high school in 2004. I went to Tennessee state university. By 2006, I'd developed Crohn's Disease. I had to drop out of school, and eventually move back to Detroit, MI. Now I owe for student loans, as well as medical bills. My debt is pretty high to due to interest.

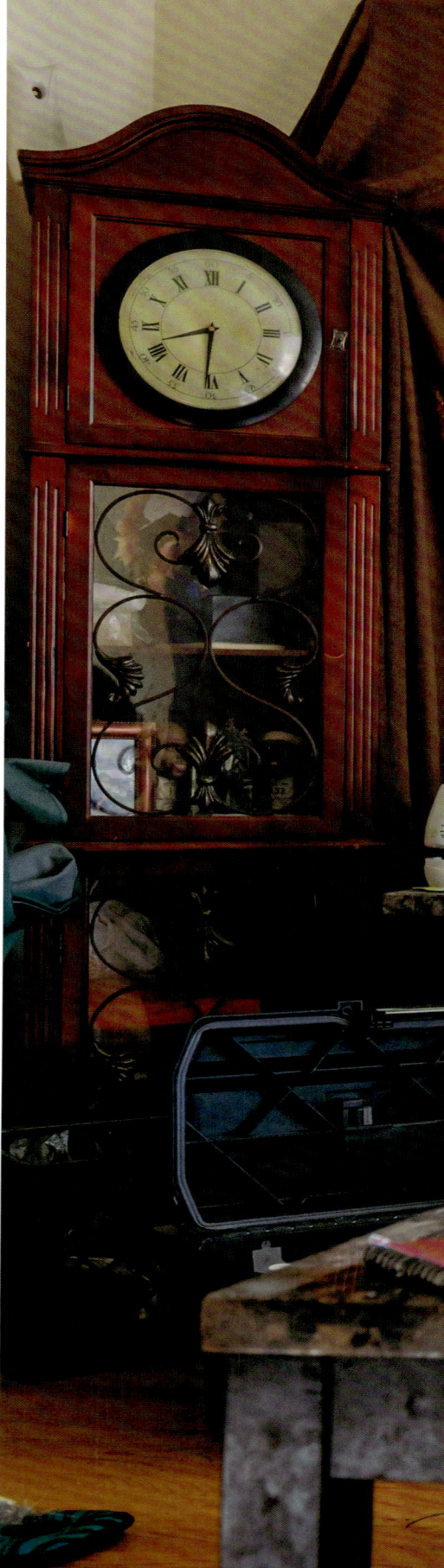

Debt Portrait #26, Detroit, MI 2014

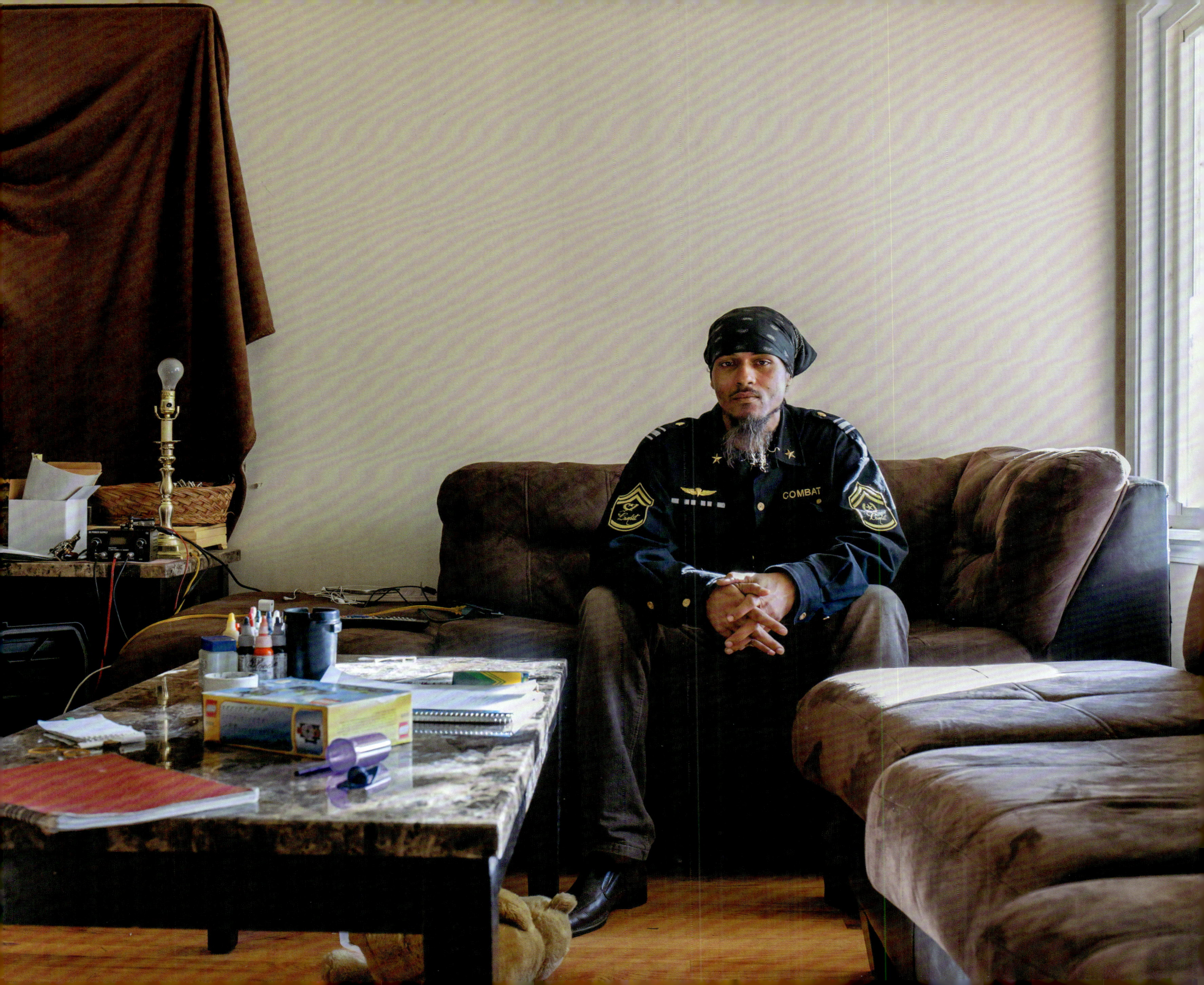

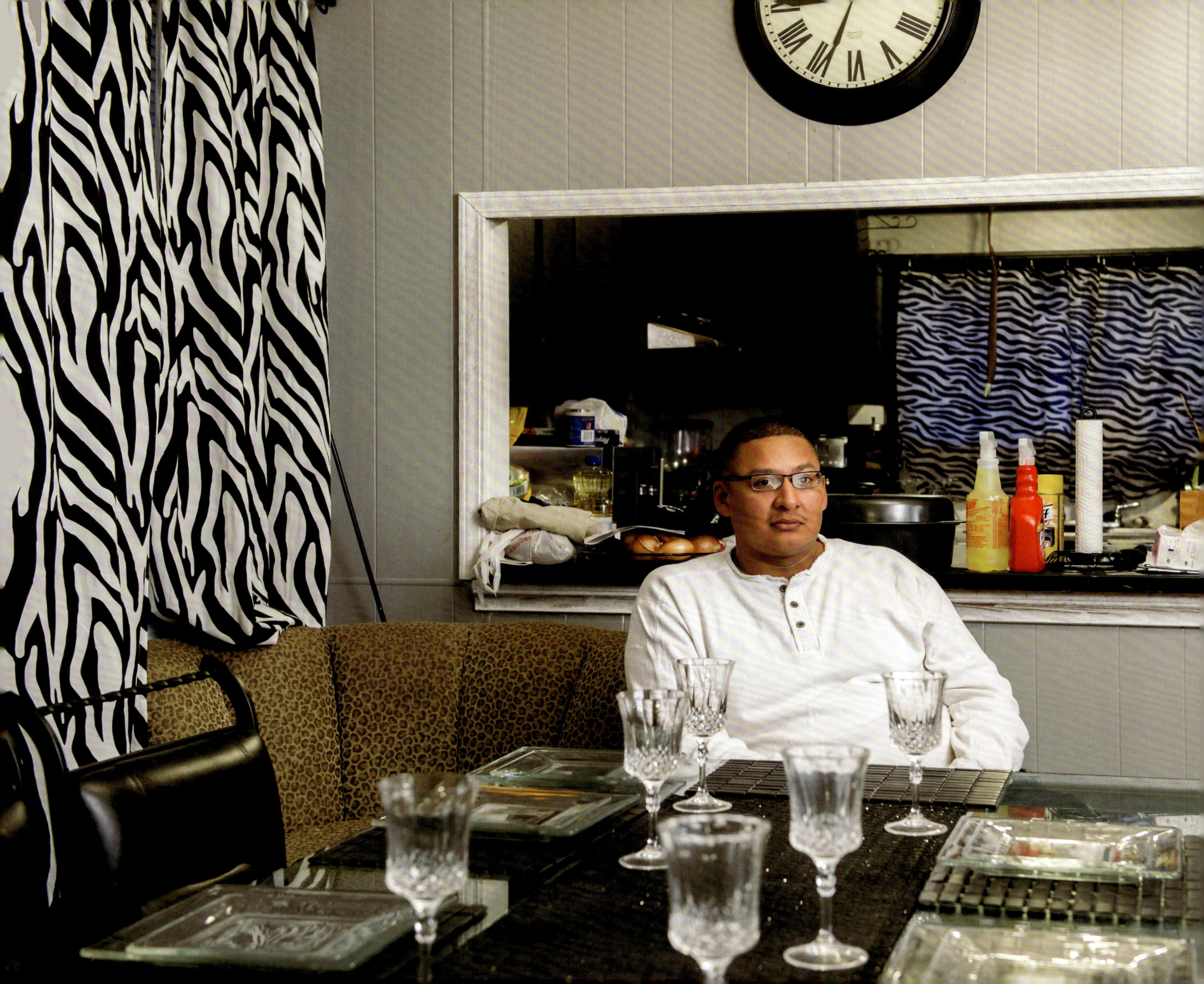

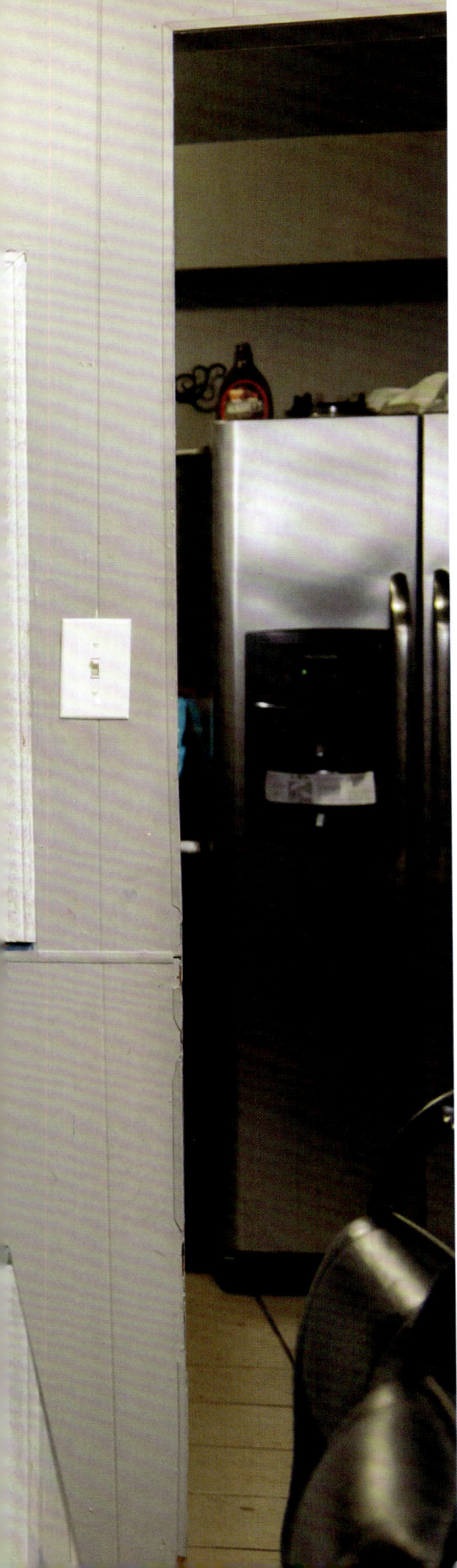

Ramon Romero   10-23-2014
                                Age. <u>30</u>

I've accumalated over $<u>250,000</u>~ in Dept.
Starting from credit cards, phone bills, & a
Laundromat that I purchased. In 9-months
my Water Bill was over $ <u>28,700</u>⁰⁰.

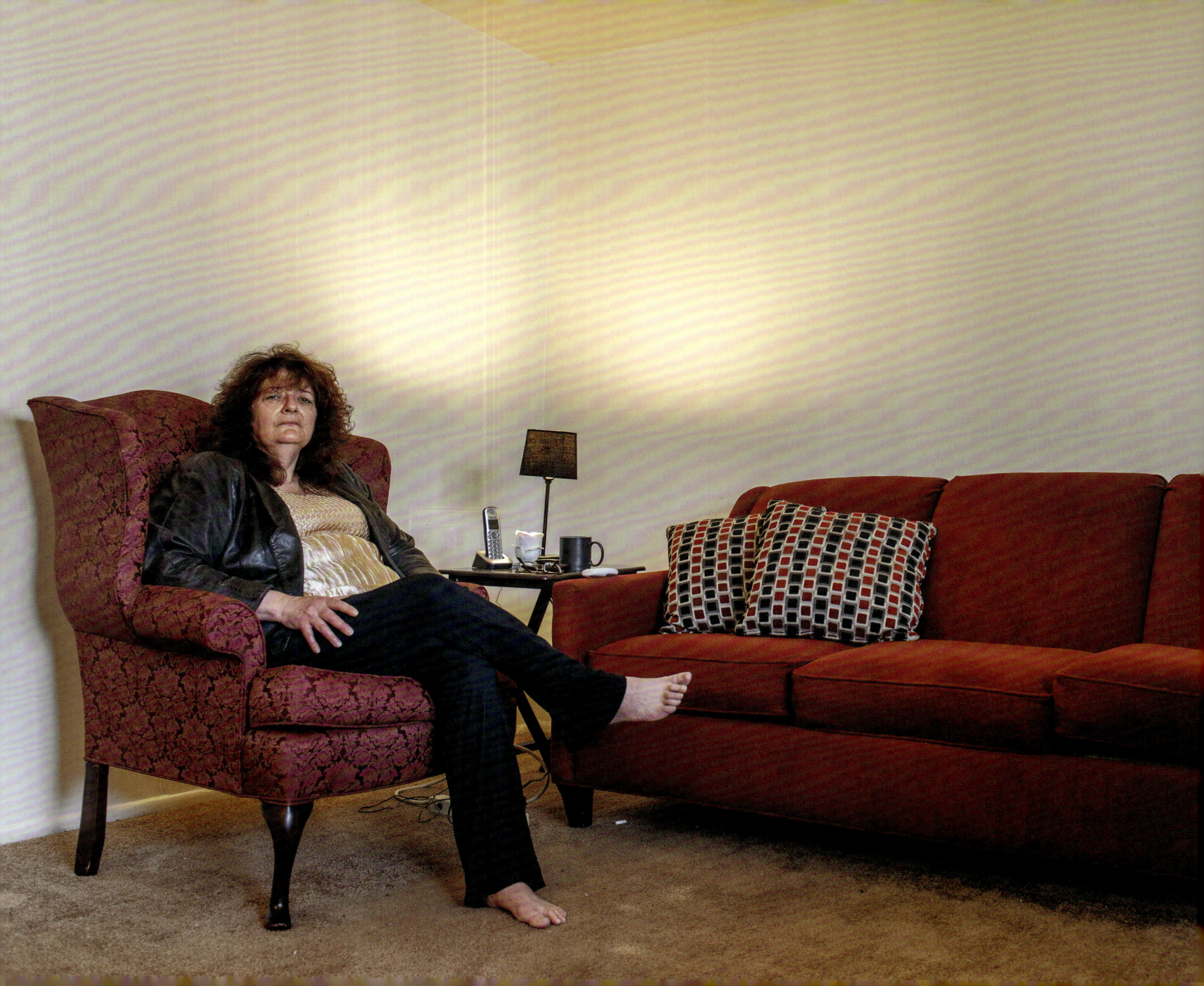

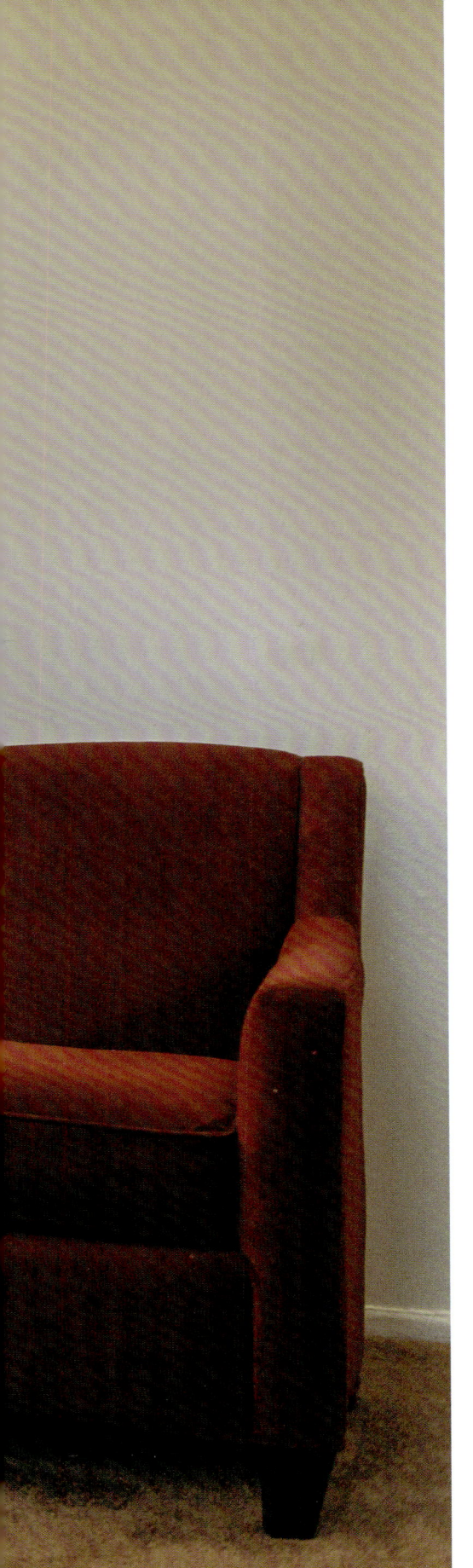

$20,000

Leasa Rosolino
unemployed

a combination of not
being able to work
and being able to
make money in the field
I was experienced in.

Debt Portrait #28, Pontiac, MI 2014

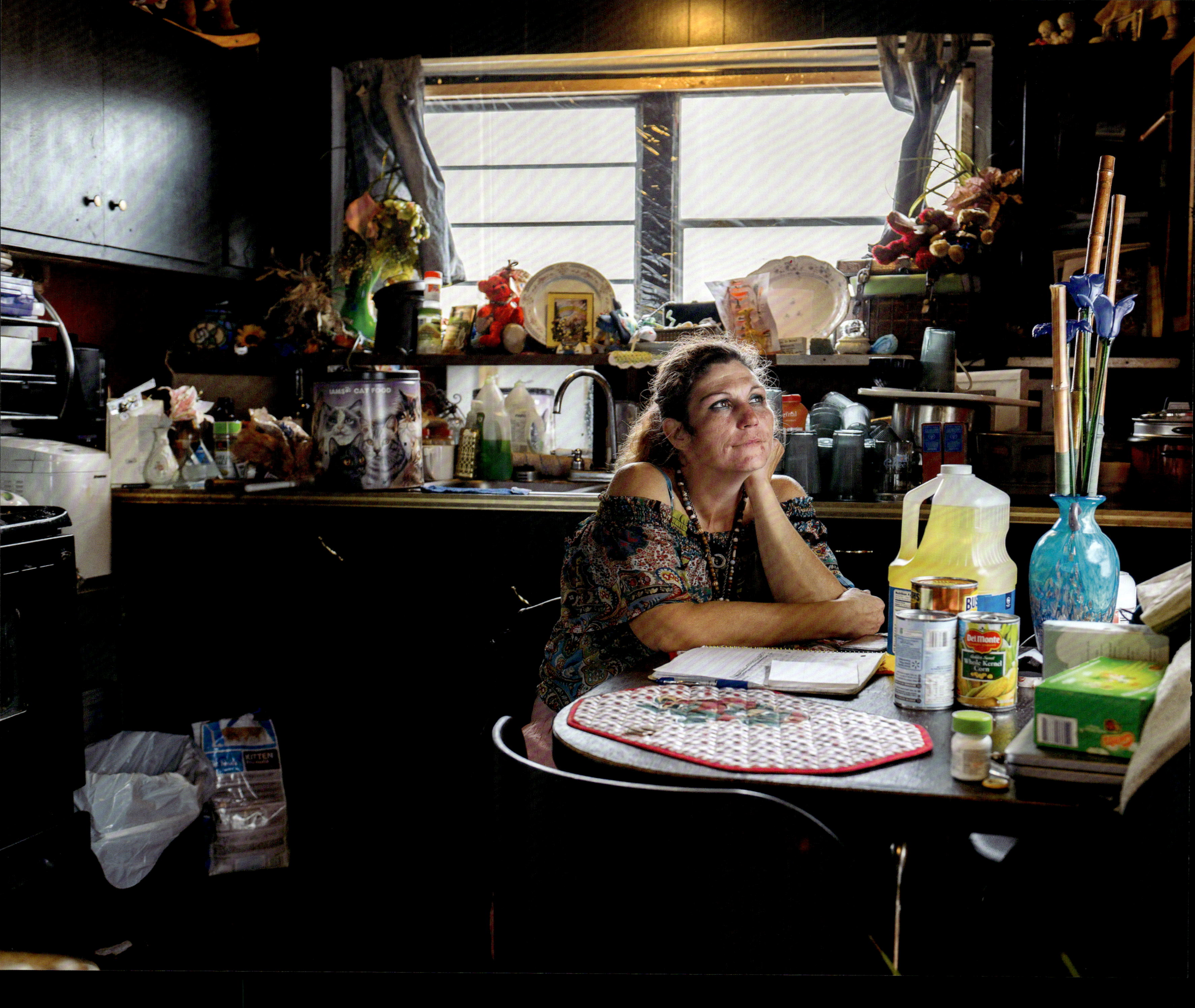

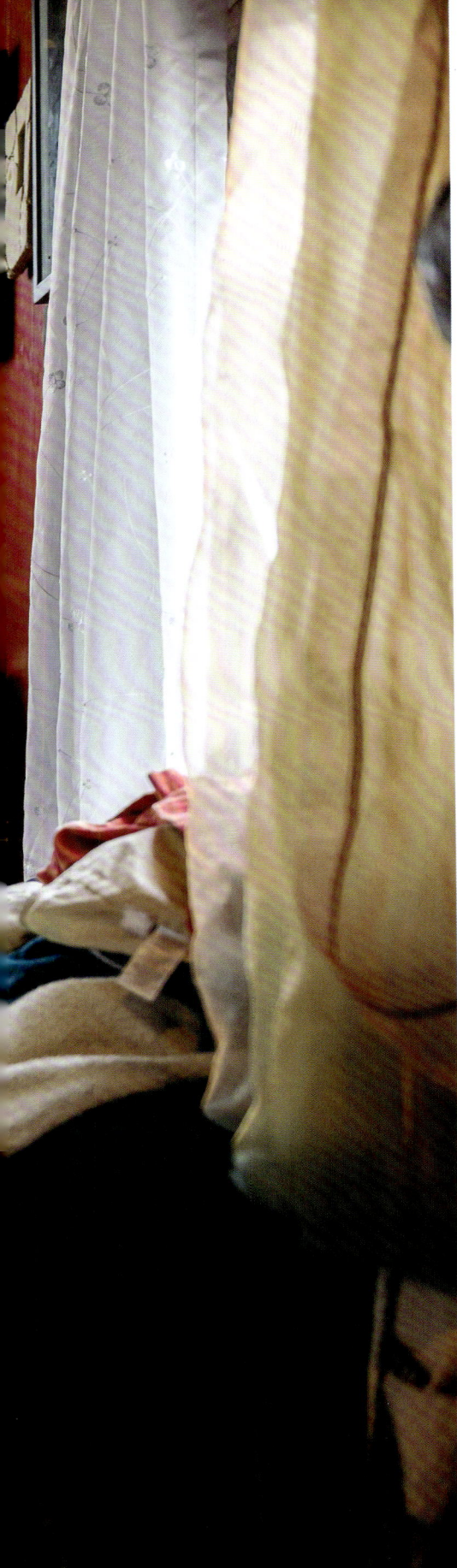

Michele Manis

House keeper /Artist

Reribe

35,000

I accumulated the last round of
debt after paying off a large amount
at 23 when I went back to college I acquired
Most of the debt. I also acquired much
of the debt there The Rest was Mail order
catalogs, debt and getting through in homeless
times Robbing Peter to Pay Paul or so they say

Debt Portrait #29, Harrison Township, MI 2014

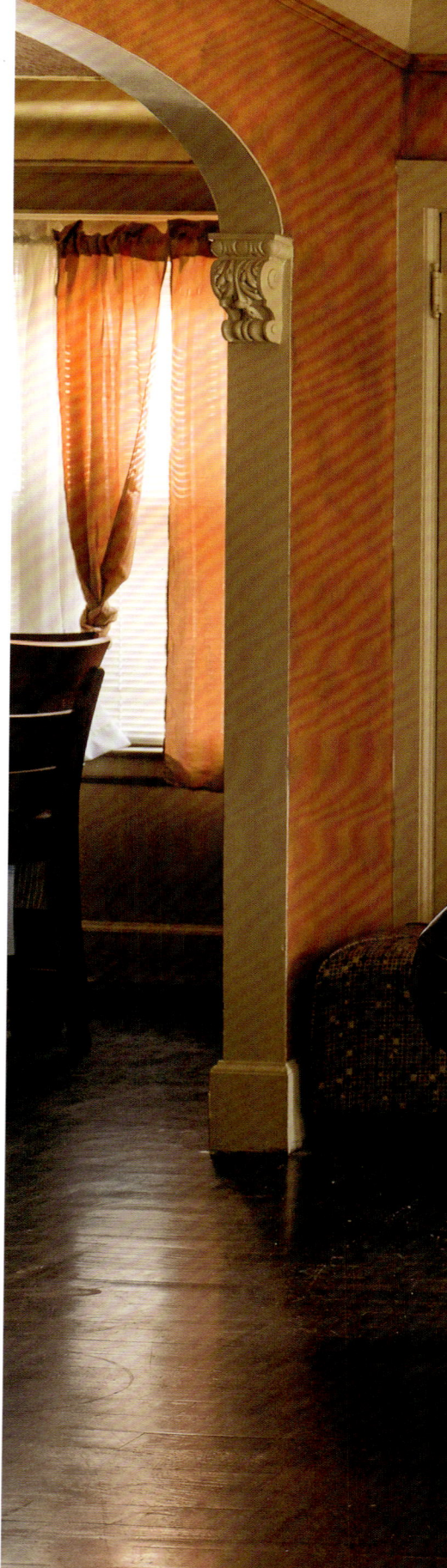

Bernita Bradley
Community Outreach & Engagement for ESD

Was in debt for $130,000 for Homes
and Cars. Now still in debt
For $26,000 From student Loans that
helped me live while I was in school.
I plan to pay them off one day soon.

Debt Portrait #30, Detroit, MI 2014

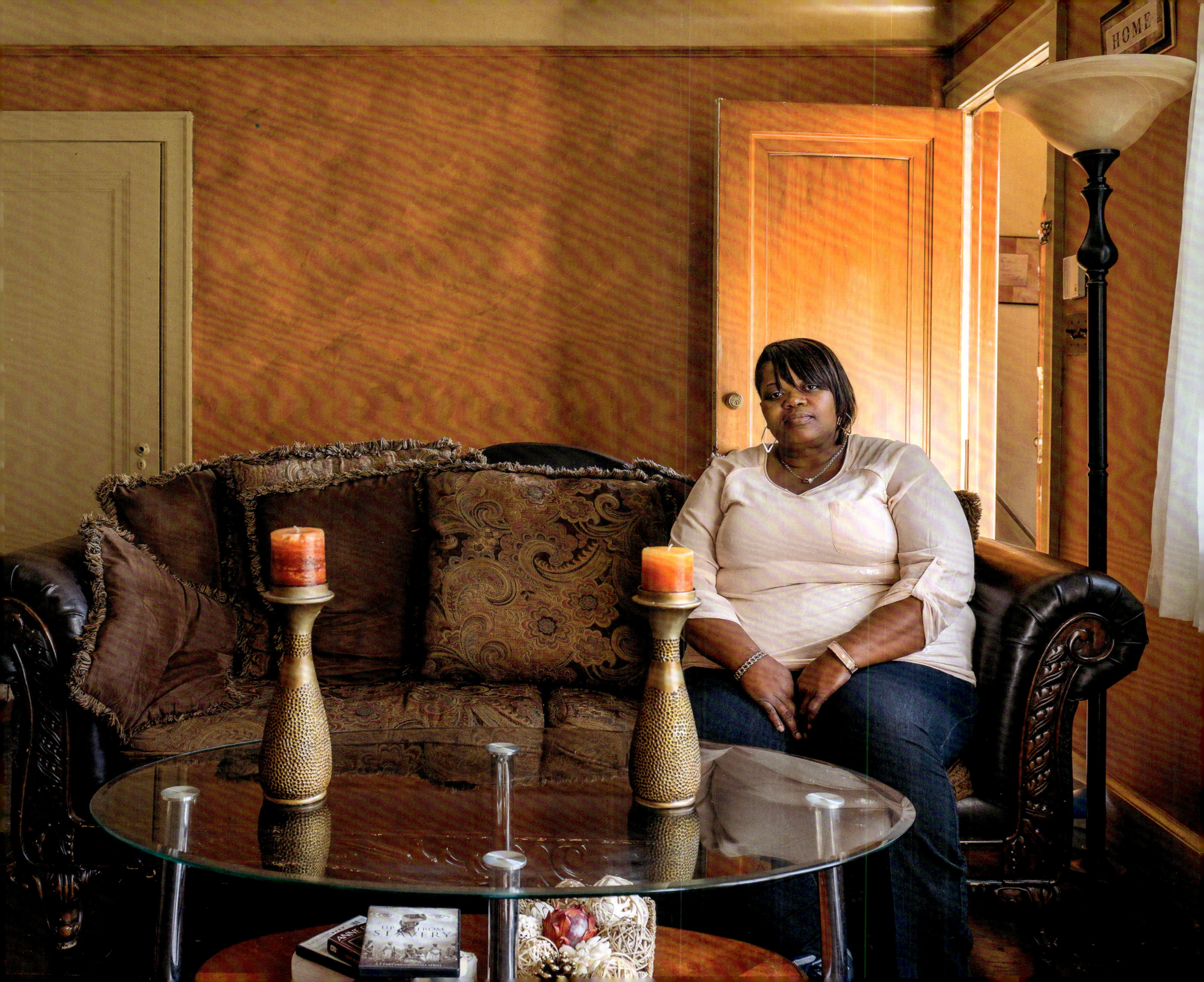

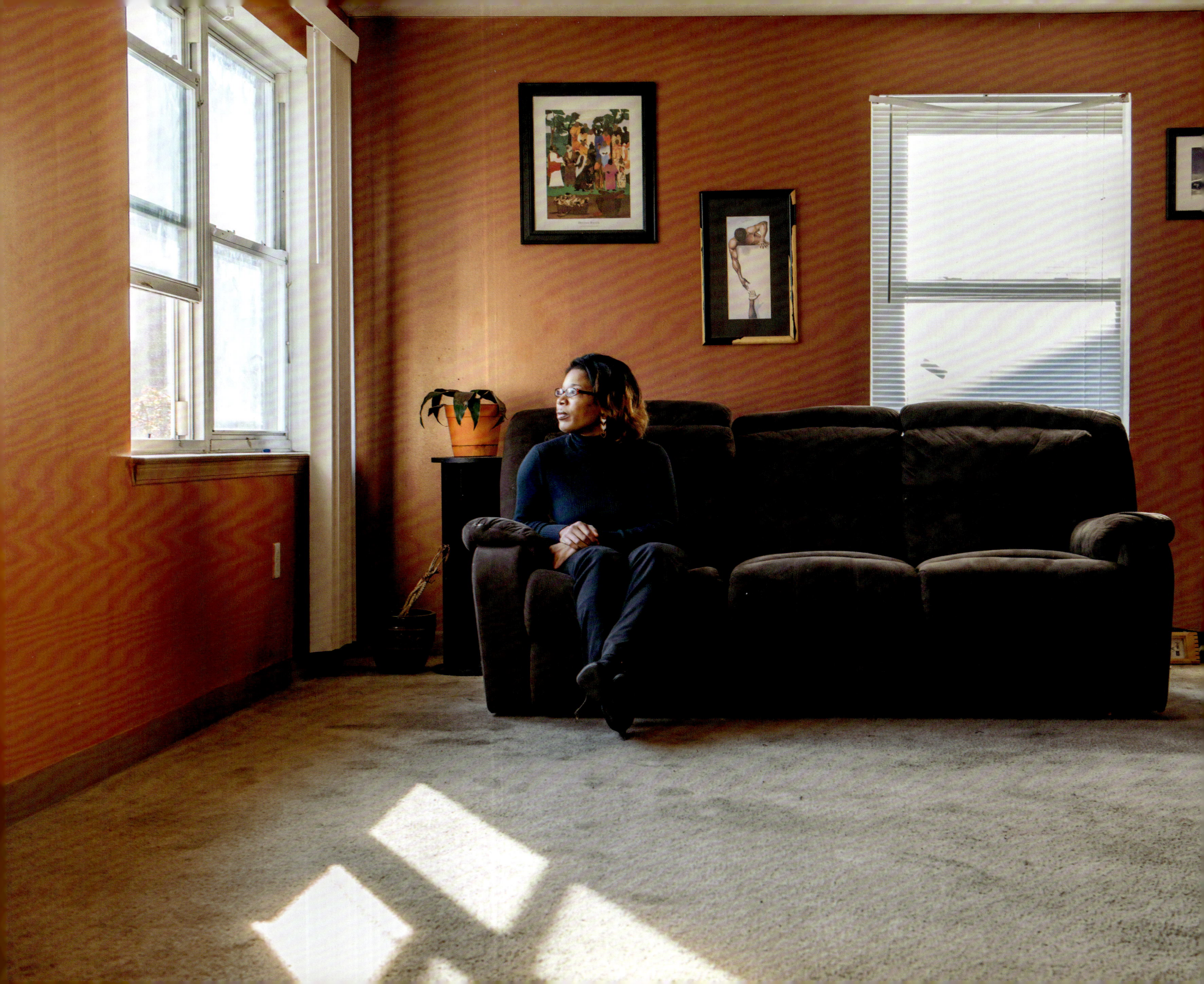

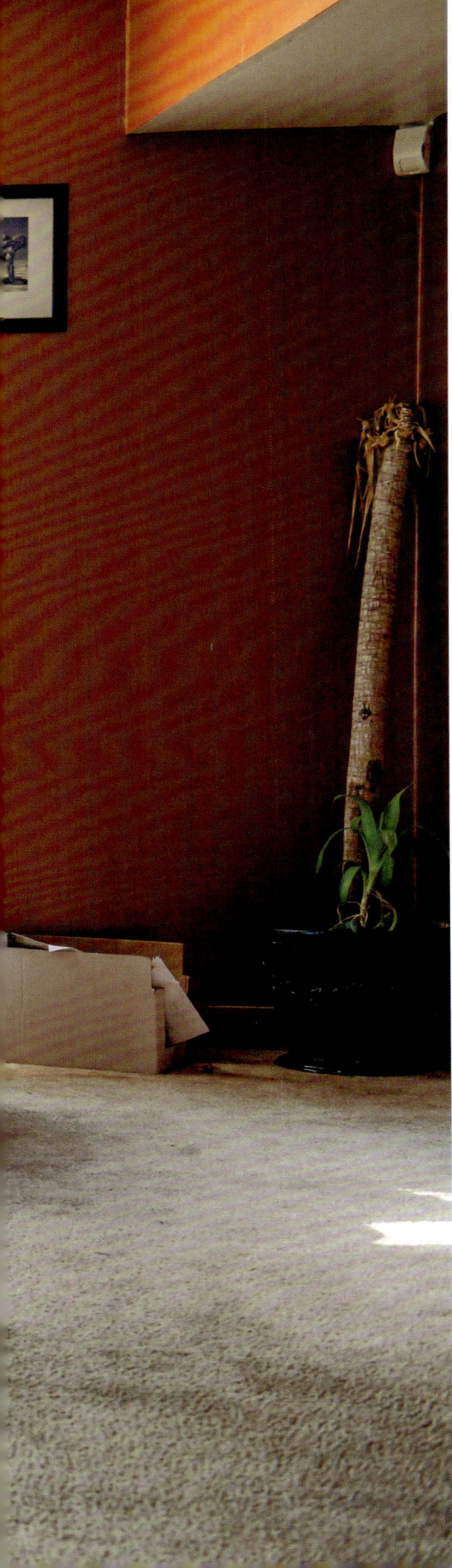

Regina Hollis
Parent Partner
AmeriCorps

30,000

I got into debt because student loans
and letting someone close to me put a
car in my name.

Debt Portrait #31, Detroit, MI 2014

My name is Katya Kilbarne I am 25 yrsold
~~to Hey~~ I am a sideshow performer ~~$~~ Street
performer & ametuer musician.

I am around $130,000.00 in
debt.

It ~~is~~ consists of medical bills,
student debt & racked up expenses
by my parents using my identity.

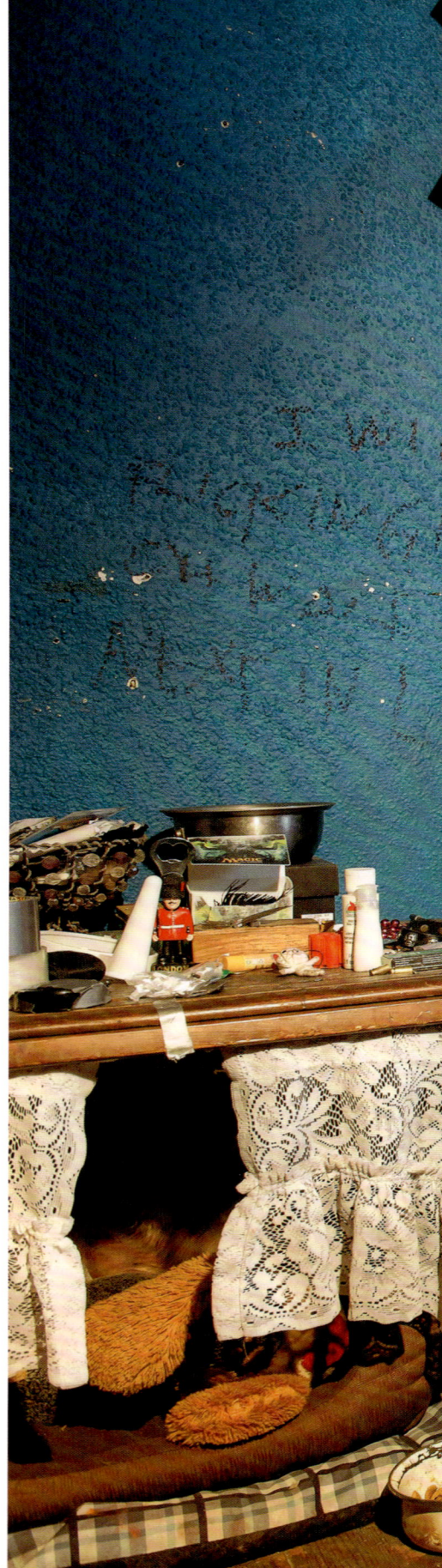

Debt Portrait #32, New Orleans, LA 2015

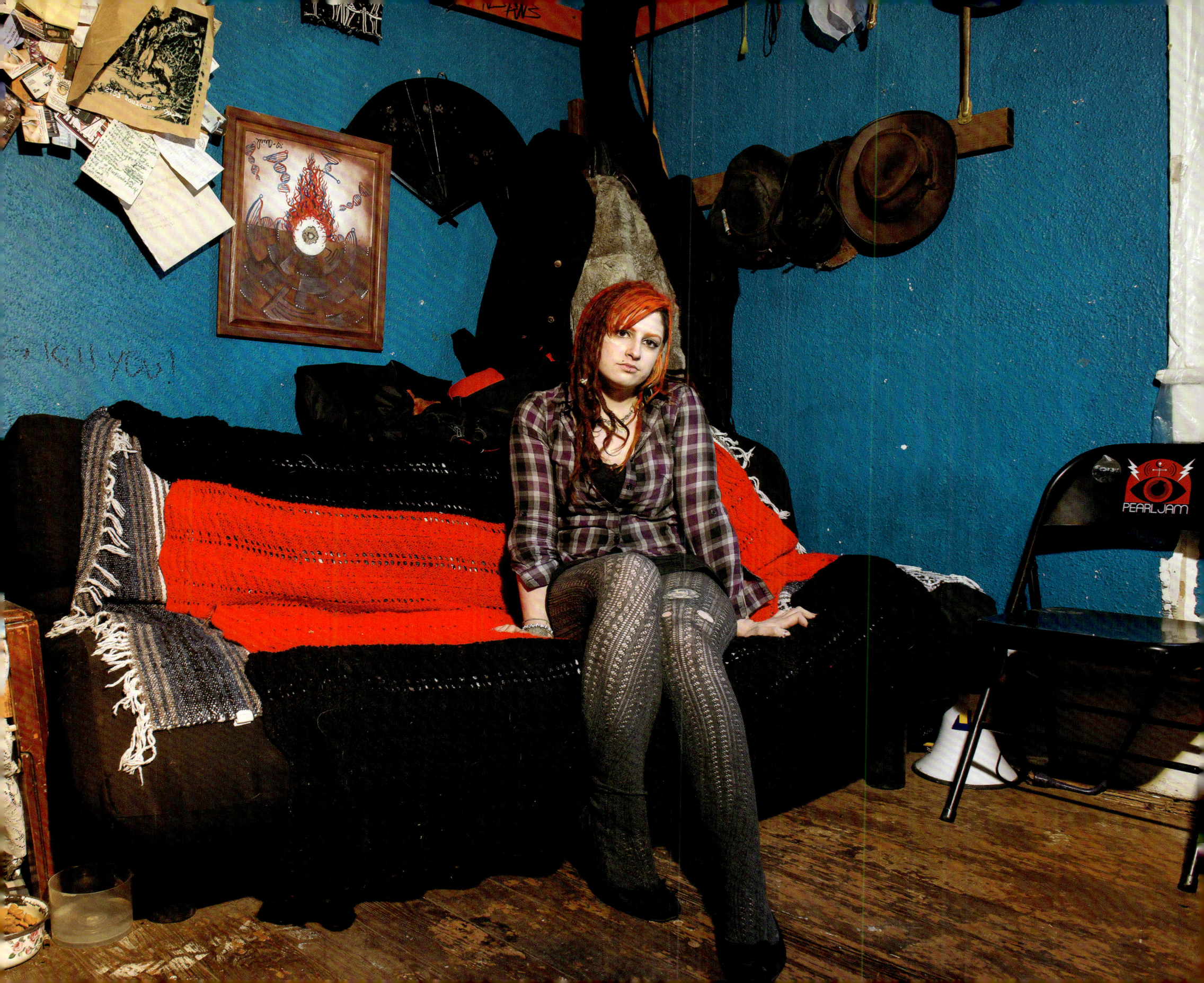

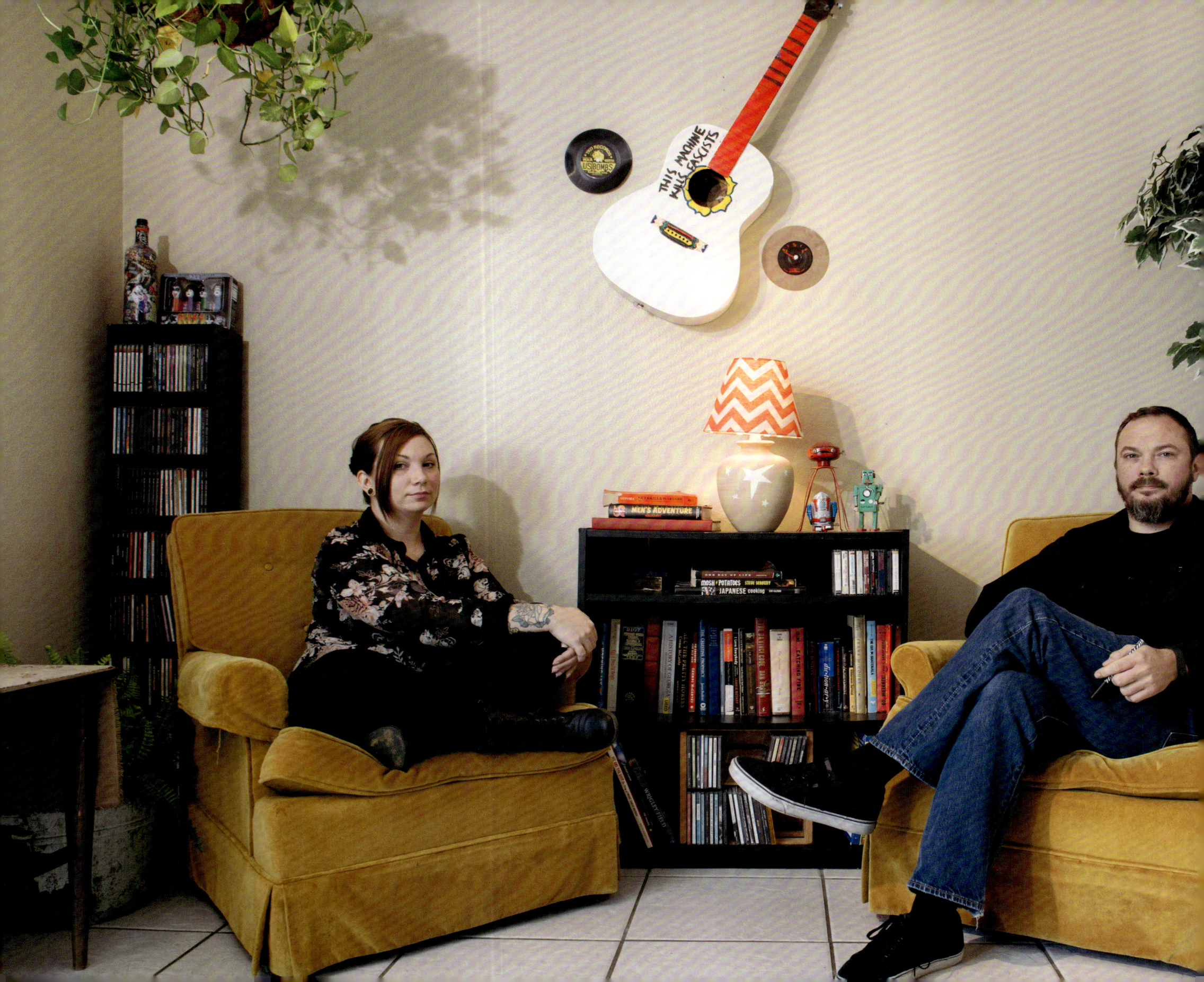

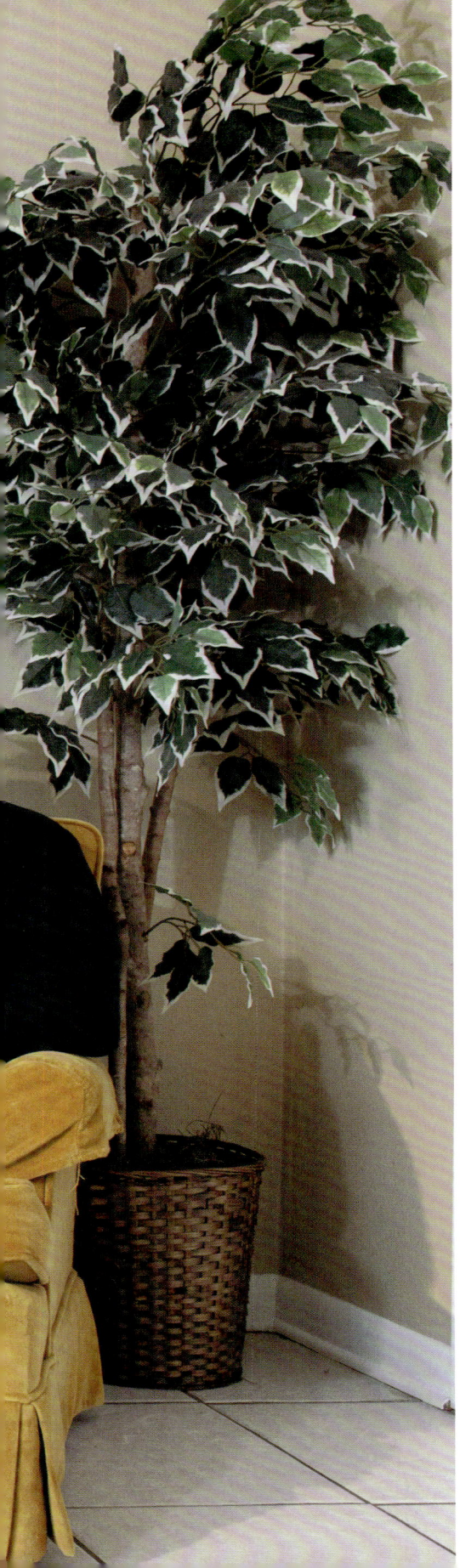

Michael Scearce

Melody Brown

$ 36,000

$ 162,000

- Credit Cards $4,000

- Student Loans $ 12,000

- Car Repossession $20,000

- Federal Student Loans - 54

- Back child Support - 27

- Medical Bills - 81

Debt Portrait #33, New Orleans, LA 2015

I have been in debt with my phone bill & student loans, since 2012. It started in the year of 2012 every since I graduated from College due to not being able to find a full-time job. I owe about 69,000 towards My student loans and about $800.00 for my phone bill. I worked many part time gigs, but not enough to get out all this debt I am in at this time.

Total Debt = $77,000

Debt Portrait #34, New Orleans, LA 2015

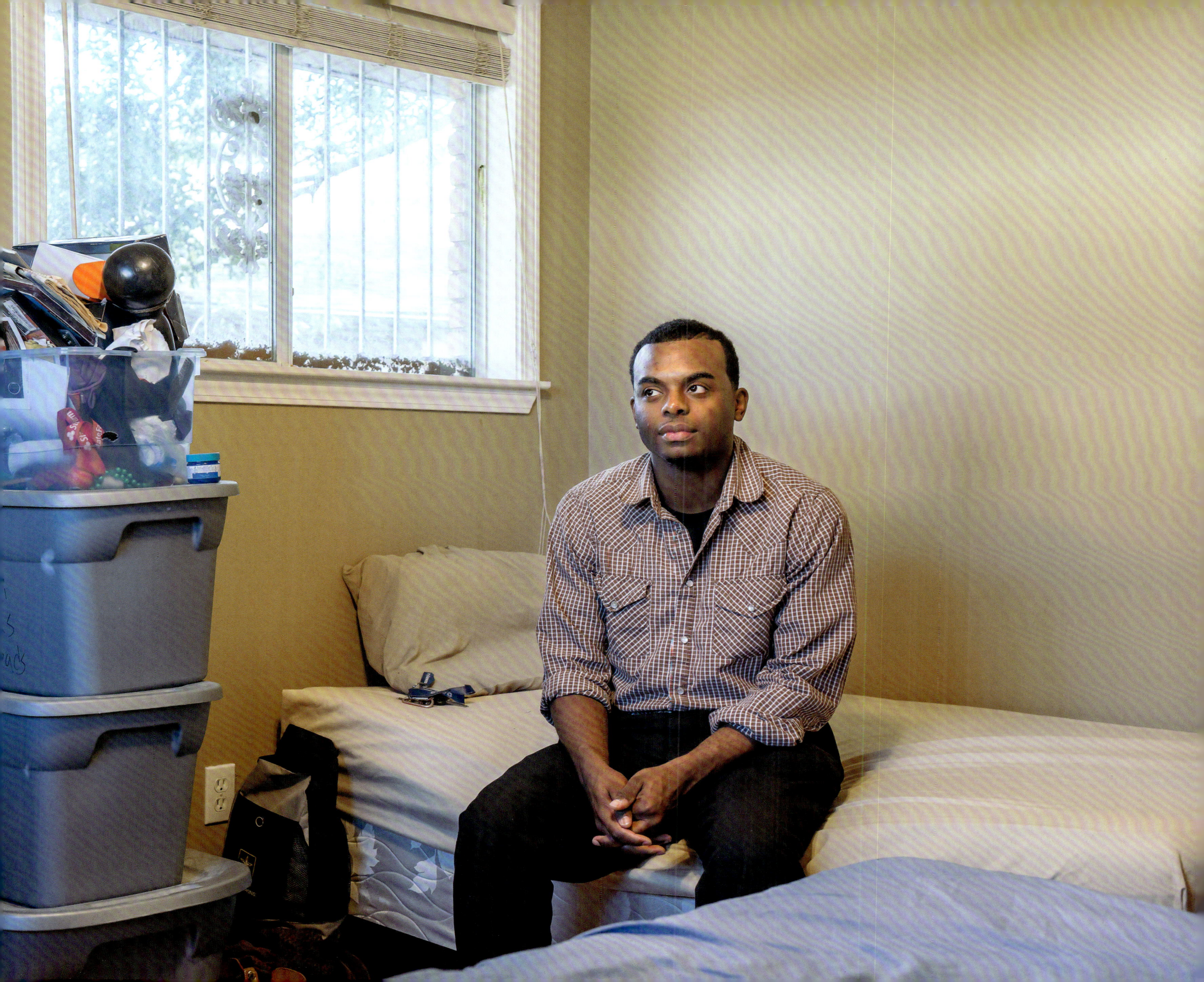

I WENT TO GRAD SCHOOL IN 2010. IT WAS DIFFICULT FINDING A JOB WHEN I GRADUATED IN 2007 SO I WENT BACK TO SCHOOL. MY LOANS ARE A TOTAL OF 50,000 AND I WORKED FULLTIME WHILE IN GRAD SCHOOL, MOSTLY WAITING TABLES.

$50,000

SARAH KING

ASSISTANT DIRECTOR, NONPROFIT

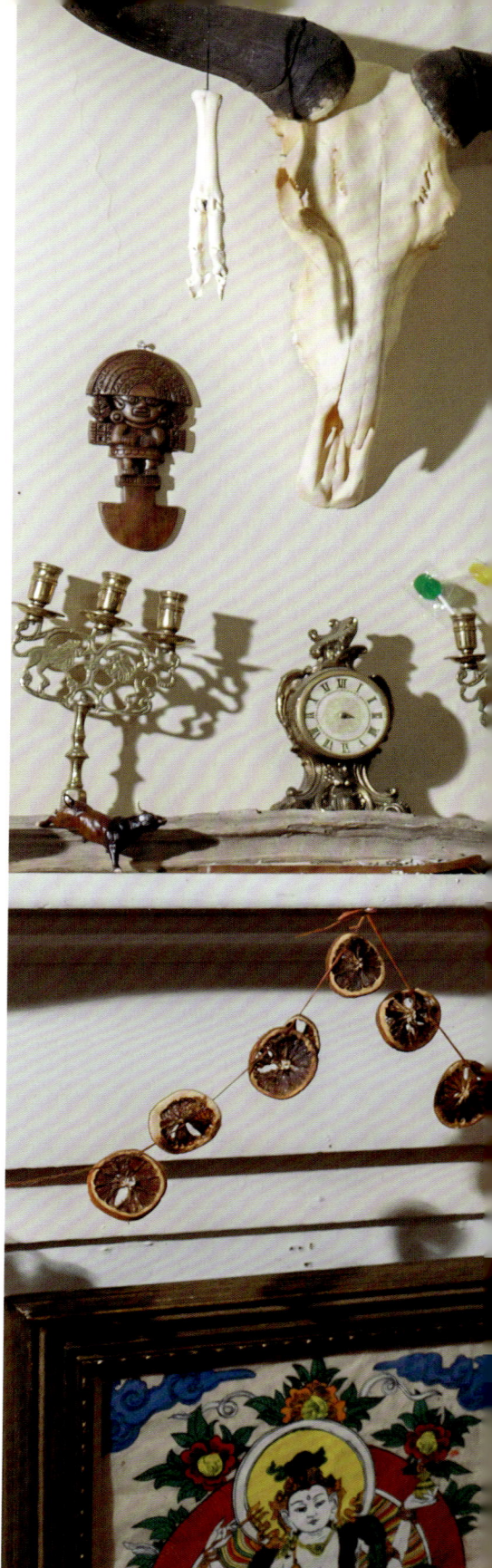

Debt Portrait #35, New Orleans, LA 2015

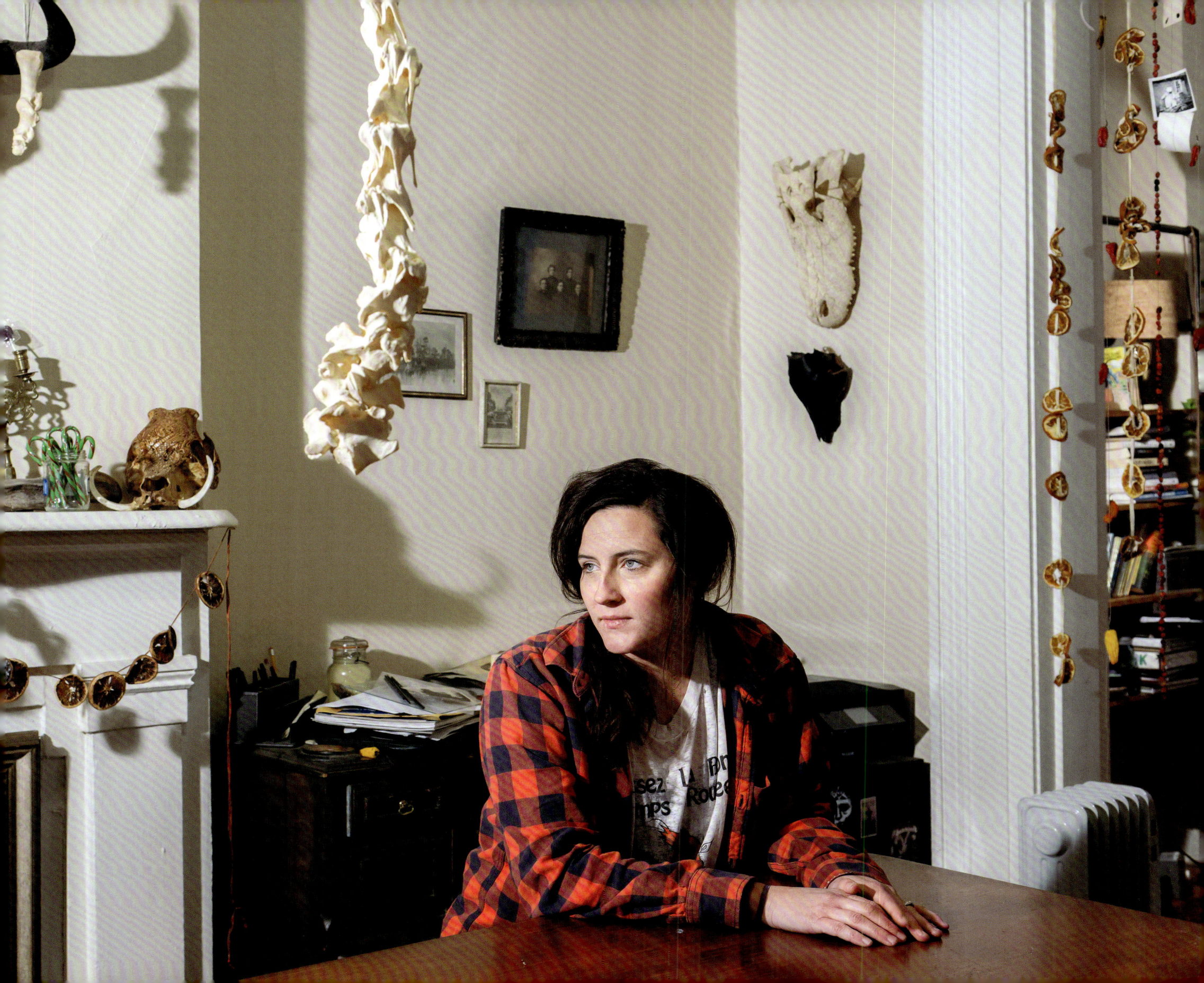

I'm in debt today mostly because
of student loans, but after hurricane
Katrina I make sure my new debt is
because of experiences... like travel, visiting
friends and long, extra special lunches!

CHRISTOPHER ARD   GIS Analyst

$56,760

Debt Portrait #36, New Orleans, LA 2015

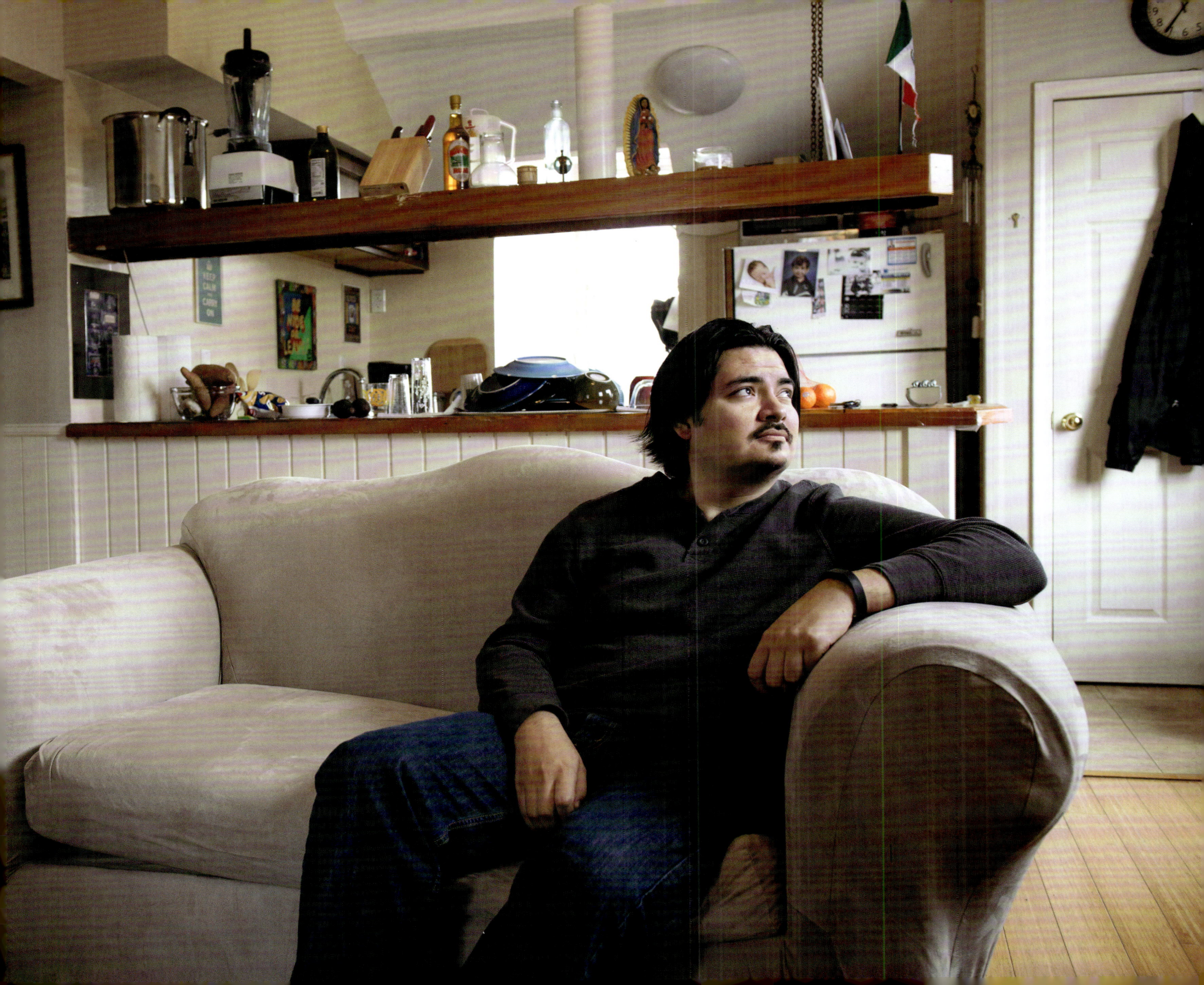

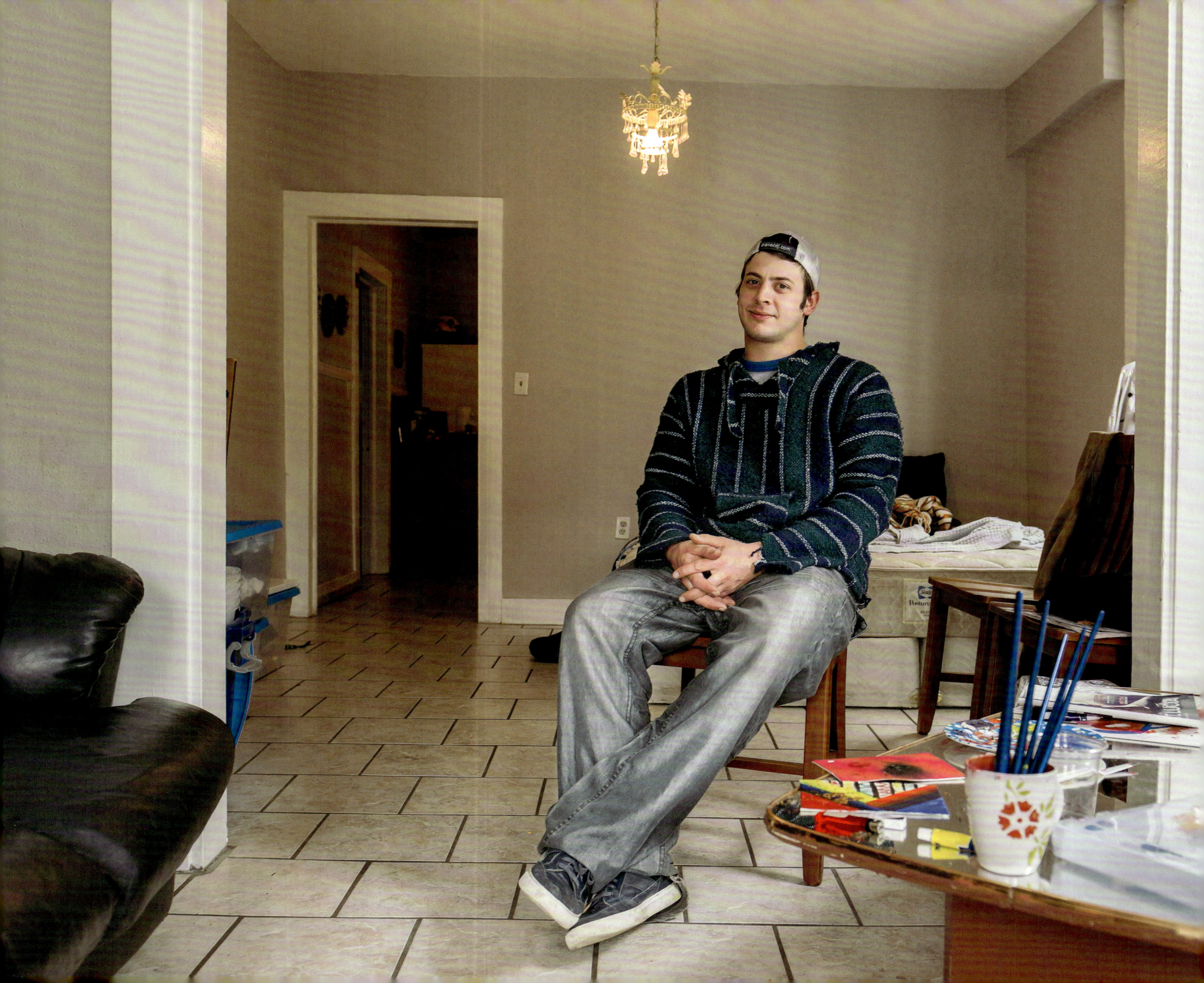

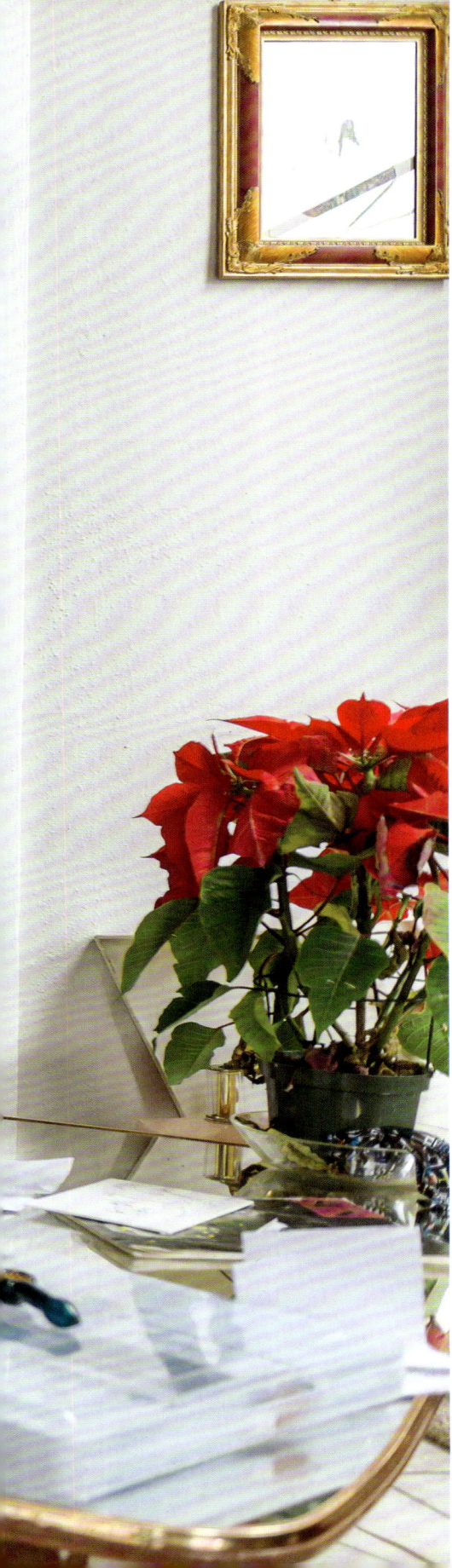

Today I'm in debt because of prior choices that I made from the first point that I lived on my own when I turned 18. I had never made it a perogative to deal with my debts until recently, and have let them pile up to a staggering amount. I have made the decision to forget the medical and focus on smaller private companies.

$140,000

Daniel Bear
Chef

Debt Portrait #37, New Orleans, LA 2015

Maria Montoya

$244,000

My debt is a combination of student loans ($23,000), a home loan for a house that lost most of its value following Hurricane Katrina ($185,000) and credit card/back taxes owed for a failed marriage ($36,000).

I am not proud of the debt, but do know a large part of my debt was accrued when I took on raising children that weren't my own. I do hope to be able to one day get out of debt and get back on track.

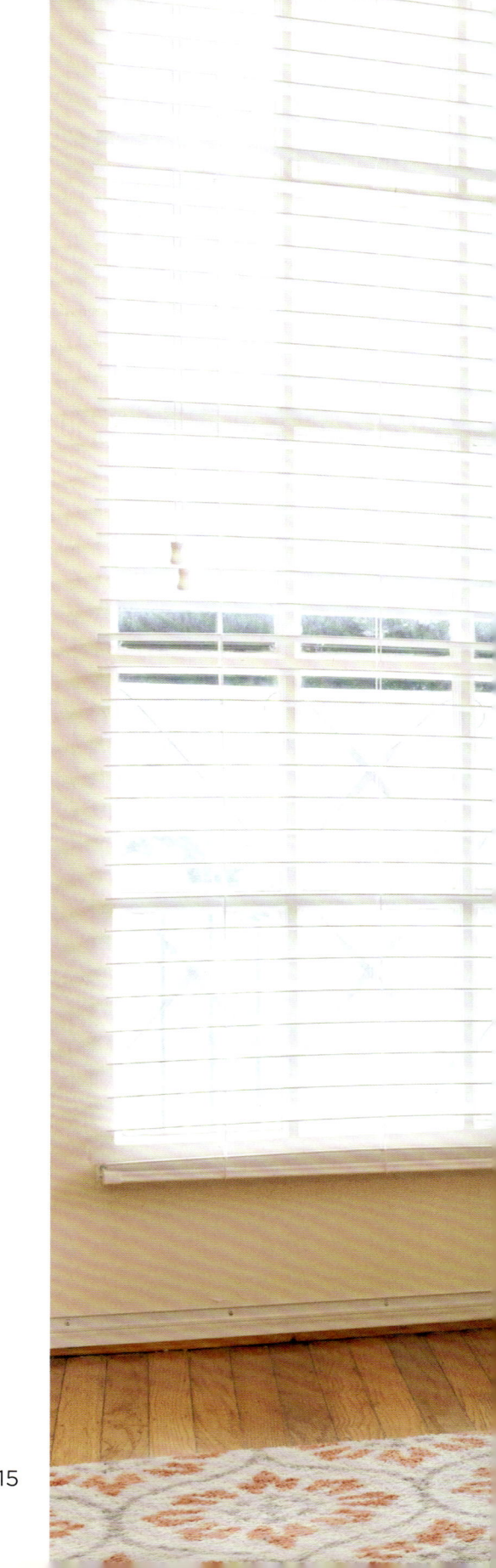

Debt Portrait #38, New Orleans, LA 2015

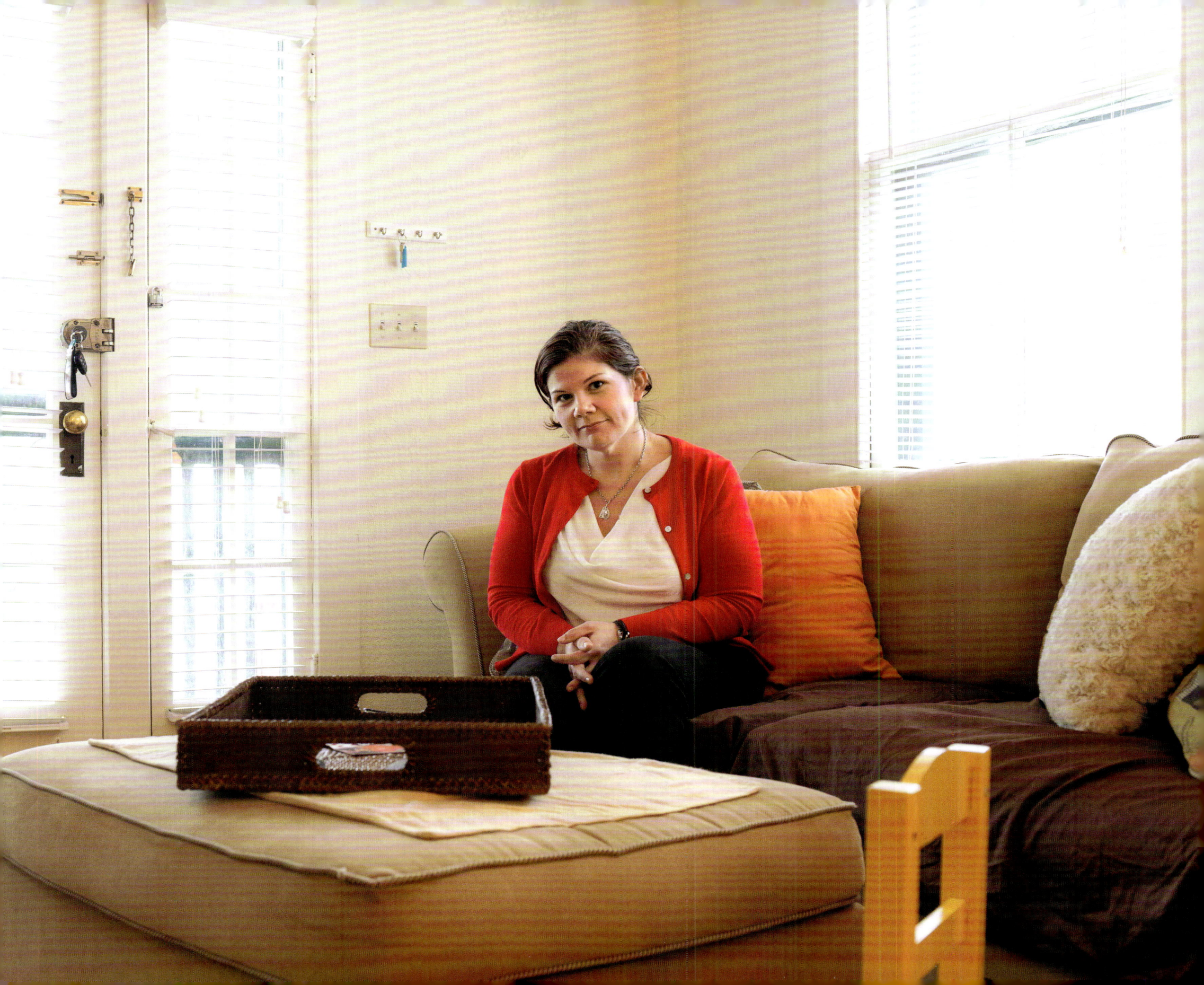

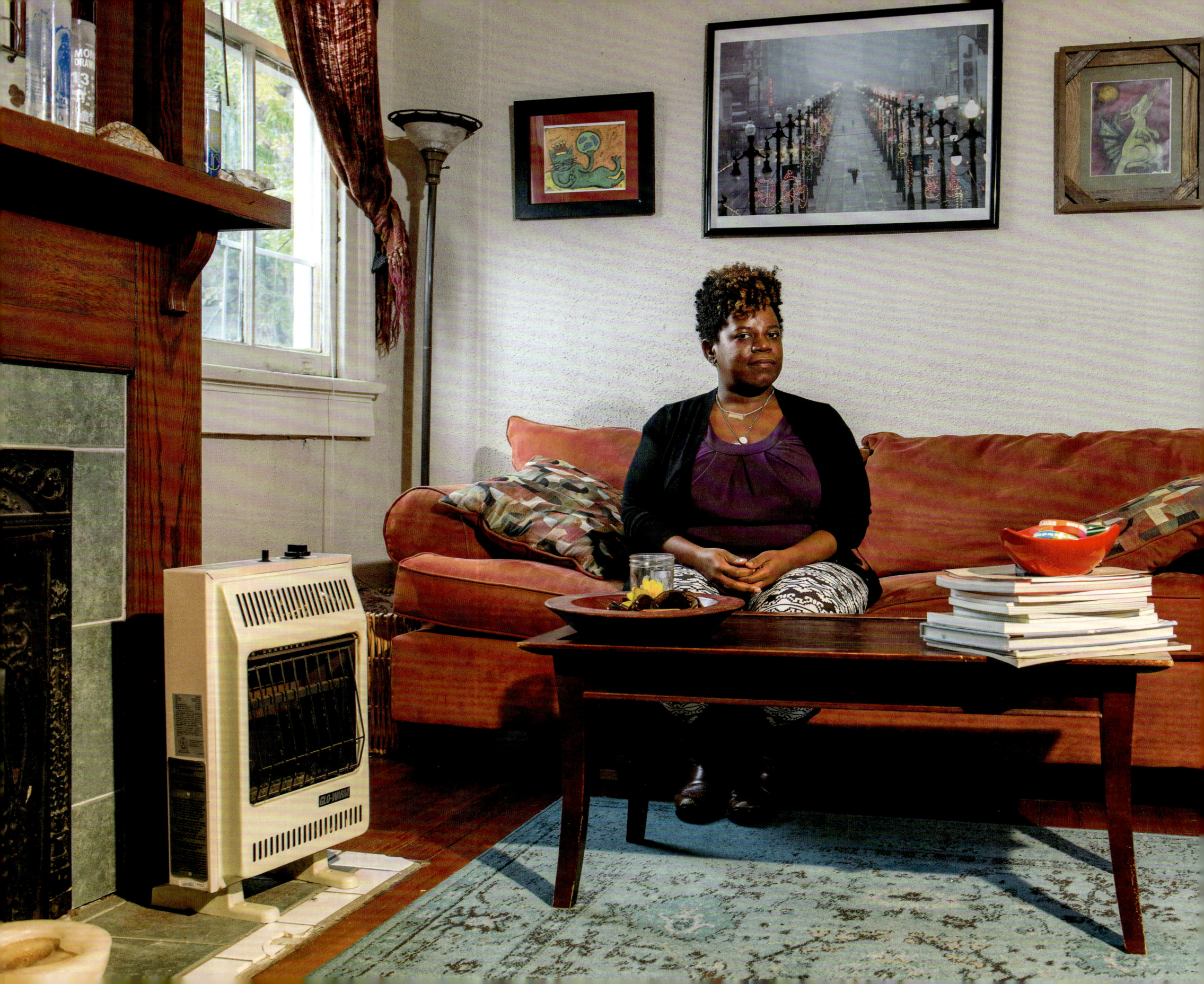

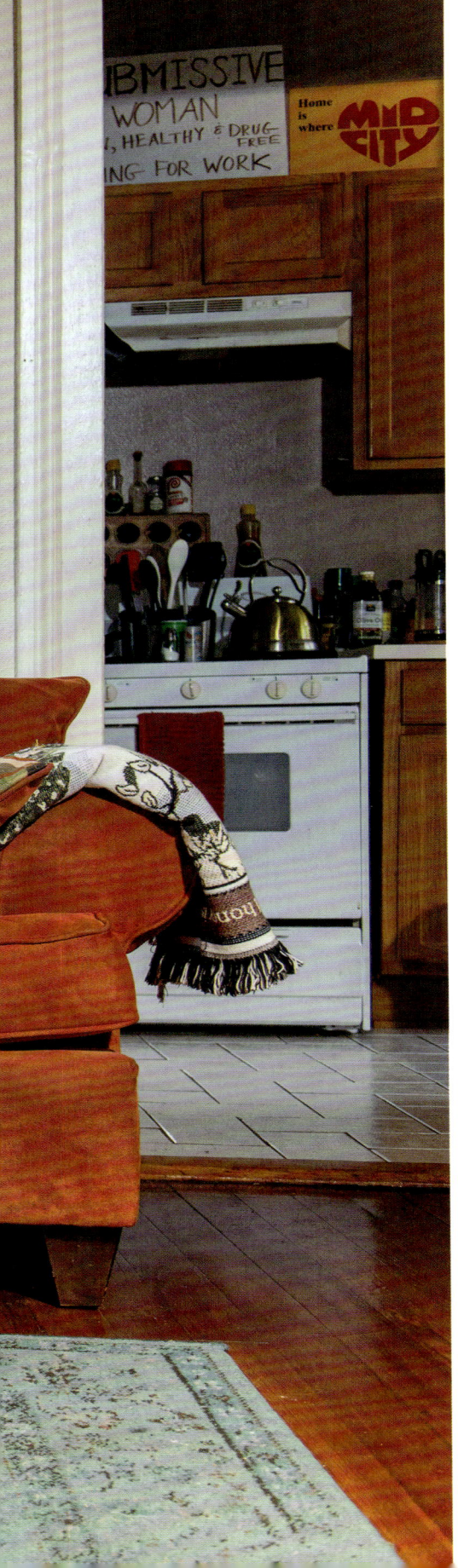

$ 120,000

My debt is primarily from student
loans and my massage therapy school.

For the most part I don't think about
my debt on a daily basis. But I think
debt and avoidance of debt is tied up
in my existence, relating to future plans.
Achieving
^ Some of my dreams and passions will
necessitate addressing my debt. In order
to continue my healing work, I need to
pay off school and become licenced as
a massage therapist. I don't know how t
do that - it seems insurmountable.

Debt Portrait #39, New Orleans, LA 2015

Alyssa Roy, Bartender

STUDENT LOANS $14,000

CREDIT $ 1,000

old electric $ 150
    BIll

                    $15,150

plan to pay
student loans,
But currently don't have
the means. not very responsible
either. :

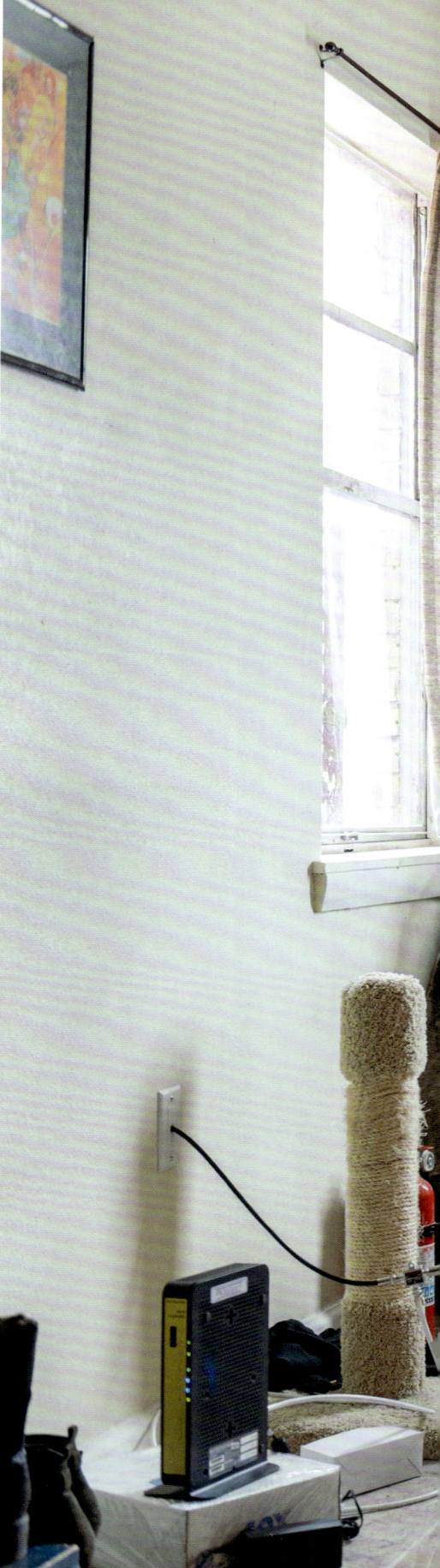

Debt Portrait #40, New Orleans, LA 2015

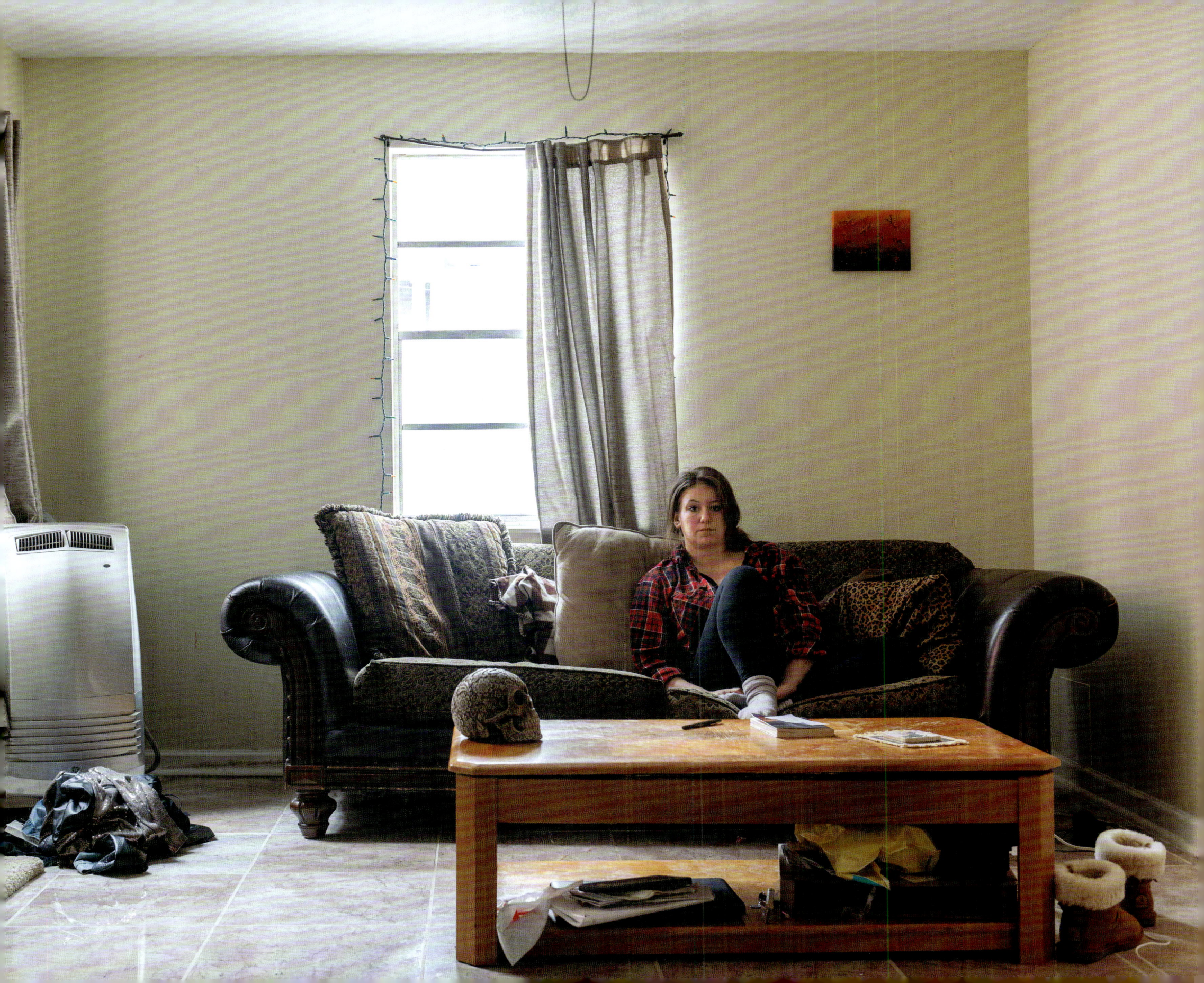

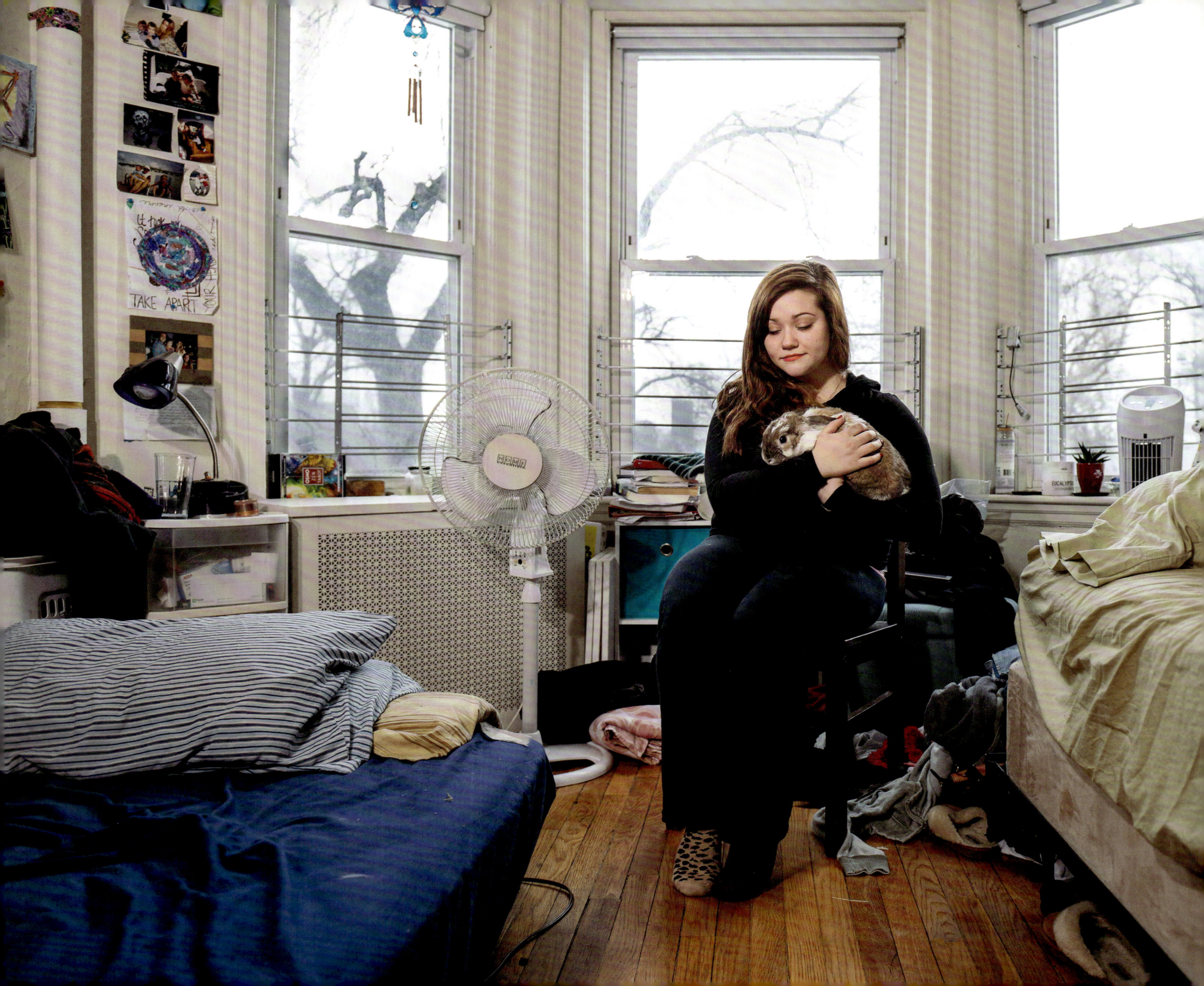

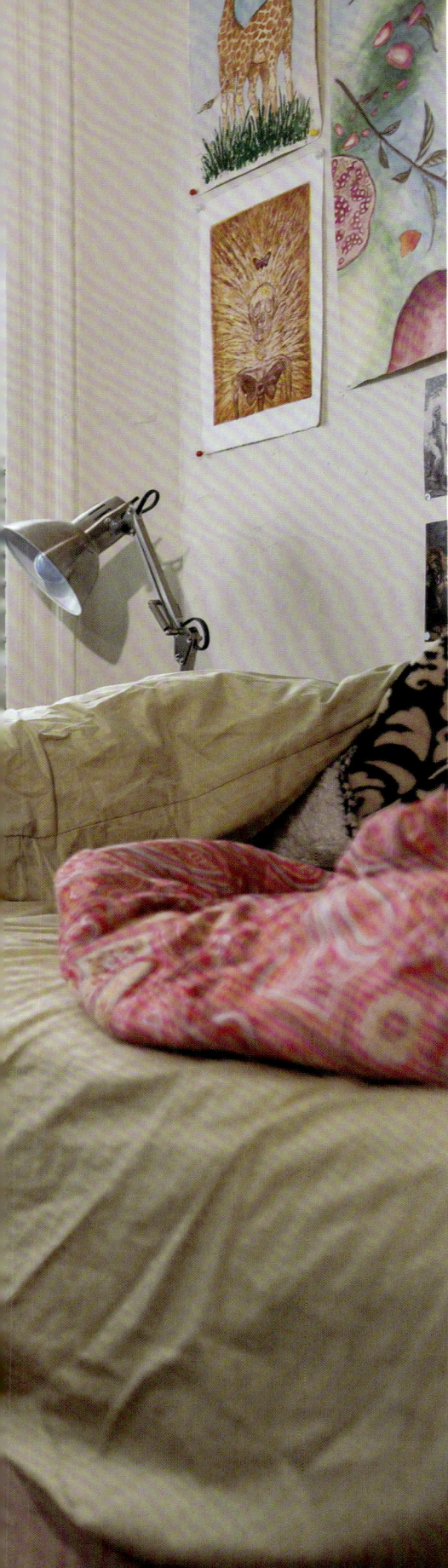

Lauren Skaroff - 19
Student/Waitress

~$64,000.00

I have required most
of my debt from this past
year of college in addition
to living expenses and my
father being out of work
due to legal and health
circumstances. I am mostly
living off of loans.

Debt Portrait #41, Boston, MA 2015

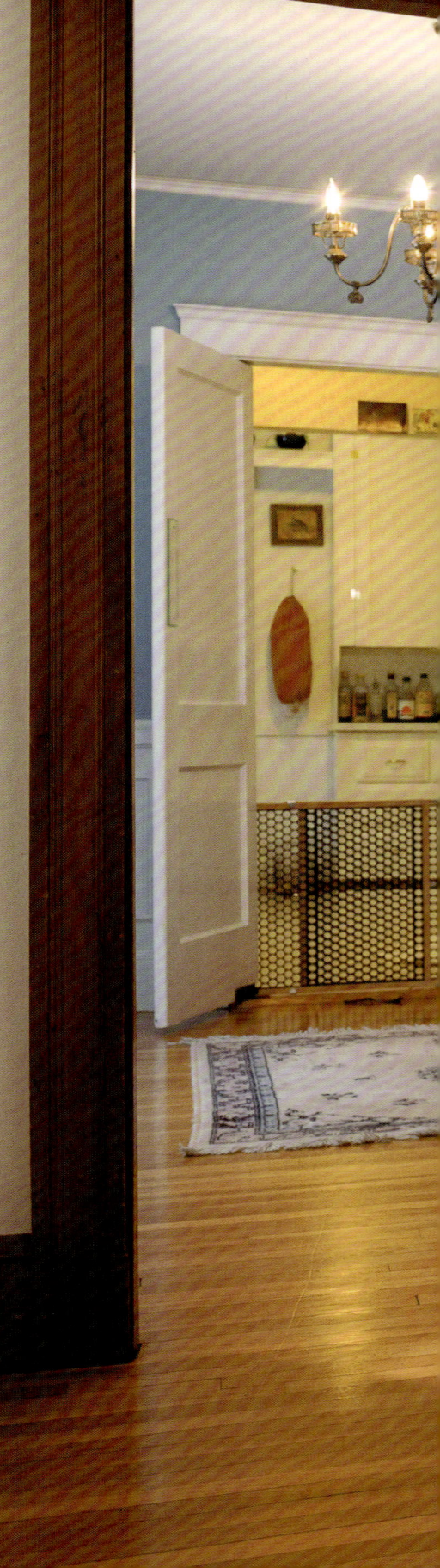

Callista Rae Womick
(24)

Artist + Figure Model

$23,699.03

My first two loans were acquired before I even matriculated to Dartmouth College: for a new laptop and for a new health insurance plan, both required because the school determined my preexisting ones to be insufficient. The total amount is an accumulation of student loans to cover mandatory expenses not covered by financial aid or work-study. It would be MUCH more if I hadn't worked full time during my undergraduate years.

Debt Portrait #42, Boston, MA 2015

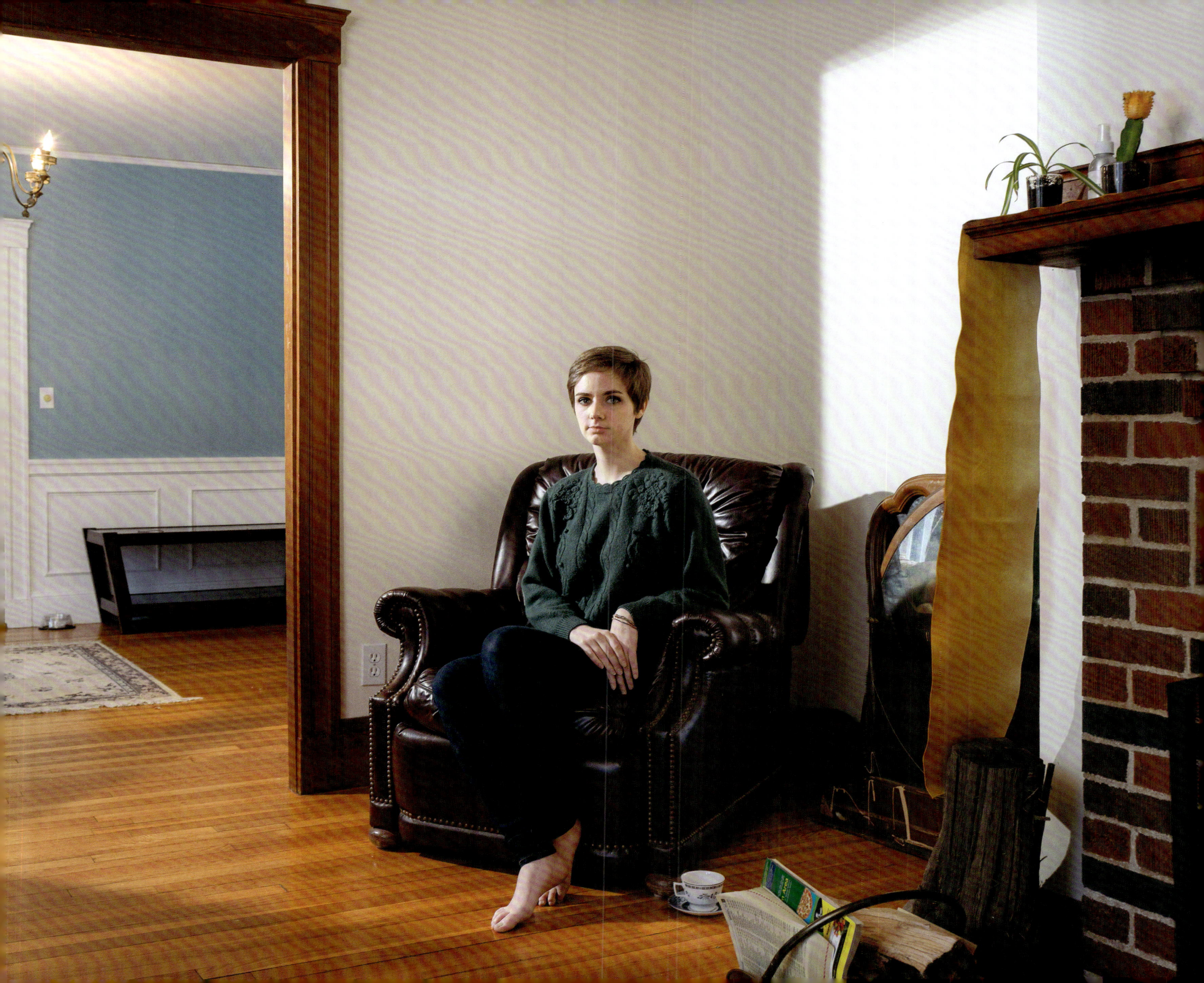

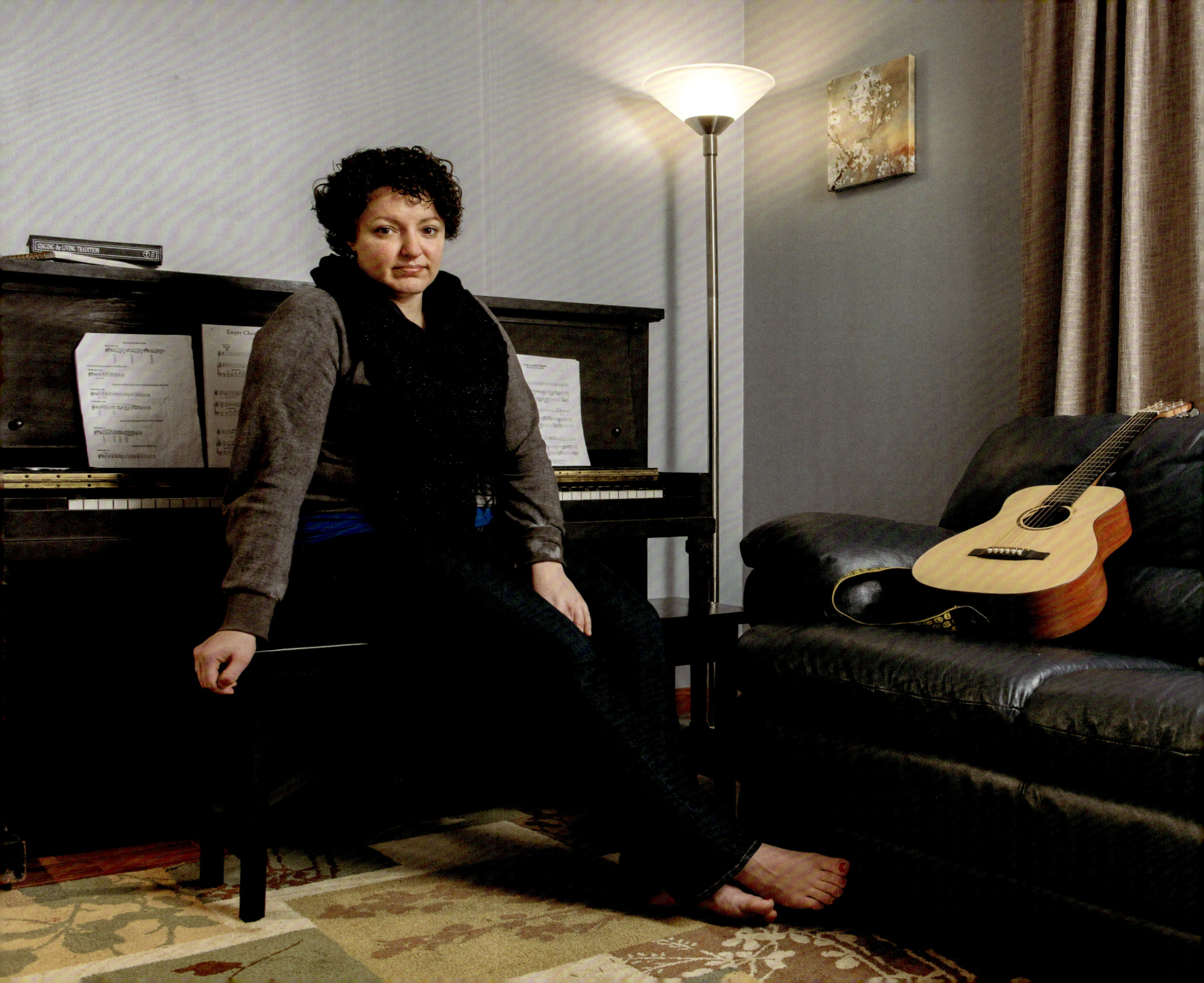

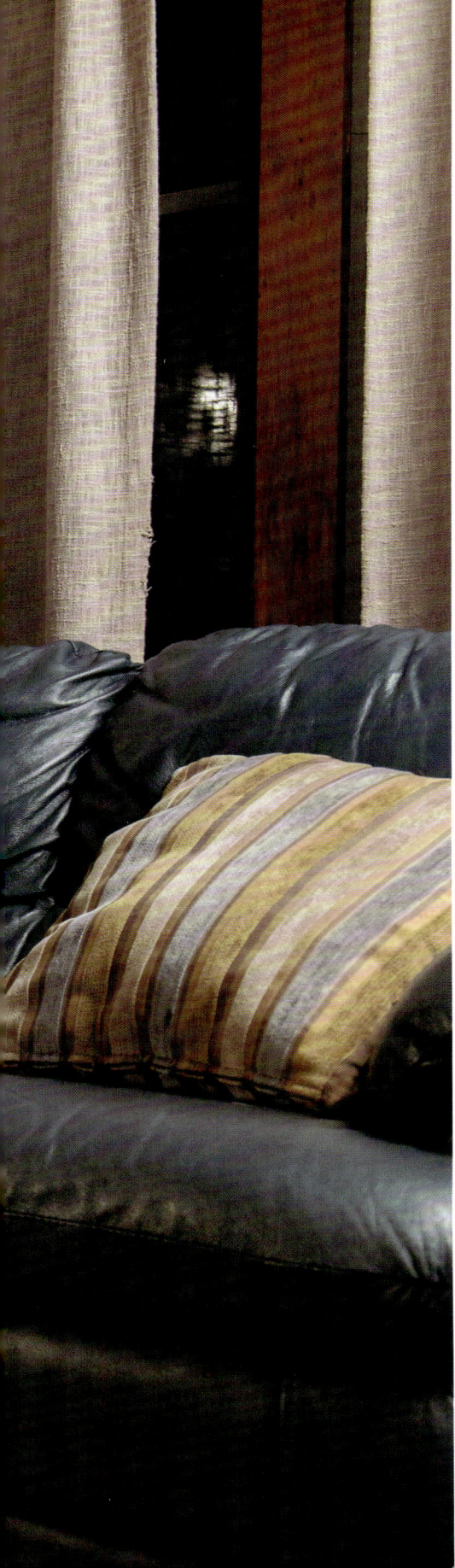

Olivia Charlian
(31)
Inventory Control /
Writer

$ 62,269. 92

Student loans comprise
the bulk of my debt, with a
few thousand miscellaneous
credit card expenses. I
majored in Creative Writing and
Biblical Studies, but I work
at a manufacturing company.

Debt Portrait #43, Marble Head, MA 2015

Cody John Laplante
2 6 y.o.
freelance writer + teacher

English degree - $15,614
credit card - $766.62
private - $350.00
Total — $16,730

I feel priviledged to be allowed such
things on the promise to pay. When you're
indentured, you know someone somewhere
wants you to succeed. My debts
are heavy, but motivate me.
I aquired them for my degree, laptop,
and automobile. I esteem them to
have been good investments. I will
pay them slow 'n' steady, like a
perseverent tortoise.

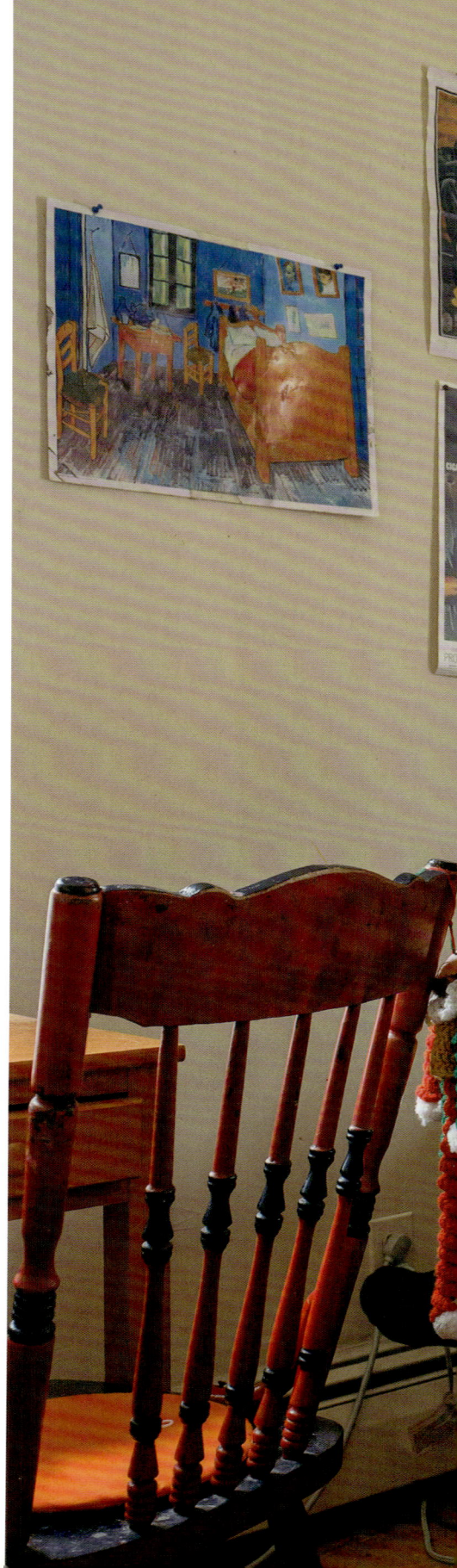

Debt Portrait #44, Portland, ME 2015

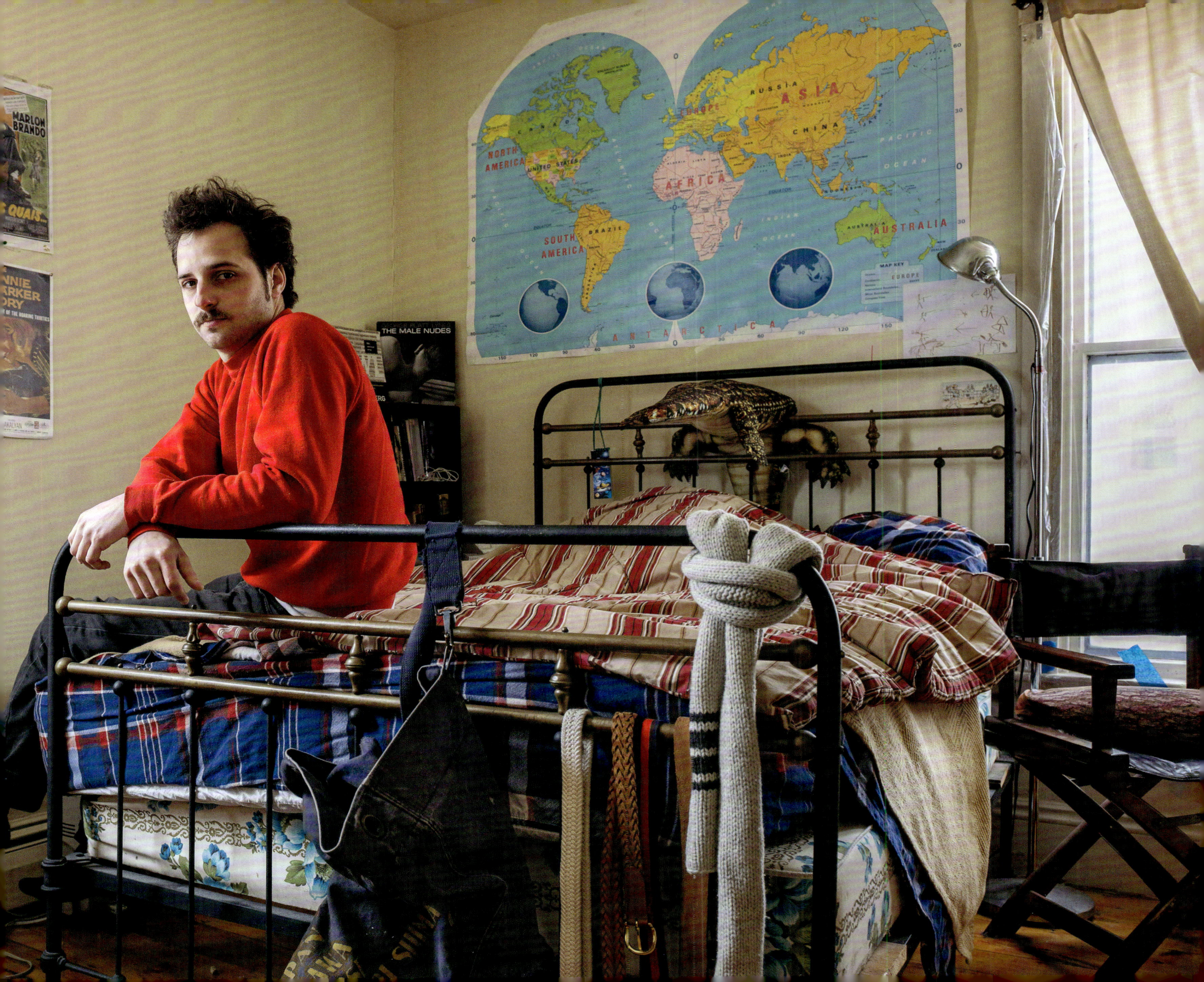

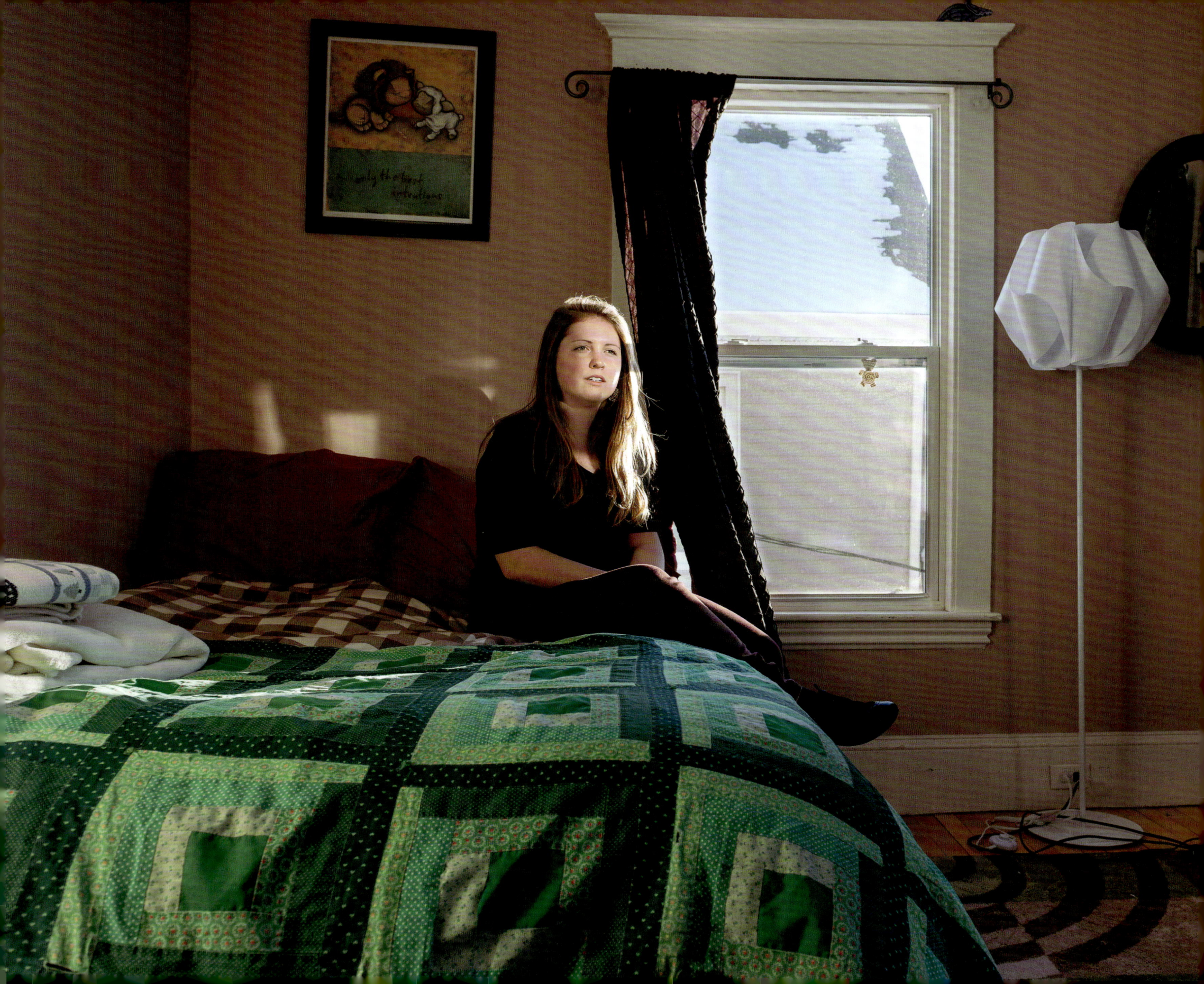

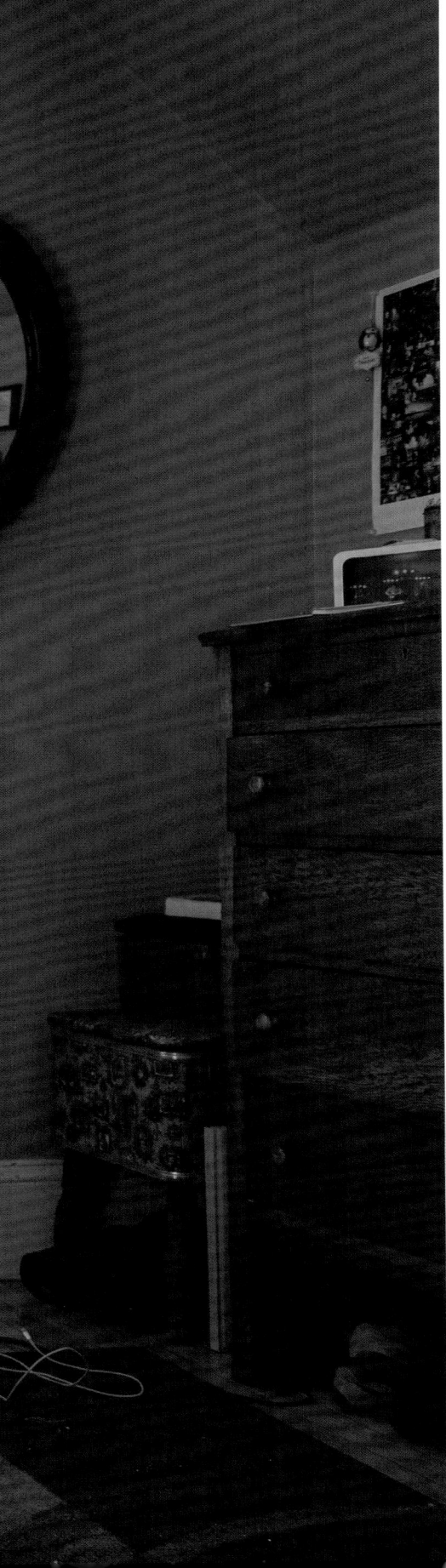

Katherine Way
(Educator)

~$42,000

A mixture of student loans and credit cards, the total amount sort of leaves a bad taste in your mouth. Finishing Grad School now, I'm still skeptical that a future opportunity would be able to pay back all of the student debt I actually have. The biggest question is what's the best way to minimalize it?

Justin Fetterman -29
Professor/Writer

~$140,000

My debt started when I
was married after college. I kept
half when we divorced. The bulk
of the debt is tuition and living
expenses for putting myself through
grad school. I finished my MFA
last semester and am finally
working in my field.

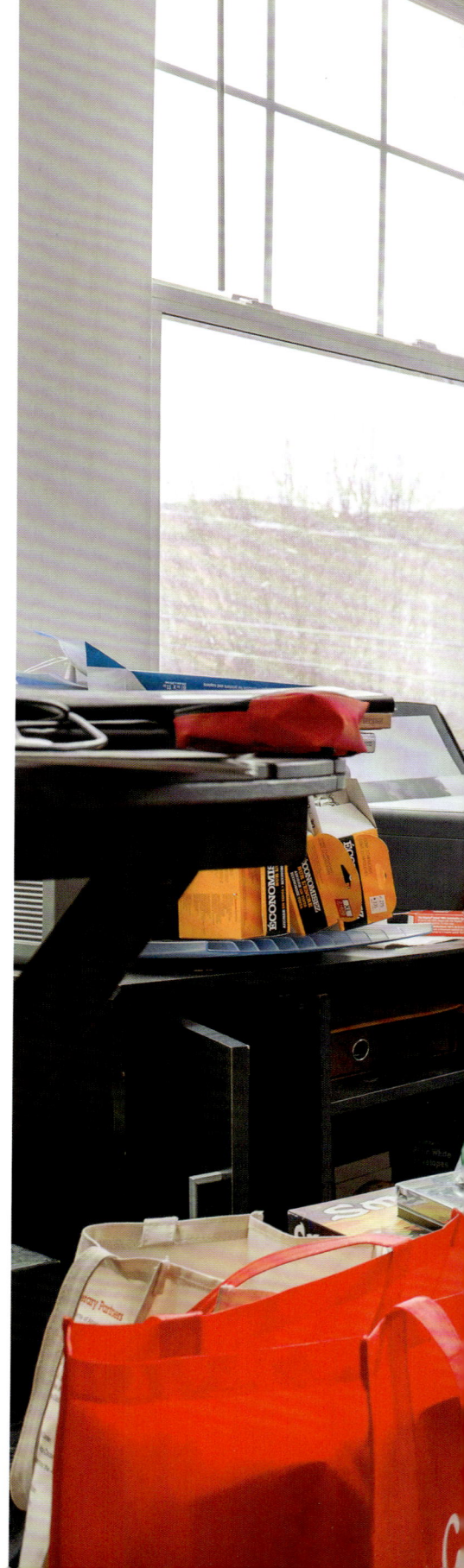

Debt Portrait #46, Boston, MA 2015

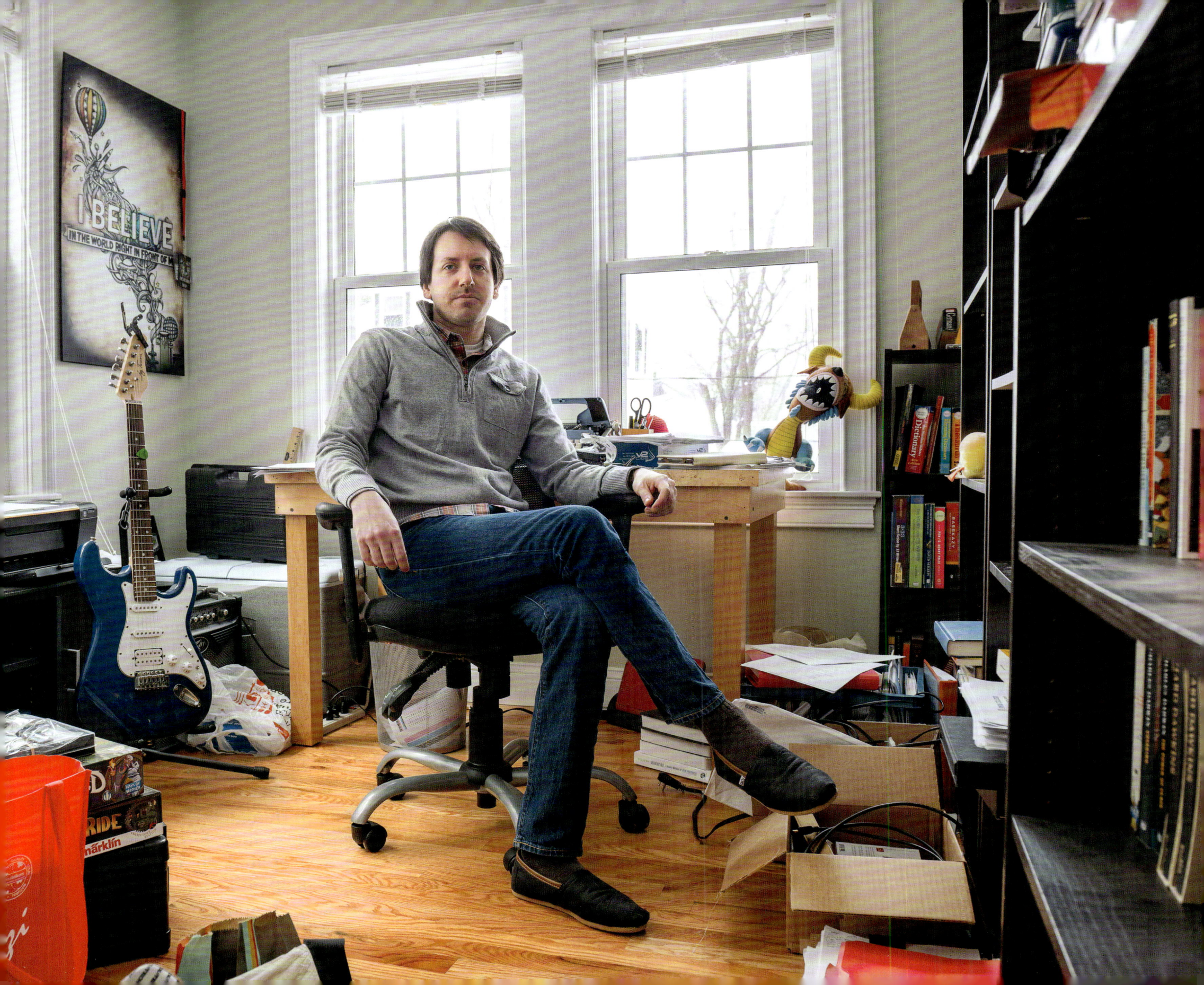

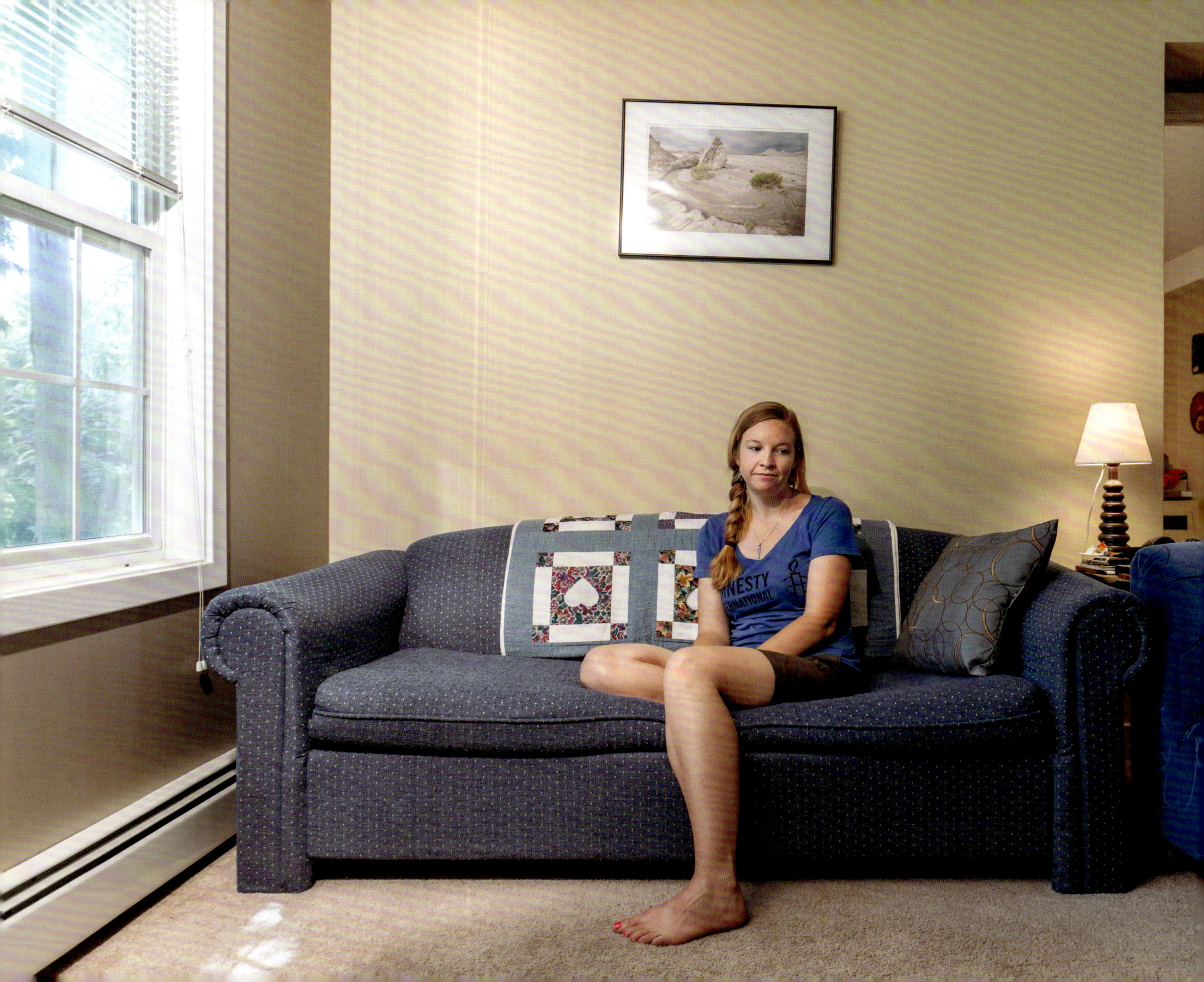

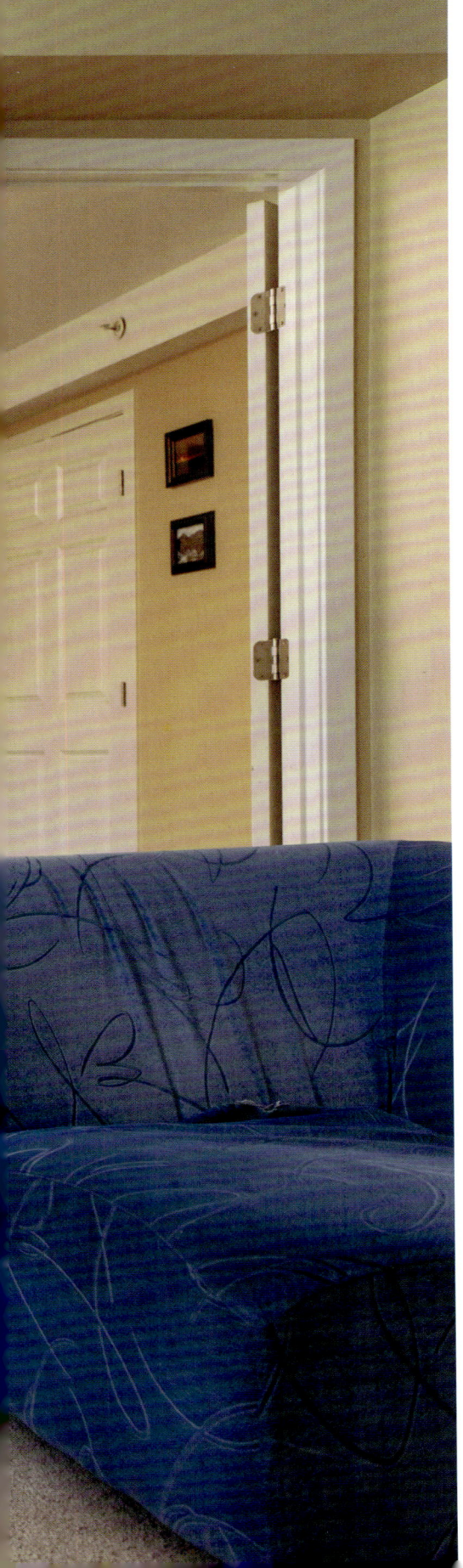

Shelby Perry   29 years old
Graduate Student

$ 26,685

My debt is all federal student
loans. I'm not ashamed of it
because I am proud of my
education, but I think my
government should be ashamed
of profiting off of my
education.

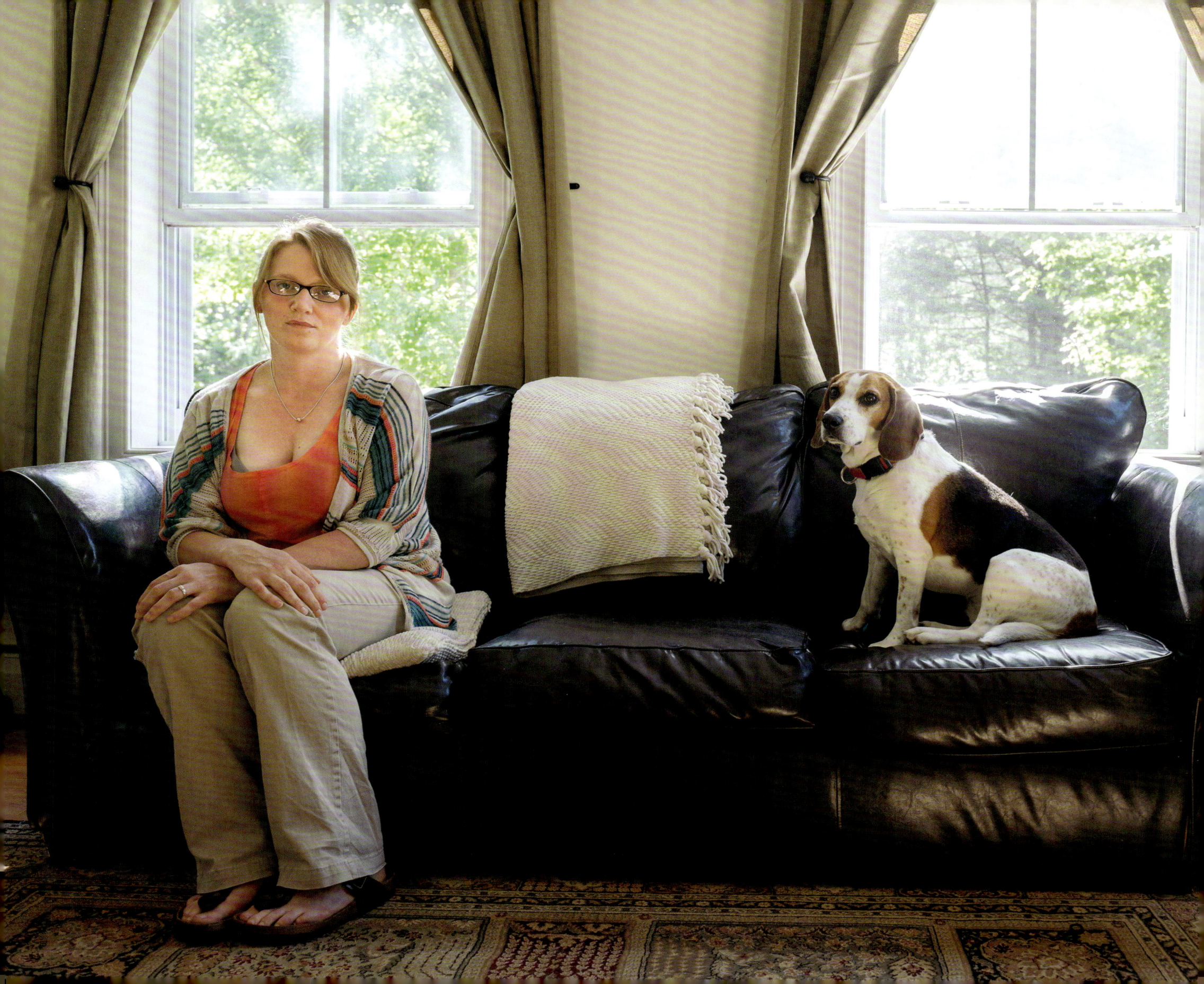

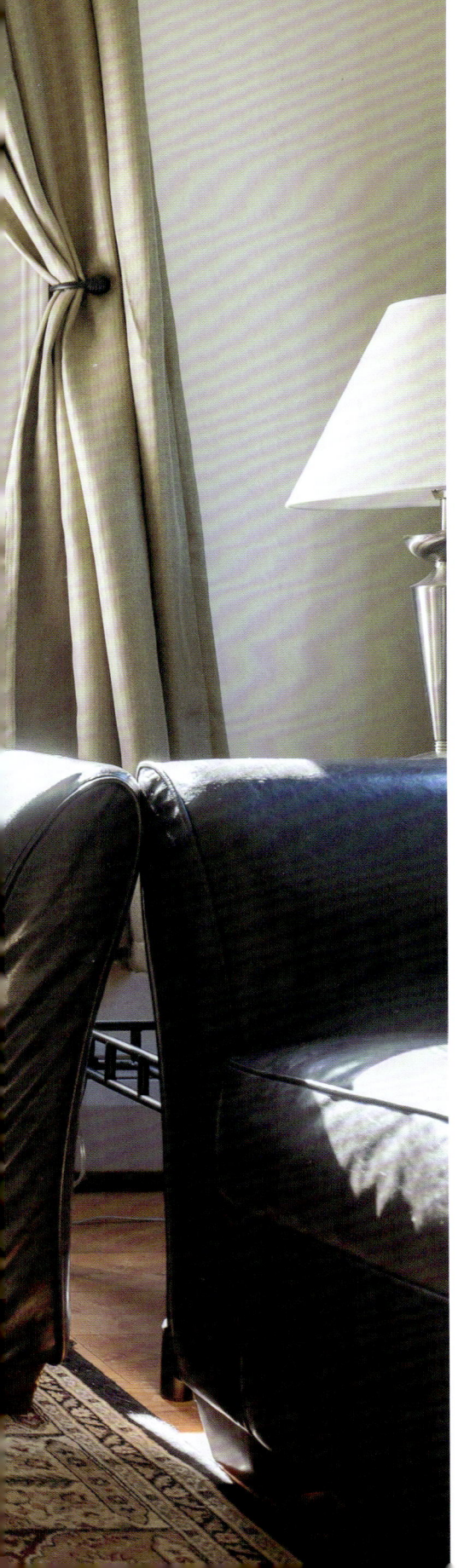

Amber Walsh   Age: 30
Insurance Examiner/Analyst

       Student loans $68,040
       Car note   1,954
                        ‾‾‾‾‾‾‾‾‾
                         $69,994
                        ‾‾‾‾‾‾‾‾‾

The debt listed above doesn't tell my whole
story. It was alot worse. I'm paying it
down by changing my behavior with
money and by saying "NO" alot. Evaluating
wants vs. needs is key. I feel less
stress every time I make a payment.
paid off $36,808 in 17 months - taking
it one pay period at a time...

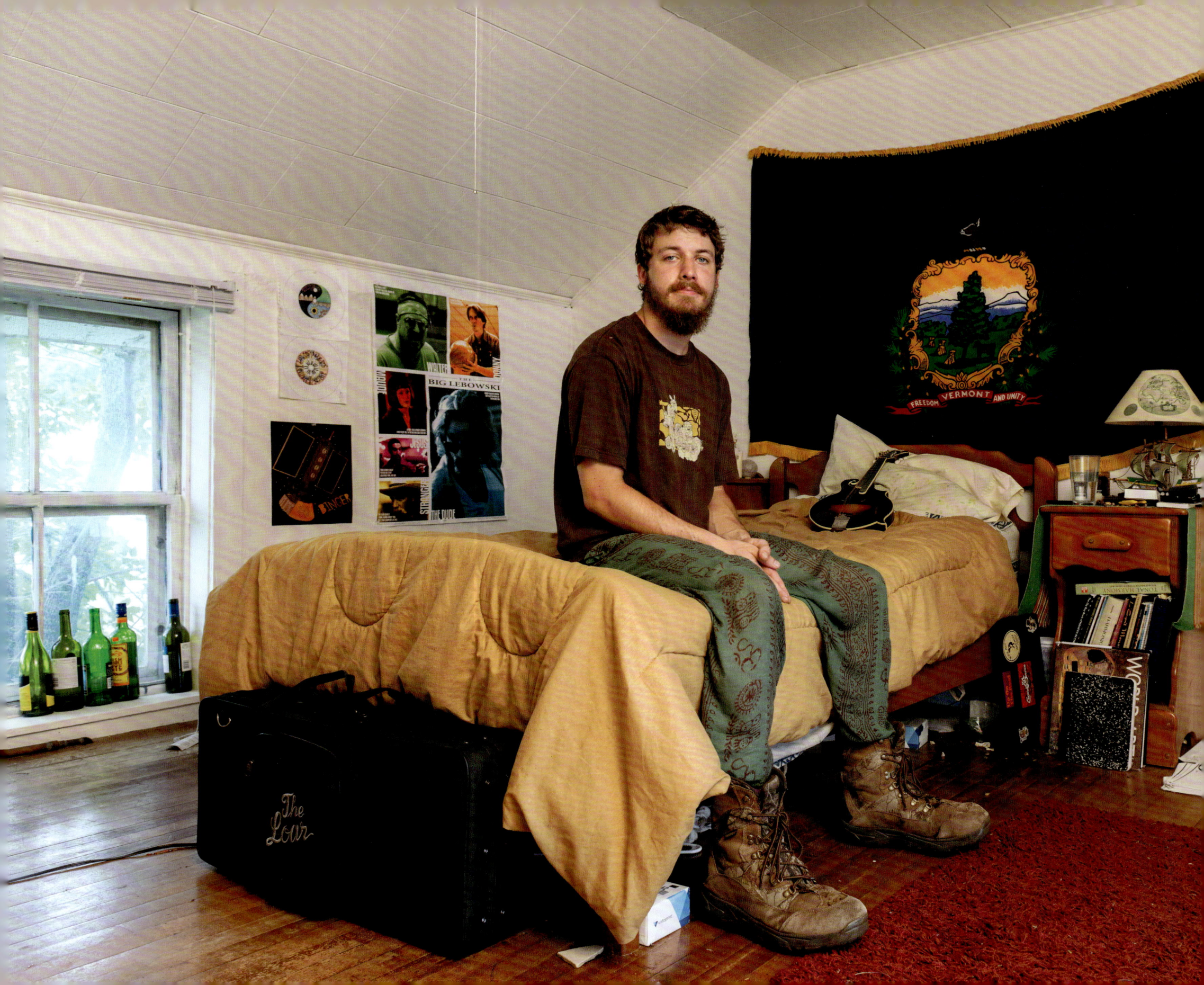

Henry Clark   22 years old

Musician - Recent College Grad.
$ 23,000

   My debt is all due to
student loans from attending Johnson
State College. Even with payment
throughout school I had to take
out loans to complete school. I
do not regret any of my debt
although I do find the government
should lessen the load for college
students.

LISA BARANYAY   AGE: 45
database manager/teacher

$196,000

    I'VE BEEN THROUGH MANY PHASES OF DEBT
AND HAVE MANAGED TO ELIMINATE ALL OF THE
CREDIT CARD DEBT, BUT AM STILL SADDLED WITH
A MORTGAGE. SINCE I OWE MORE THAN THE
HOUSE IS WORTH I FEEL VERY "STUCK". THE HARD
PART IS JUGGLING MULTIPLE JOBS EVERY MONTH TO
MAKE ENDS MEET. MY GOAL IS TO RETURN TO
TEACHING SO I CAN HAVE A LARGER INCOME AND
BE ABLE TO KEEP MY HOME WITHOUT NEEDING
A ROOMMATE AND MULTIPLE JOBS. BABY STEPS!

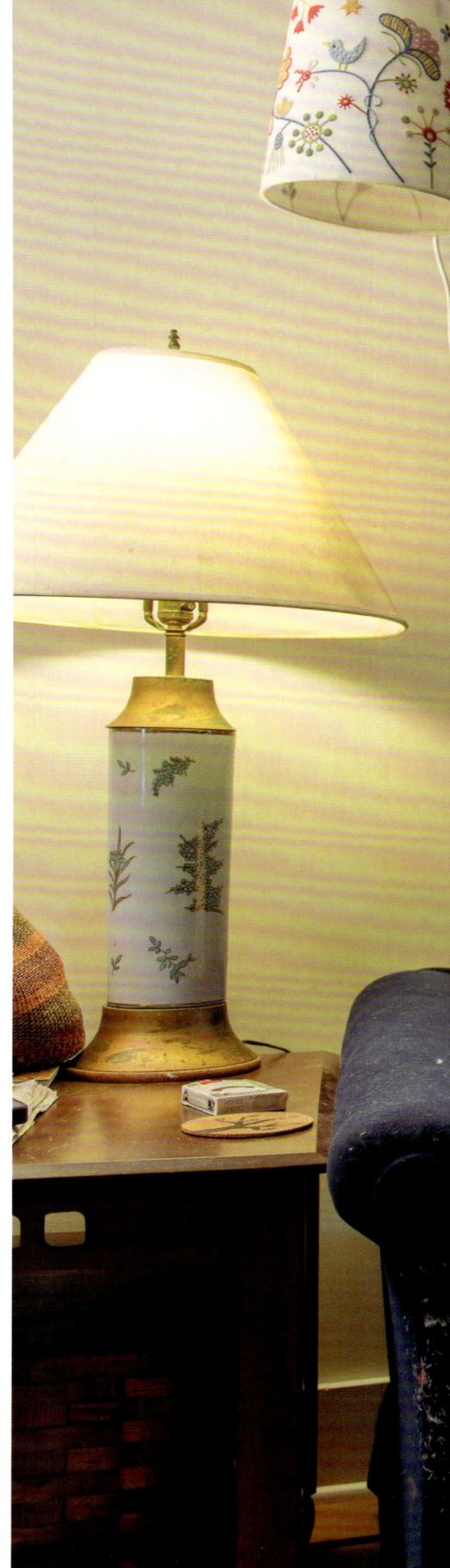

Debt Portrait #50, Morrisville, VT 2015

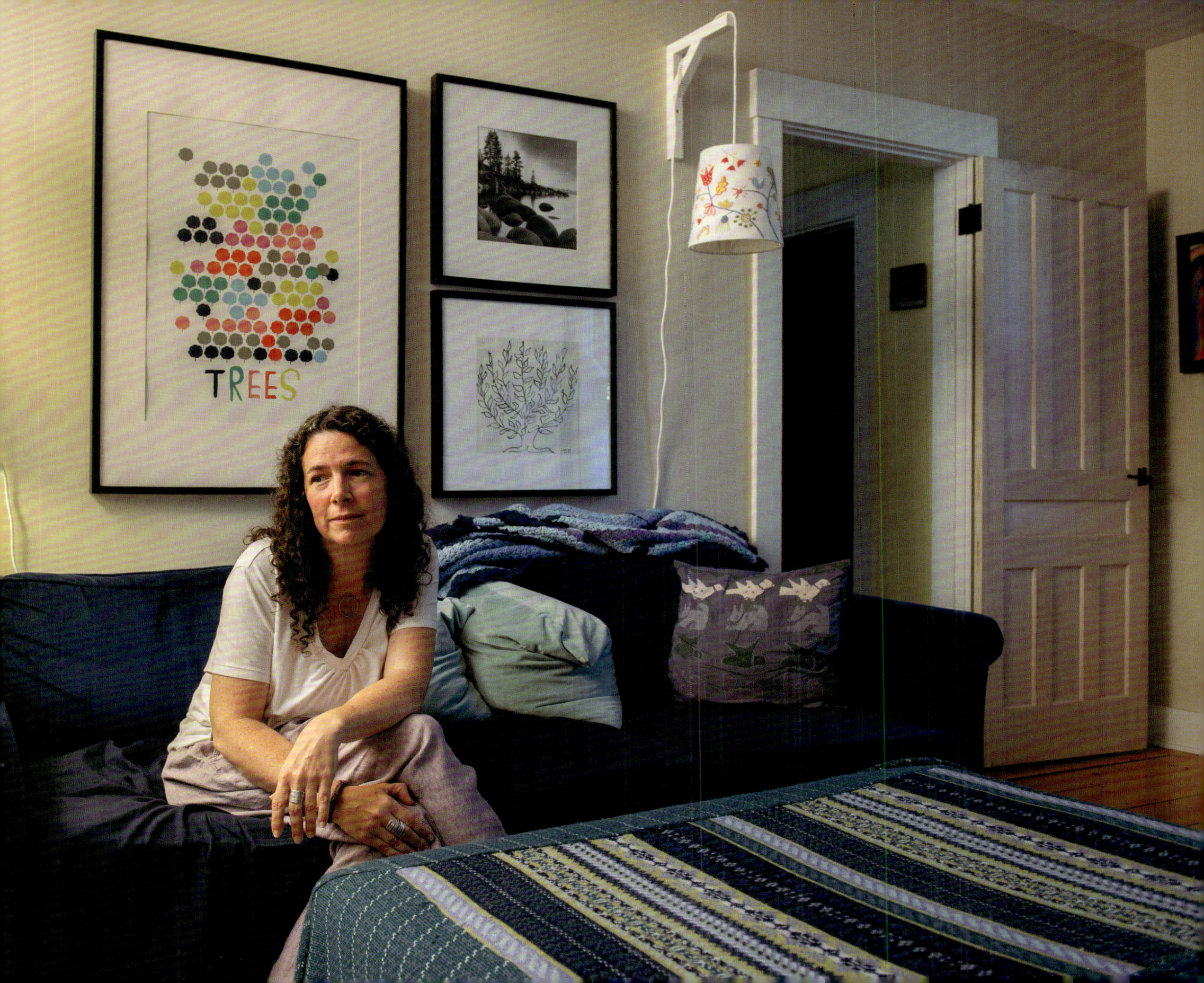

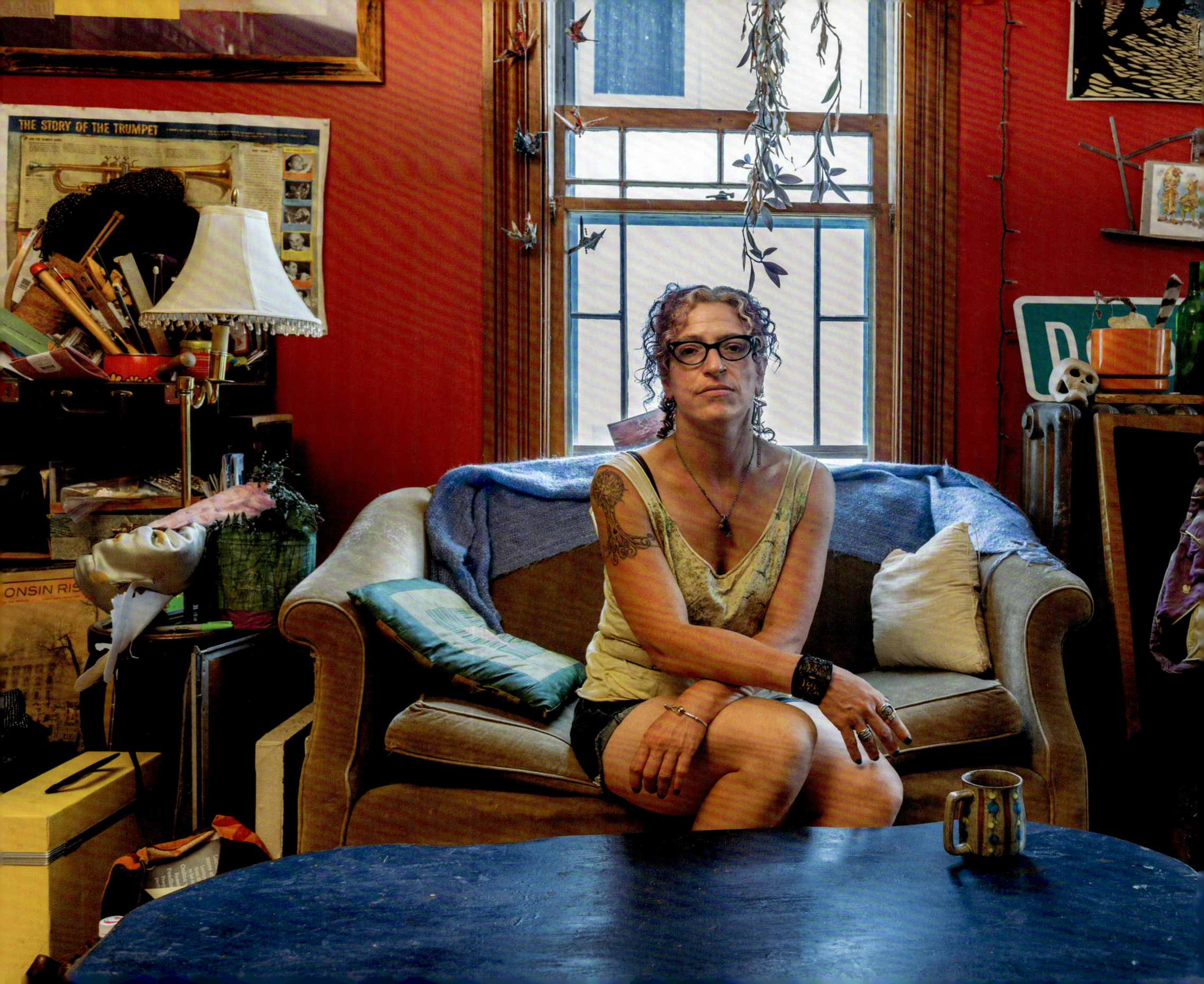

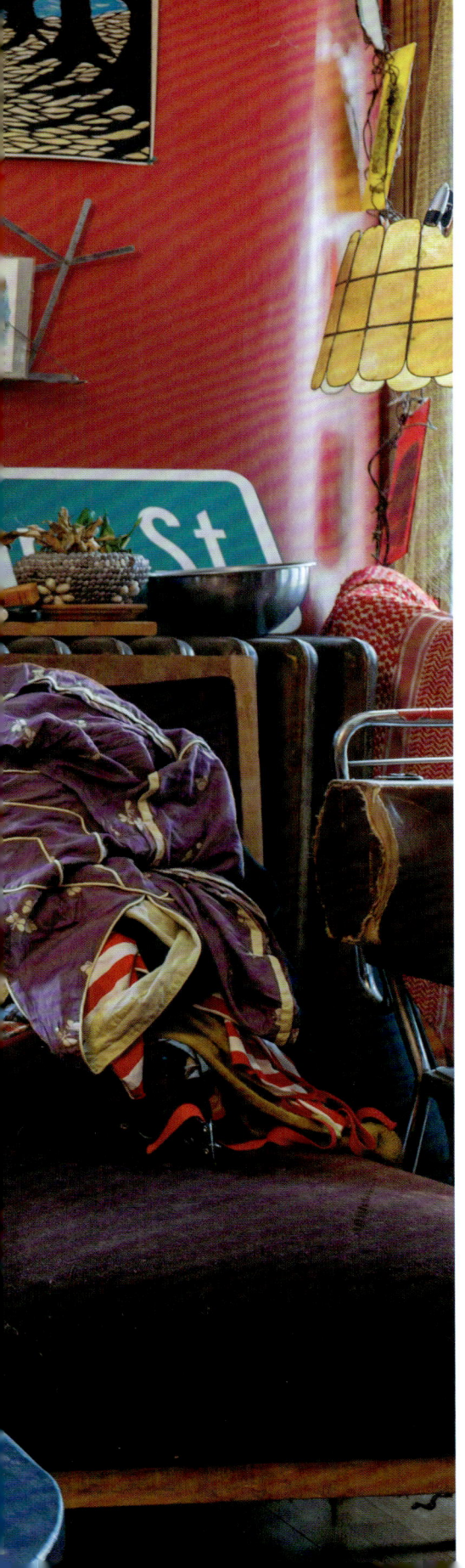

jen berger   Age: 43
educator/artist/activist

~ $100,000

Even though I am no longer in
the economic crisis I was in 15 years
ago, due to education loans, catching
up on prior debt, and the cost of
living - and even though I have
stable housing and a master's
degree - I find myself perpetually
in debt - still struggling to move
forward and NOT be tied to
money & credit in the decisions
I make.

Debt Portrait #51, Burlington, VT 2015

Simone Crfuentes   Age: 32
Unemployed /Future Education Fellow

Mortgage   161,000
Student Loan   ≈140,000 +
Car Loan   17,000
Intra Family Loan   4500
    (for education, car repair, etc.)
+ Varrous Credit Cards 9,500
                    _____
                    332,000

    I started 2014 with about $16,000 of debt not counting
my house and student loans. My mortgage isn't changing and
I'll never pay off my student loans so although I obsess over them I
don't really "worry" about them. That 16,000 grew to 27,000 and by
the end of 2014 was back down to about $10,000, I think. Every time
I got ahead of it something else happened like the loss of my job
in December 2014, a week before my birthday. Although debt
payments continued they were smaller and the debt remains high.
I've had to stop paying off May loan from my dad in favor of ones
that either accrue interest or will be soon. I'm planning on having
every thing (not house/student loans) paid off by December 2015 after
starting my new job in September. I'm hoping to go back to teaching
full time in fall 2016 and with no more "bad" debt I can finally
afford to live in my own house w/o four roommates just to
make the note. I have a plan and just hope everything goes according to
plan.

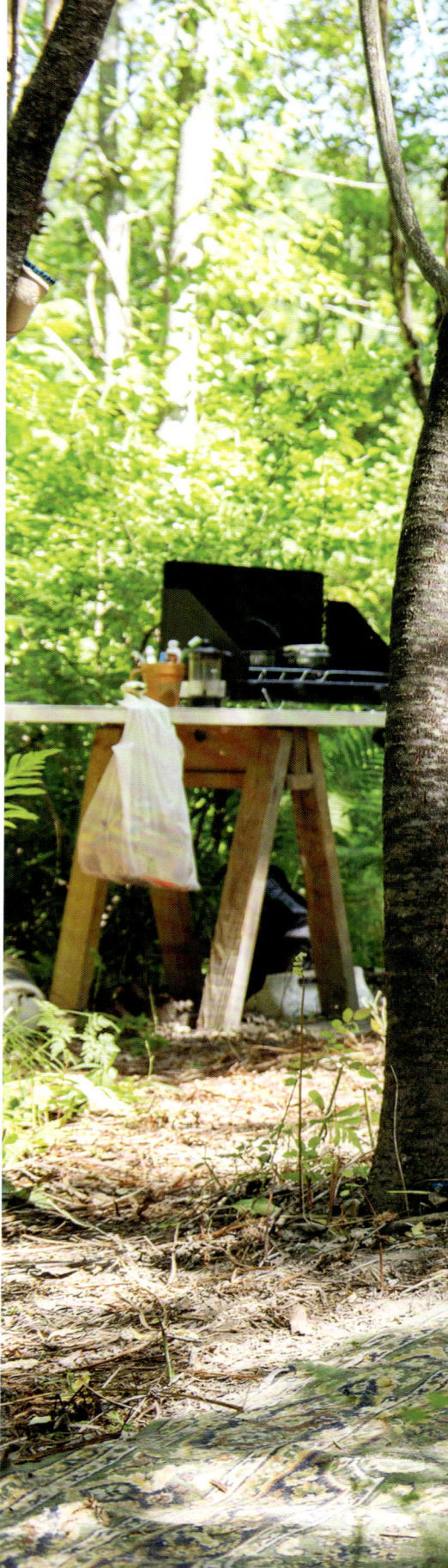

Debt Portrait #52, South Royalton, VT 2015

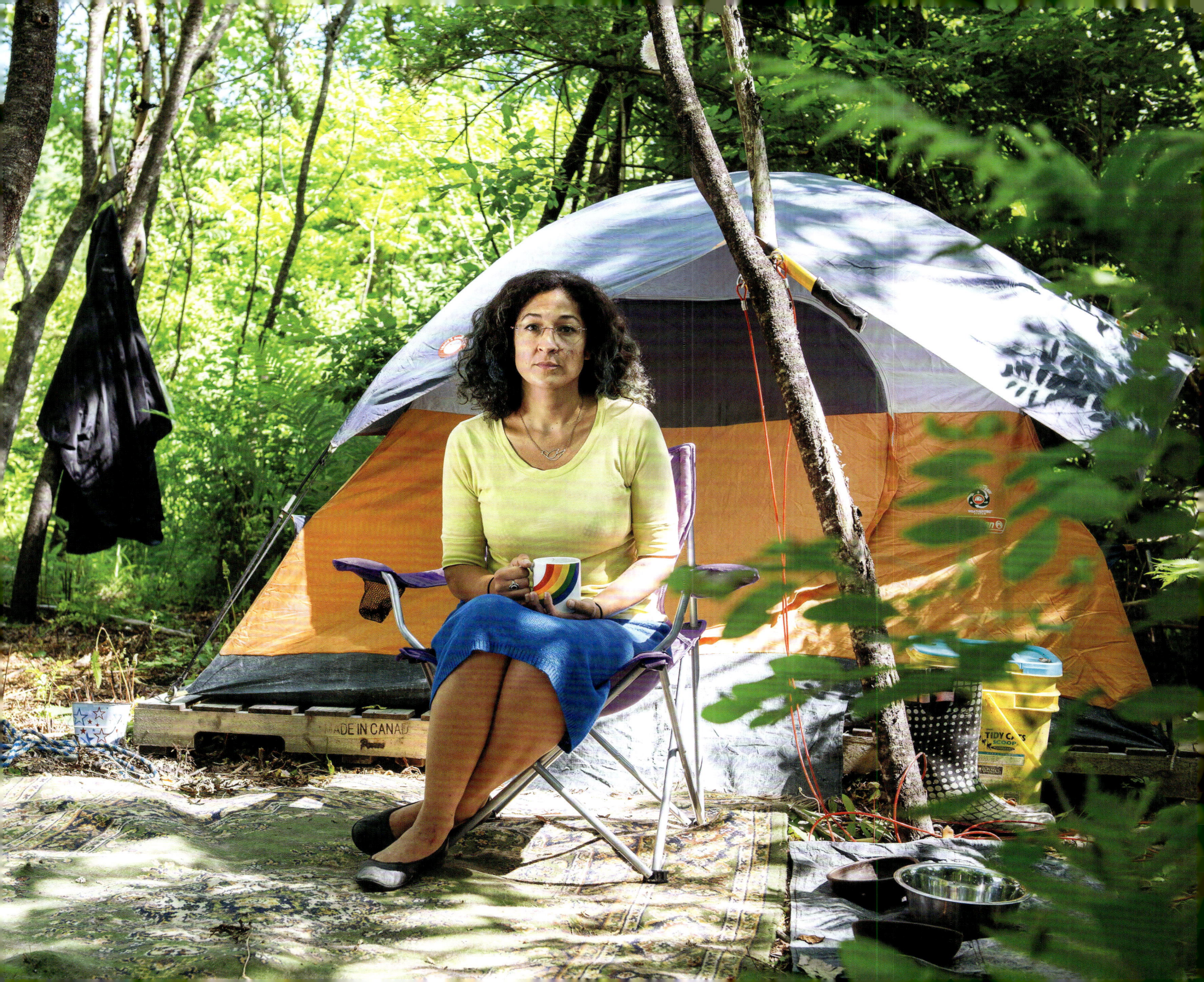

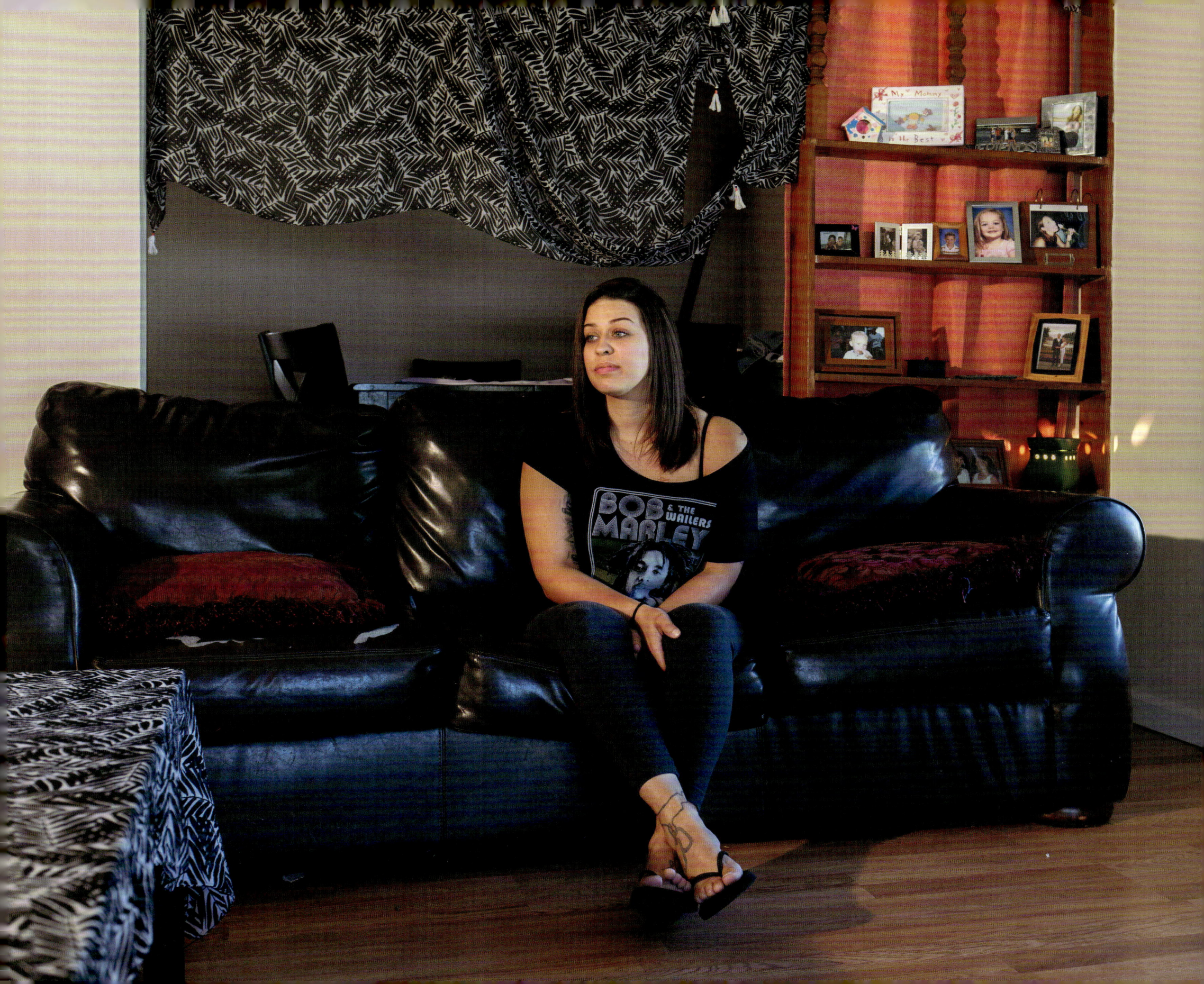

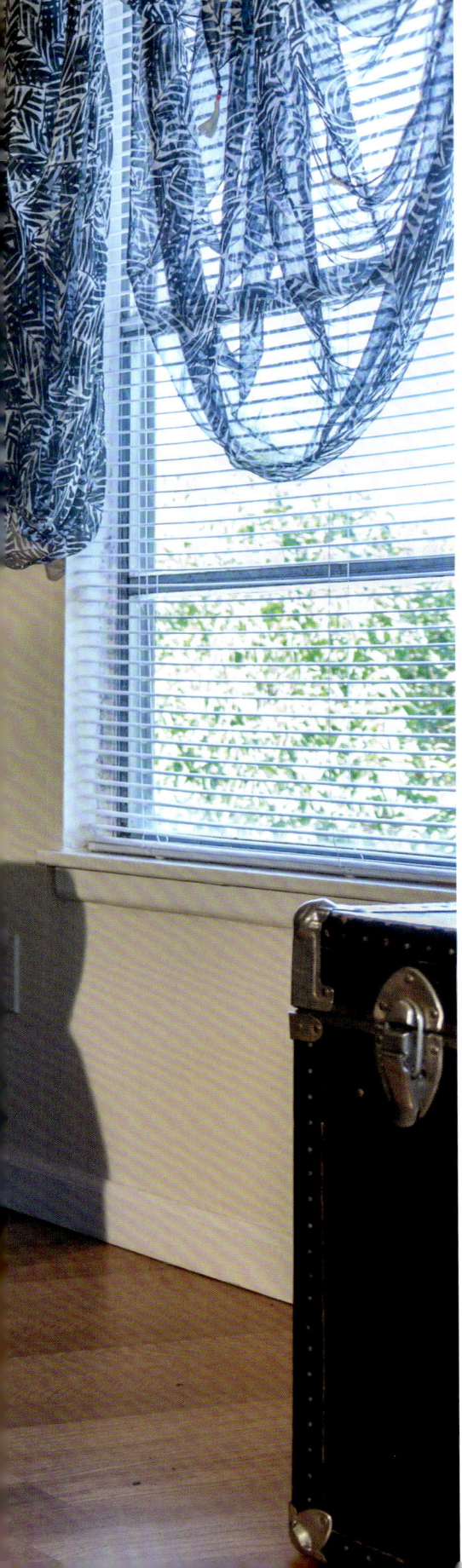

Mary Blackstock
120,000

School loans
Evictions
Toll charges
Legal fees
Medical bills
Ex Husband

Debt Portrait #53, Taylor, TX 2015

I walked away from over 2 million dollars of Realestate debt. I filed chapter 7 Bankruptcy after working 7 days a week for 5 years as a remodler and home builder. I was allowed to keep my home + Truck and a few other things that had debt equal to their value. some of those things were property that I still have Today. I held on and fought to keep them. Today they cash flow and it was worth the work to hang on.

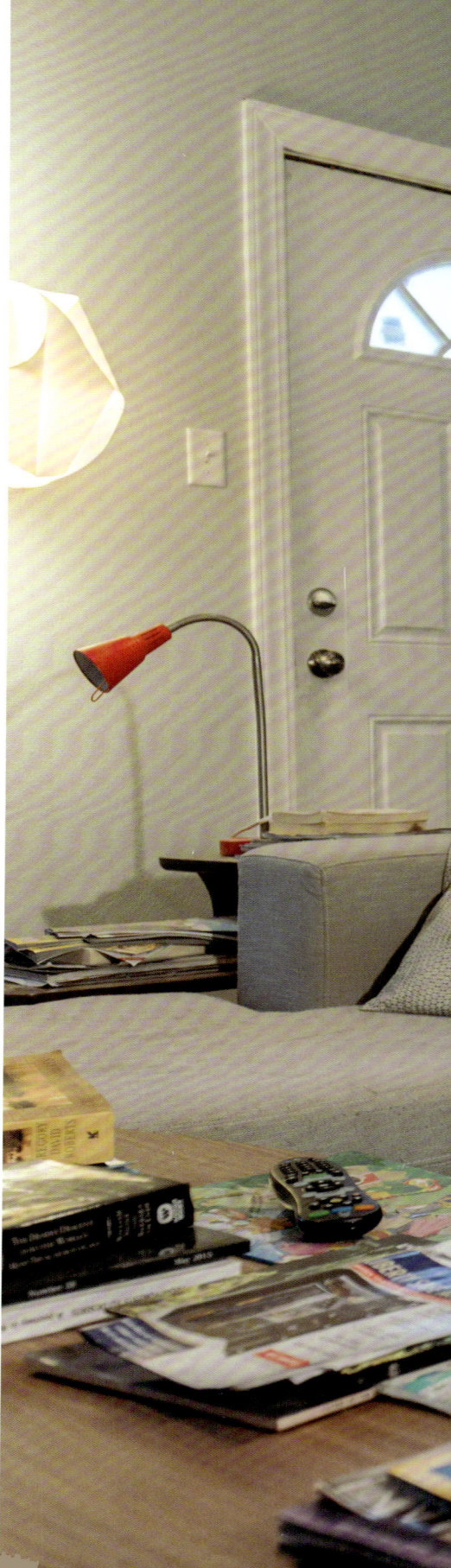

Debt Portrait #54, Austin, TX 2015

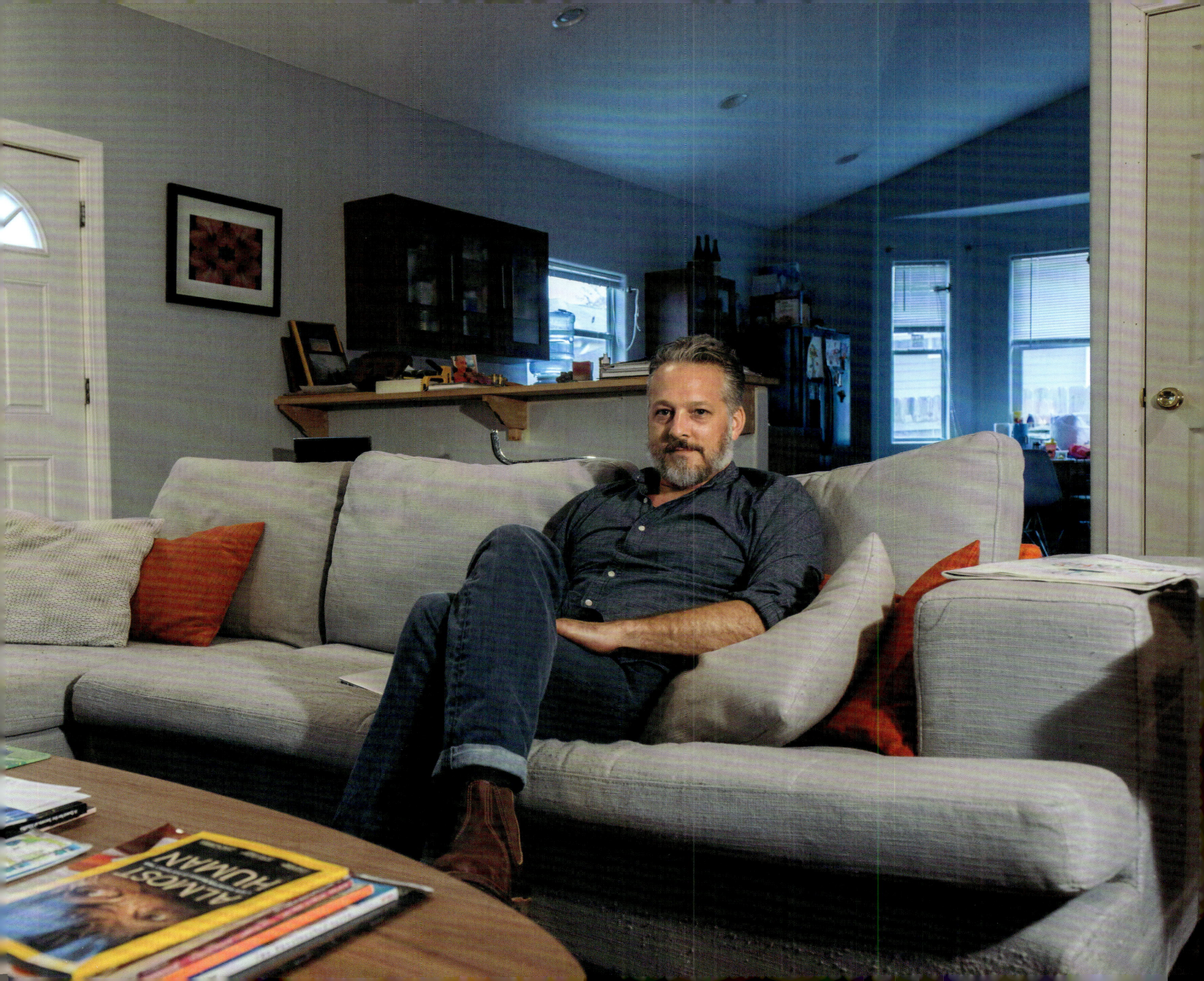

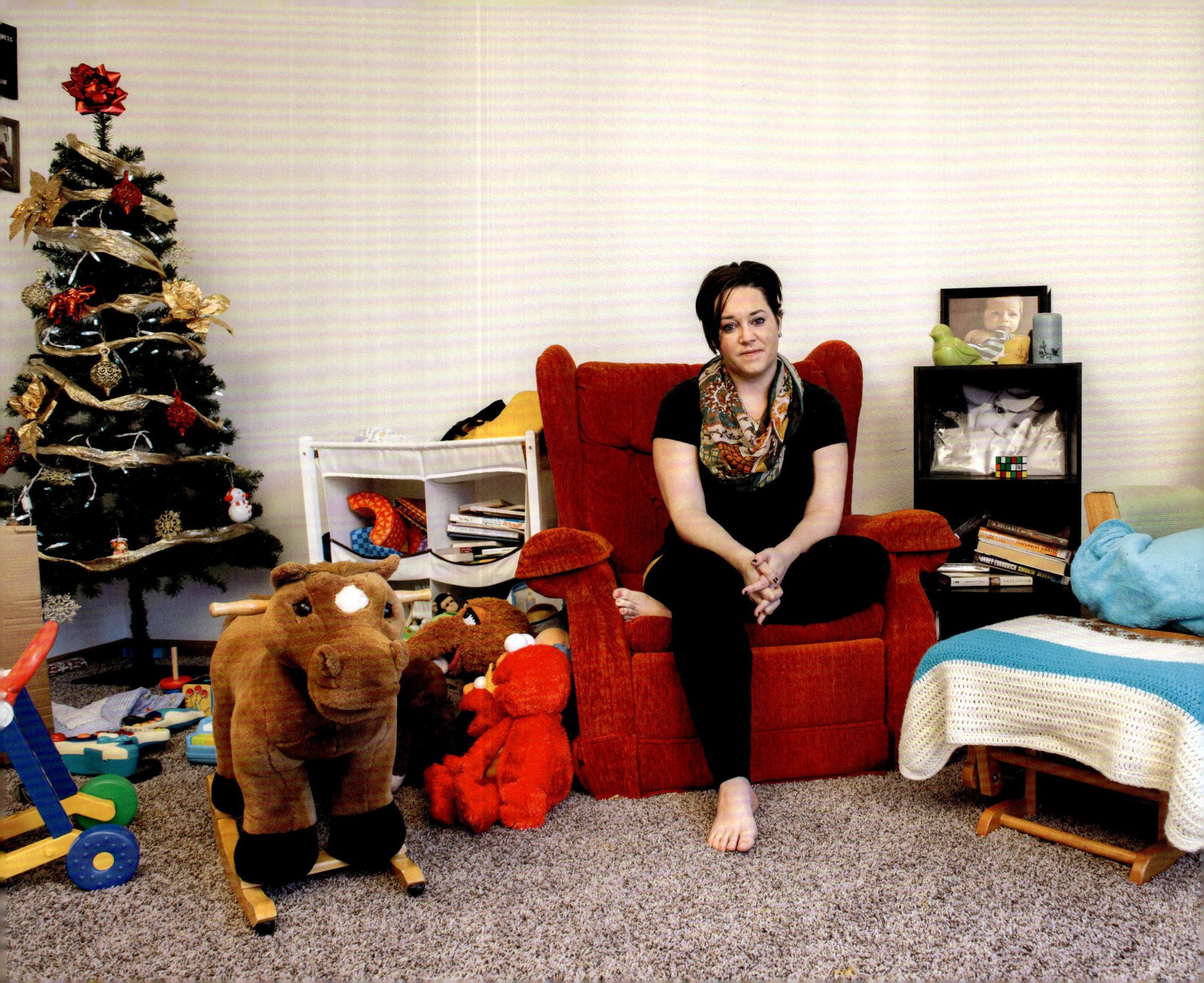

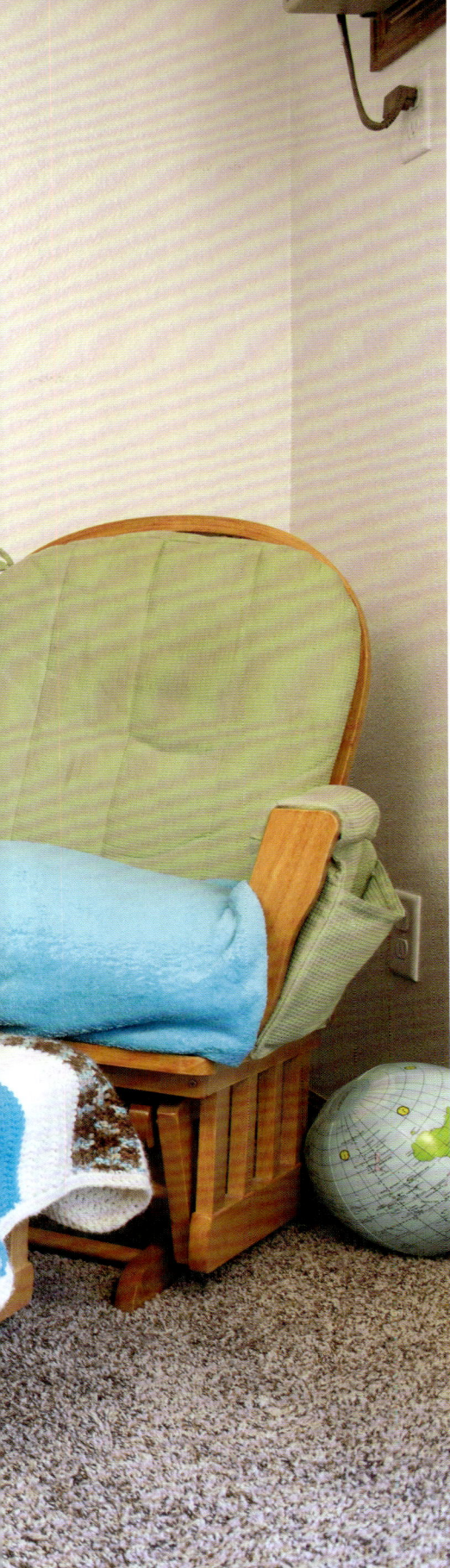

Amber Zenor   Stay at Home Mom

$40,000 debt

When I turned 18 I had no idea what credit was or it's affect on my future. I went to Community college and was offered loans, which I took out, being optimistic about my future. I had no clue what I wanted to go to school for and went just because that's what everyone else was doing. I ended up failing and withdrawing from all my classes, eventually defaulting and being ineligible for future financing. I also feel I was taken advantage of by a loan company that I had my car through. Every time I went in to make a payment, they offered me more money, and at 19/20 years old, that sounded great. I was basically refinancing my loan, til it grew to around $30,000. I was able to pay on some of that, but have come to the conclusion it is out of my hands. All of that accumulated with medical bills, I have realized my only way out is to declare bankruptcy

Lauren Pesta

Debt
$20,000

In 2013 I lost my job & wasn't able to find another one that could support my son & I. So I decided to go back to school. I chose a community college because it was cheaper. Now 2 years in, almost done, I owe $20,000 & will soon transfer to a University where my debt will double in just one semester. I have 4 more years to go & wonder if when I'm done will I have the same problem finding a job to support us with all this debt.

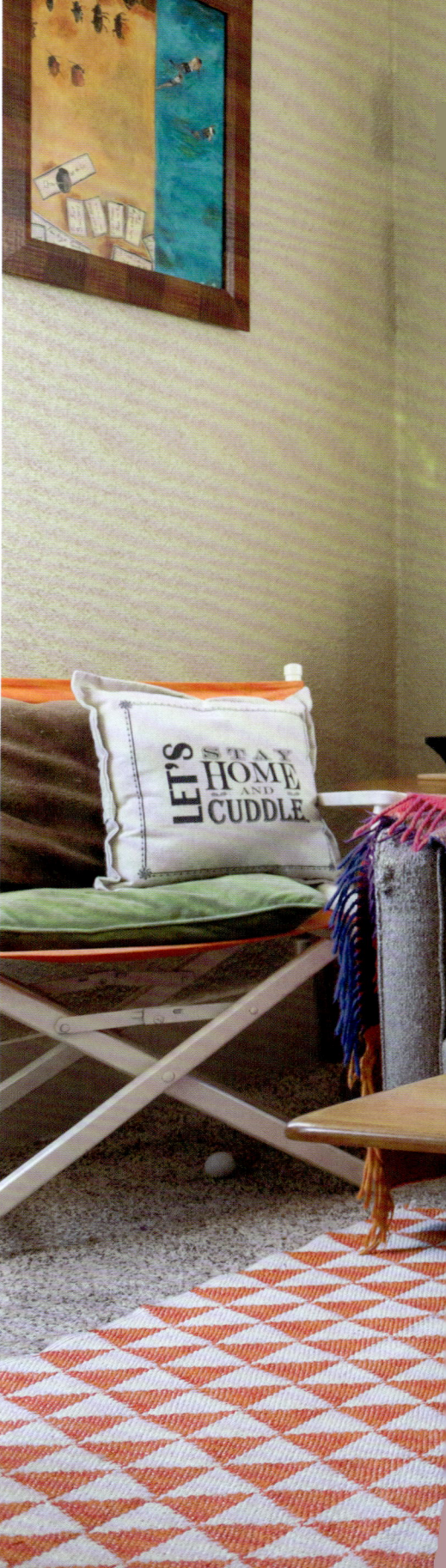

Debt Portrait #56, Des Moines, IA 2015

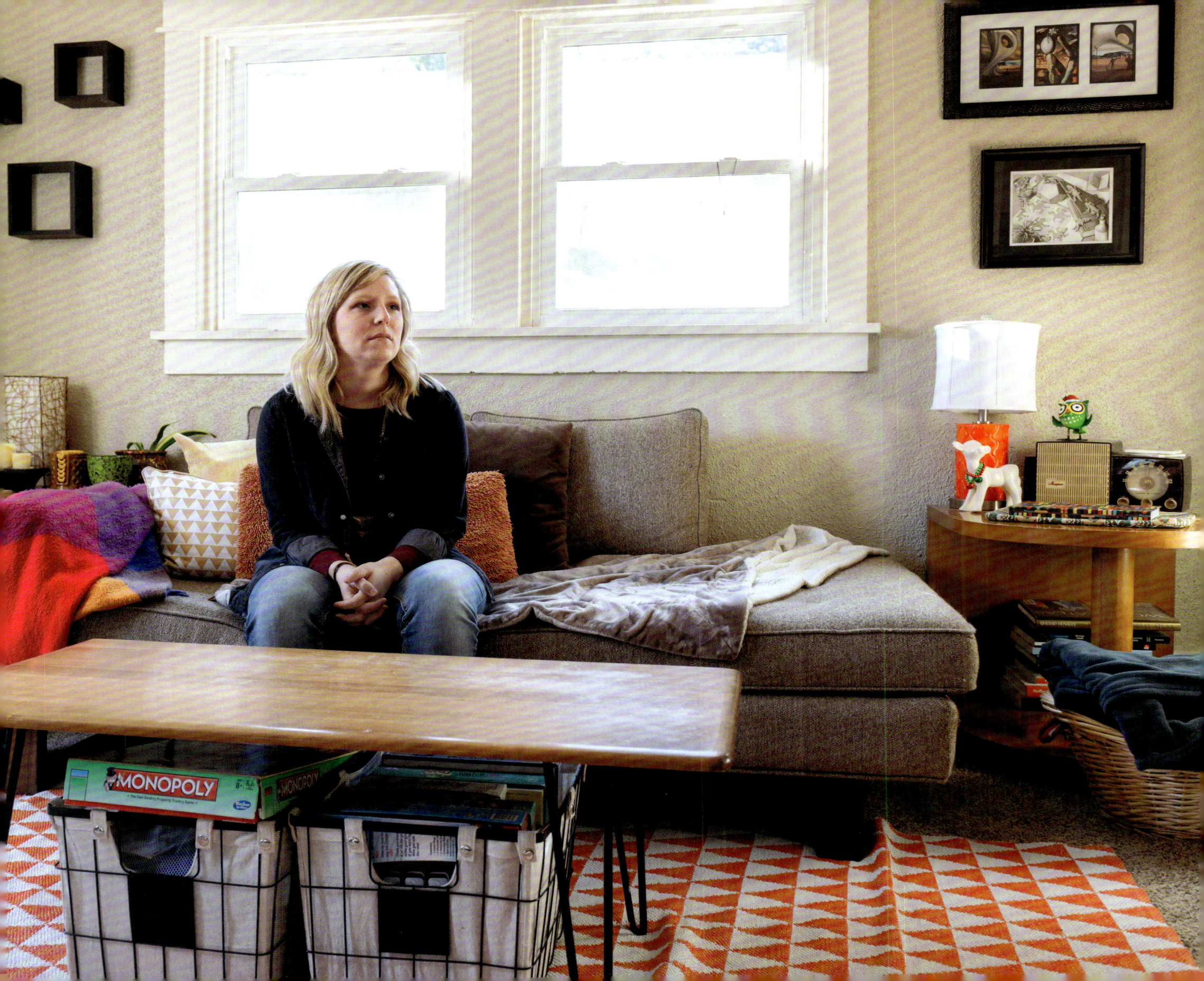

an. c

?????
. . . . .

debt is a kind of dread,
& one of its arms is capital.
in the hand is money, or, where
money should be. debt isn't
quantifiable ; it isn't a person.
who is the debtor? to whom
to i owe the performance
of negligent payment? i am
made a fraud, until the debt
is _in_ me. part of the body.
i wake up every day & try
to be a person. to afford
to be a person. who feels
like me. i am trying on
empty.

Debt Portrait #57, Iowa City, IA 2015

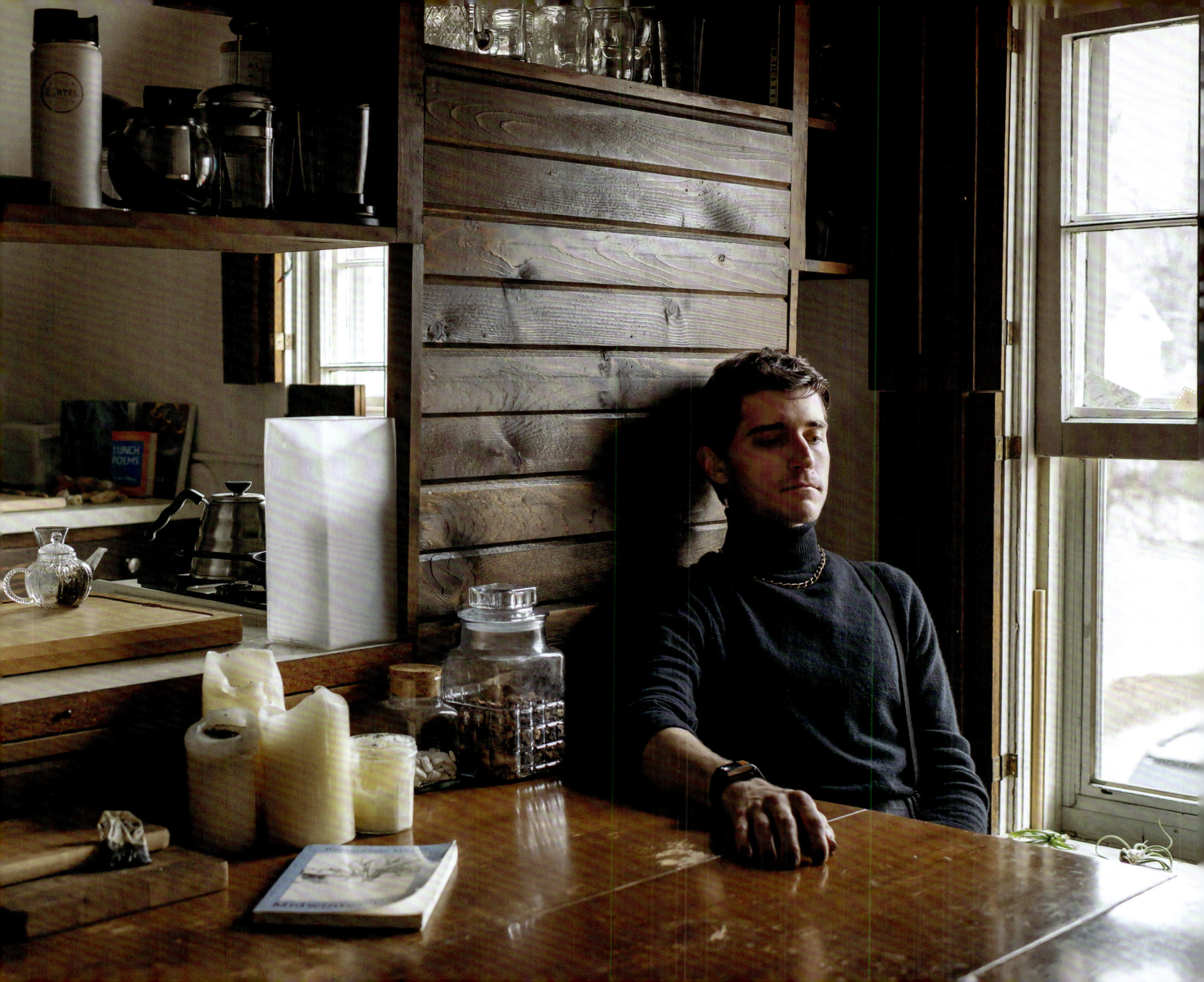

Lisa Steenhoek

About #55,000

I started my debt with student loans.
and then progressed to medical bills
after loss of a marriage that never
happend. I tried to Consuladate debt
Cecunceling and they told me it was
My parents cespociblity I have had job
loss and family loss. Trying
too simply trying too Keepin forward
and Always taking one step back
My dept has been like a spiral
that keeps going despite My efforts
to improve it.

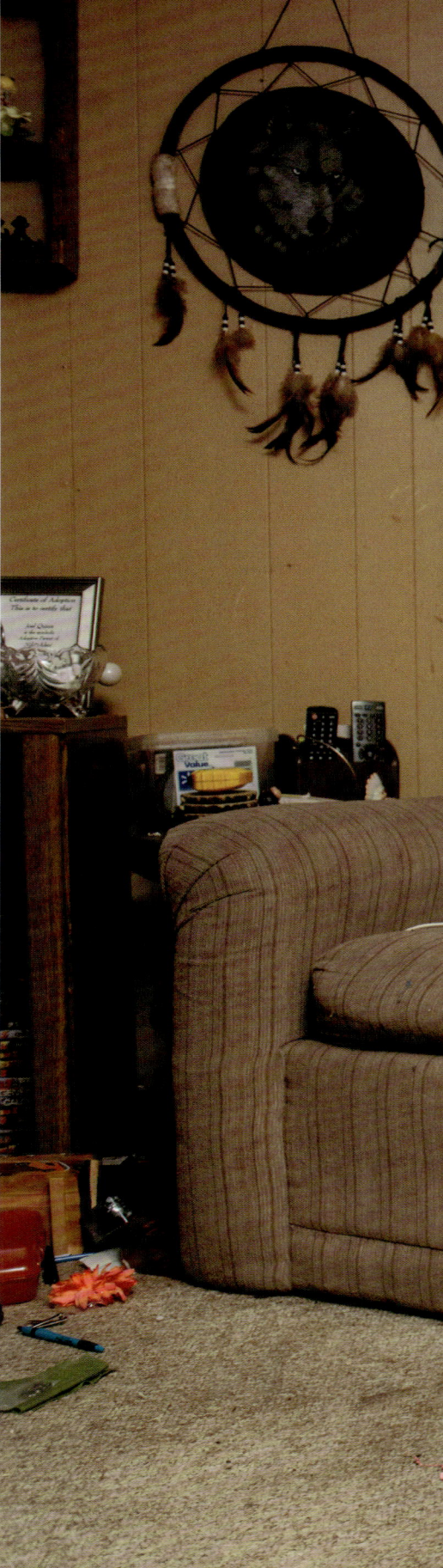

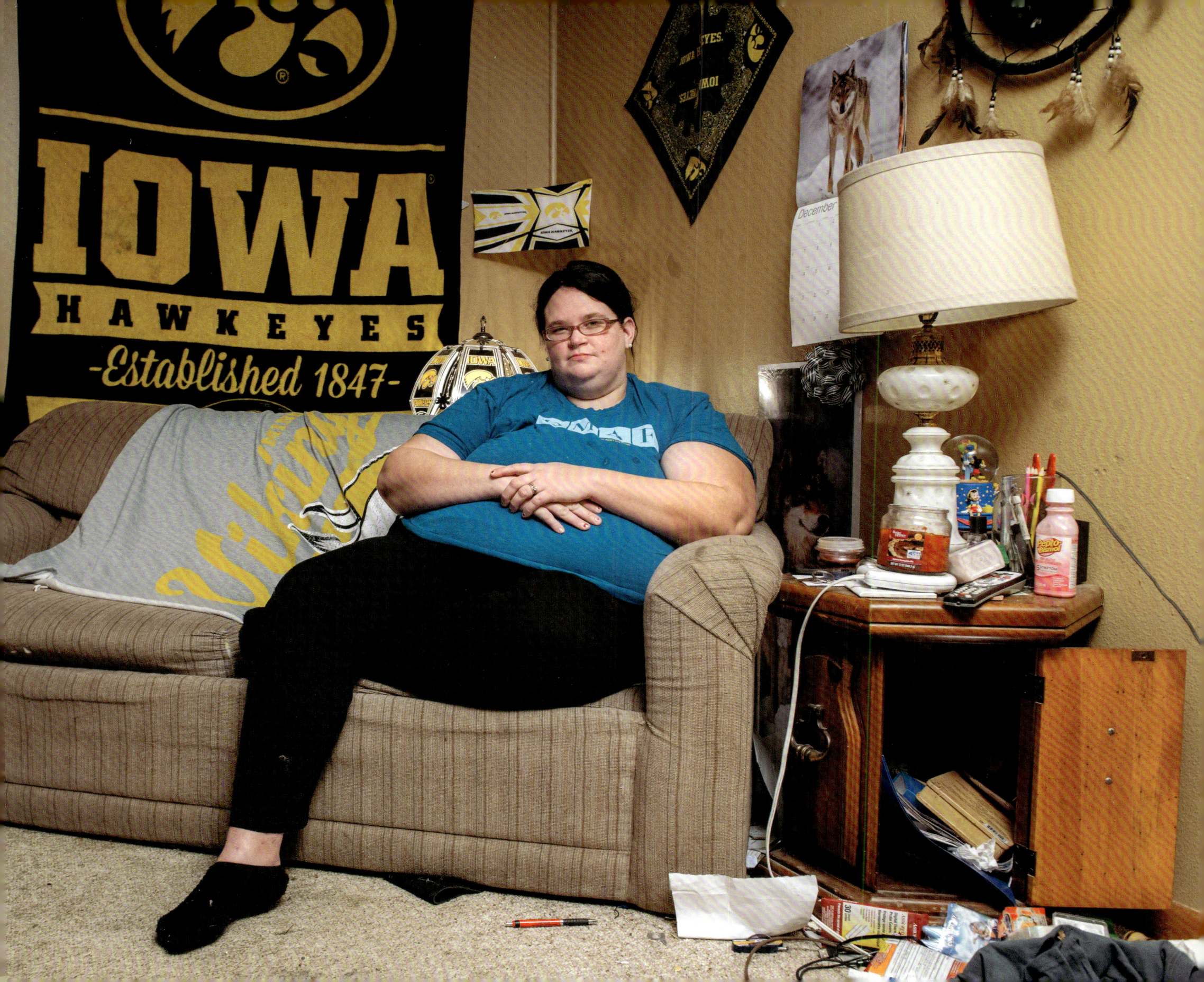

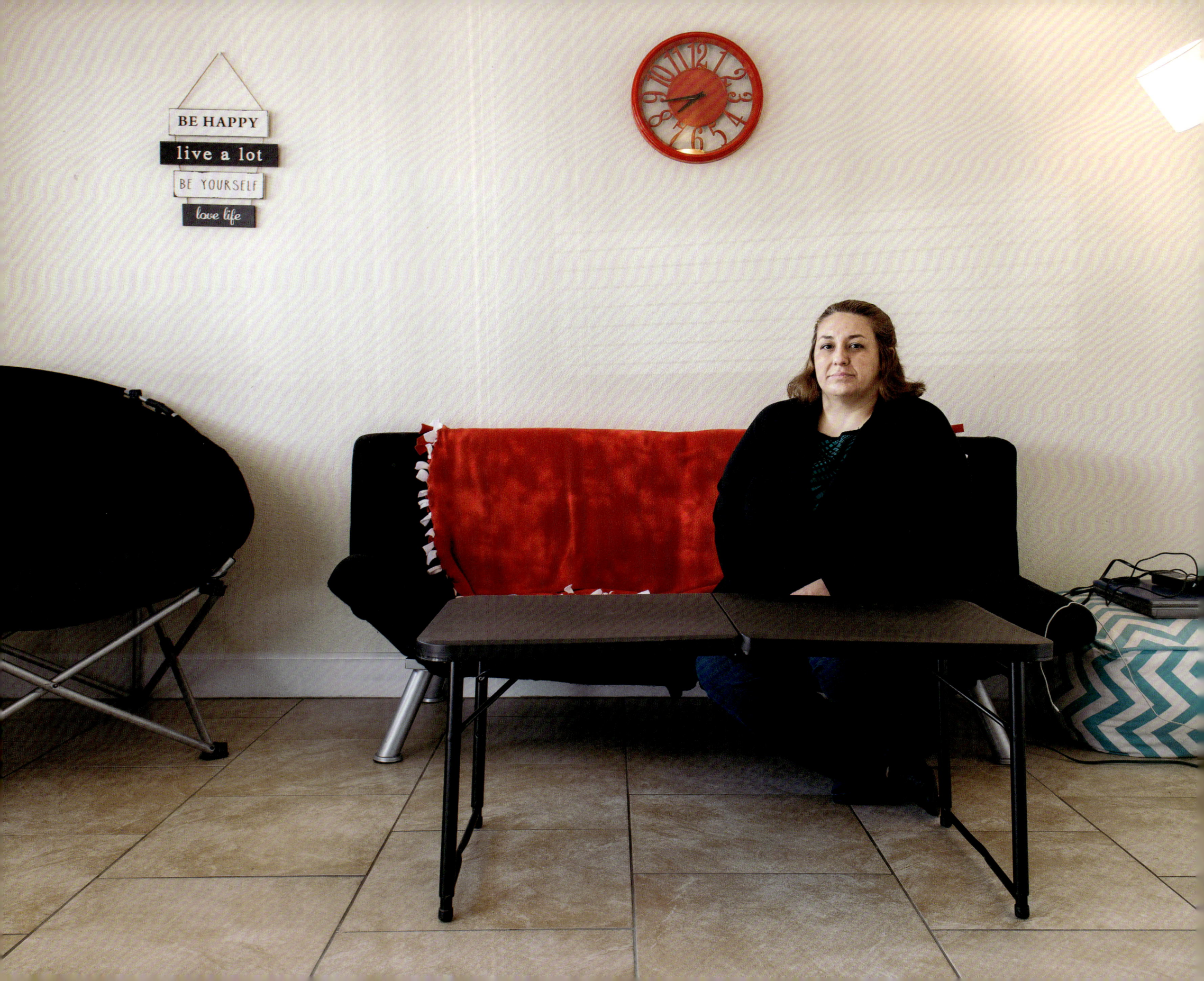

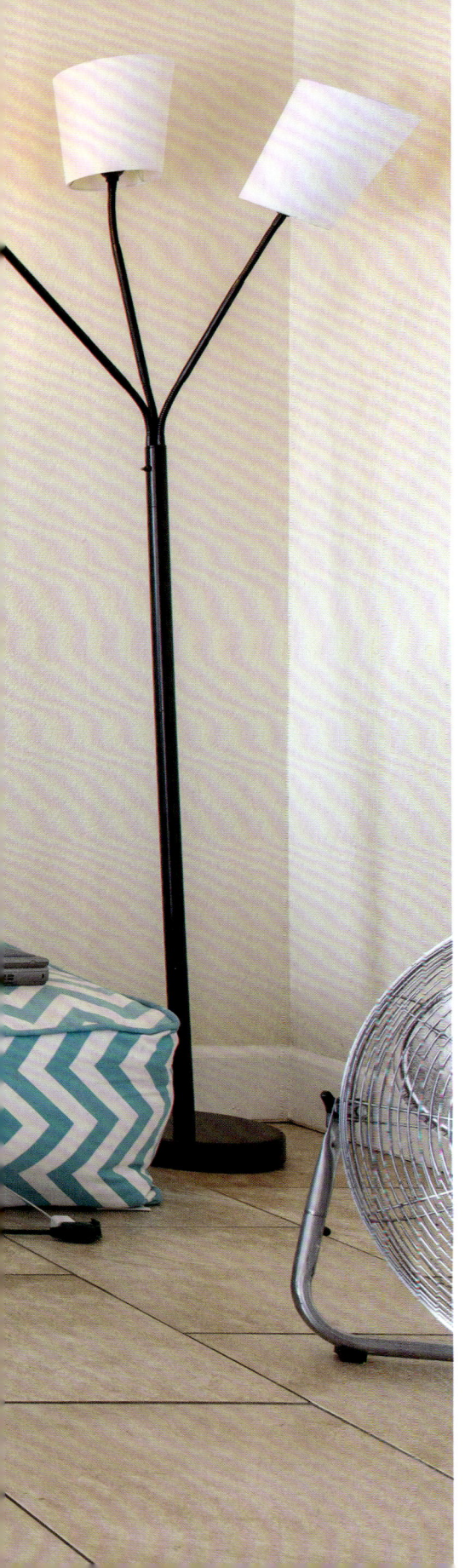

Kim Payne   39
Unemployed

$10,000

I filed bankruptcy in 2000.
   It was hard to get a good
     job based on my past.
   In the last 5 years or so,
employers are becoming more
concerned with a potential employees
credit. Thus, experienced
people are being passed up
based on issues in their past.

Debt Portrait #59, Reno, NV 2016

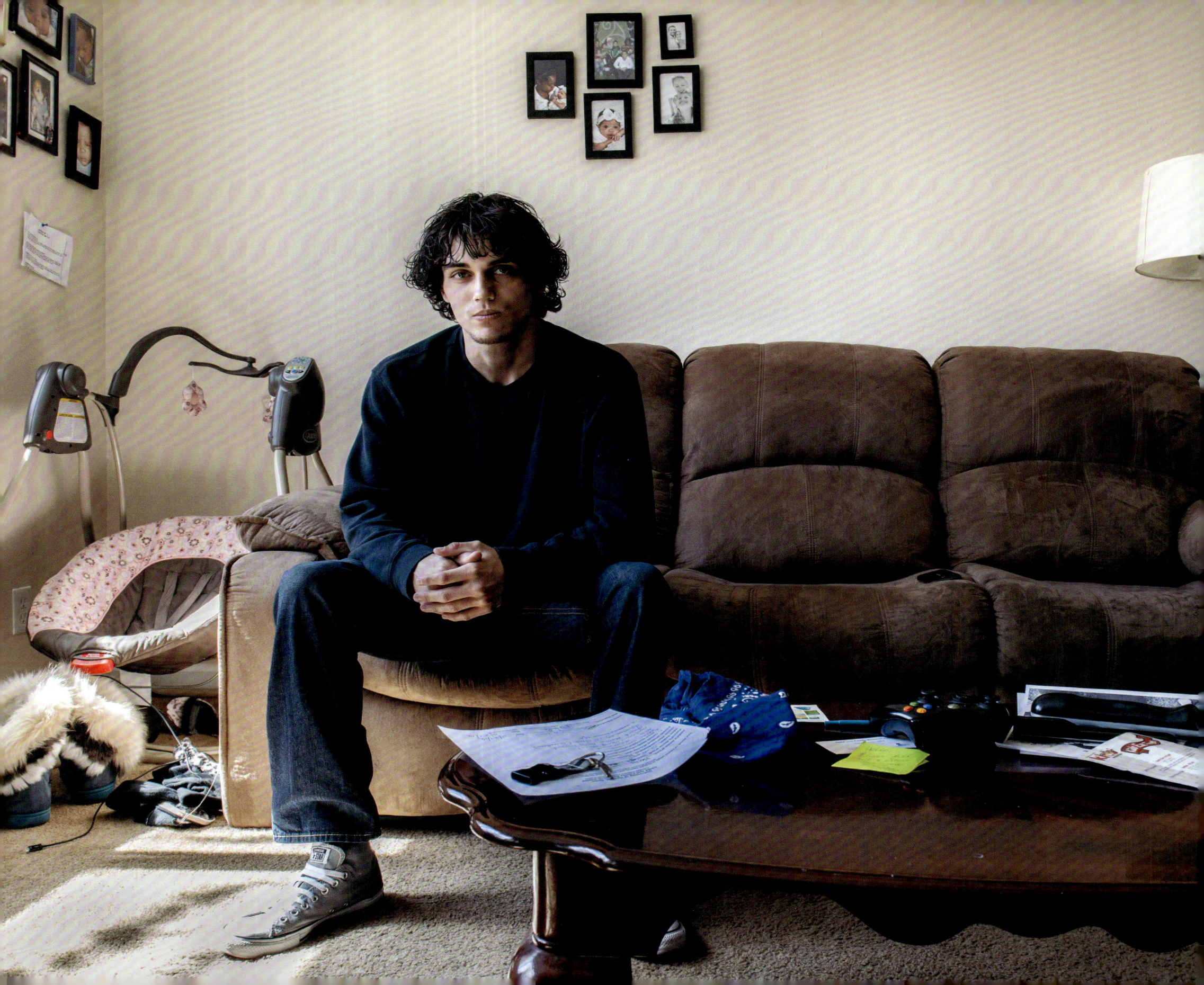

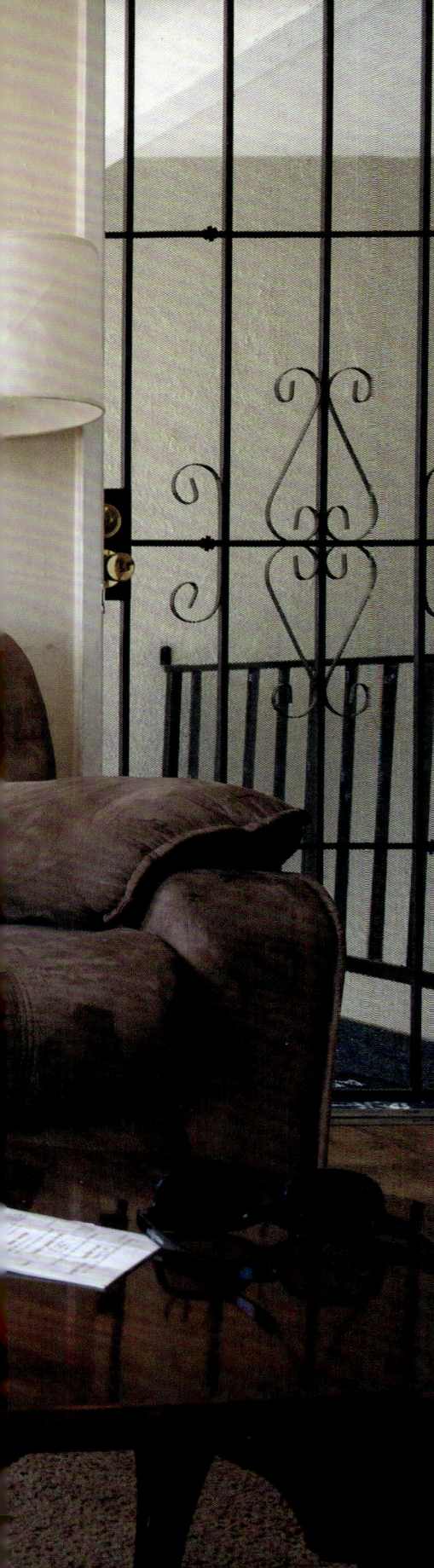

Devan Edmonds
warehouseman

2,500

The reason I am currently in debt is when I had my first apartment I lost it because I was fired from my job for missing work to deal with family issues & my second apartment was lost when my fiance lost her job so we could not afford our place at the time.

Debt Portrait #60, Reno, NV 2016

3-26-2016

My name is Lewis E. Gross, and I owe between $80,000⁰⁰ and $90,000⁰⁰ in student loan debt.

I have been harassed, garnished, and left feeling criminal. All because, I wanted to better myself.

I don't regret completing my education, but I do regret not focusing on the cost of it all! Hopefully, there will be a less costly alternative in the future for kids!,

Lewis E. Gross, J.

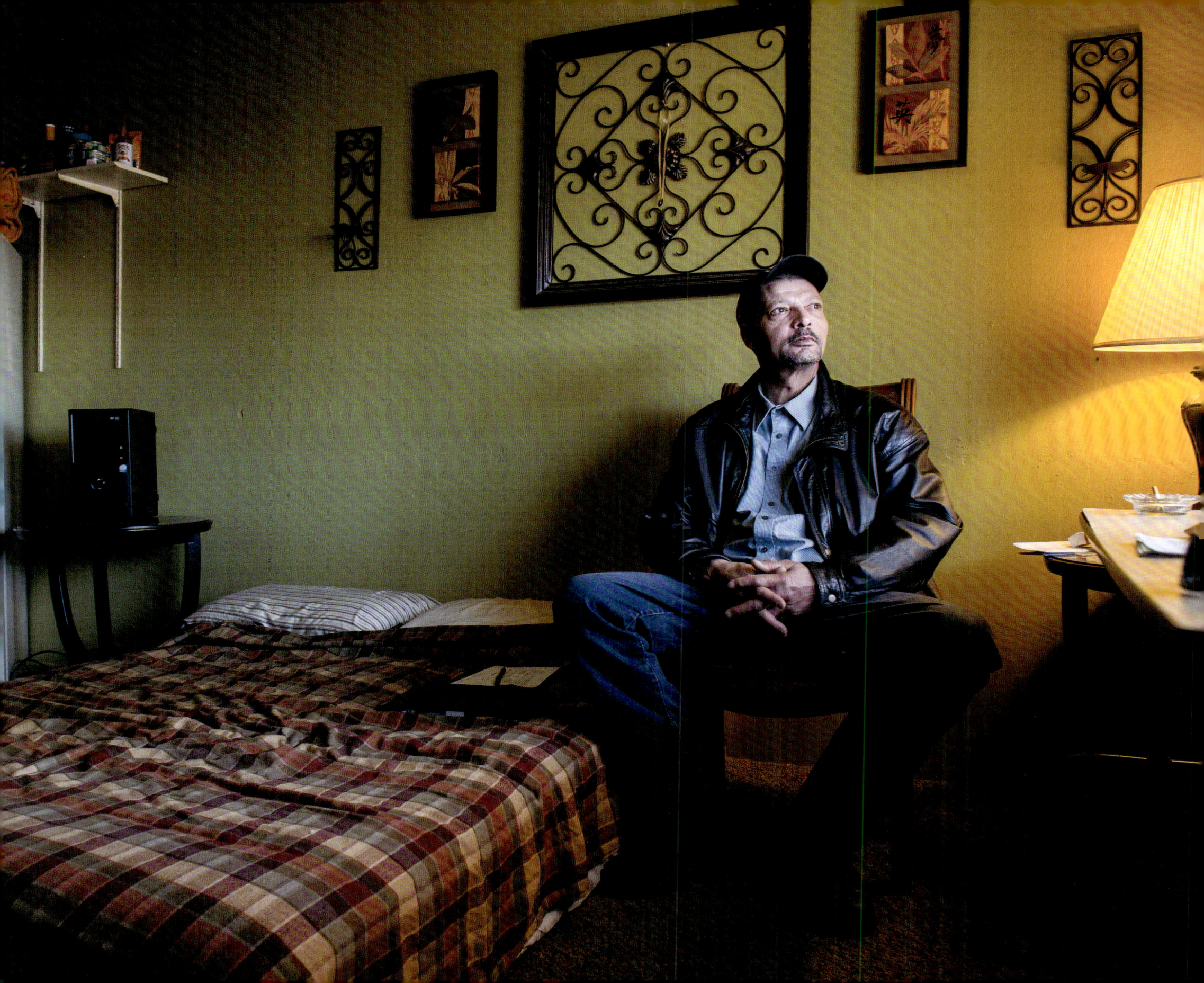

Michelle Hopkins

① Short Sale 70,000
② Jayflight trailer 8,000
③ fingerhut etc. 10,000
④ Pay day loans 5,000
⑤ Bonced 2,400
⑥ MISC. 2,000
⑦ 5,000
                102,400

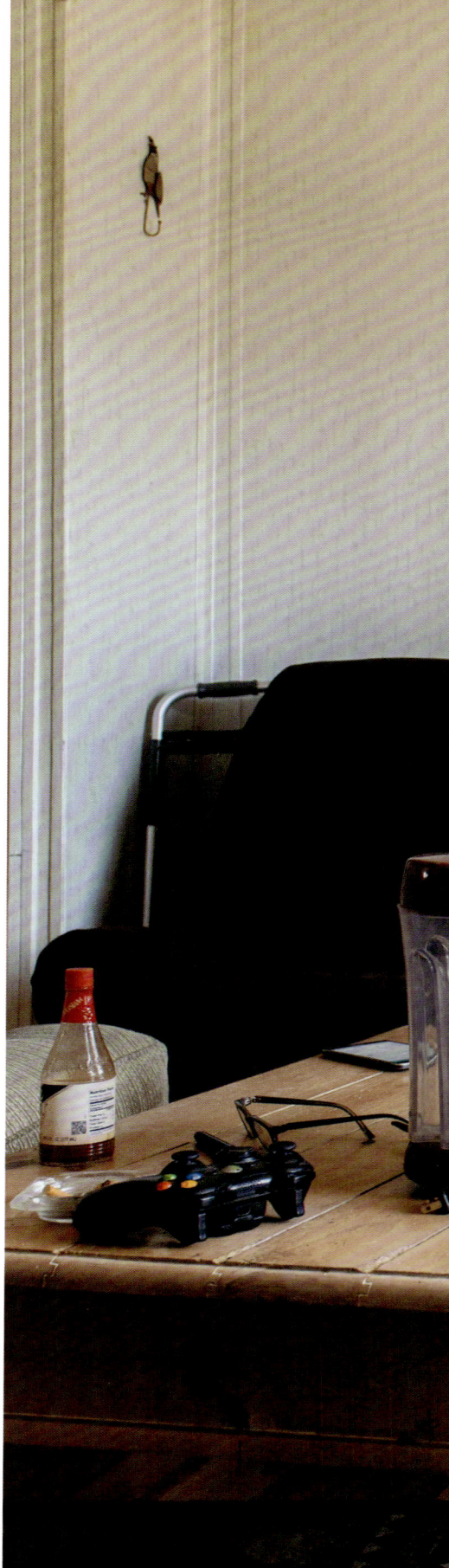

Debt Portrait #62, Reno, NV 2016

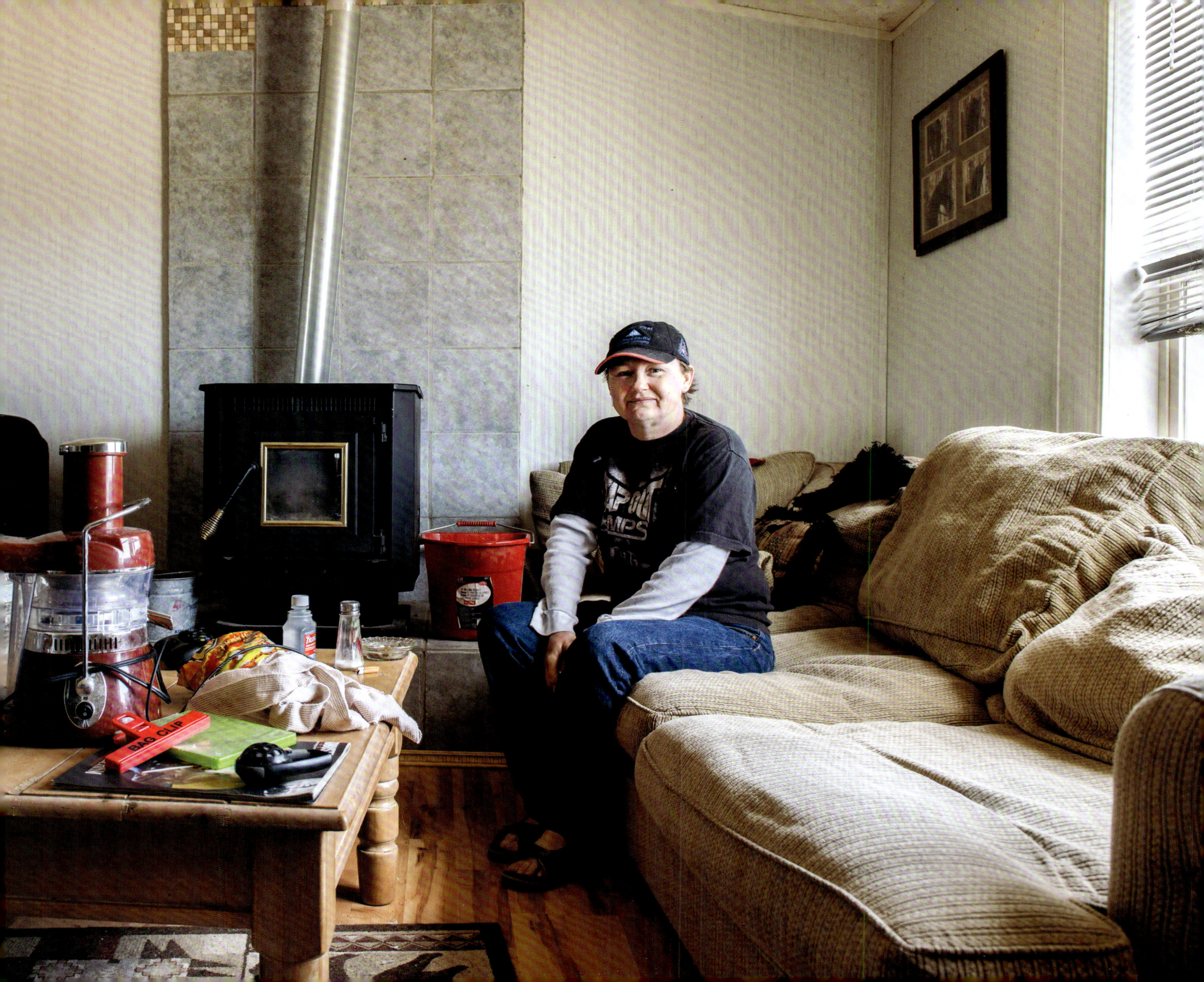

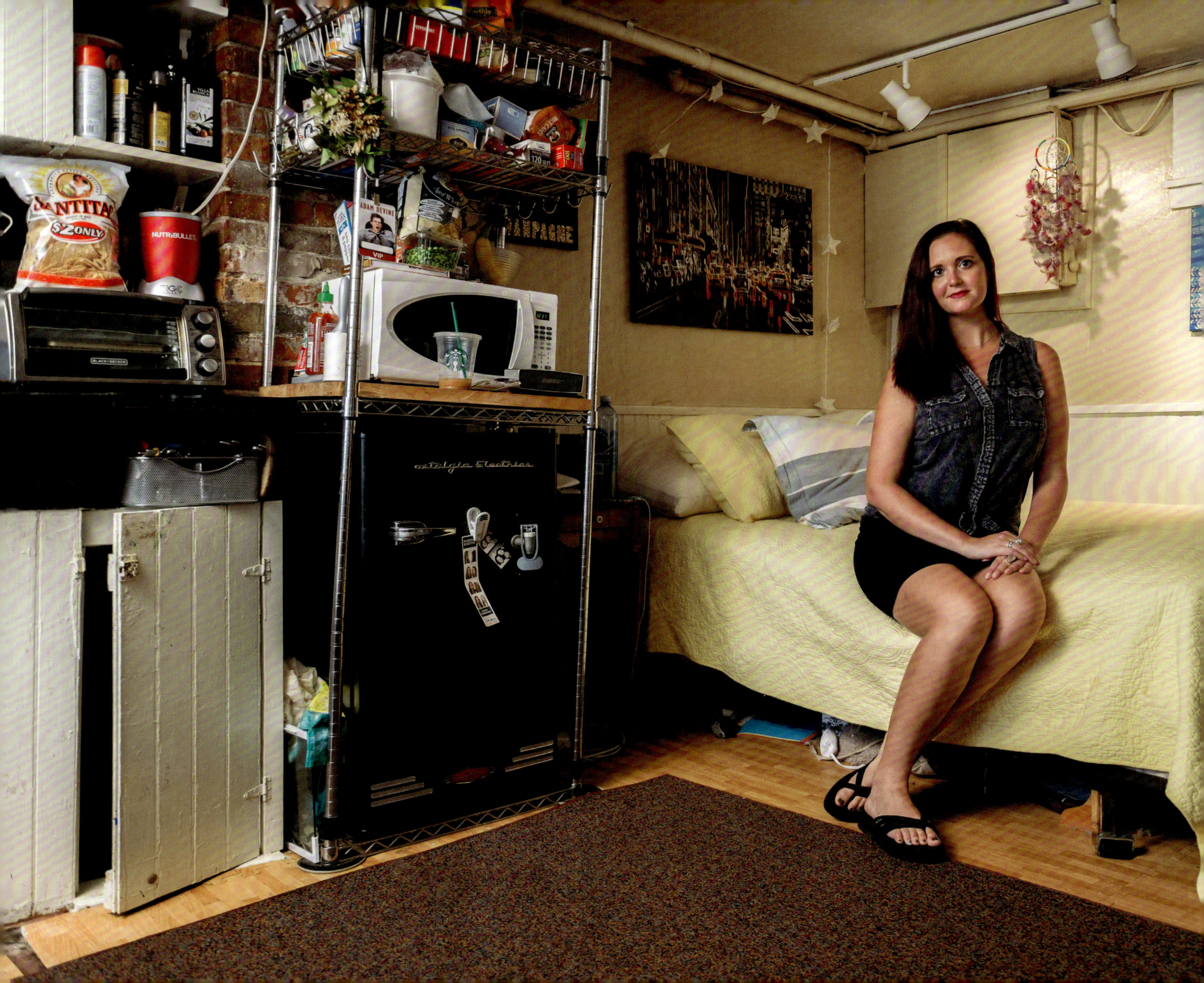

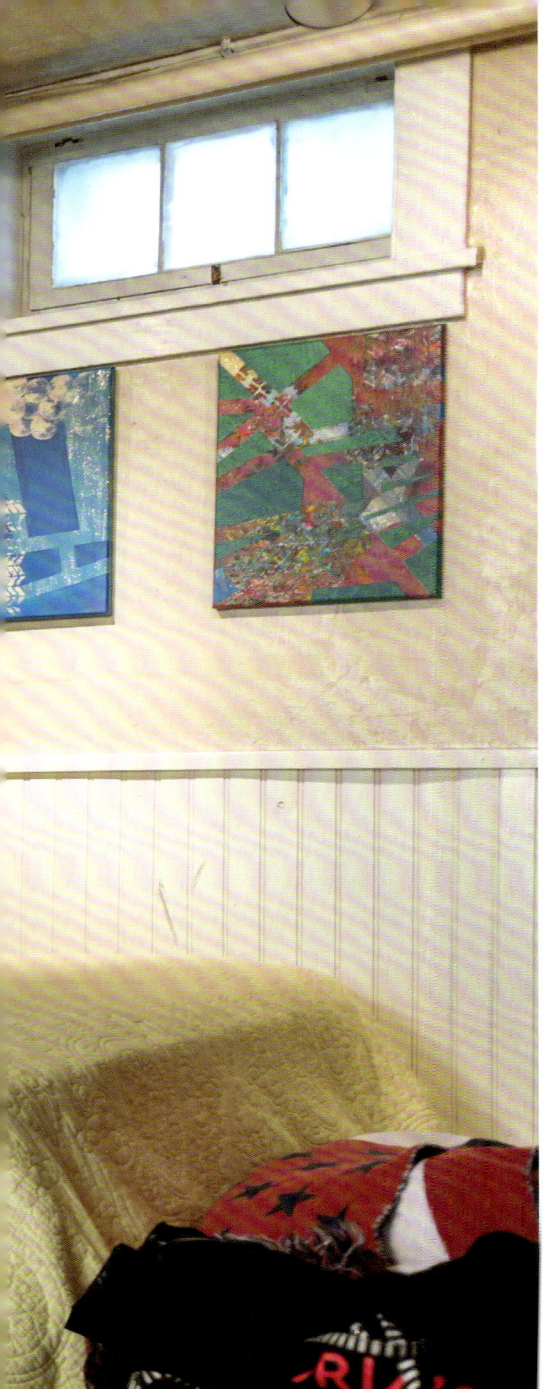

Casi DeSarro
Bridal Consultant
Age 26

DEBT AMOUNT : $40,000

At the age of 18 is when I took out my first credit card. I should not have been allowed. Going to college is not something I would like to regret, but unfortunately because of the debt that it has caused is making me wonder if it was worth it. Debt plays too big of a roll in my every day life because it is extremely limiting. I hope that there will be a day that I become debt-free!!!

Shanita Walker.
HOTel Night Auditor
90,000

Being in debt, I feel like I am limited
to what I am "accepted" for. My
credit score is now the main factor
in Housing, building a business and raising
a family.

If I Knew then what I know now I would
have at least waited until I was sure
of what I wanted to do before taking
out loans.

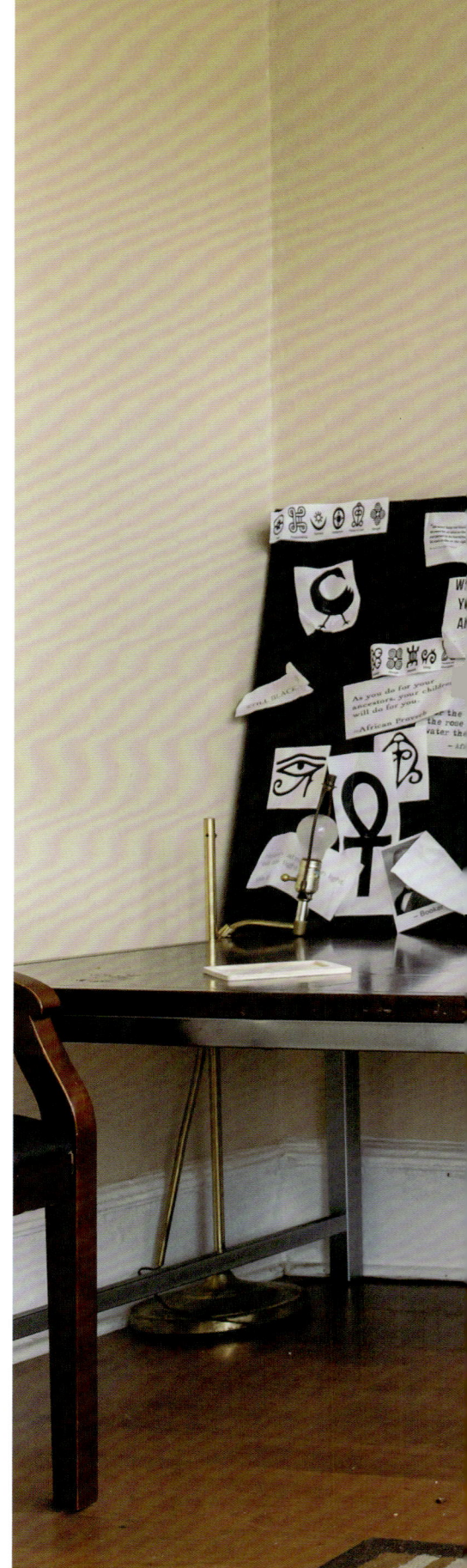

Debt Portrait #64, Philadelphia, PA 2016

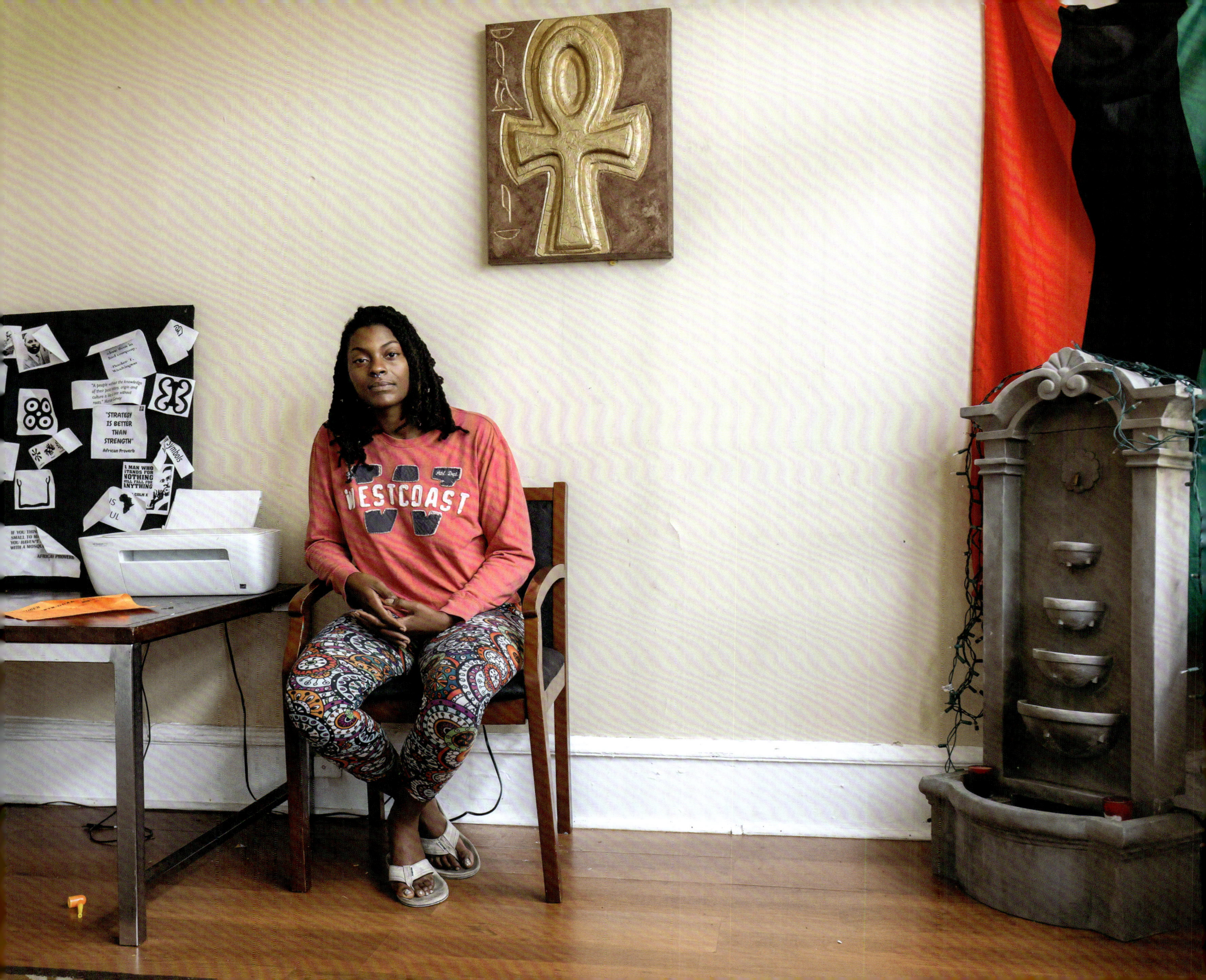

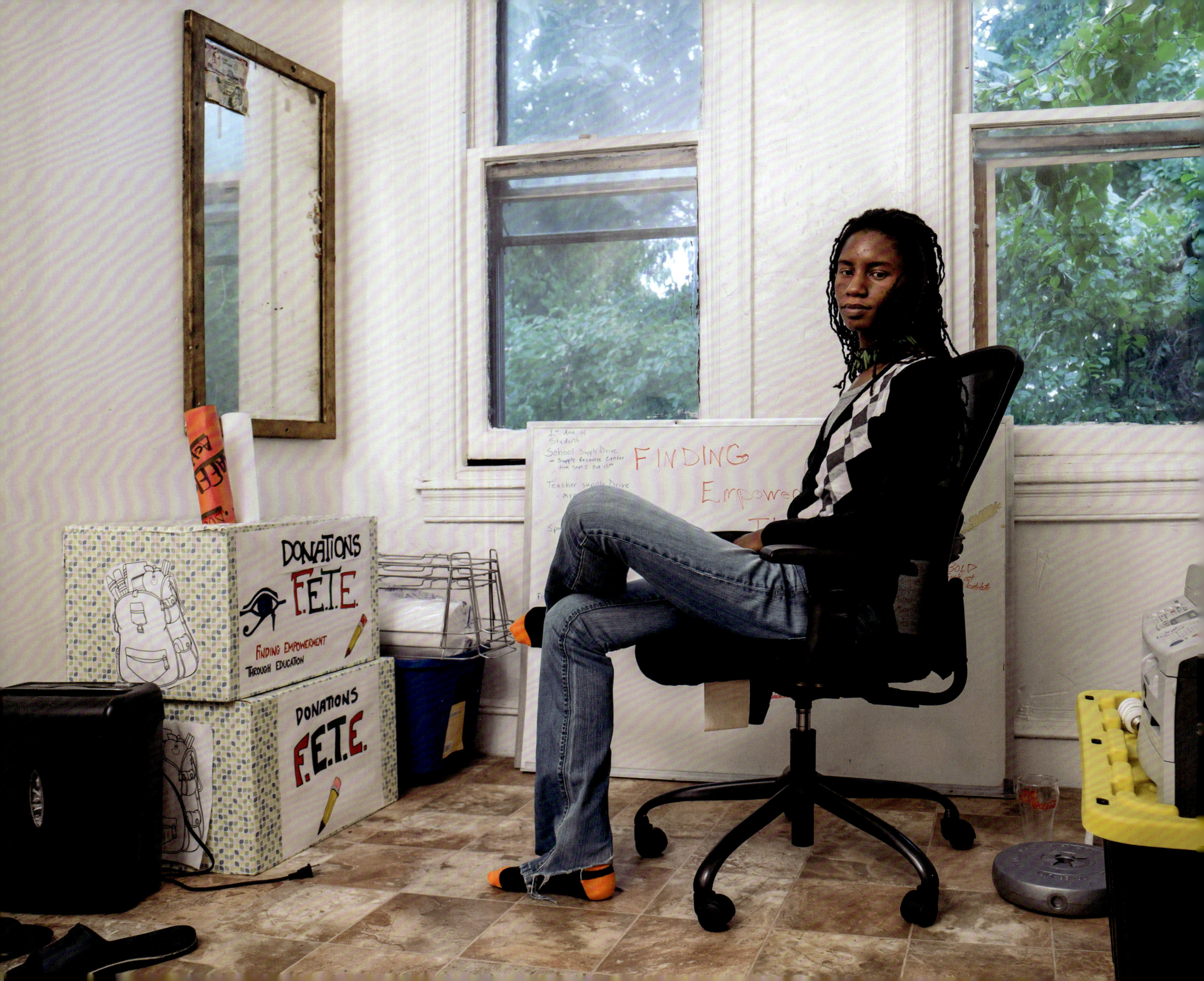

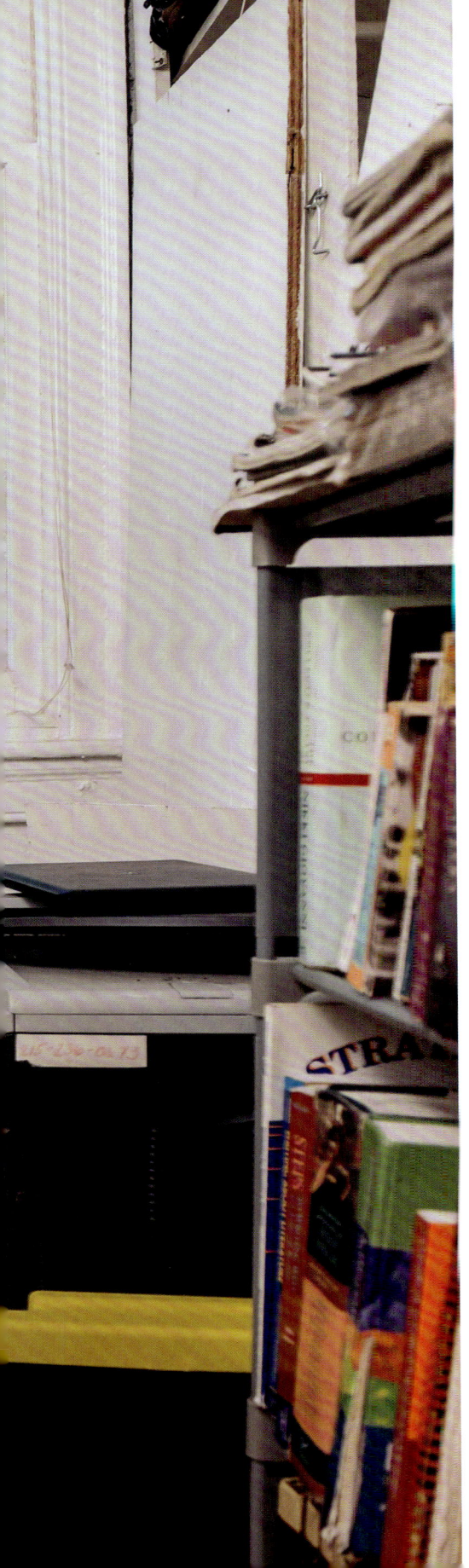

Lori Chambers
Health Insurance Agent
Debt $130,000

I have a 6 figure debt mainly due to attending college from 2003-2007. I had dreams of becoming a lawyer but instead graduated with an English degree and founded a not for profit Education foundation. My mission is to now eliminate the social and economic restraints of a lack of education by giving children the tools necessary to exemplify: scholarship, leadership and accountability. I create curriculum that reinforces critical thinking, appreciation of nature and virtues and financial literacy. My dream is that my K-12 curriculum will eliminate the need for college debt, in the next generation.

Debt Portrait #65, Philadelphia, PA 2016

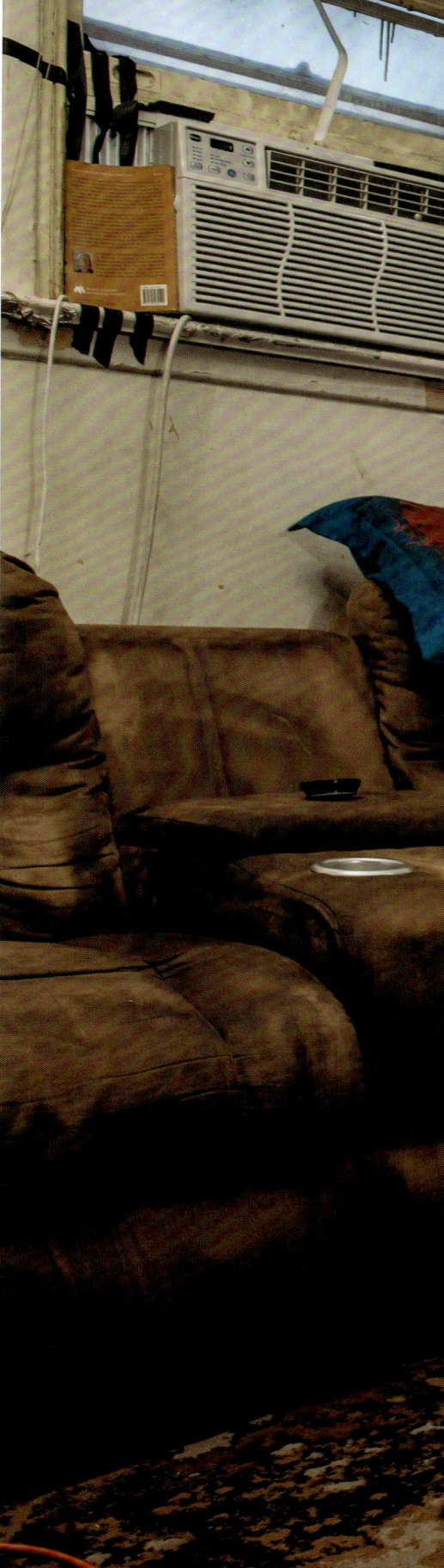

Brandon Wallace
Free lance Artist
Debt 25,000 est.

I acquired my child support debts because of an ongoing negative court ordered stipulation. Example - 59.00 a week for every week working and not working. If i didn't work for two weeks, by the time I received a check I would be deducted 18.00 and etc. Child support debt was stopped by child's mother. Debt is now at arrears of 9,000. I was fined 10,000 for an altercation with law enforcement a few years ago. I paid about 800.00 of this before I fell behind. Various debts for citations ranging 300.00-600.00 an offense. I am not sure as of now, through the sheriff's department, collections, or other enforcement agencies, if interest is accrued at this point in time. I marginally check my credit report to see where the debts stands out.

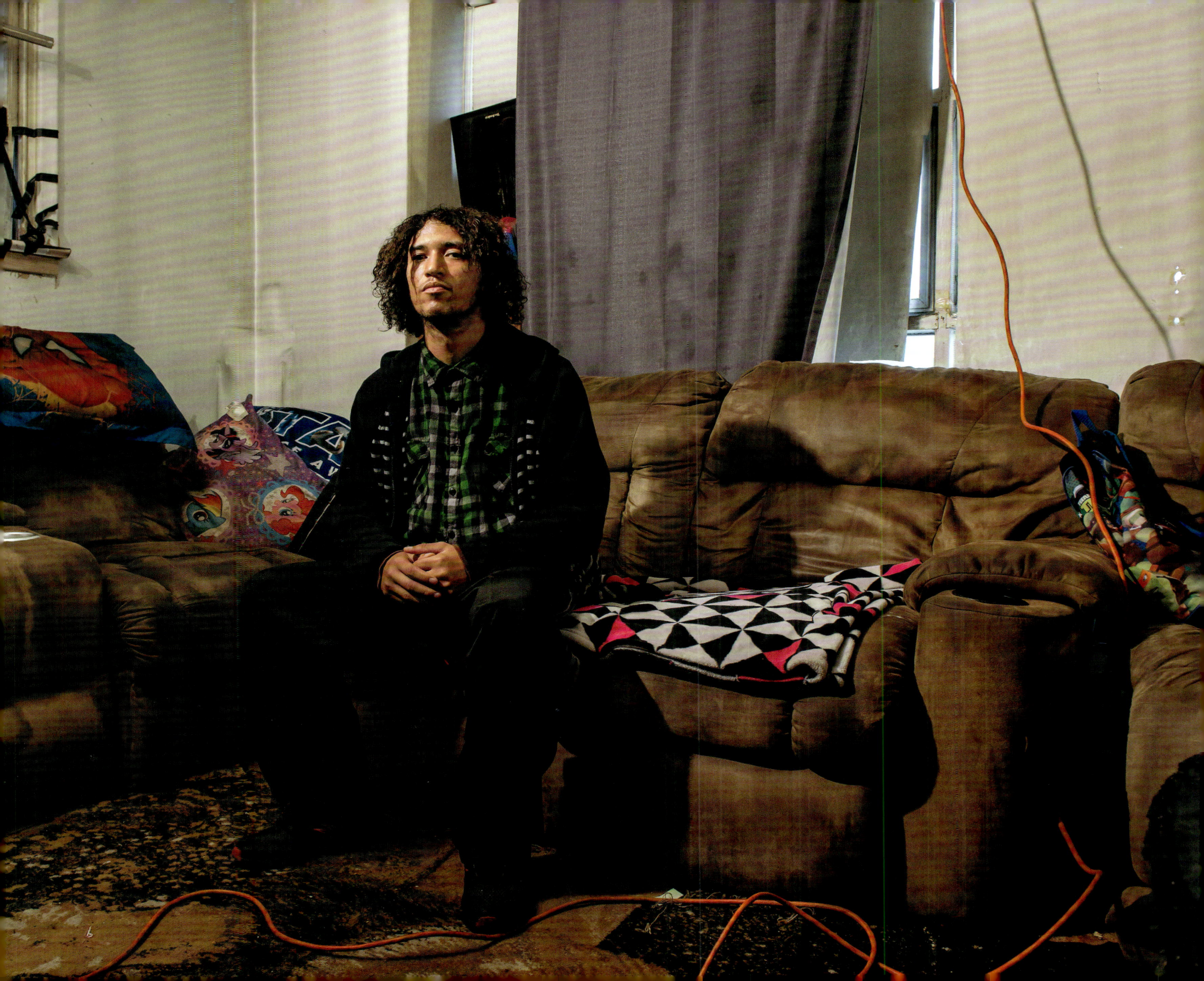

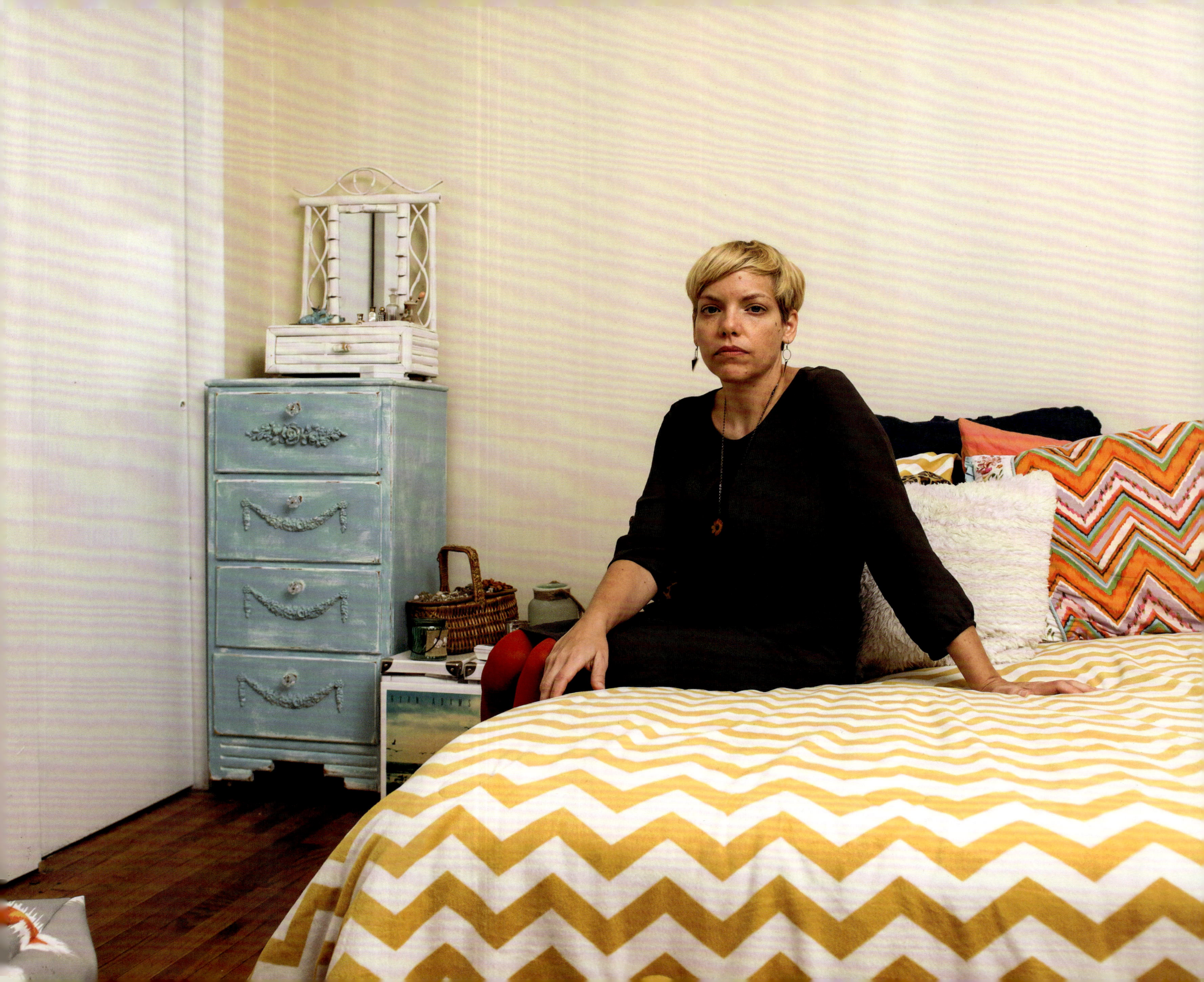

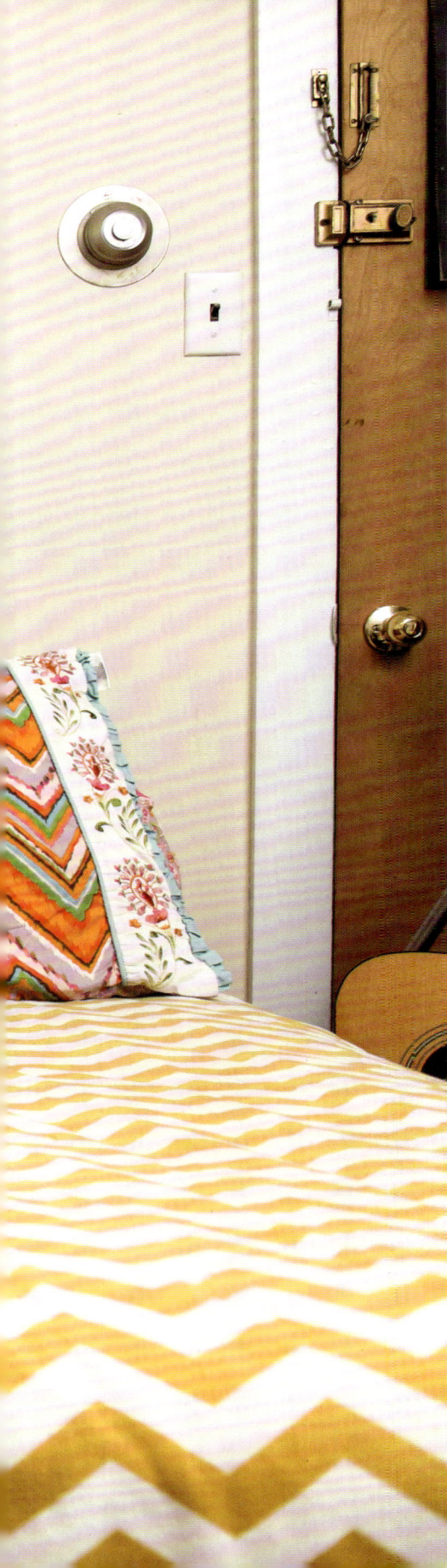

Jill Mumie
Server/artist
Debt $9,000.00

    I have a BA in Studio Art/Photography and upon graduation was the bright eyed, starving artist, loaded with loans and jumped into society, full of debt. I began to work in the restaurant industry. At age 28, the debt I was in was significant, accumulated from poor consumer purchases, education expenses and missteps in my personal life. I found myself engaged to an addict, his problems affecting my financial and emotional stability. At 28 years old, I made the decision to file Chapter 7 bankruptcy. With the bankruptcy discharge i was able to move out, leave him and start life anew.

But not without burden. I've been afraid to admit this failure and have carried this shame with me for 13 years. The shame is the emotional burden that has kept a better life from being realized. I felt like a failure. As consequence, this moment affected the trajectory of my life. I have yet to marry, i never had a child. I resisted accruing debt again—. going back to school, investing in myself.

Debt was a lesson learned, but living in a society that values wealth so highly, it has been a struggle to overcome the feelings of negative self-worth. Perhaps this story can comfort another. You are the sixth person i've told this story to, perhaps telling my story is the final step in making peace with the person i once was.

    Current debt— $9,000.00 due to medical bills/expenses from a surgery.

Debt Portrait #67, Collingswood, NJ 2016

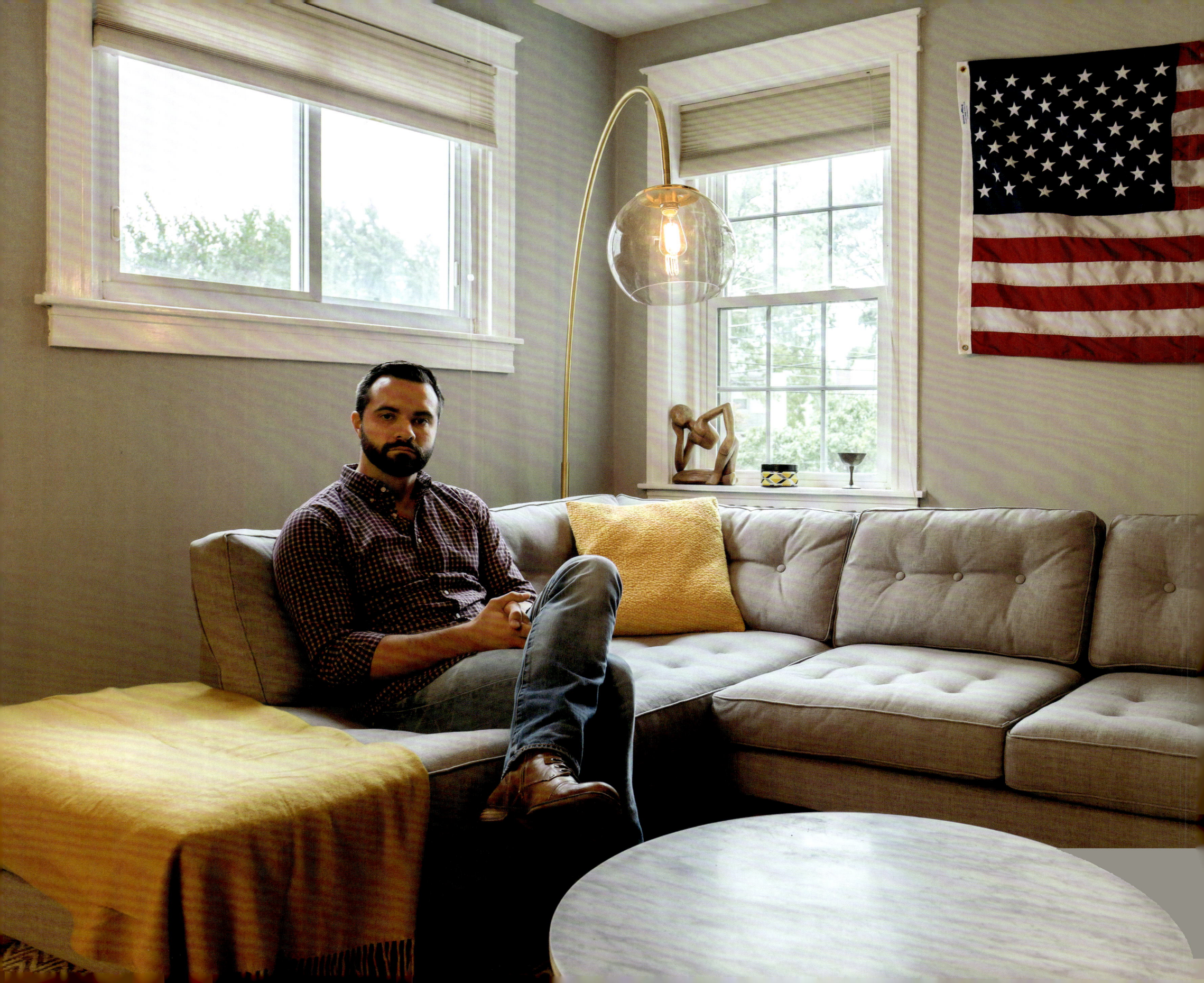

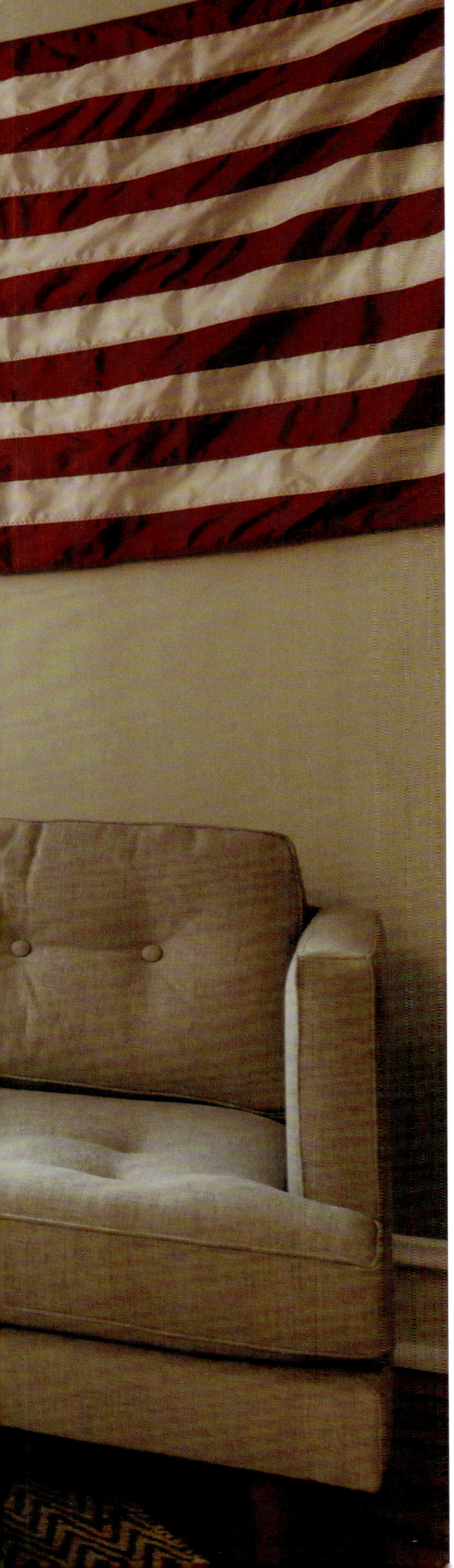

Nick DePrimo

Scientist

~ $140K Student Loans
$3500 Credit card debt

Applied / didn't get into Med School. Opted to attend a post-undergrad, pre-med program — 1 year of grad school & $70K of debt. Applied / didn't get into Med school (again). Stayed in program (another $70K) to at least earn an M.S. Finished & took $35K salaried job ASAP. Making a better salary now, but spend $800/month on interest alone — did math, & it will likely take into my 70s to get to Net worth = $0.00. Wish me luck.

Kate Wheeler
Server

$35K Student loan debt
(mostly private, some federal)

I signed a MPN when I was 17 so I have lived my entire adult life with debt. The meaning of this debt has shifted over time. It started as a meaningless figure, moved to a panic inducing weight and then just another bill to pay. I see it as a mix of all three now. I hope that someday it leaves me alone.

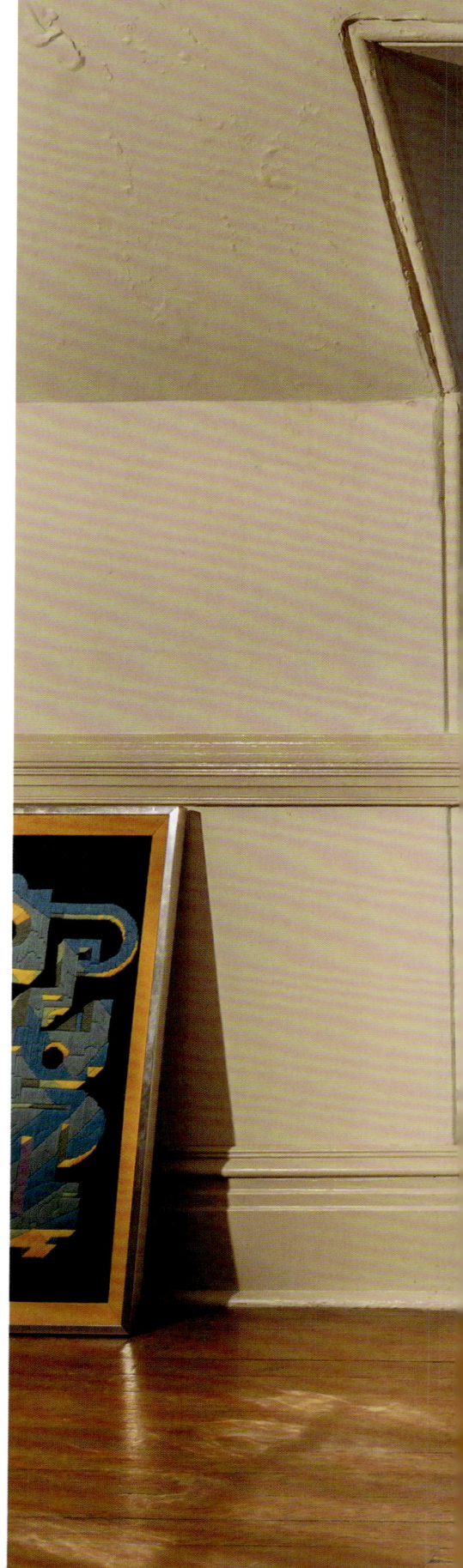

Debt Portrait #69, Philadelphia, PA 2017

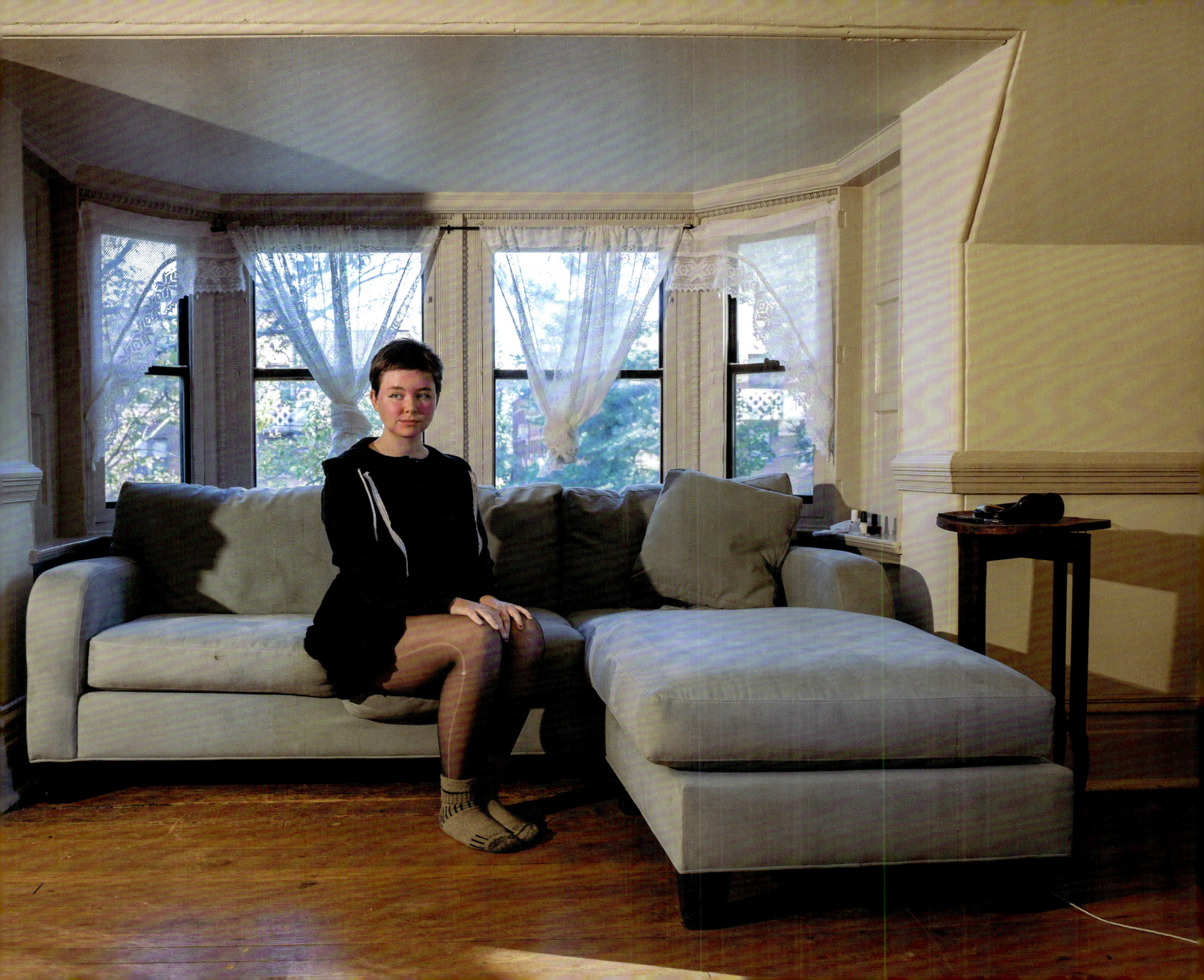

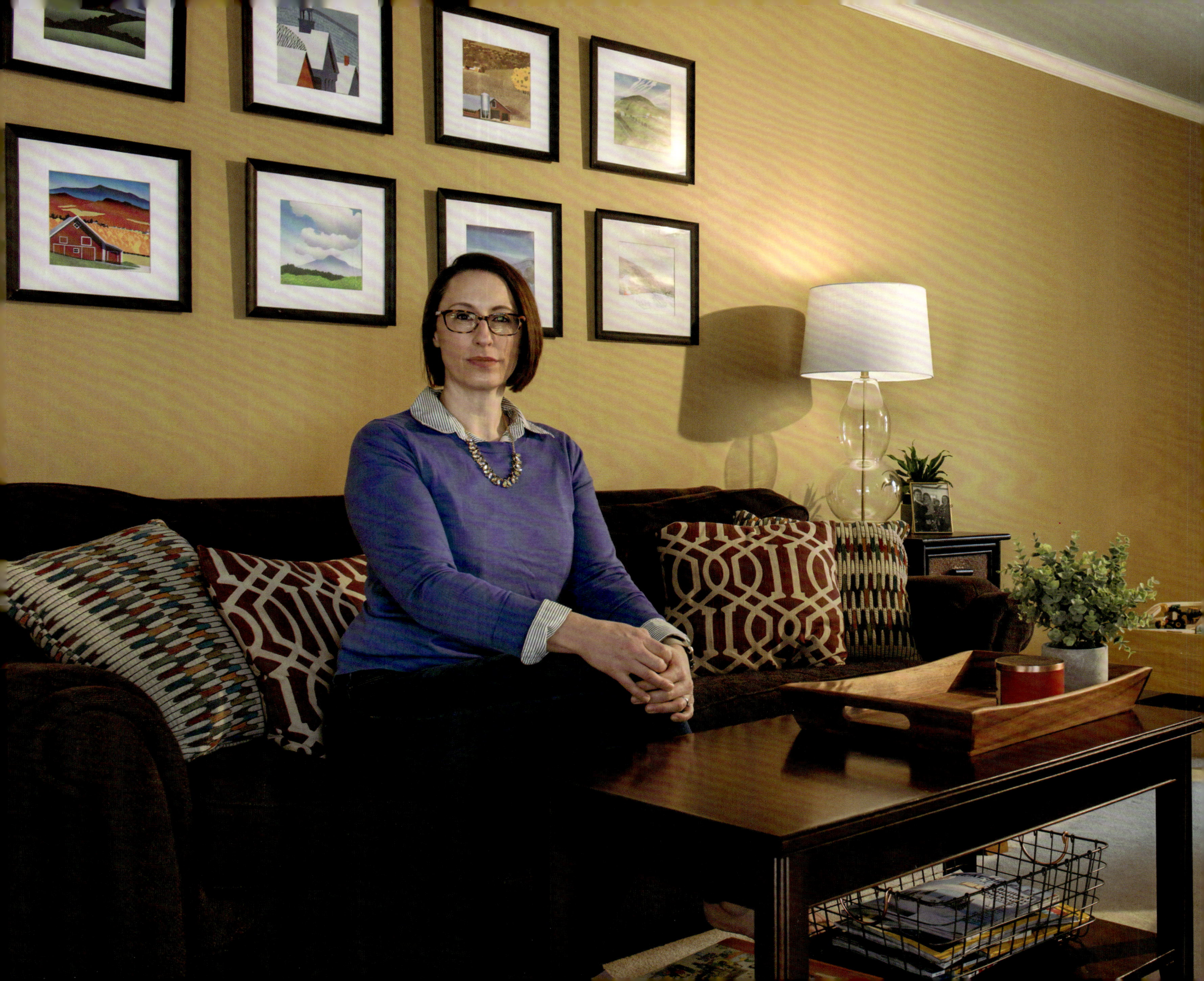

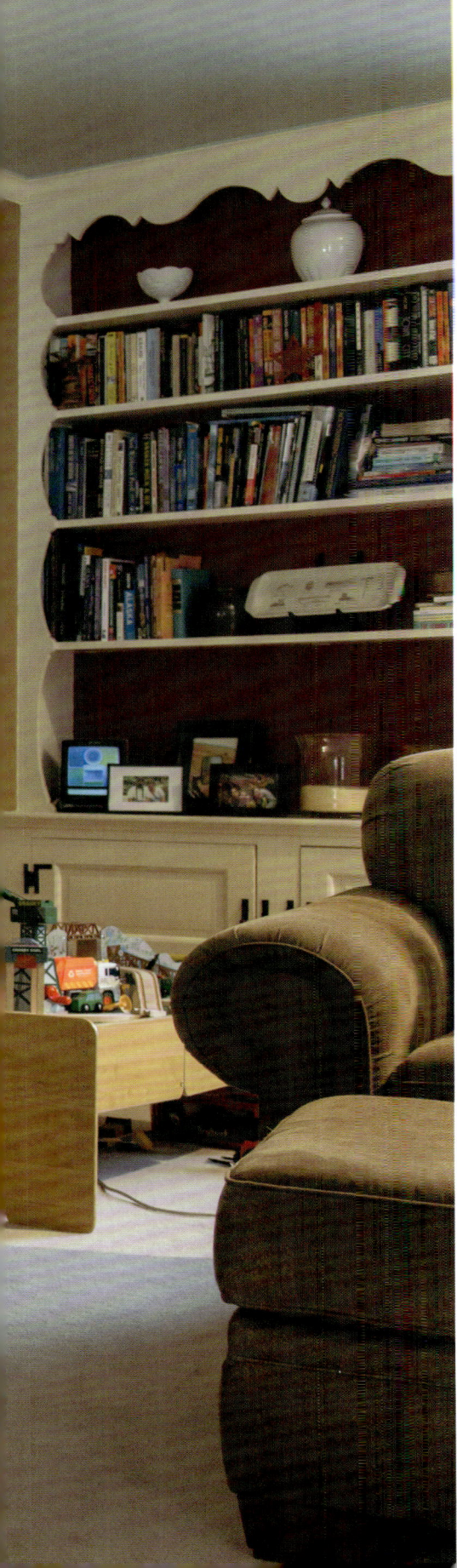

Beth Wagner
Physician

$200,000 Student loans
$300,000 Mortgage

My student loan debt feels like a
heavy weight. It is present in any
financial decision we make as a
family. It keeps me awake at
night. While we have the luxury
of being a single-income family,
our debt is a heavy burden. I would
love to use the money I spend on
my student loans to save for my
kids' education or retirement.

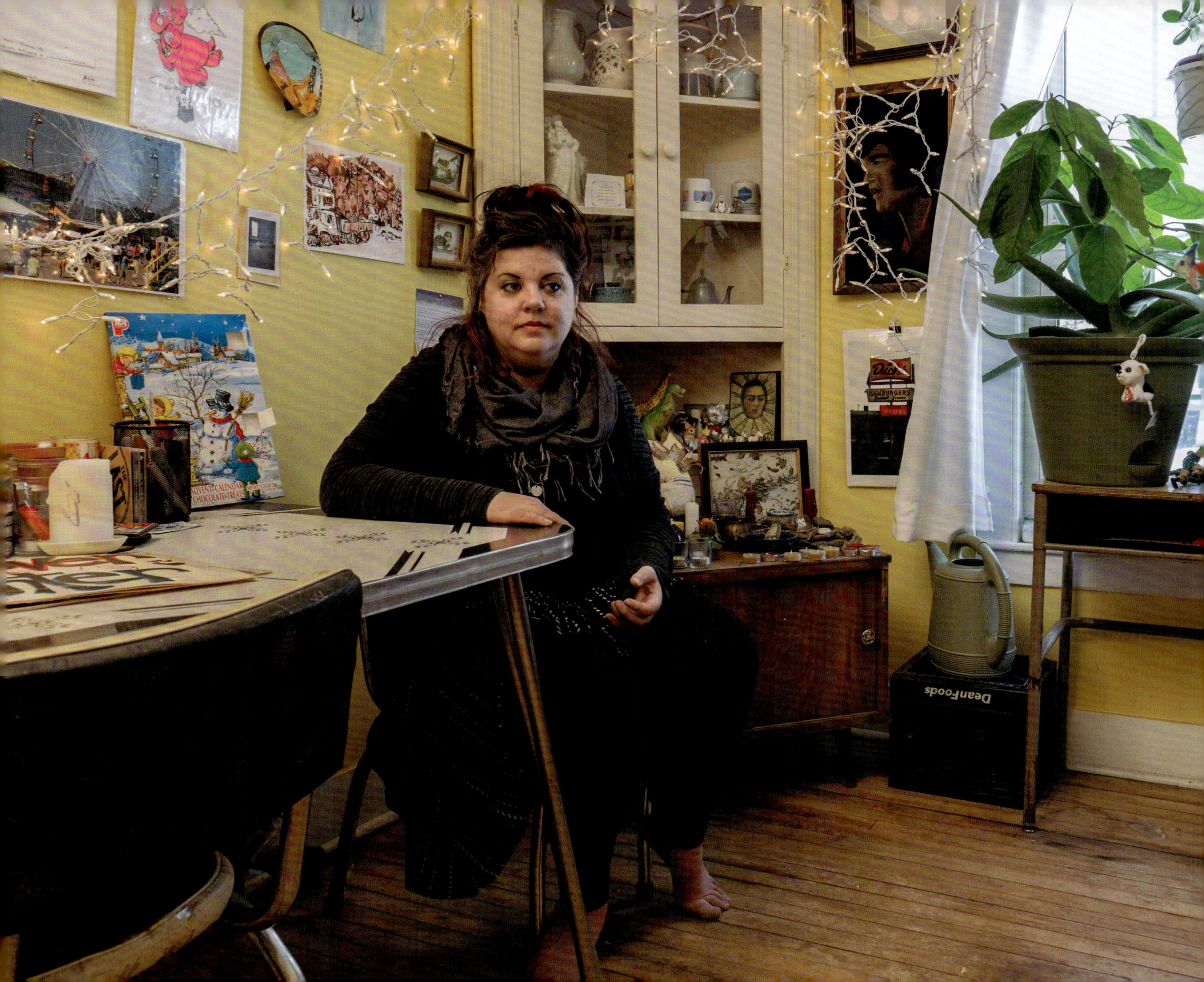

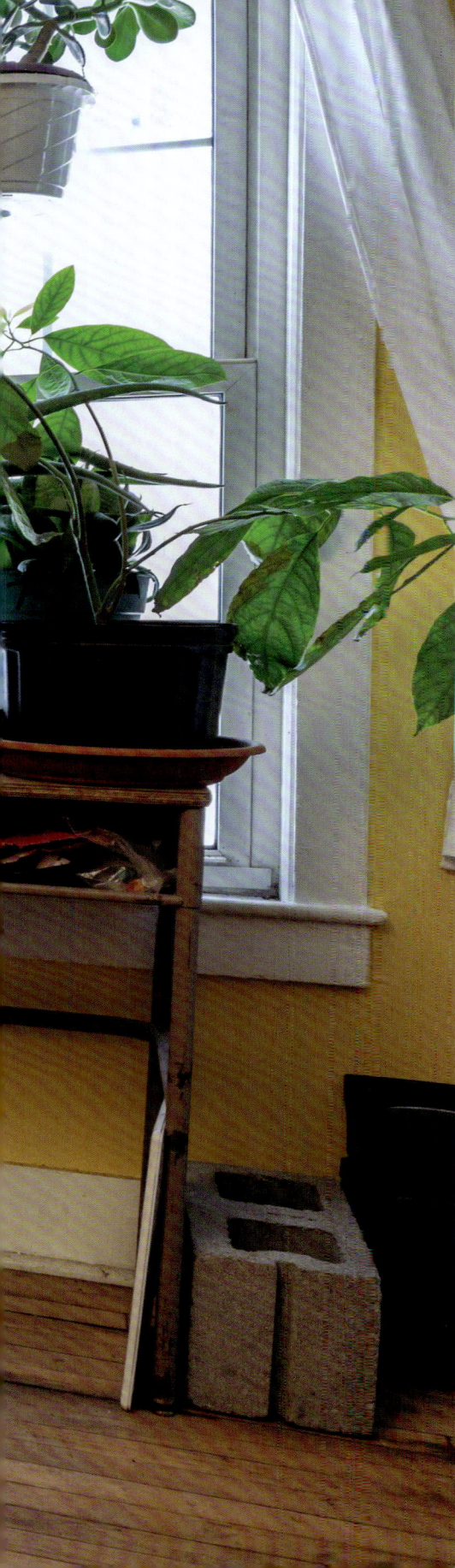

Robyn Joy Peirce
Community Relations + Membership Assistant
@ Hunger Mountain Co·op
Yoga Teacher
Model for Art classes
Musician

$18k   student loan
$24k   credit cards
$4k   401k loan

I graduated from UVM in 1998 with a student loan for $7k. I put off paying it for many years (without defaulting) until it doubled. After paying regularly for ~10 years, it's back to the original amount more or less... Credit cards have never been something I could use responsibly - I destroyed my credit in my 20s with them. I rebuilt my credit by not having any for 8-10 years, + then with my high credit score was able to start all over. At first I used them for extras + paid more than the minimums + did really well but inevitably got in over my head, using them as supplemental income. I am 100% with my minimum payments, so I'm not in trouble per se, but half of my payments go to finance charges + it is barely manageable. I got sober 2 years ago + no longer ingest things that intoxicate me, but it has become apparent that I am financially drunk.

Debt Portrait #71, Montpelier, VT 2018

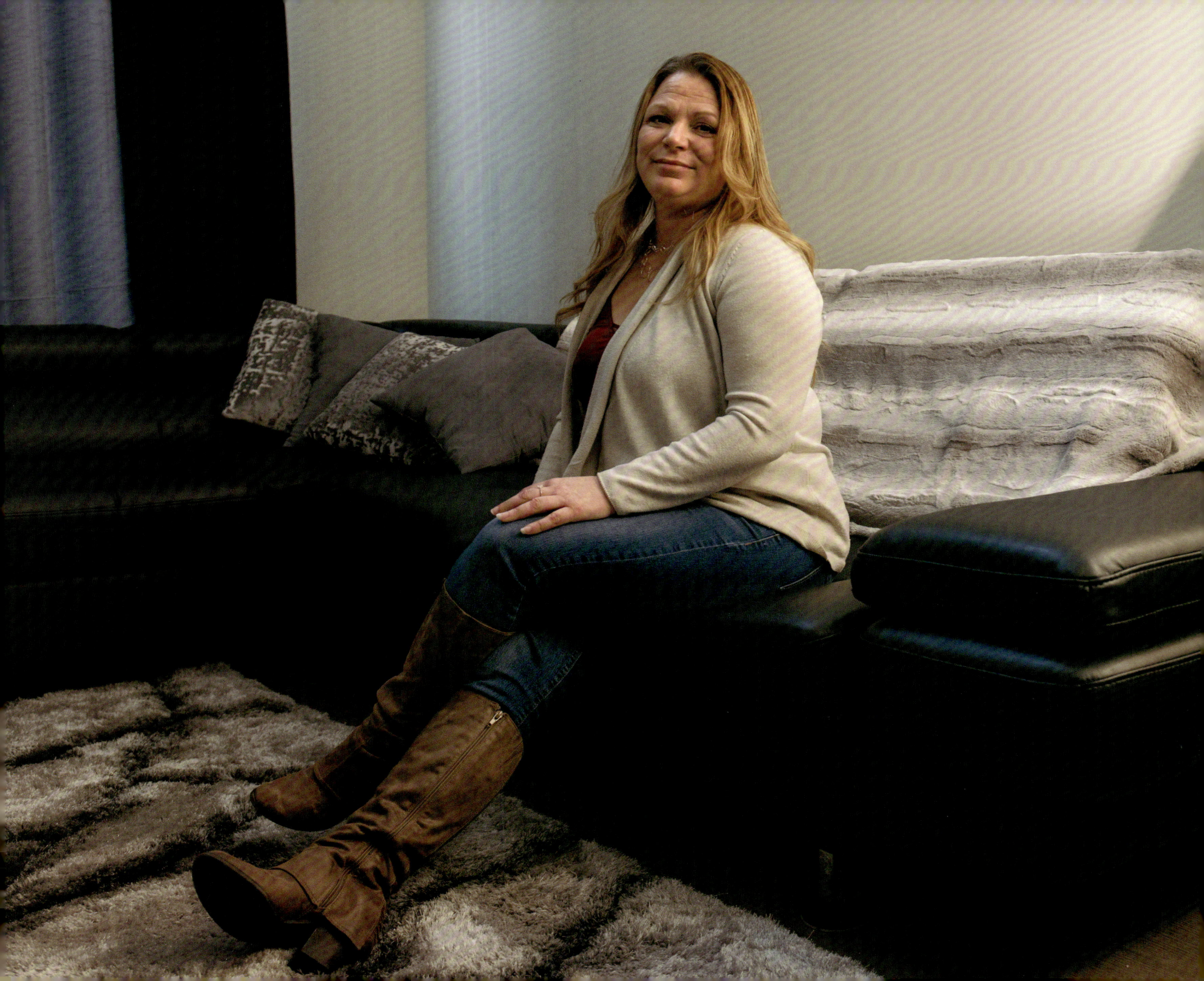

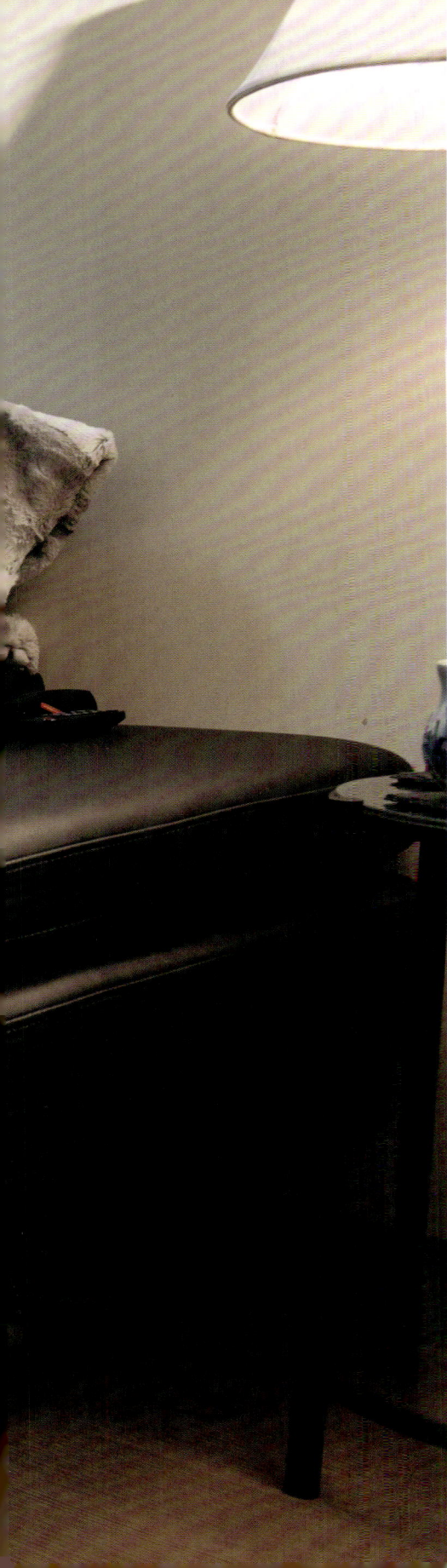

Rebecca Holca ~ Business Development Rep
& Graphic Designer.

$78,000 Debt - Plus. Student Loans
$14,000 Car Loan.

Hard to Put a Hard # Number on the Debt I have
accrued. Each Month it grows larger. After
a bout of unemployment and a car accident
I have not been able to even make ends meet.
Employers do not want to compensate for experience.
Have found that poverty level offers continue to
impact my ability to make enough money. And actually
~~considerations~~ contributes to ongoing debt. Buying
my most basic needs on a credit card continues,
as will the debt. No end in sight.

Melissa Harris -42
Mother / Daycare Provider / Artist
Teacher / Costume Designer
LOVER OF LIFE
$267,000 in debt

Debt is... so many things.

It is an ever present looming force
    threatening to take over at any moment.

It is the feeling of being buried and
    not knowing how to get out.

It is a thing we fear that can
    dominate our actions.

I use my creative strengths & resilience
    to lessen the power it holds on me.

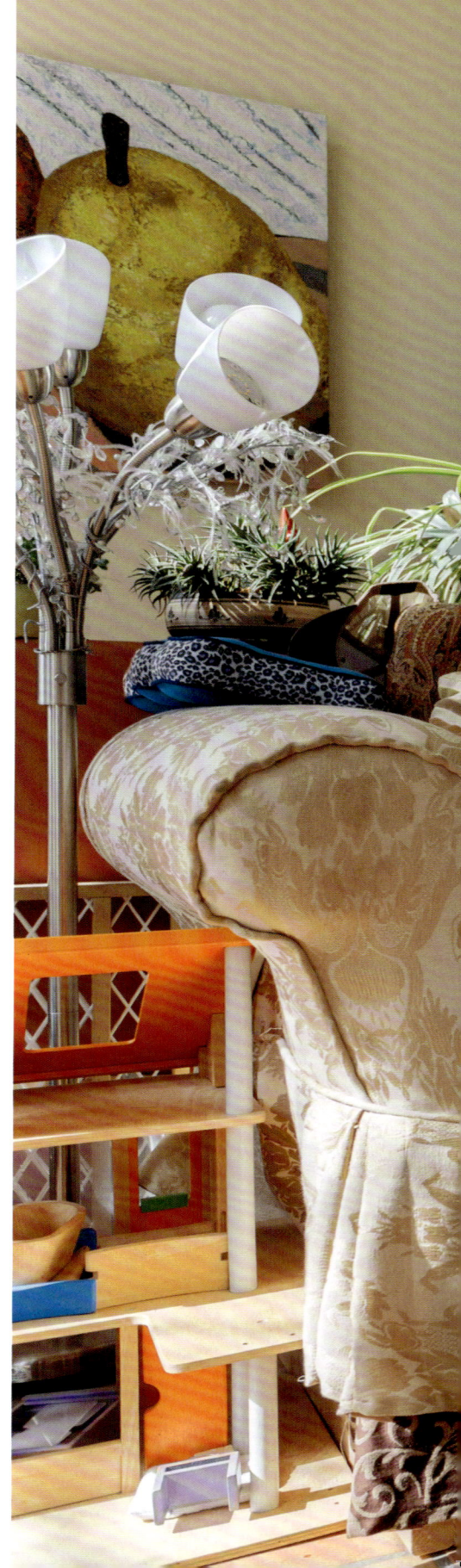

Debt Portrait #73, Telluride, CO 2019

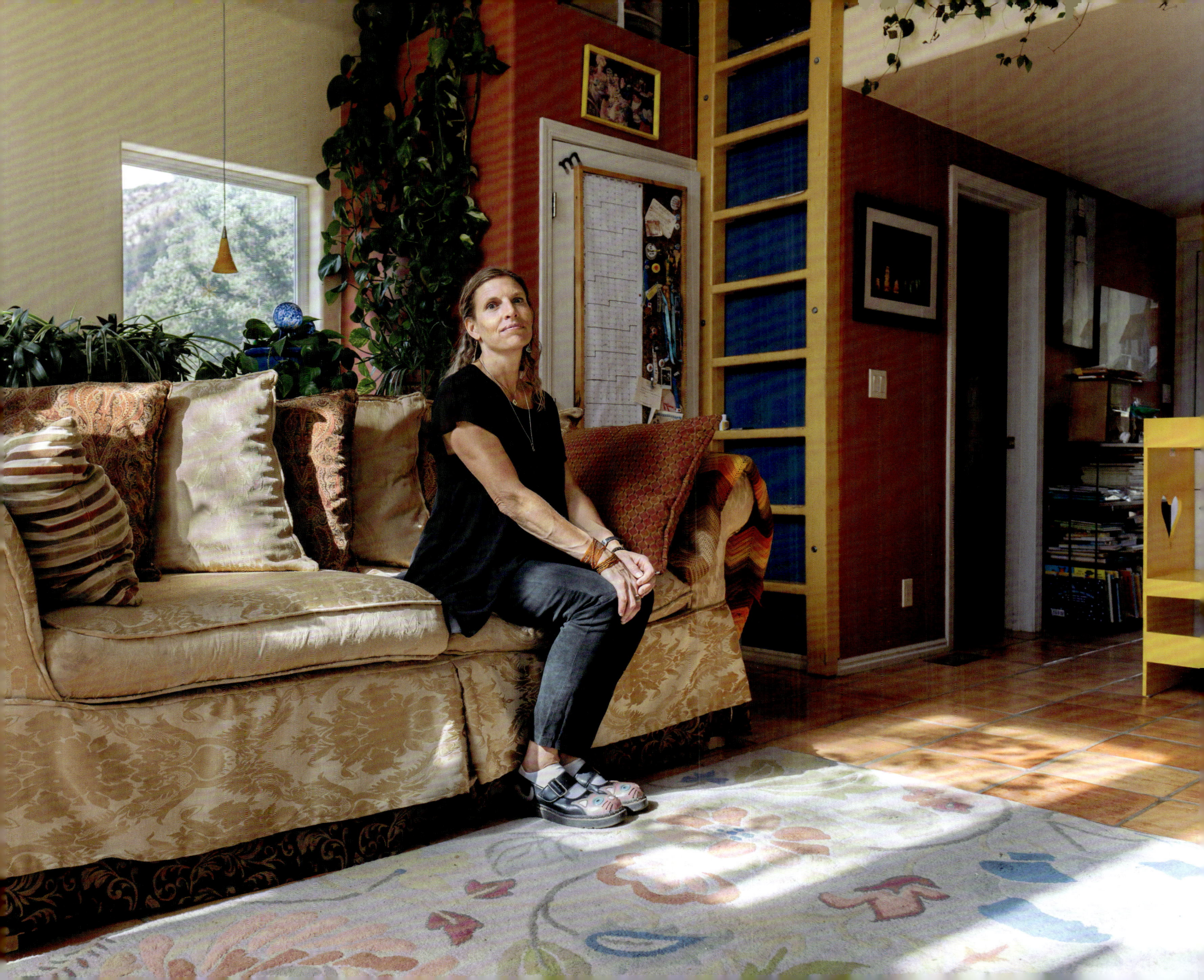

Sierra Hawksley - 28
Dog behaviorist| W-EMT

$104,000

I racked up this debt from student loans over 7 yrs of Medical school. After a head injury caused me to drop out, I added more debt from the medical bills. I now spend my time doing what I love - wilderness medicine and volunteering for Search + Rescue - which is all volunteer/ non-paid work. I live in a van year-round with my dog & partner just to be able to survive financially.

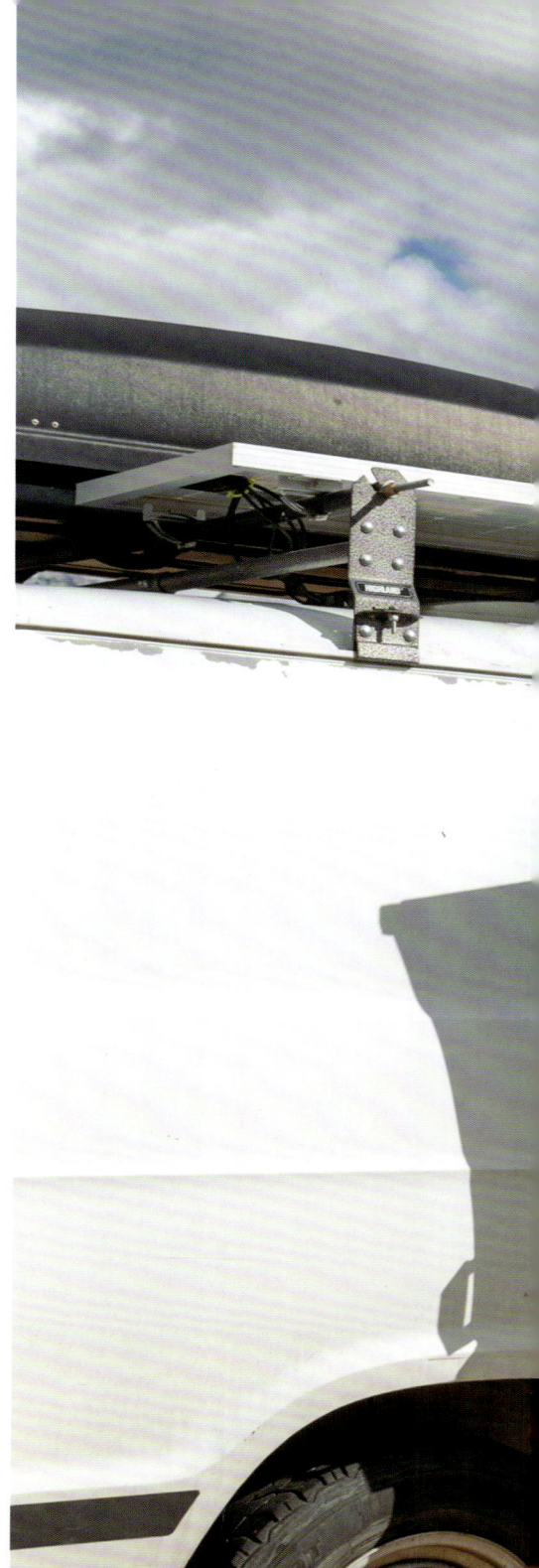

Debt Portrait #74, Telluride, CO 2019

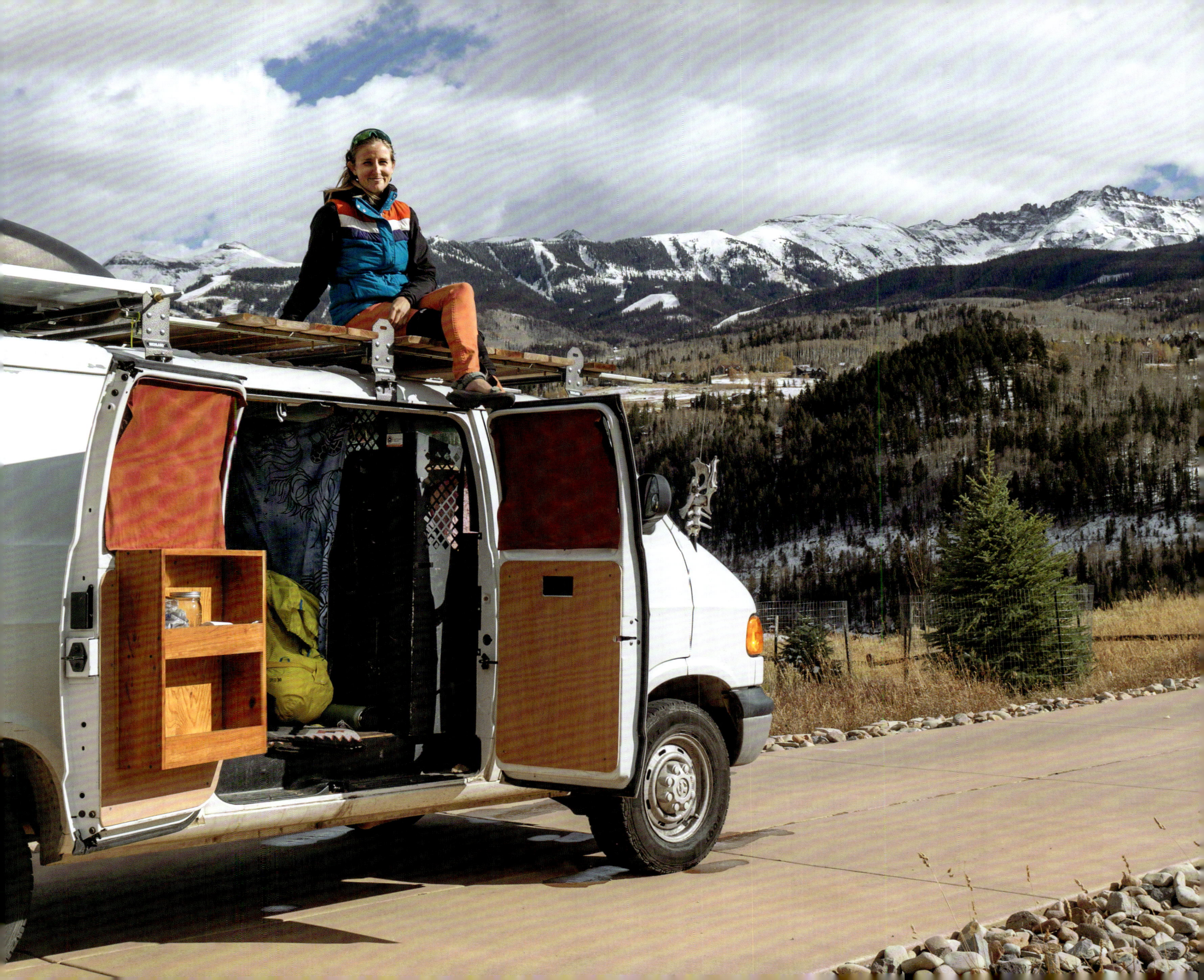

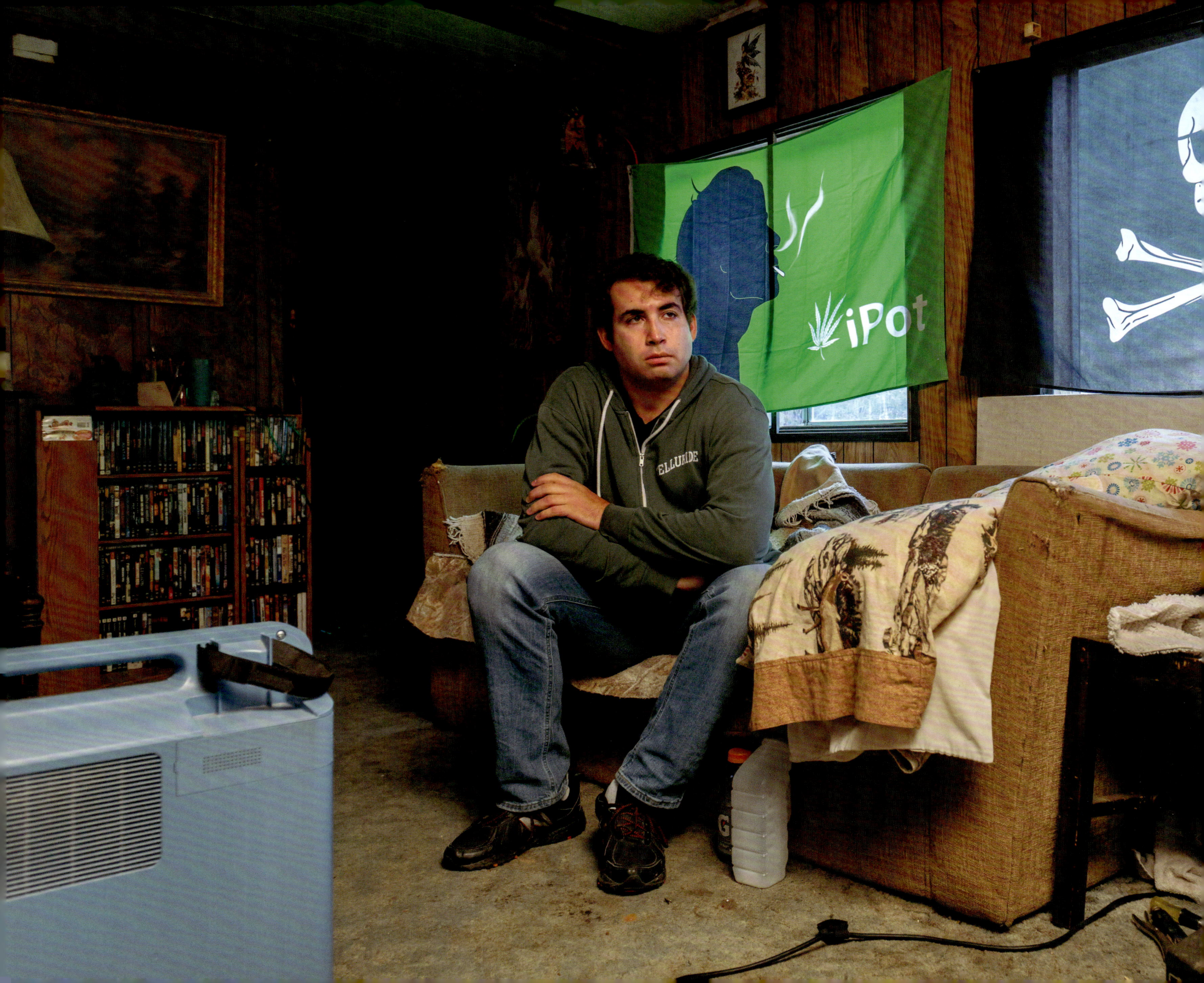

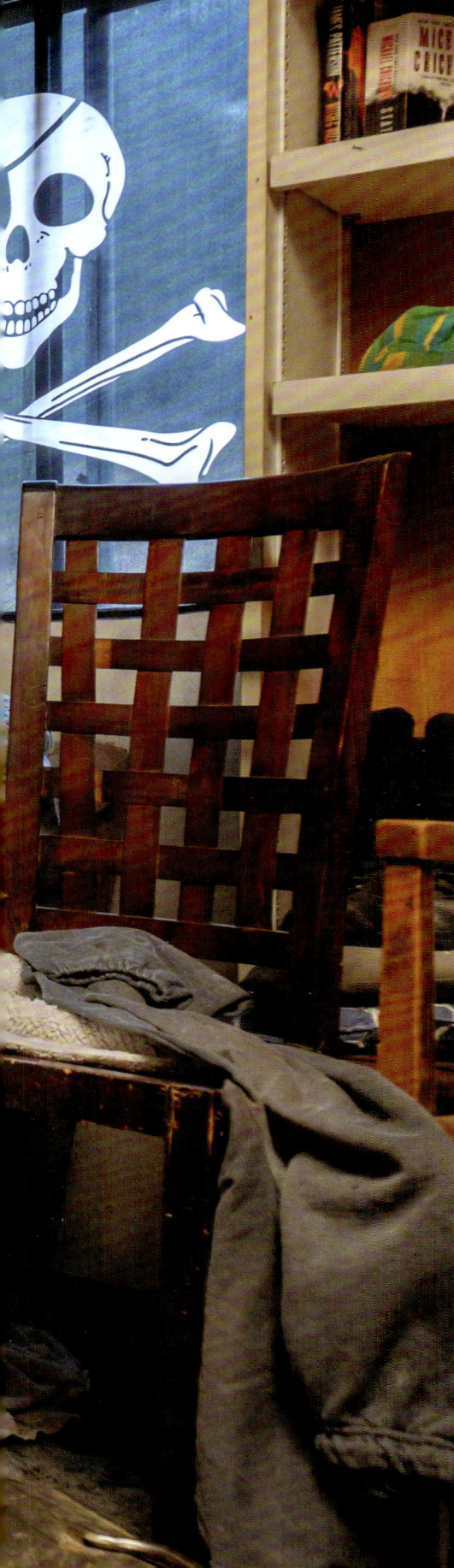

Eric J. Freeman, 28
unemployed
$6,500

I am in debt for medical
Reasons. I have had difficulty
with gainful employment because
of chronic health issues
which have sent me to
the hospital countless times $1500
I have had other debts, including
The social security administration
over-paying. There is no way
I can pay back $3500 for their
mistake.
Thankfully, my folks have put
up a tab, and have helped me financially
over the years. I have to pay them $5500+
but because of difficulty in gainful employment
It will be a struggle. DEBT SUCKS!

Debt Portrait #75, Ridgway, CO 2019

Kile Wetlaufer

$18,500

A COMBINATION OF

I AM IN DEBT DUE TO MY STUDENT LOANS. AND CREDIT CARD DEBT ACCRUED IN THE COURSE OF A SERIES OF UNFORTUNATE EVENTS. I LIVE OFF THE GRID IN A ONE ROOM CABIN TO MINIMIZE MY BILLS. I HAVE FIVE JOBS, AND HUSTLE CONSTANTLY TO REMAIN SOLVENT.

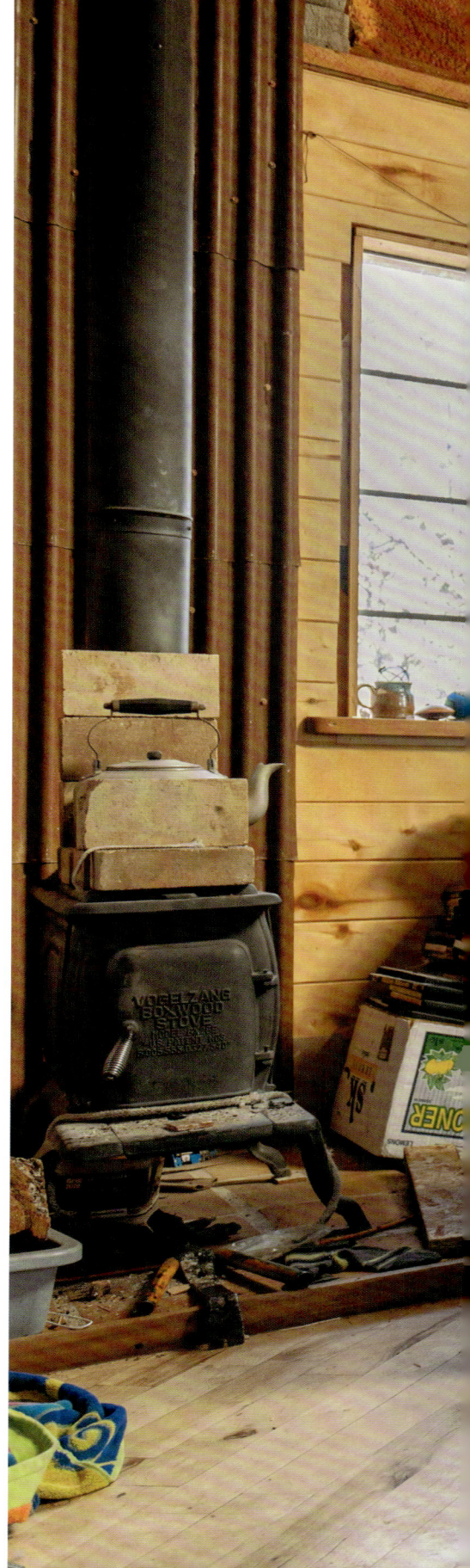

Debt Portrait #76, Montrose, CO 2019

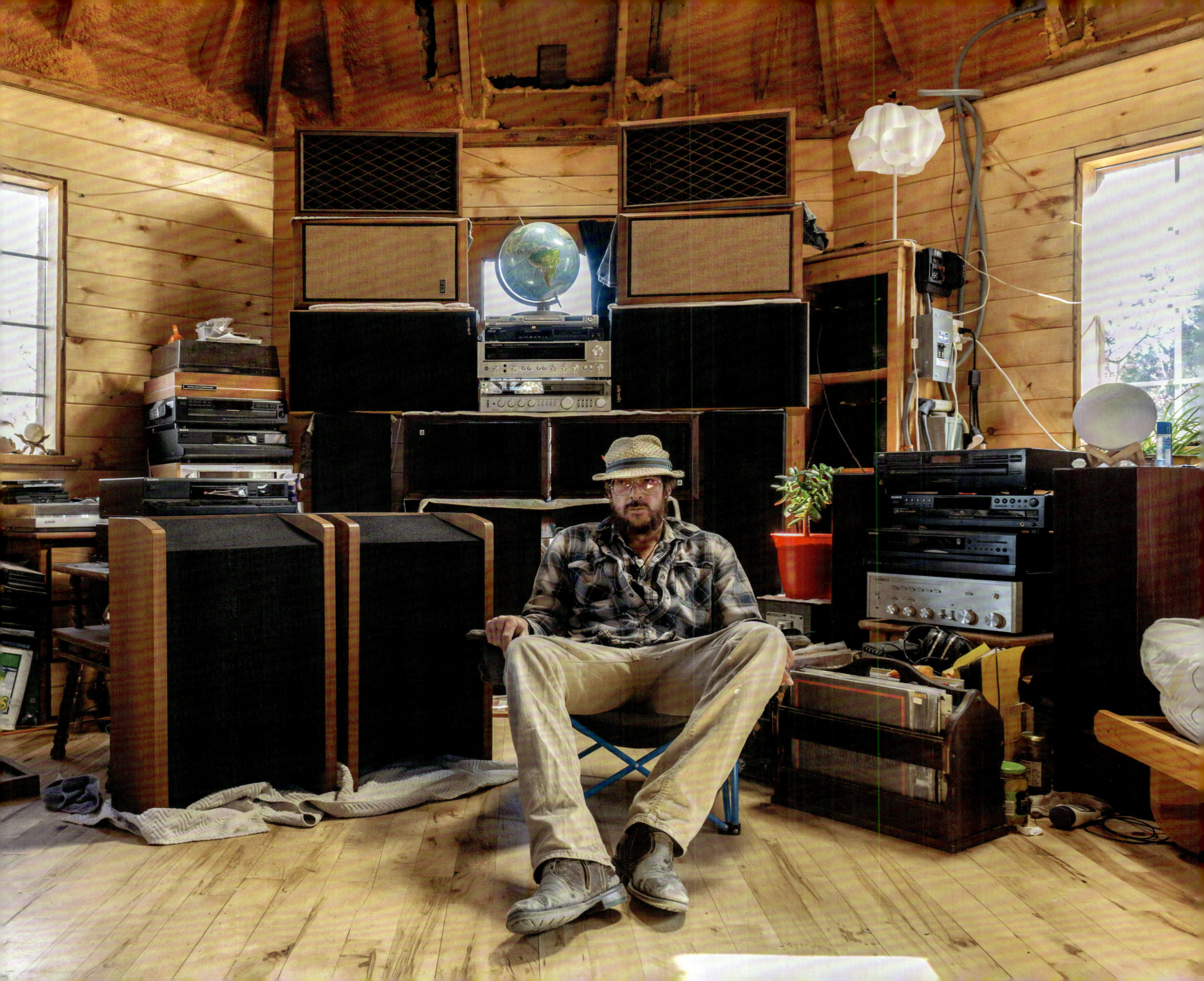

Heather McClary Chase - 34
$136,000

My debt is from a mortgage on our condo,
credit cards and, primarily, medical bills. I am
kind of proud of the mortgage debt and getting to
own a place in an amazing location that I love.
My credit card debt is mostly from emergency
spending. My medical debt is (and likely always will be)
a part of staying alive as a type I diabetic with
infertility & thyroid issues. We aggressively pay our
mortgage down and have a plan for our credit cards -
so I look forward to seeing this number, and the
emotional stress I carry because of it, decrease in years
to come.

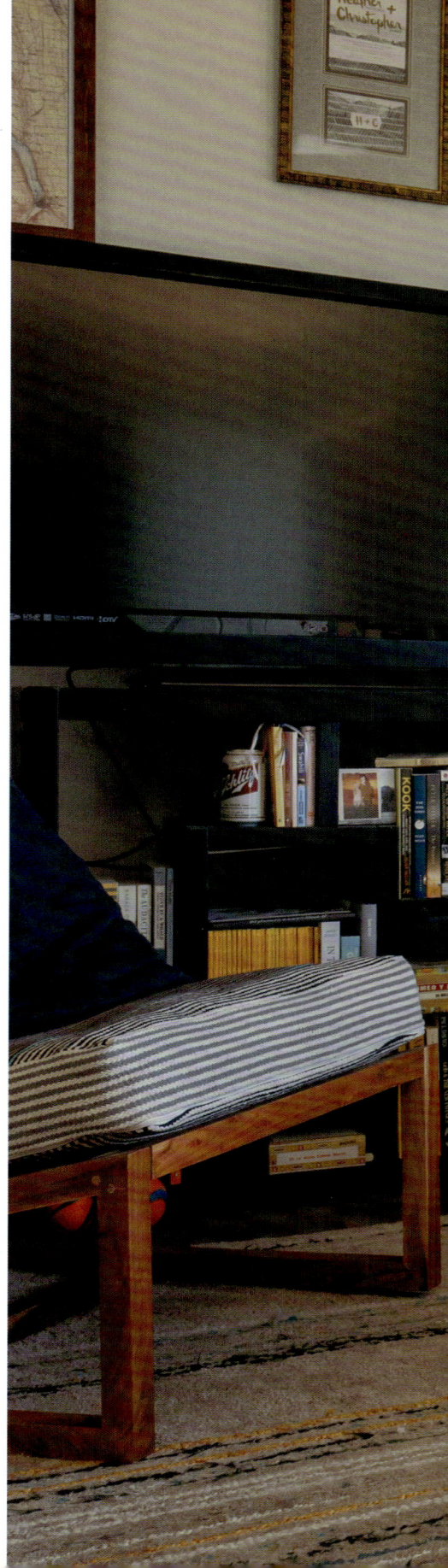

Debt Portrait #77, Telluride, CO 2019

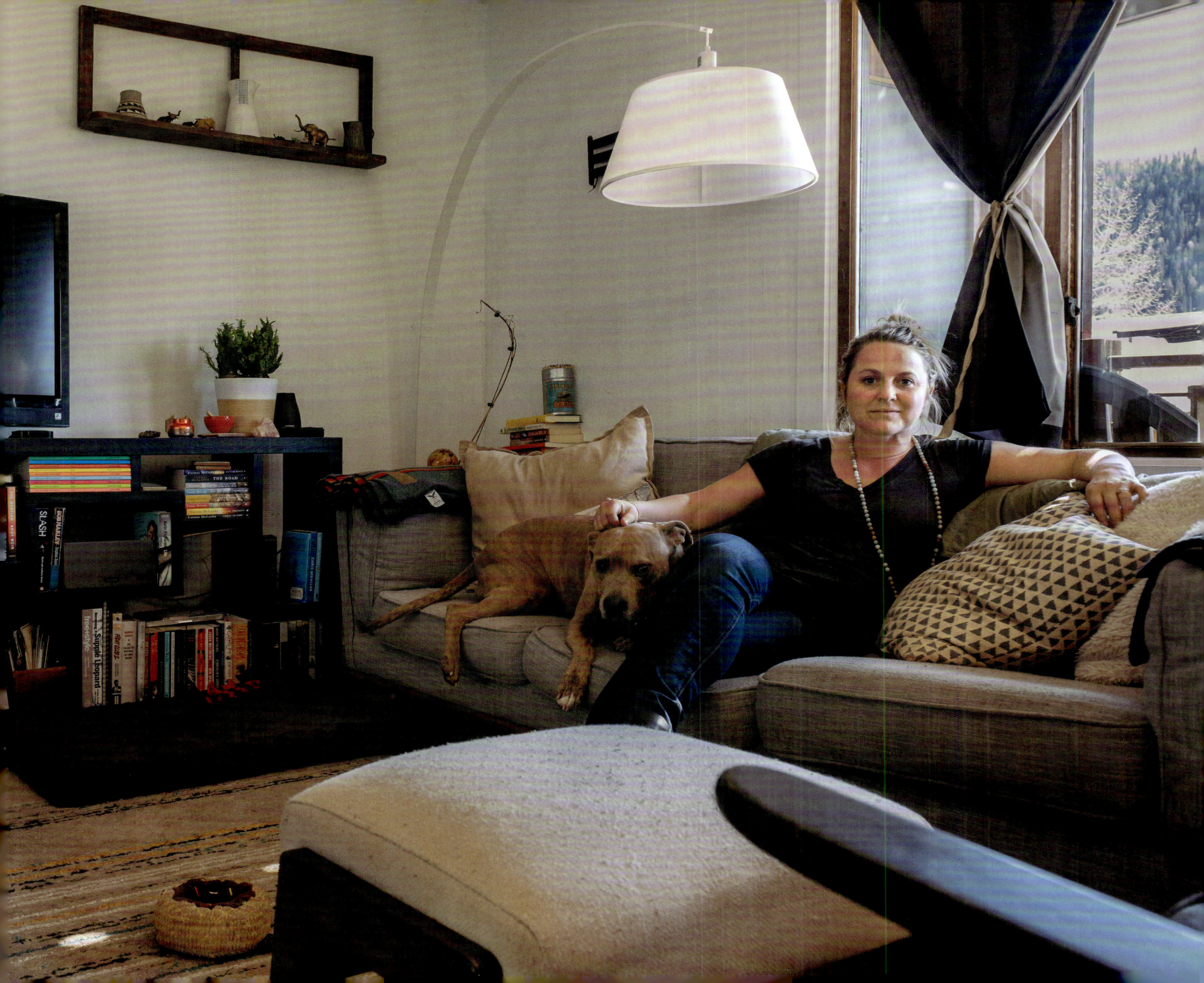

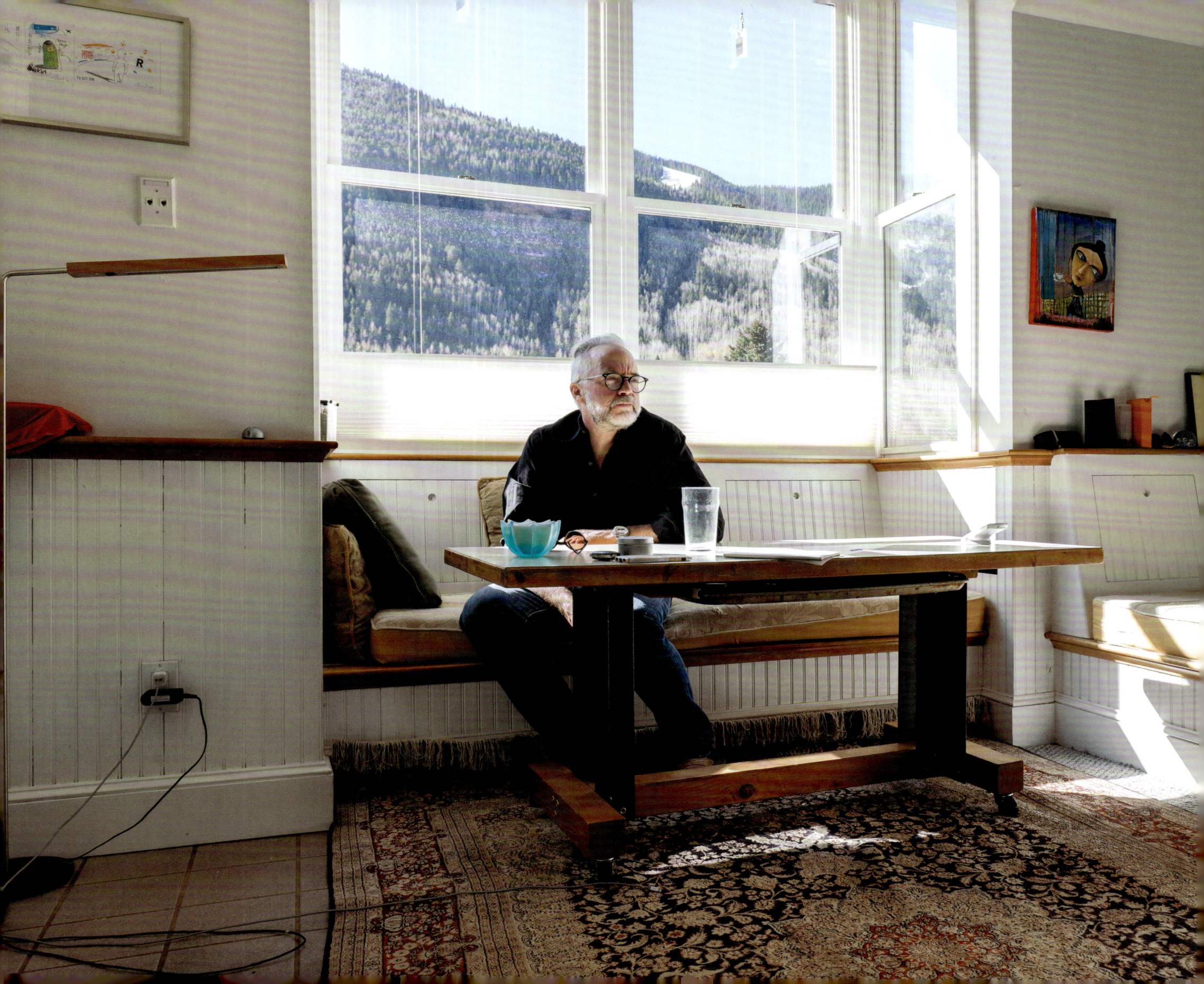

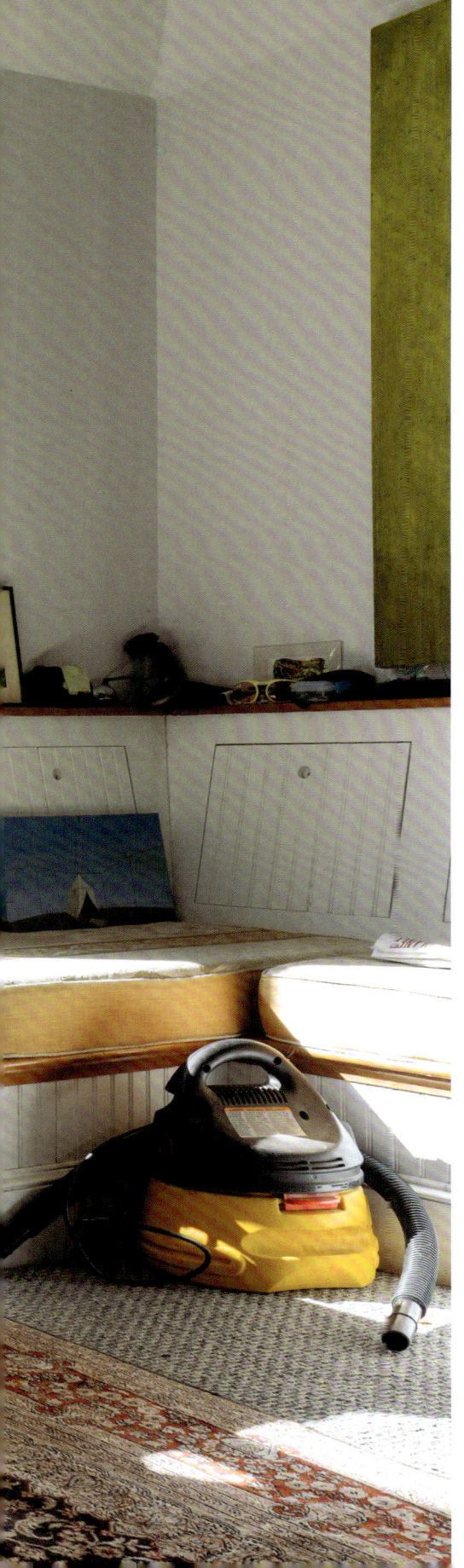

~ 45G in debt.   Brian Young, Telluride

Debt is something I have assiduously worked to avoid my whole life but here I am @ 55 with about 40 45 G in debt.

My work shifted and large parts of my clietele were lost to divorce and relocation. I am a private chef and have been for about 20 years w/ an occasional year or two at a restaurant. The perfect storm of shifting biz and debt, easily so serviced in the past, happened at once as I extended myself too far to help a friend and her kids.

The anxiety of the next, most pressing bill is overwhelming at times. The feeling of failure is overwhelming at times. I had never before known depression — I do now. Even approaching the situation w/ my usual idiotic blind American opptimism it still causes me great anxiety and dread. At my age age the future/retirement looms large— and the future looks dim from these indebted eyes.

Debt Portrait #78, Telluride, CO 2019

Mark Sturdevant

We worked very hard to keep a simple-streamlined existence. Other than a few small credit cards (from living in Telluride, CO) the large majority of my debt is just from student loans. I've always worked, rented, bought used cars, fixed things that broke, and contributed to my communities. I like to eat locally when possible, ride my bike, compost and play music.

After high school, I took out the max student loans for about 10 years. I was a quadruple major (philosophy, psychology, musiced. music therapy). I used the money to afford my rock and roll life style. Now I have to work more consistently to pay back this early retirement.

I've paid back way more than half of it, but still owe $50k. That's a lot of tacos.

♡ Mark

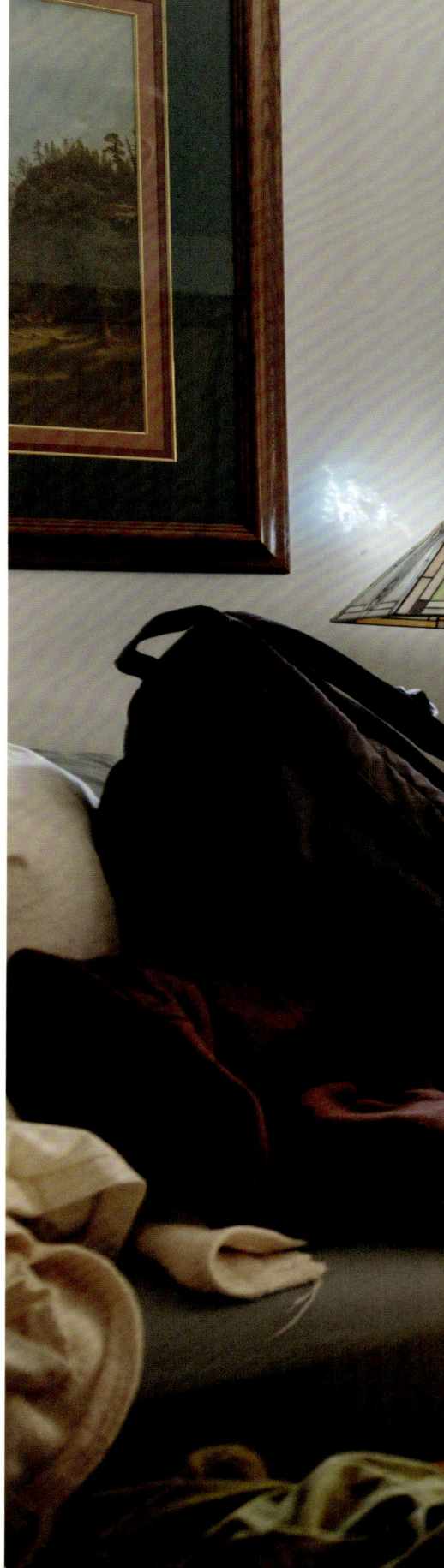

Debt Portrait #79, Telluride, CO 2019

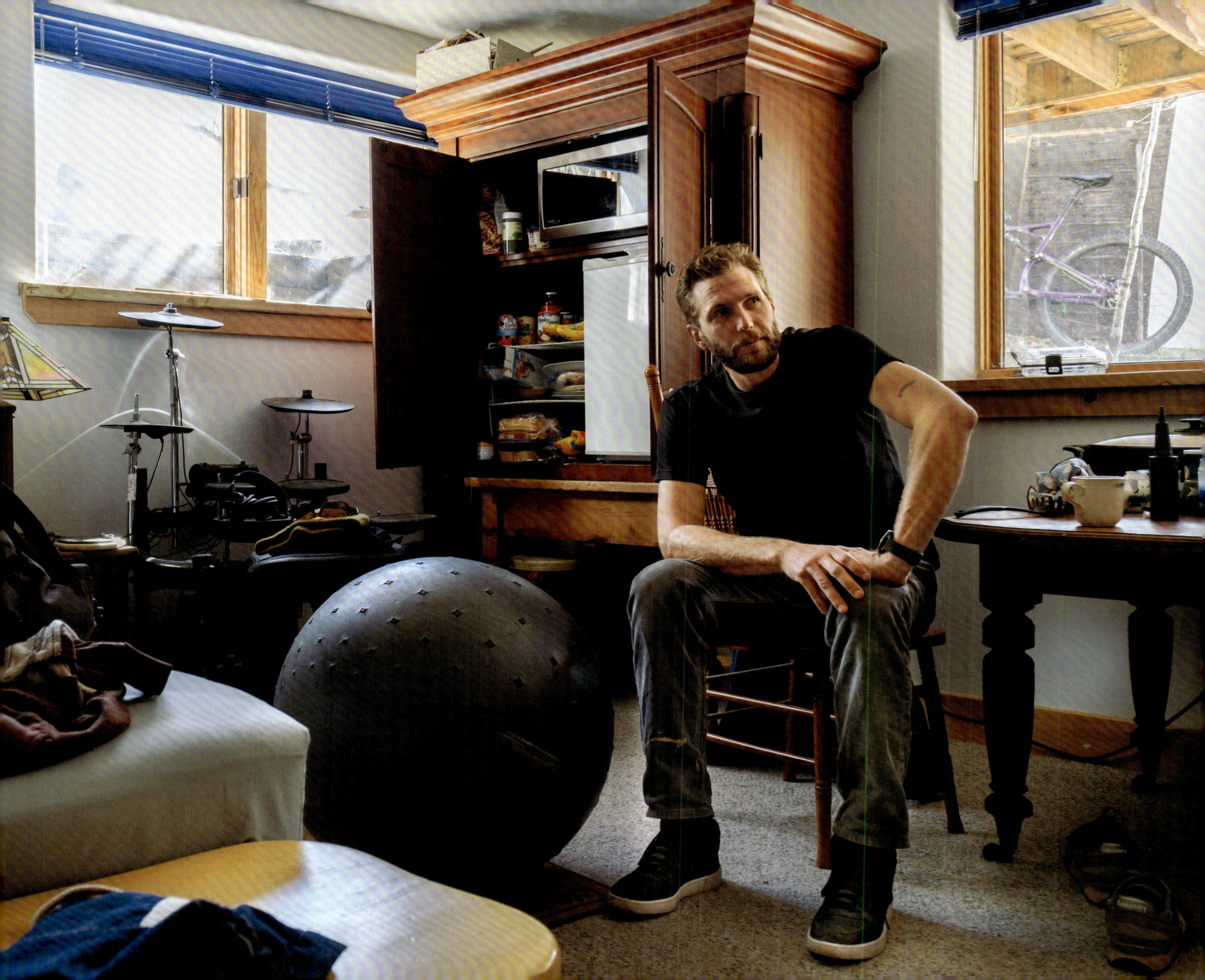

Christine Richards
$111,000
Physical Therapist

It could have been a lot worse. I made the last payment on $18K of undergrad loans the month before starting grad school in 2014. Working full time as a massage therapist, I was able to pay out of pocket for prerequisite courses for my doctoral program. My husband supported us both during three years of grad school, and I got a research assistantship that covered half a semester's tuition. But I still came away with $145,000 in debt, with interest rates between 5.5 - 7.2% in 2017.

I have a handle on it, but I don't own a home. We don't have kids, and probably won't. I need to be able to support my husband in his retirement 15 years from now. My goal is to get my federal loans ($103K + interest) under six figures by the end of the year (it's late October now).

I still do massage therapy on the side, after treating 50 patients/week, to make extra payments on these loans.

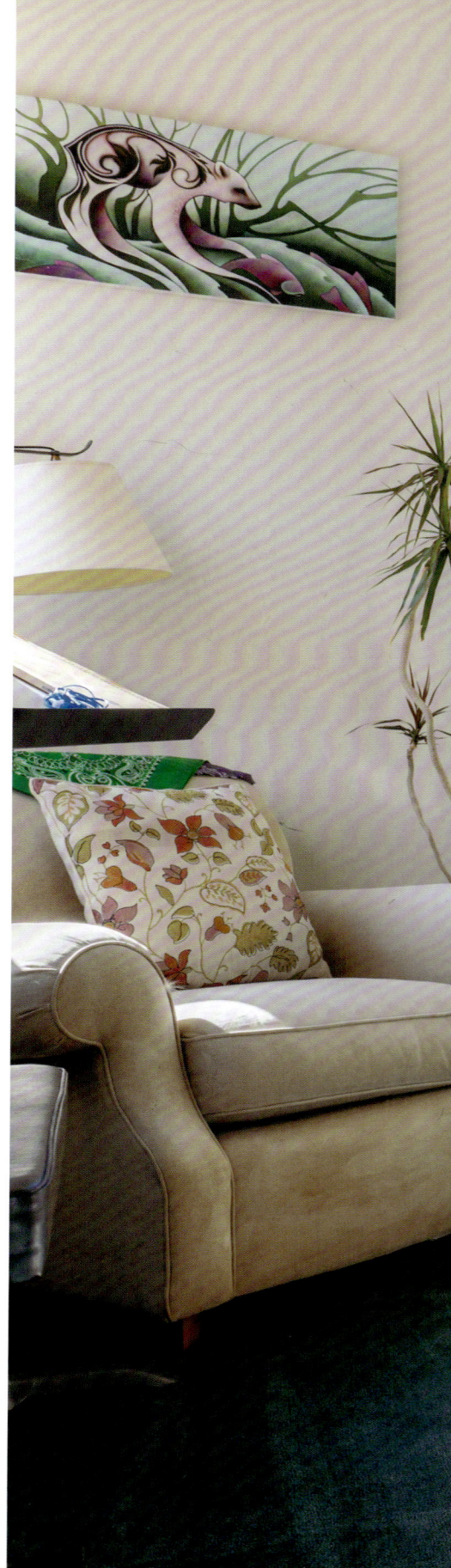

Debt Portrait #80, Trout Lake, CO 2019

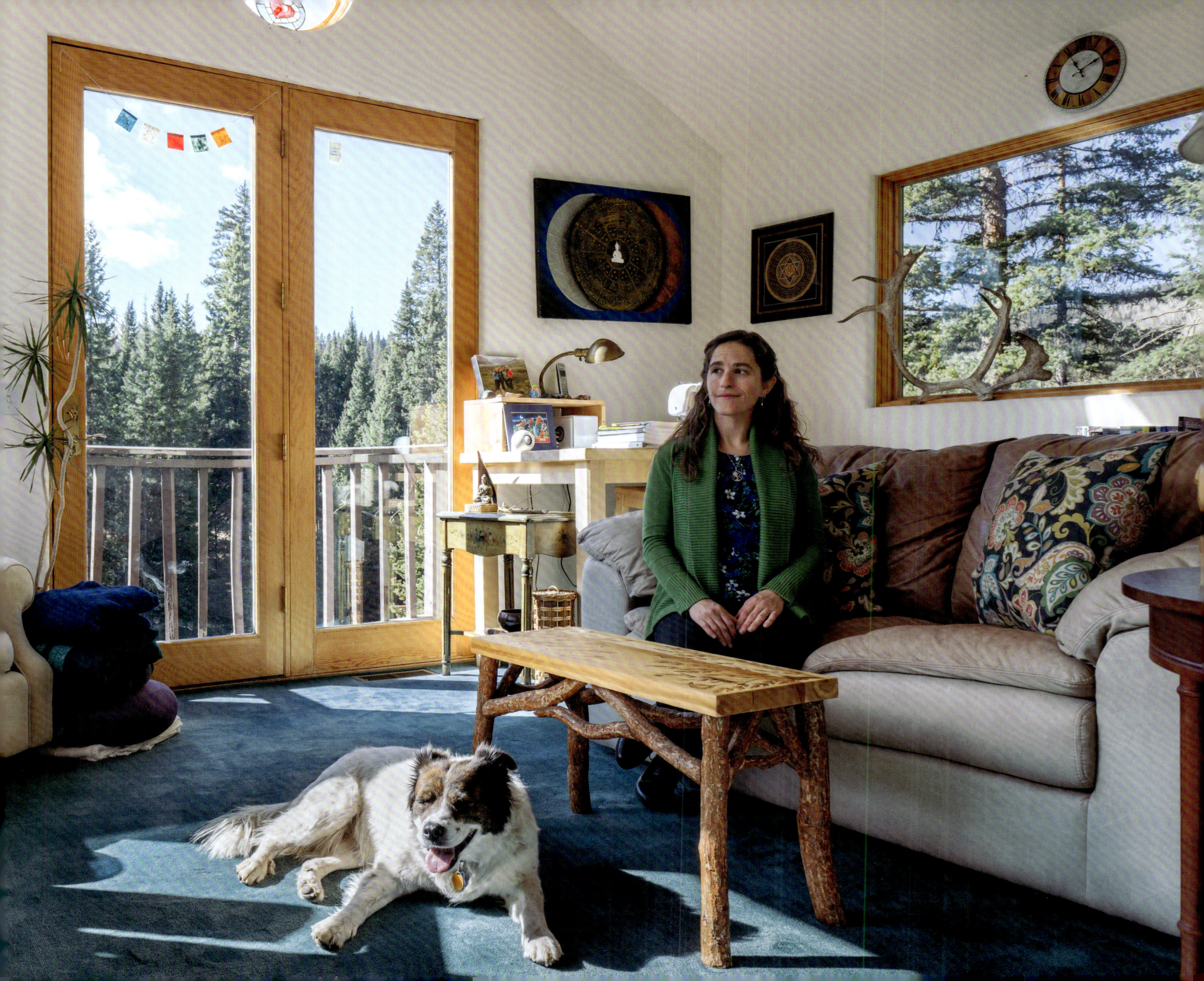

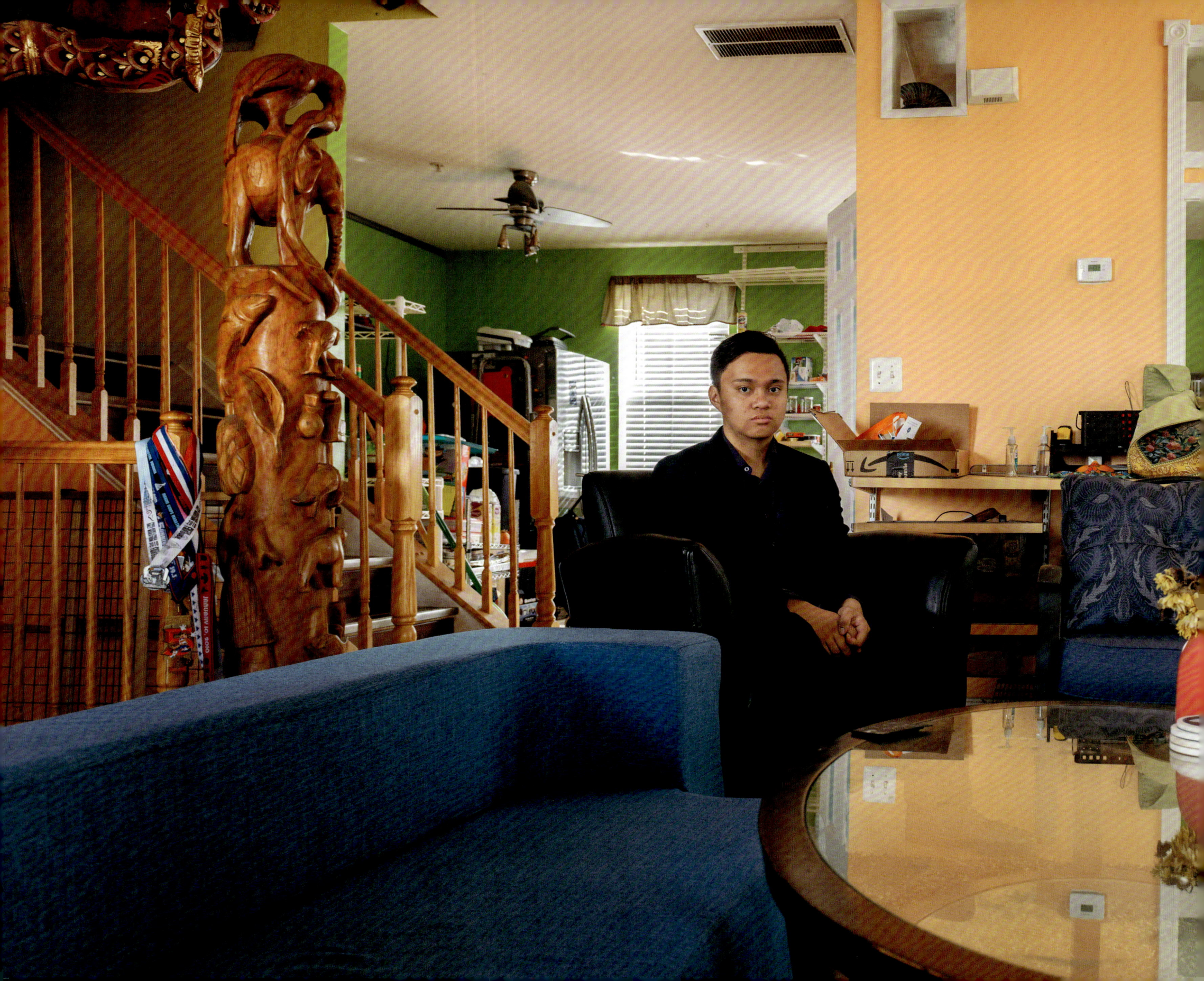

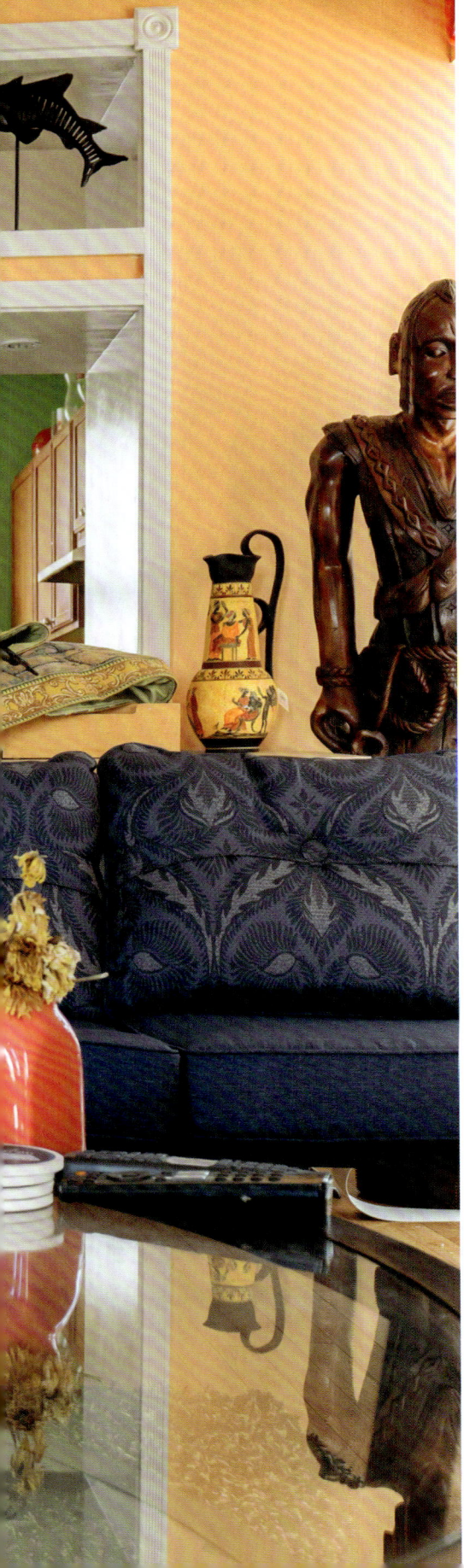

John Camara, 22
Unpaid Intern
$43,000

My debt is a combination of student loans ($35,000) and credit card debt ($8,000).

Obtaining a job has been difficult. I still want to pursue my passions, but I wonder sometimes if I made the right decision. Thankfully, my parents are supportive of the choices I made, but I worry about disappointing them. I tell myself I do these things such as an unpaid internship in order to develop my skills and network, though I question if it is worth it.

Debt Portrait #81, Washington, DC 2019

Ariel Gómez
~$31,000

combination of student debt
and growing credit card debt.

graduated six months ago and
have been on a seemingly endless
on and off job hunt.

with loan payments starting next
month and still no income it is a
number I fear will only grow.

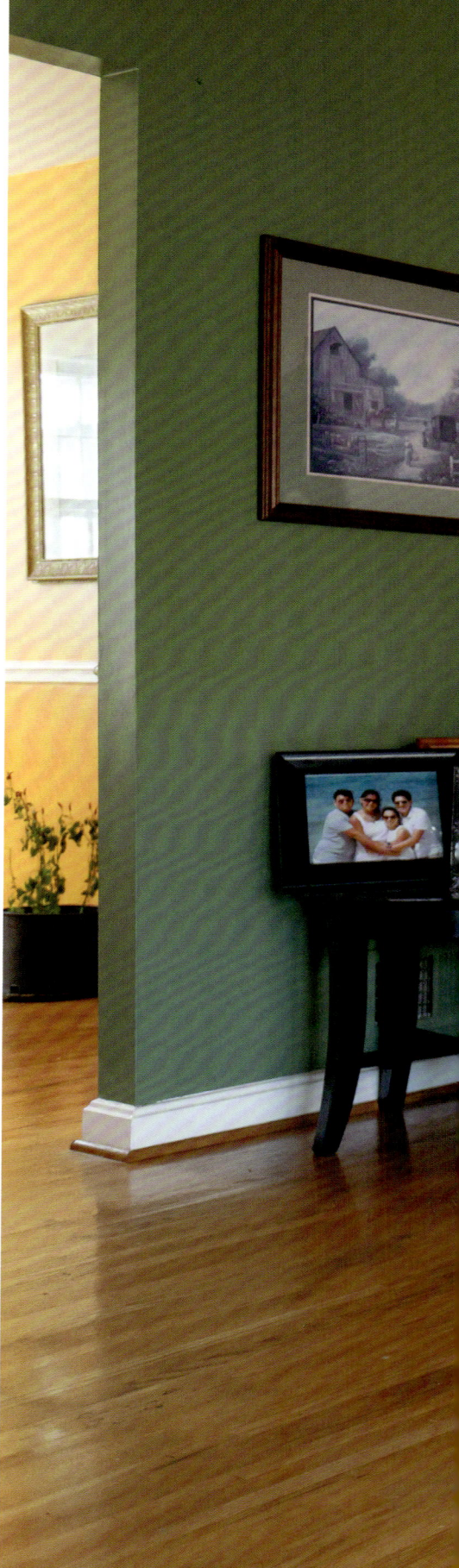

Debt Portrait #82, Laurel, MD 2019

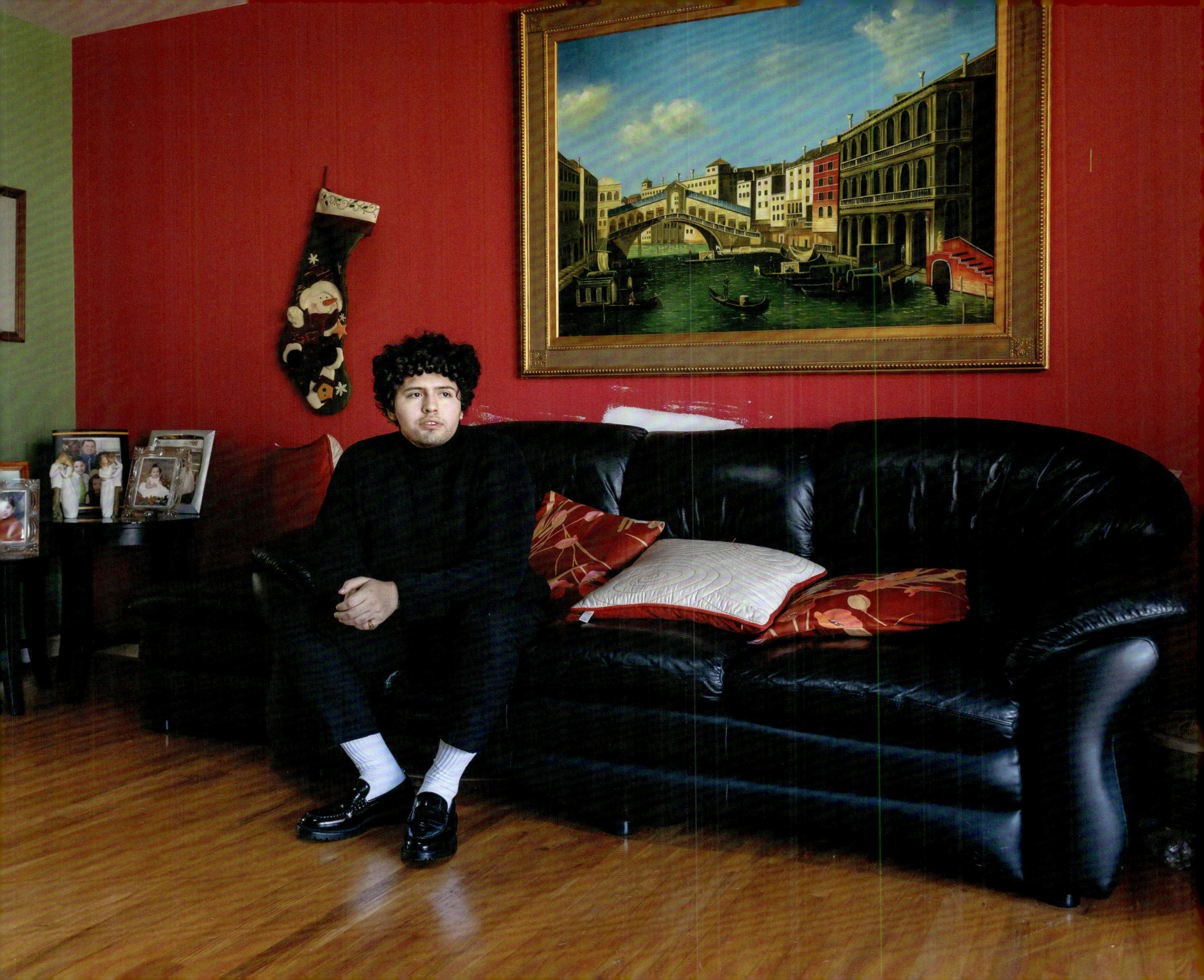

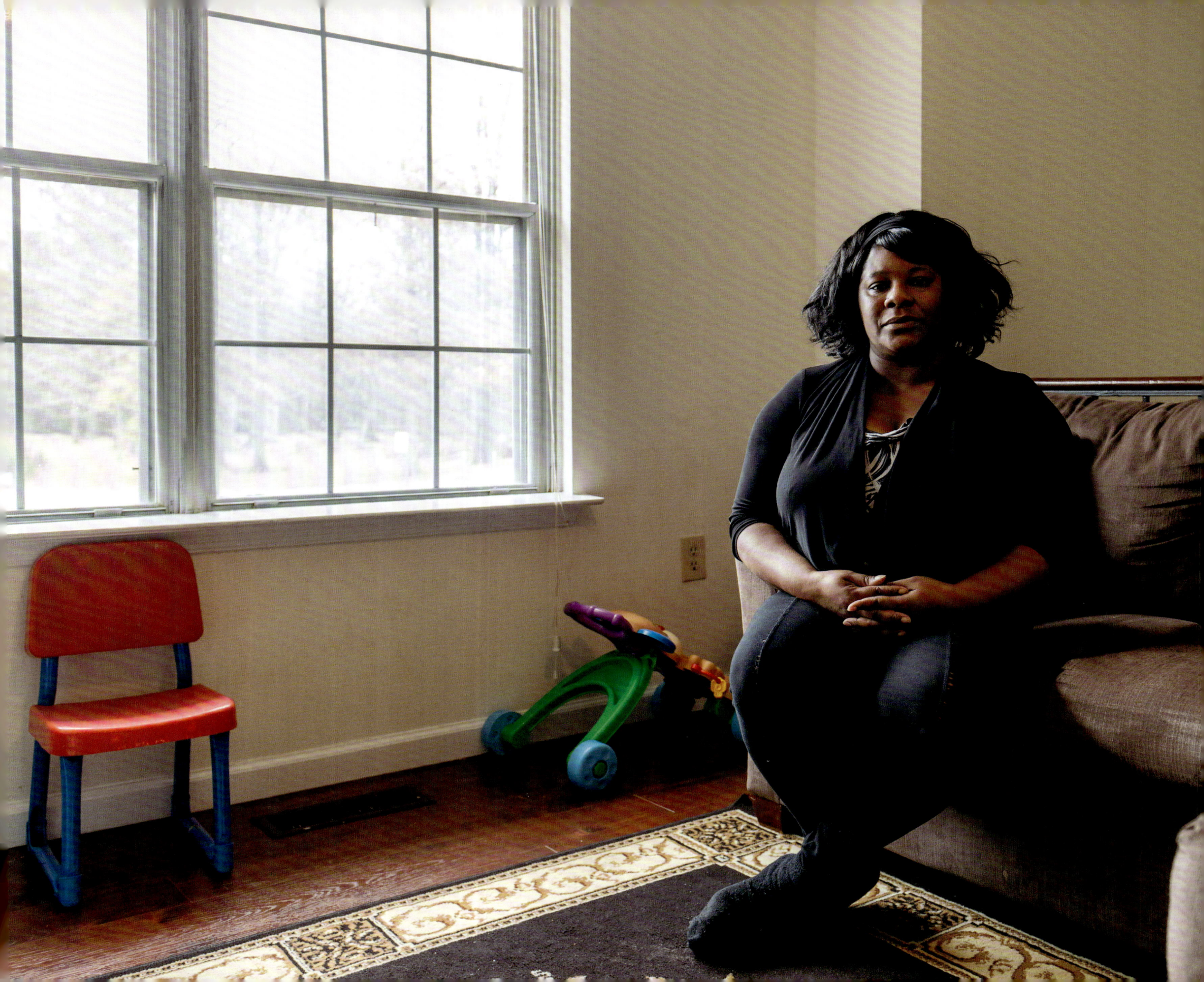

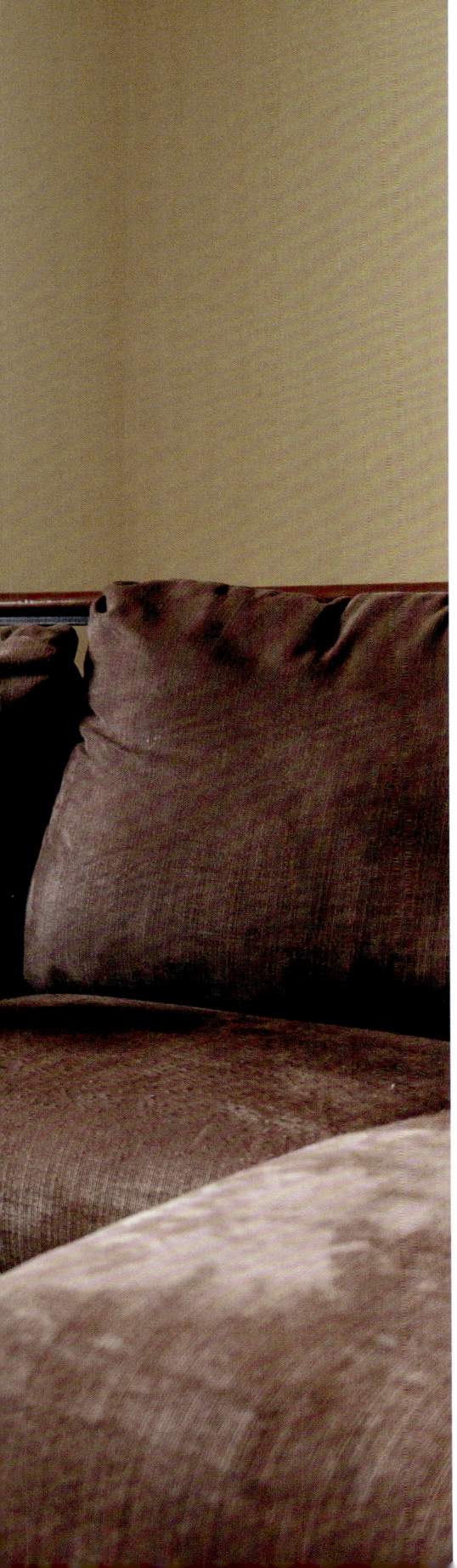

Renae Brown
Teacher
370,000

- I have 245,000 in student loans. The repayment is $500+ a month

- I purchased a home and became unemployed and my home was foreclosed. ....

- Filed Chapter 7 (twice)

Debt Portrait #83, Waldorf, MD 2019

François Bessing

— Freelance Performer —

* $55,000 *

- Graduated top of my class in 2017 with B.A. in Music (Vocal Performance)
- Can't find stable work in field
- Had legal troubles. Was incarcerated.
- Did AirBnB to make ends. Was evicted.
- Borderline homeless. — living with friend.
- Struggled with finding a relationship.
- Doing therapy and singing often.
- Decided to focus oh healing and pursuing my calling

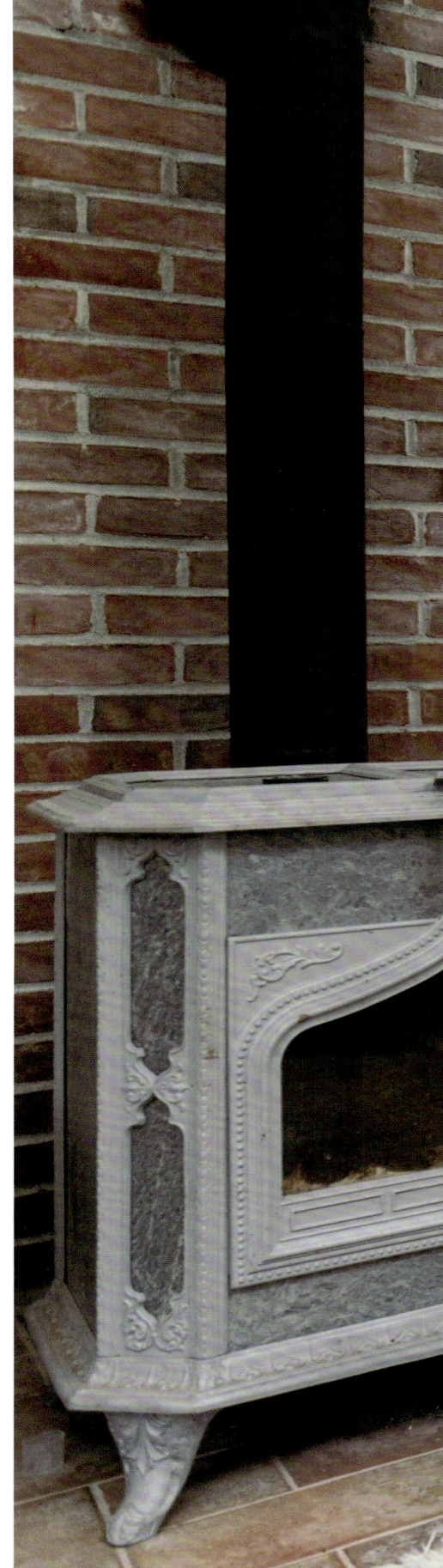

Debt Portrait #84, Waterville Valley, NH 2020

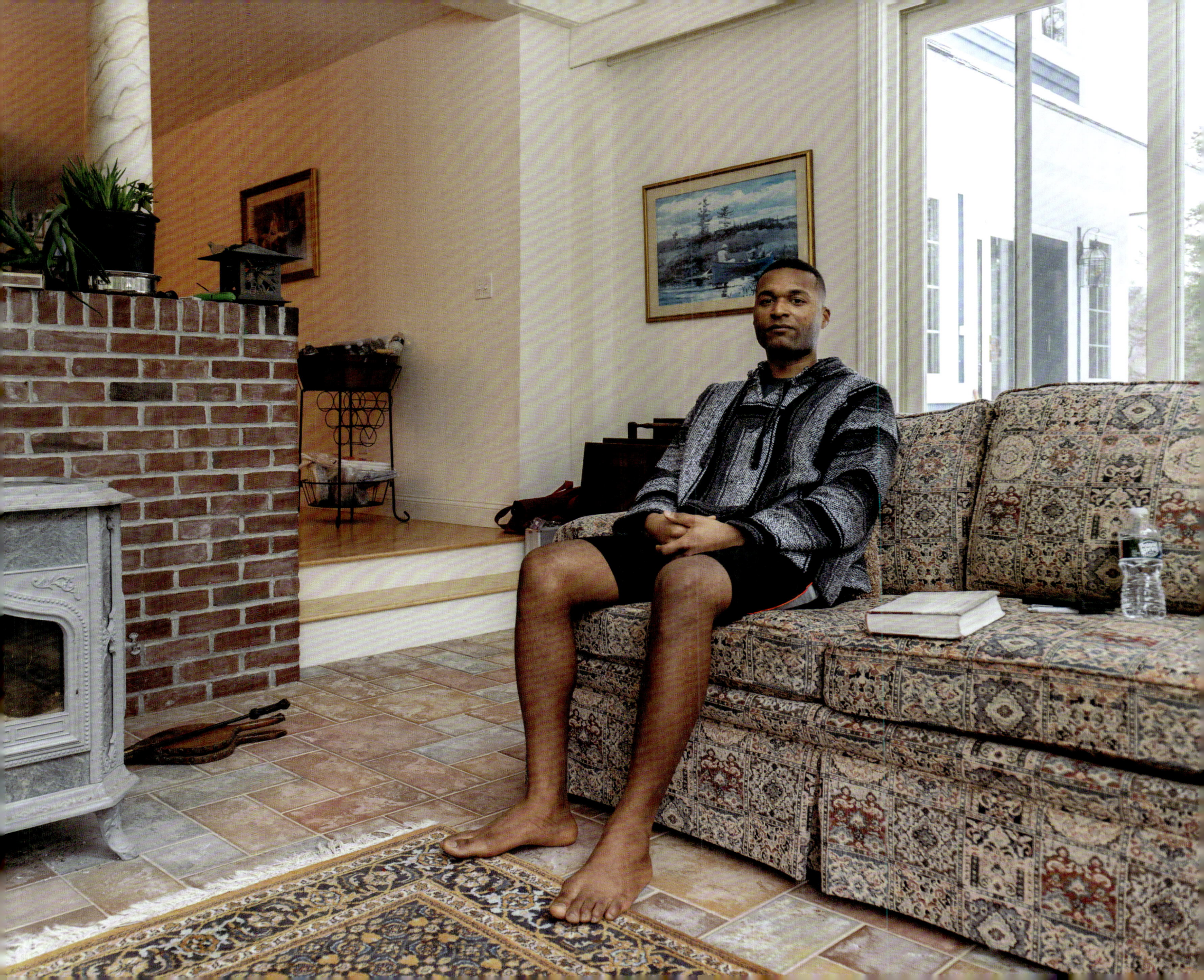

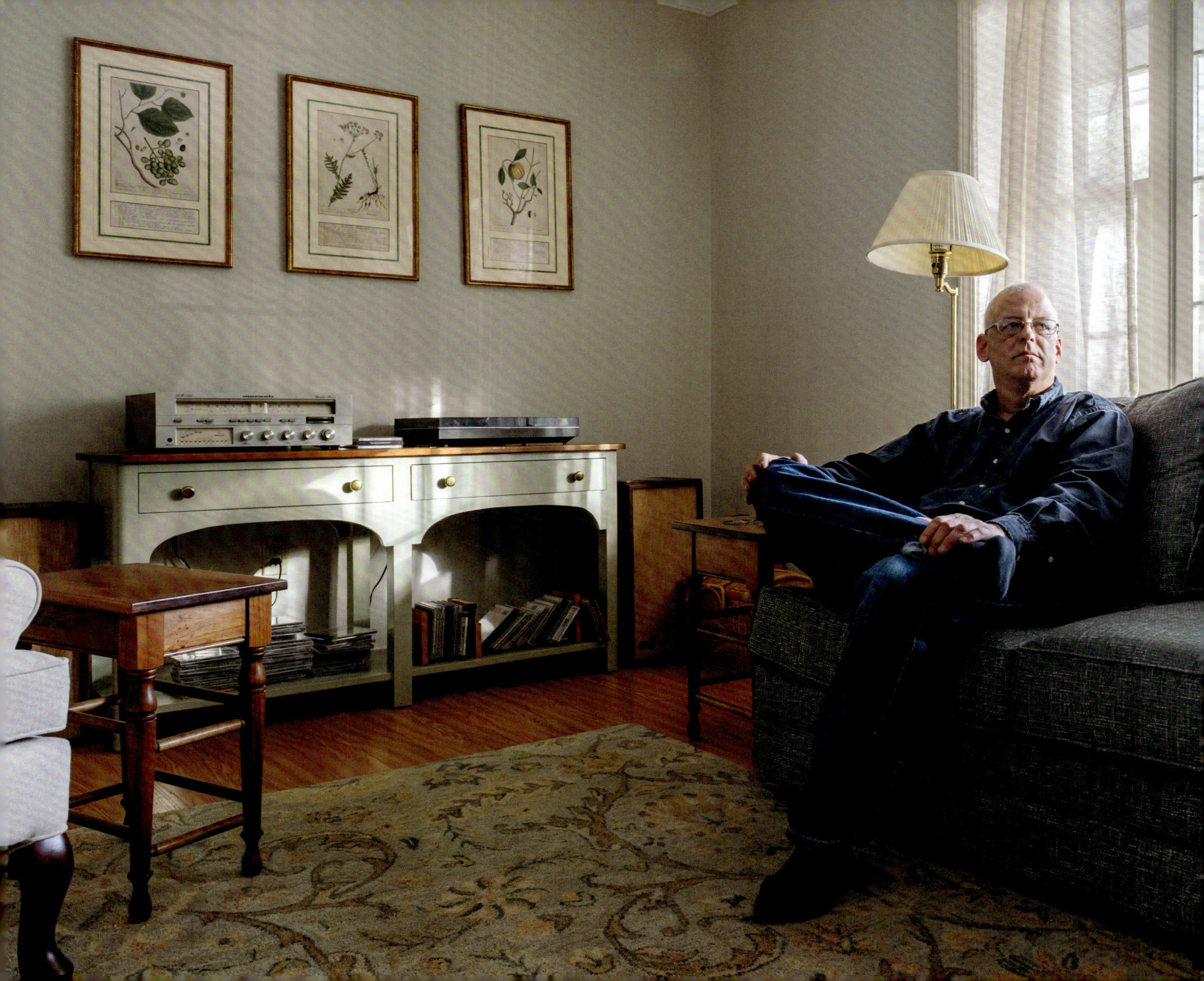

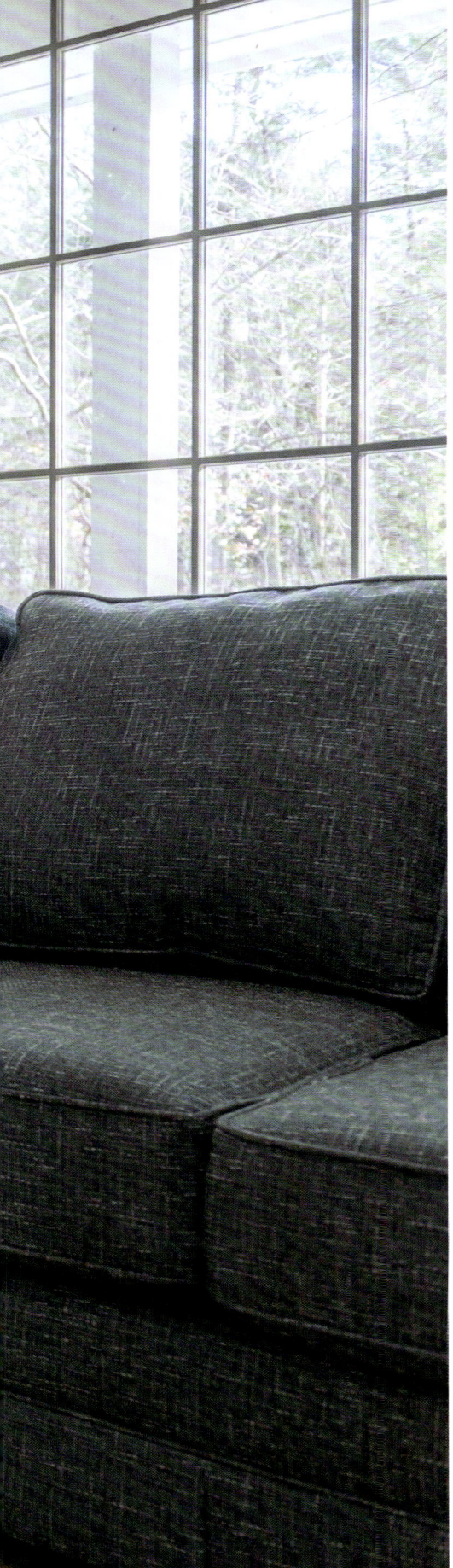

Robert Kuhl

$126,311.19 is Law School student loan debt.

- Changed jobs (just in time to be laid off in the 2000 dot.com cash. so....
- went back to school (like everyone else) and graduated into the 2009 recession!
- Like everyone else in my class, I am not practicing law (Hated it anyway).
- will have this debt for the rest of my life as I'm 56 now.
- Life goes on, Resigned to it but will make the most of the rest of my time here.

Bob

Debt Portrait #85, Bedford, NH 2020

Kahlia Shmerer
$ 209,784.89

My debt started as just student loans, for a degree I'm not really using. In an effort to feel more grounded and secure, I decided to buy a house, substantially increasing my debt. I was only able to buy the house because I lived with my mom for 7 months following an illness. I love my home, but I fear I will never pay off the whole thing.

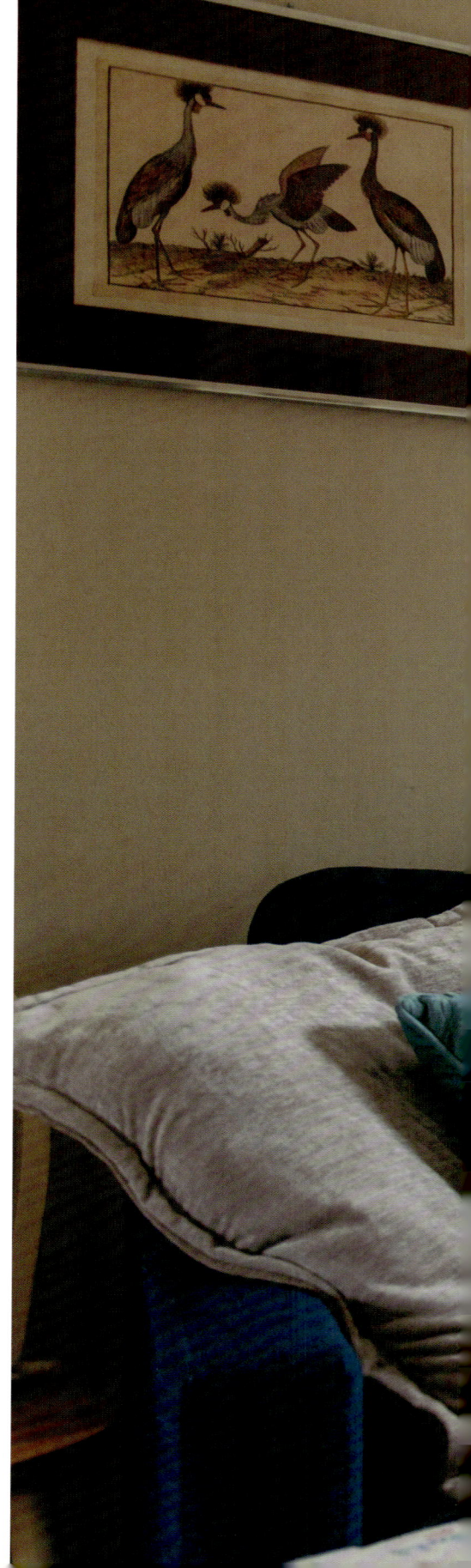

Debt Portrait #86, North Kingstown, RI 2020

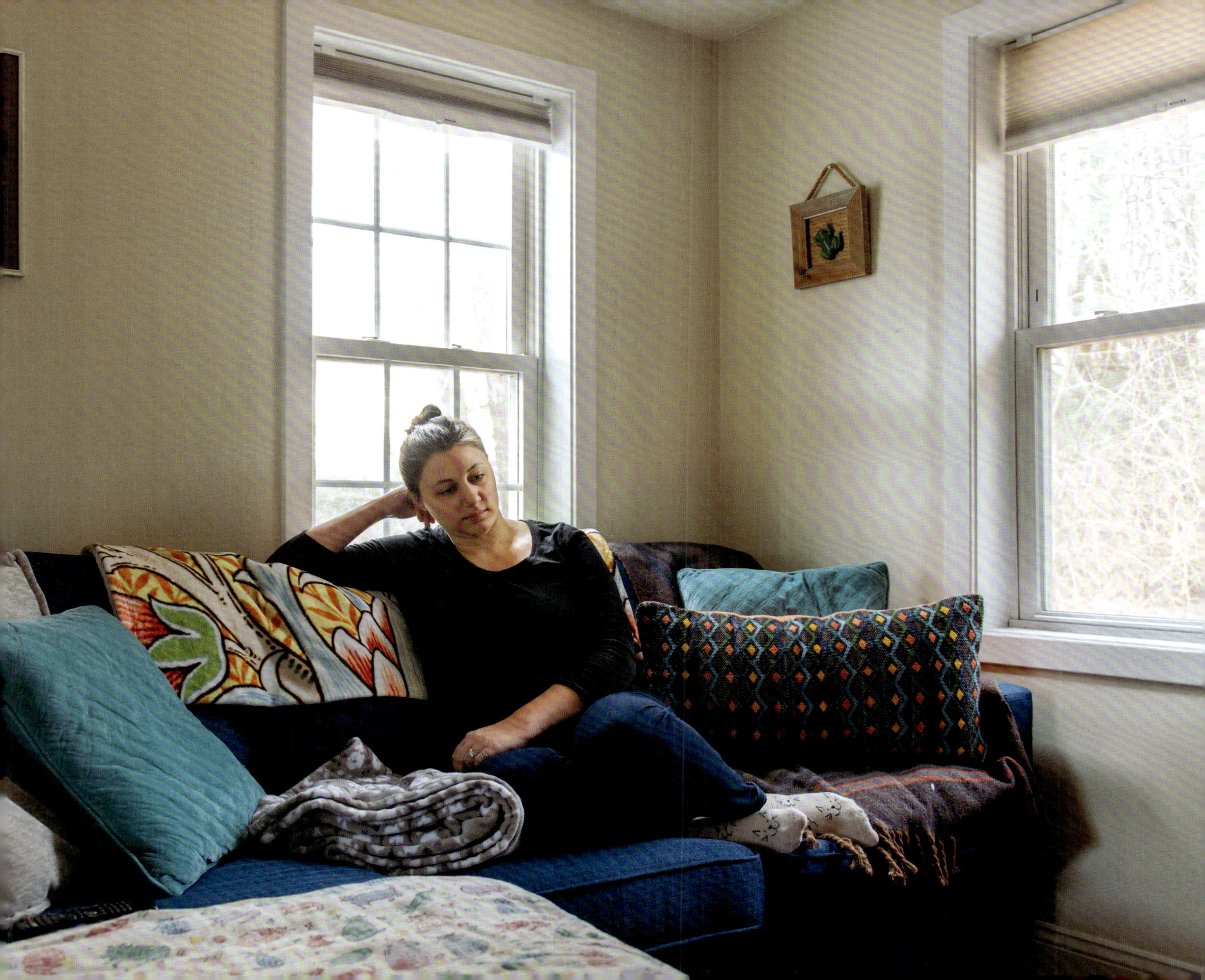

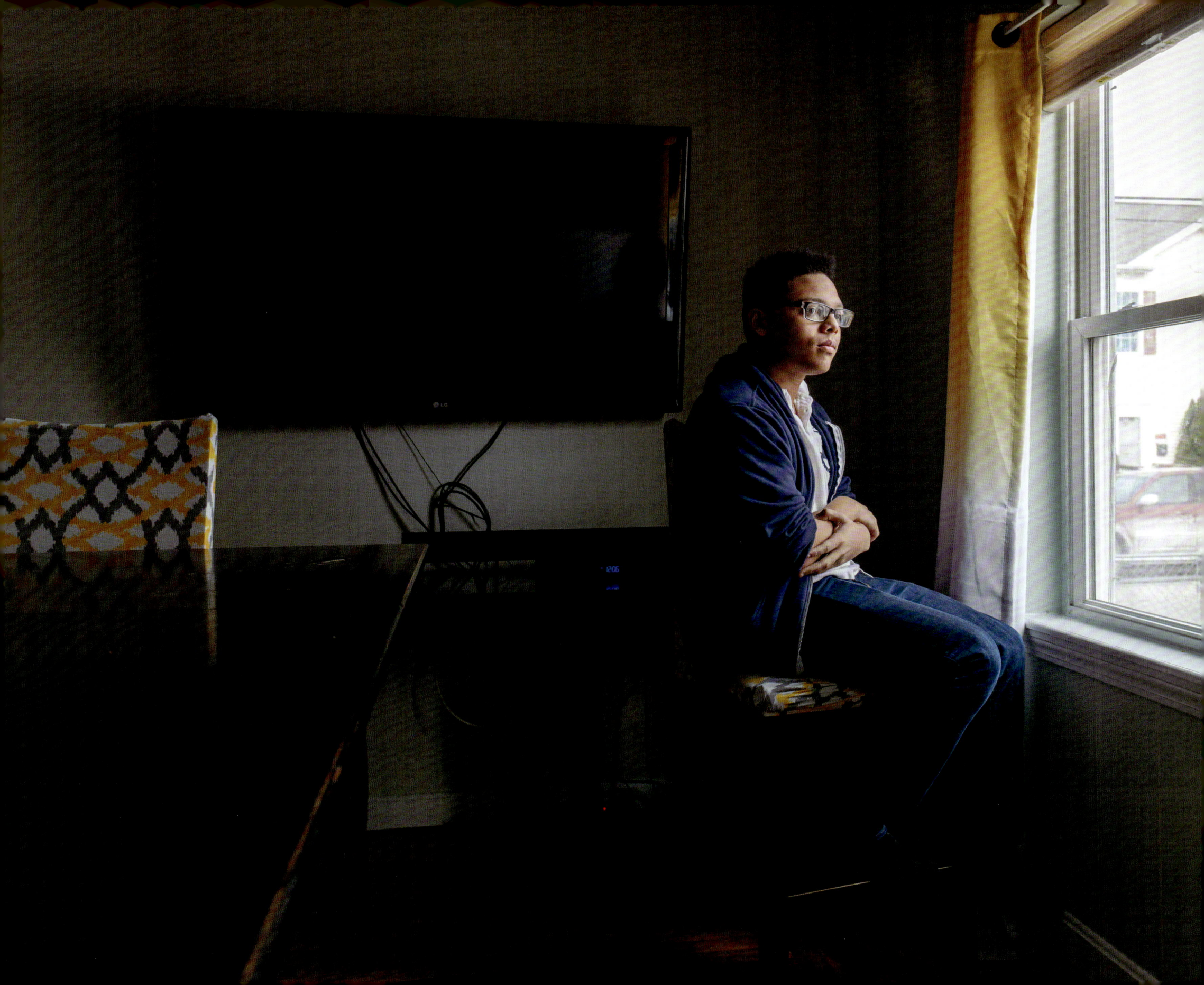

Steve Poueriet · 22

Unemployed

$ 50,000

My debt started with student loans
and then I was selected by my school
and government for extra paperwork I could
not attain. So I did not get aid/grant
money and once I graduated, I was told
I could not get my degree until I pay out
of pocket costs. Now I am job hunting with
no success and with student loans, a private
loan and out of pocket costs that I didn't
have control over.

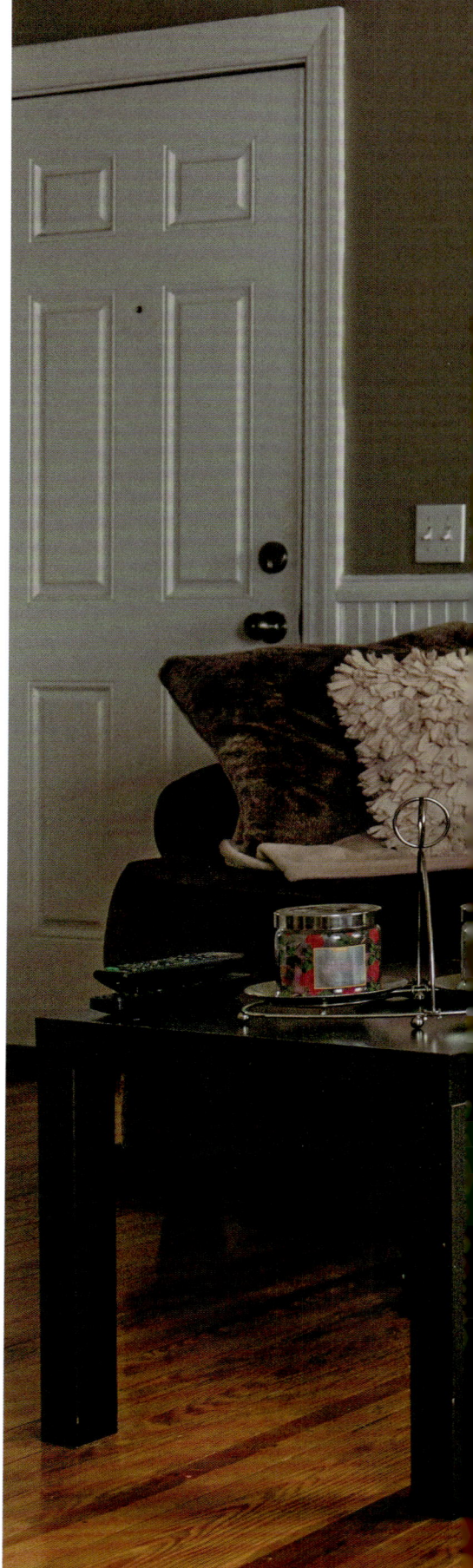

KATIE TAYLOR

$17,141.48

- STUDENT LOANS
- MEDICAL BILLS
- CAR PAYMENT

I AM STIFLED BY THE
WEIGHT OF THIS DEBT.

I JUST WANT TO BE FREE

Debt Portrait #88, Providence, RI 2020

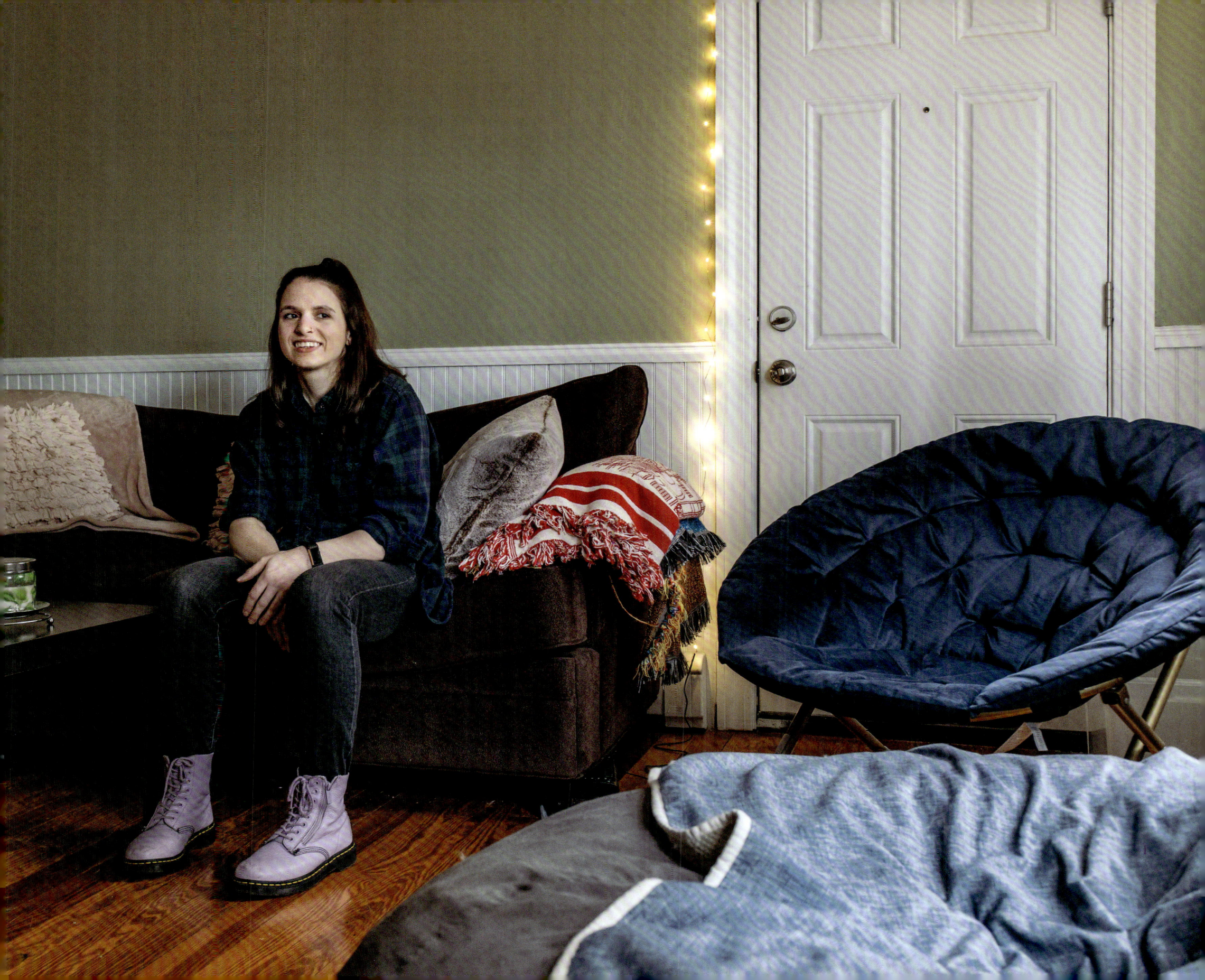

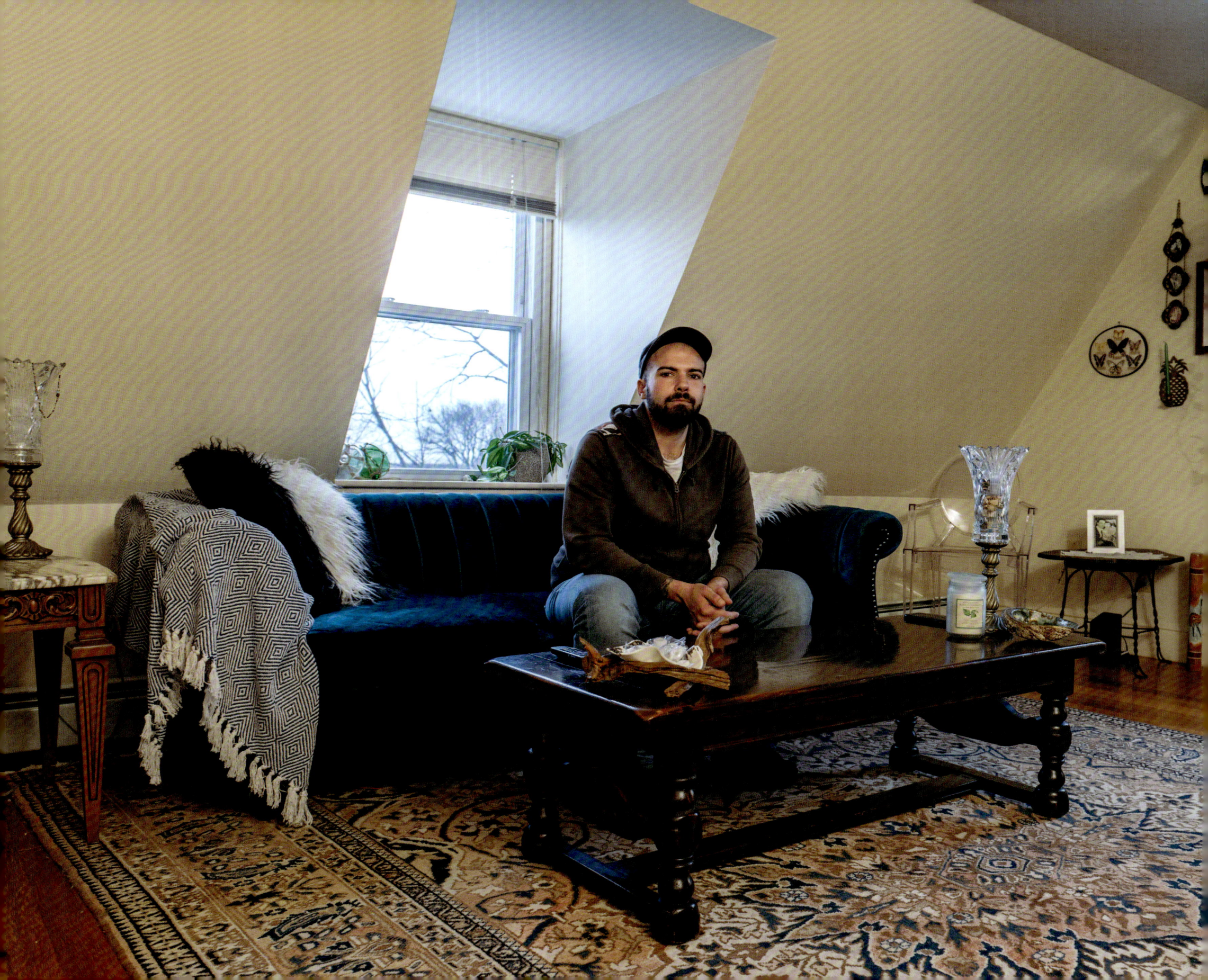

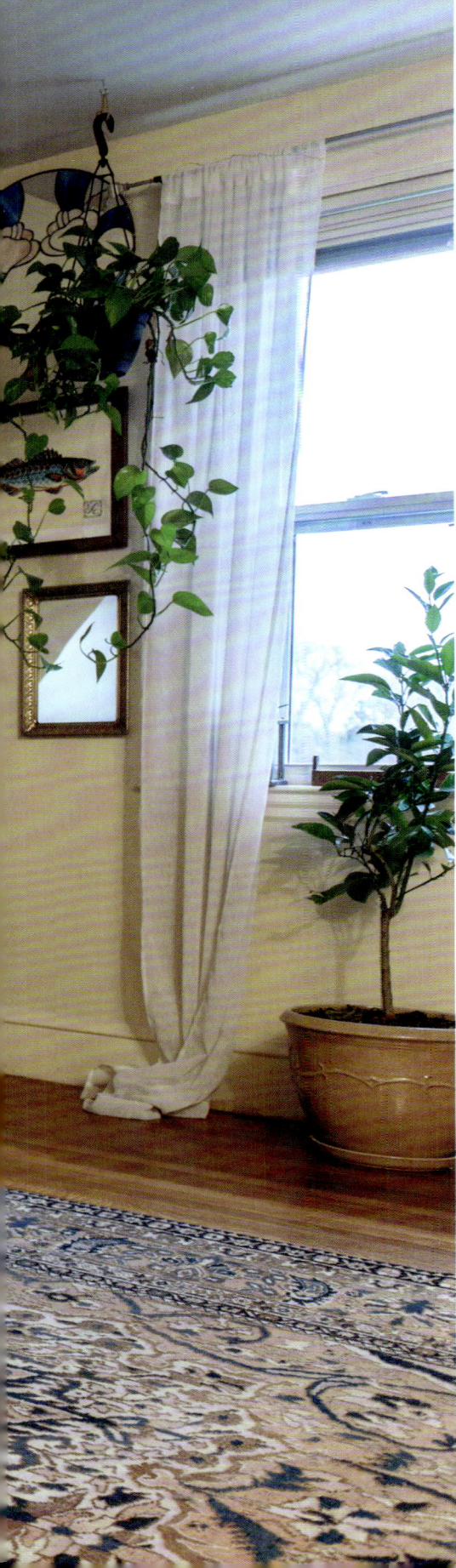

CHRISTIAN DI GERONIMO

CREDIT CARDS - $6,000
CULINARY SCHOOL - $15,000
COLLEGE - $45,000

$66,000 :-

Debt Portrait #89, Warwick, RI 2020

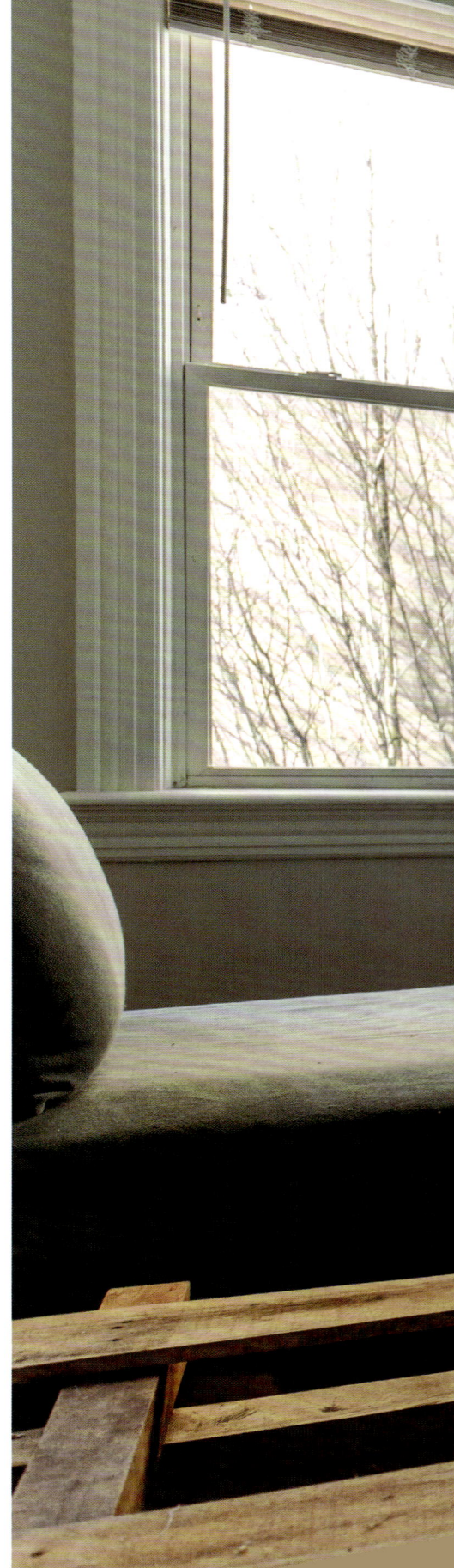

Spencer O'Neill
~100k
Software Quality Assurance Tester
My parents were awful with
budgeting so I'm not surprised
to be here.

I've done everything asked of me
(school, job, family) yet I feel
like I will never escape this
debt.

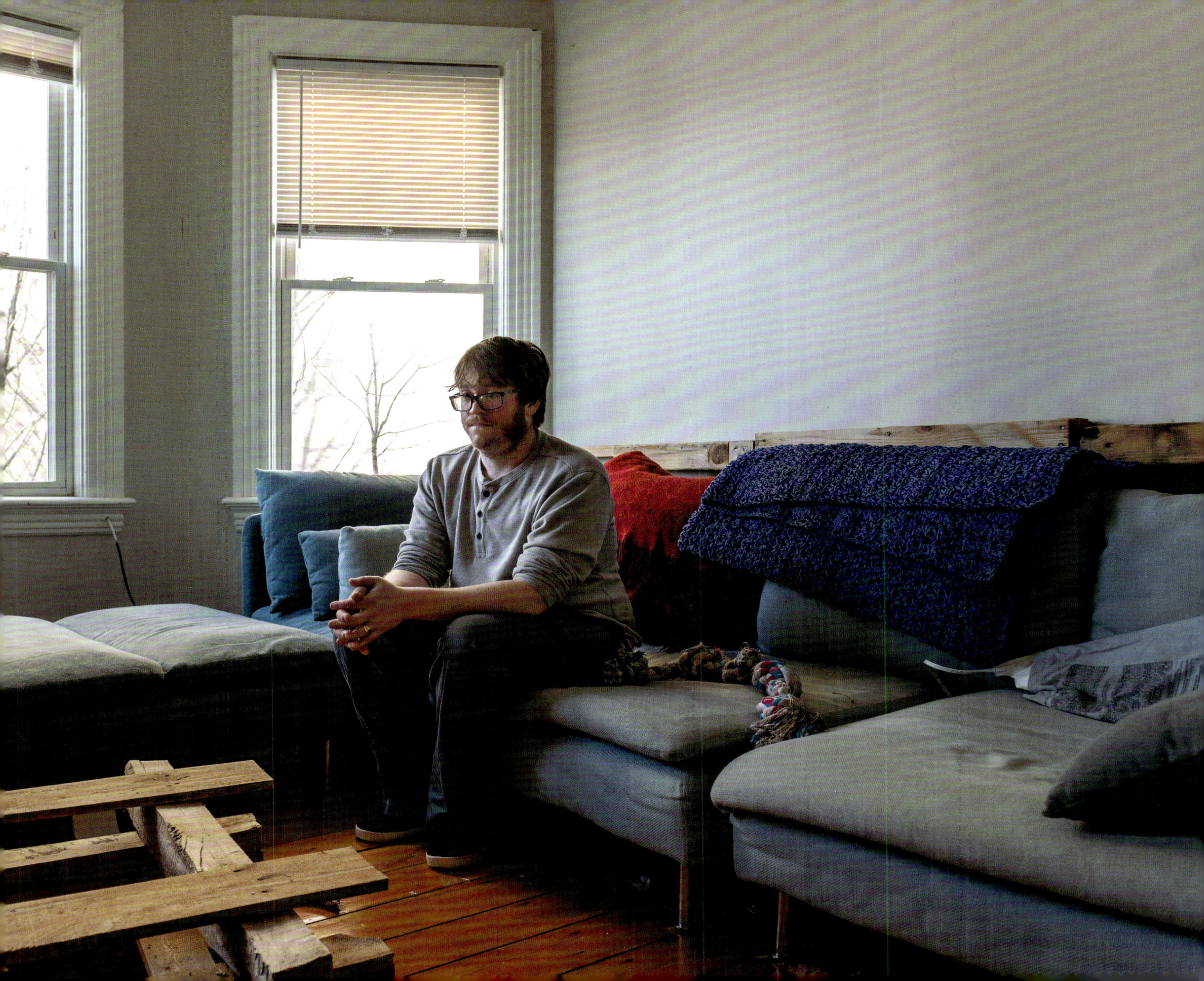

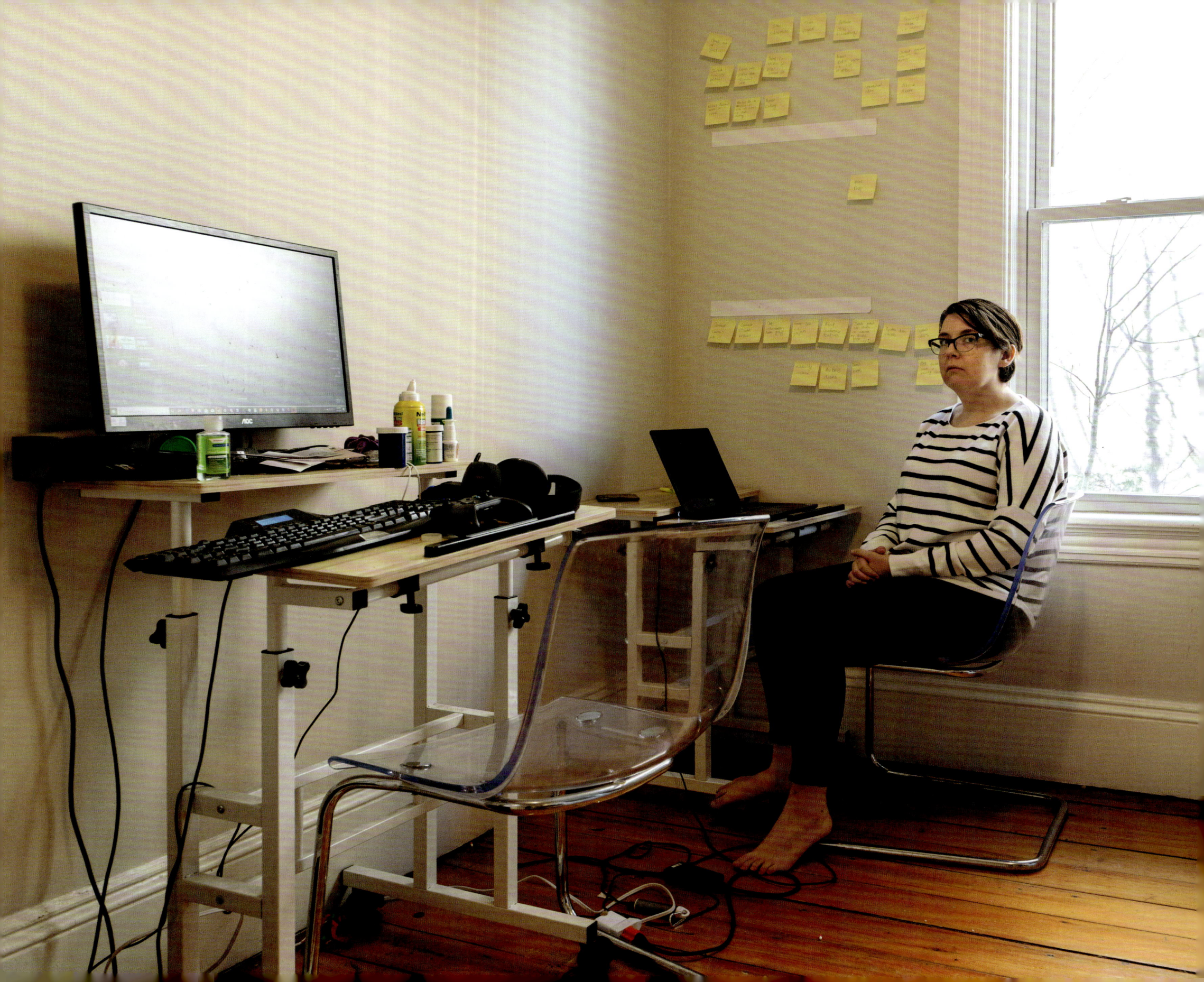

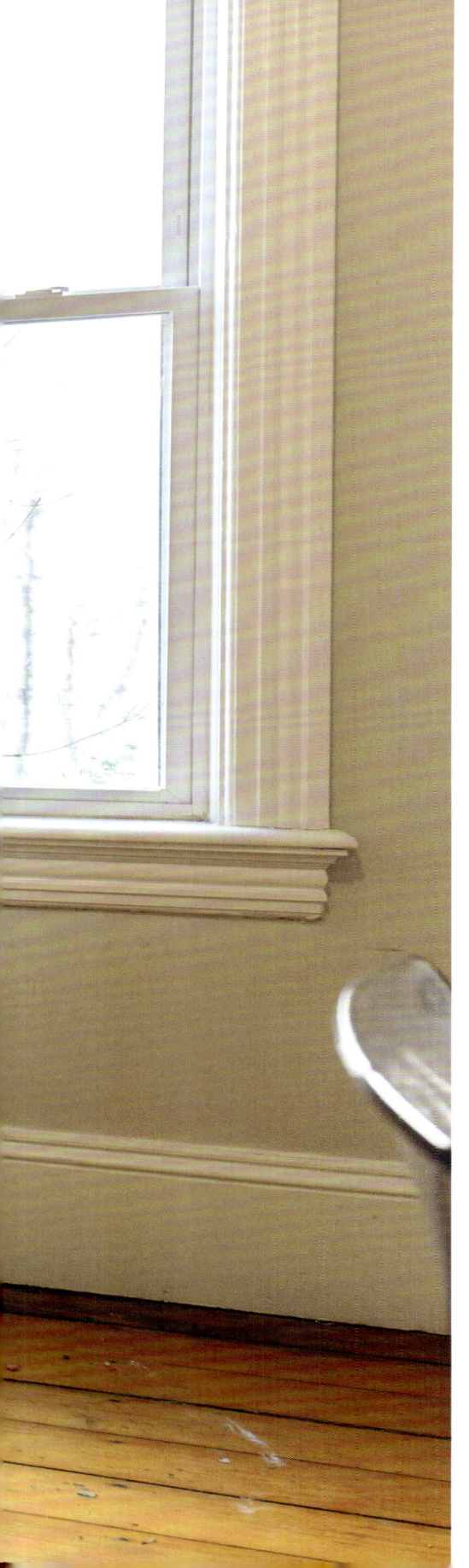

ALISON ATHEY
~$126,000

MY DEBT BUILT UP
WHEN I WAS IN GRAD
SCHOOL. I TOOK LOANS
SO I COULD DO UNPAID
WORK WITH SUICIDAL
ADULTS + KIDS. MY
CAREER PROSPECTS ARE
GOOD NOW, BUT I
DON'T KNOW IF I
WILL EVER MAKE IT
OUT OF THIS HOLE.

Debt Portrait #91, Providence, RI 2020

Jennifer Skinder
Administrator: Graduate Arts Education

$ 232,648.86   mortgage
$ 31,433.12   student loans
$ 4,148.00   credit card
$ 9,000.49   auto loan
                _____
$ 277,230.47   Total

   I took on Student loan debt when I began attending a private college in 1987. I graduated with a BA in political science + was only able to find work in the service sector. I spent a number of years working as a potter, a ceramics instructor and a baker & had to put my loans into forebearance several times. I returned to school to earn an M.A. in education + to get certified to teach art & took on more student loan debt. Bought a house, had kids, work at a "good job". I'm still paying my own loans while helping my oldest son pay his college tuition.

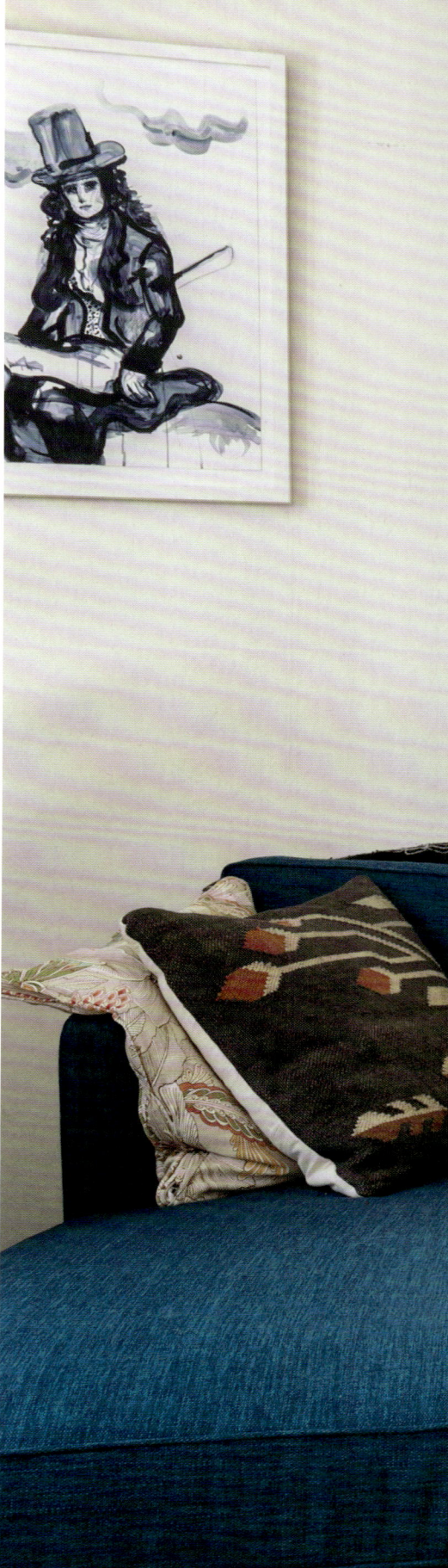

Debt Portrait #92, Montpelier, VT 2020

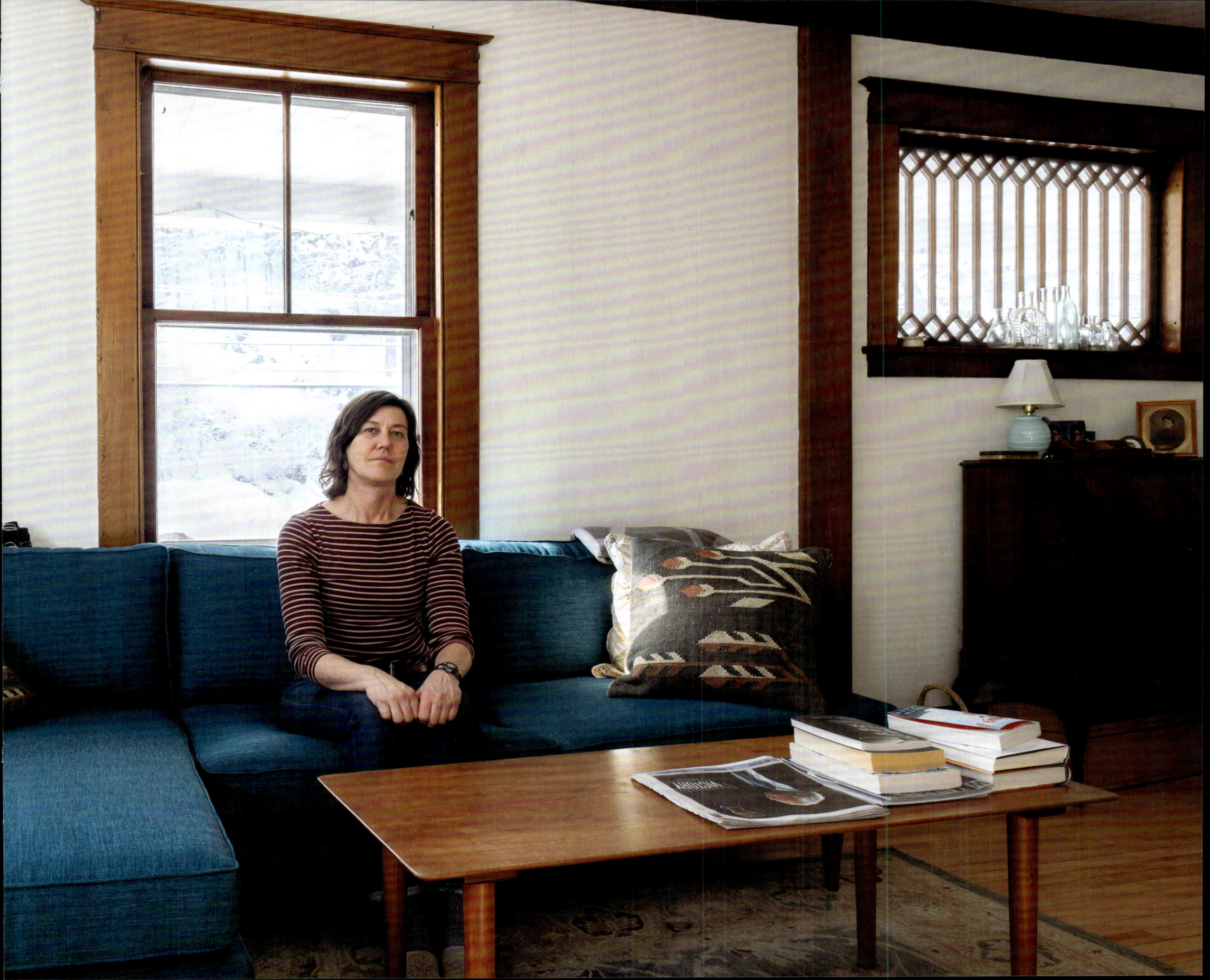

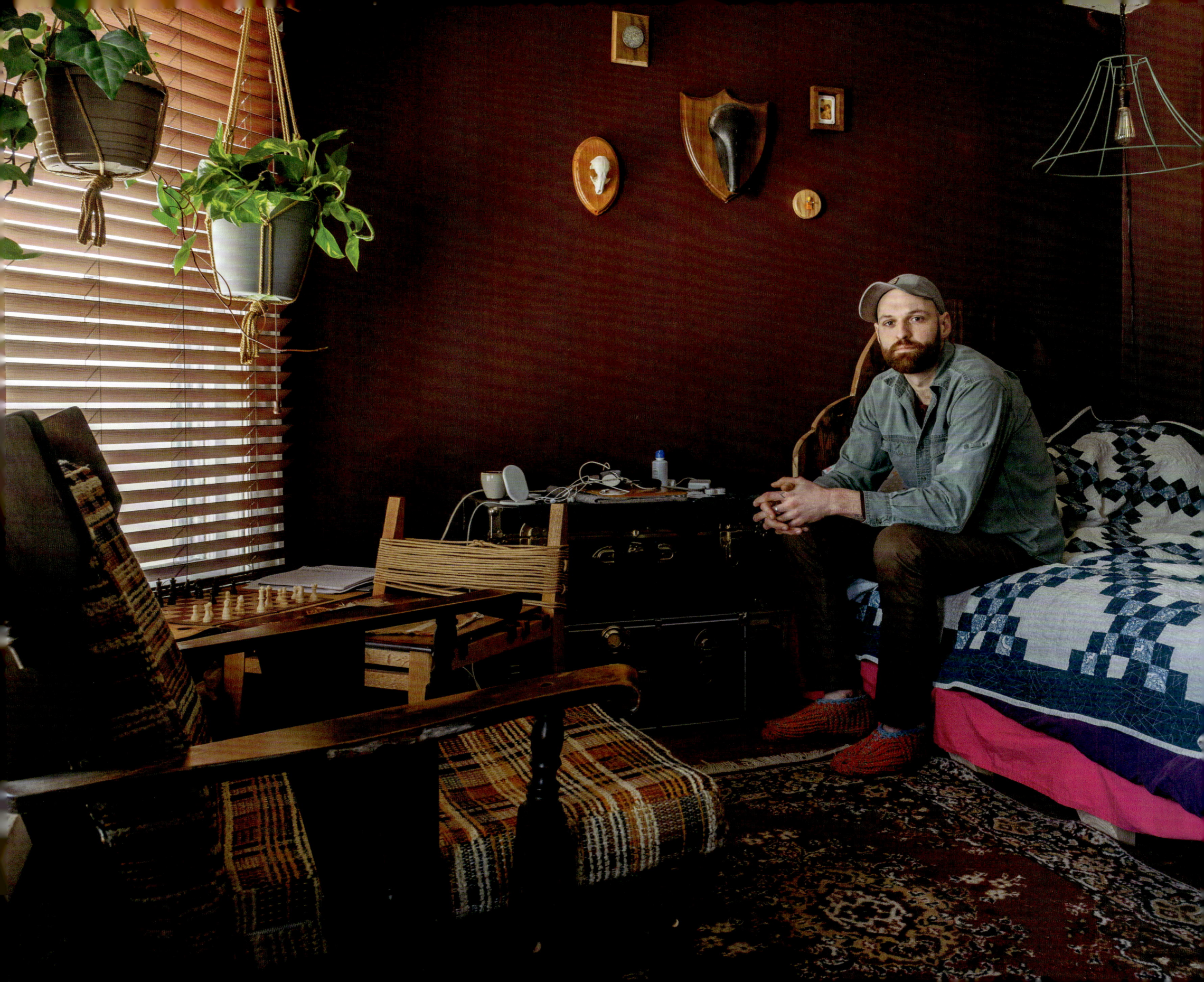

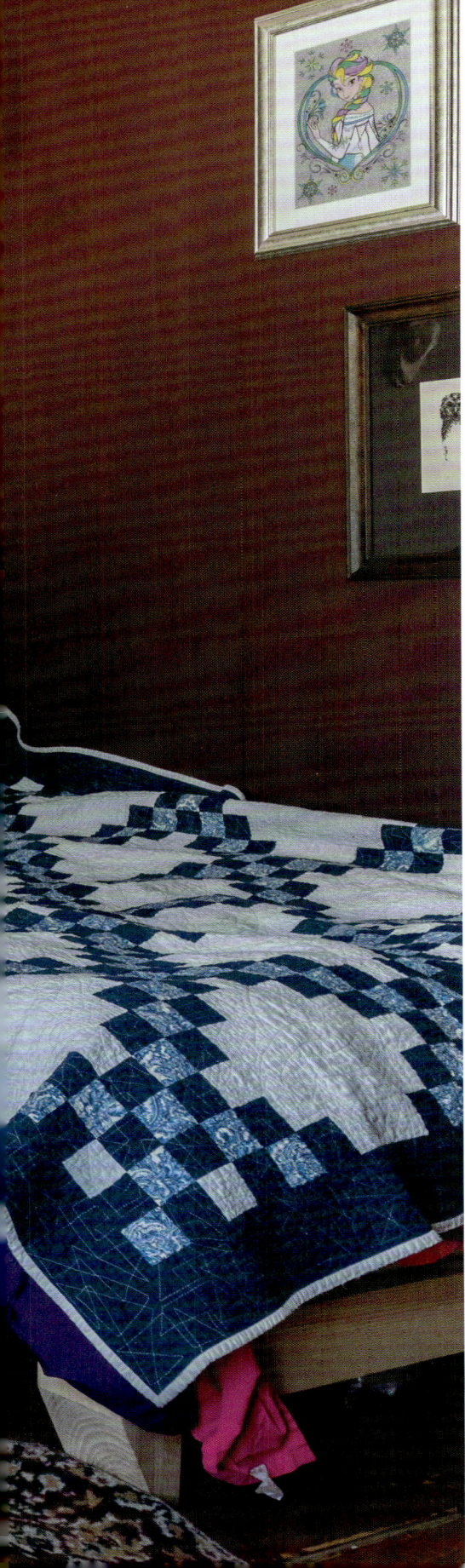

MICHAEL BADGER

$105,015.30 for a master's in creative writing. I don't feel much of anything a/b it, ambivalent, It's an exorbitant amount, it's basically not going to go anywhere so I've blocked it out.

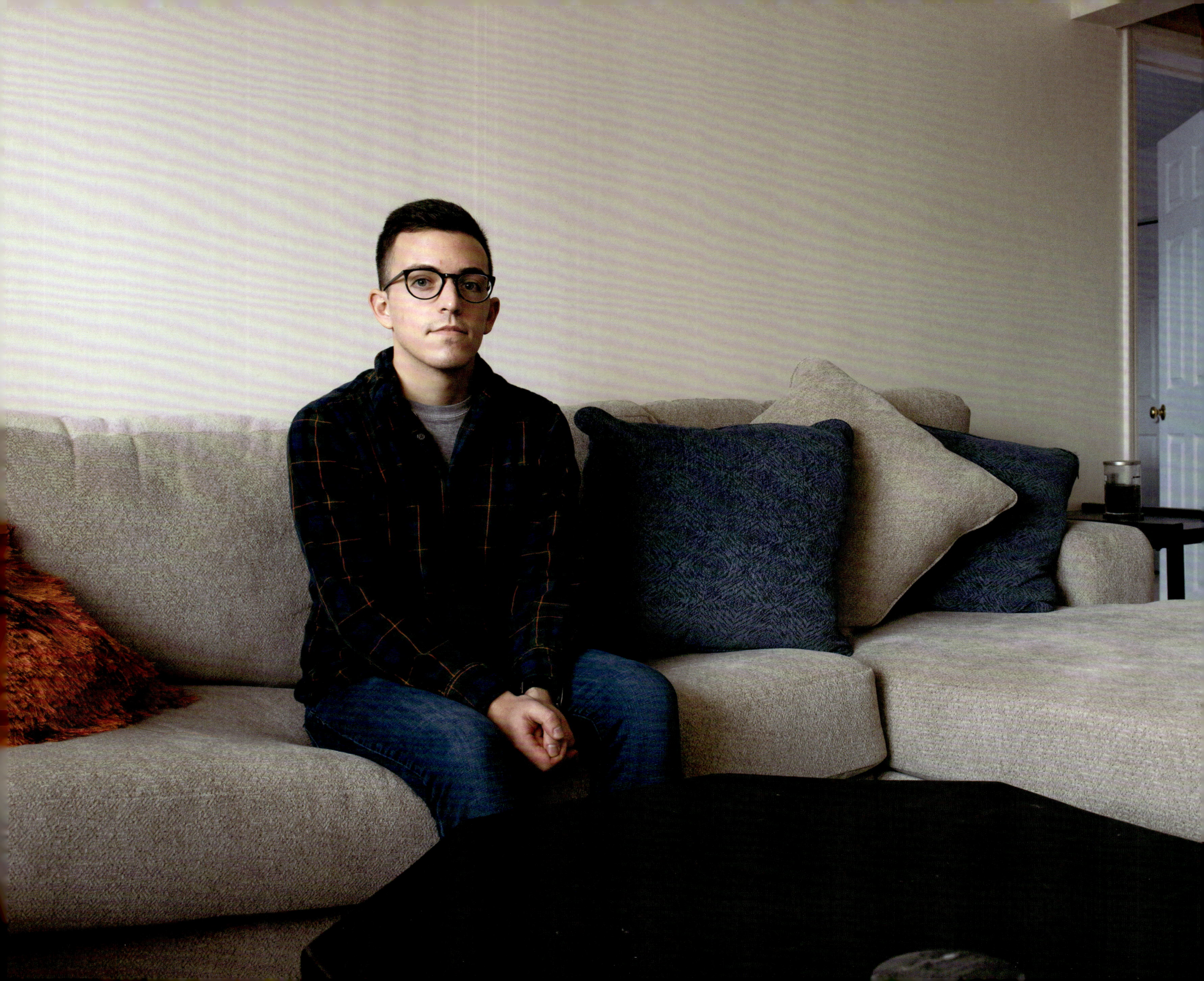

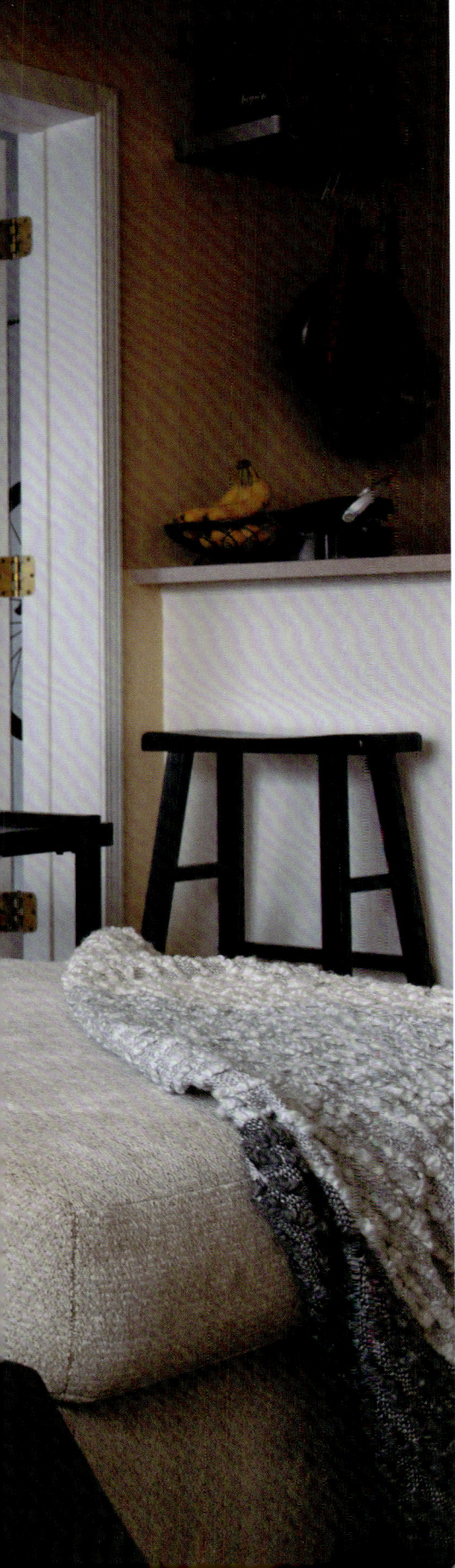

Ian McHale

$ 152,000

Clinical Research Coordinator

I graduated College with $150,000 in Student loans and after completing my Master of Public Health I had a total of $170,000. In the last two years I have been able to pay off $20,000 of my loans, but with high interest rates the total keeps going up. I work hard to Save up money, but most of my income goes to my student loans.

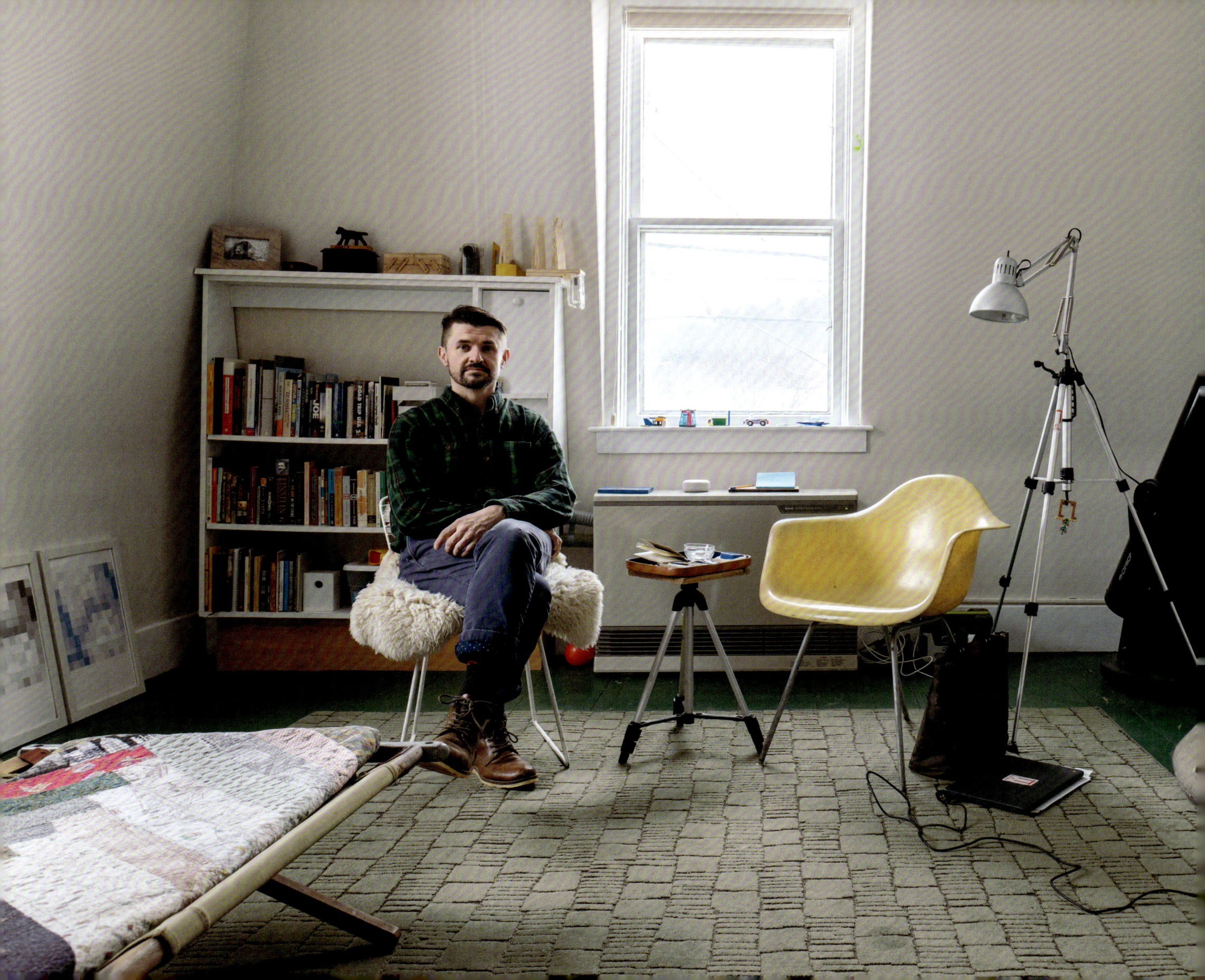

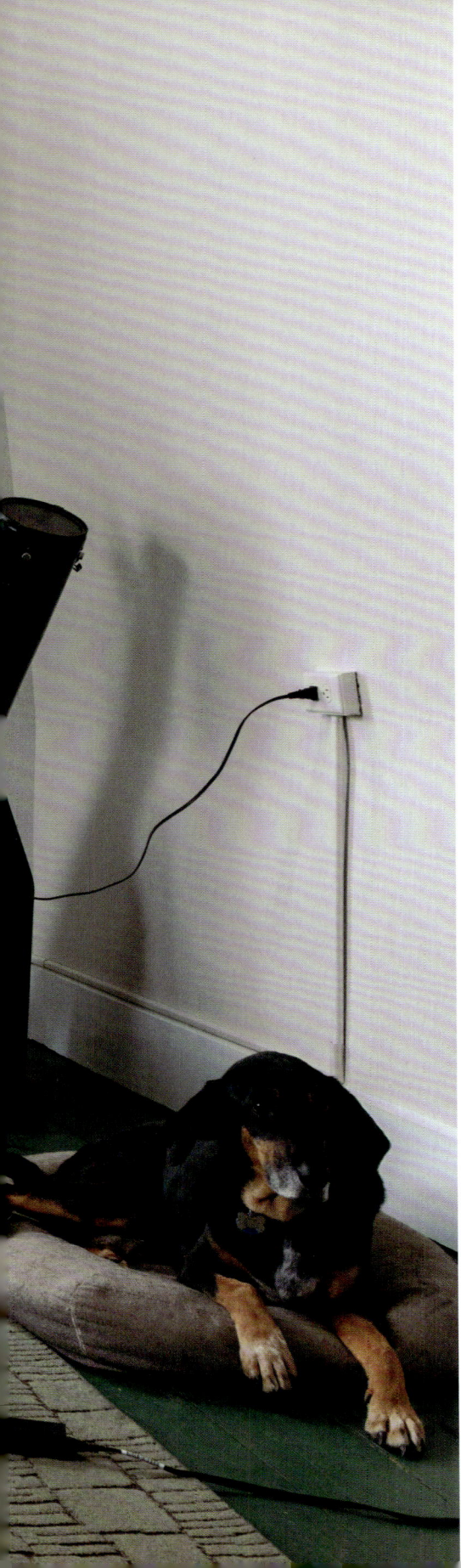

Michael Zebrowski

$228,150

From a graduate degree, a bad real estate venture, divorce, unemployment and poor self employed business practice.

Debt Portrait #95, Johnson, VT 2020

Harlan Mack

1) Student Loans 30K paid off ~~█~~ in 2019

2) 1st Mortgage debt 58K 15yr fixed (9 yrs ago)
on the backside of that equity loan and
really just paying down the principle @ a good
pace...

3) 2nd Mortgage with my ~~partner~~ ^{wife} roughly 125K
remaining.

— At this point I'm feeling pretty at ease about
my debt. I ~~am~~ an artist with a full time
job in my field. I have two houses in Vermont
the state of my birth. Things seem to be
moving along on schedule and hopefully the
choices I made around ~~debt~~ acruing debt
prove to be positive. ~~xxxxxxxxxxxx~~
when I get my debt to income ratio improved
maybe I will buy a tractor :·)

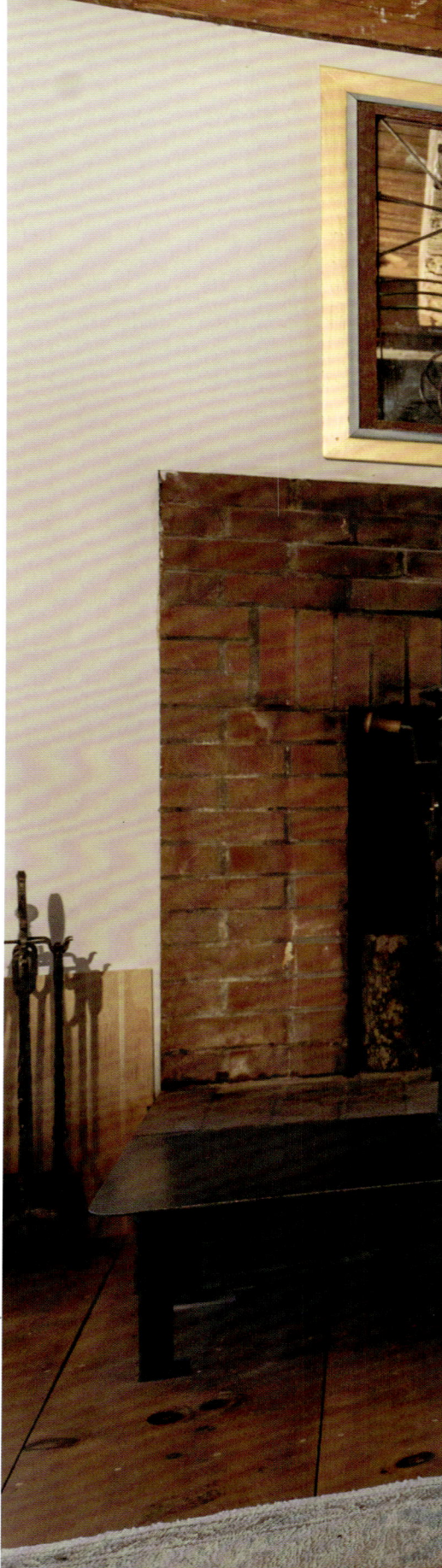

Debt Portrait #96, Johnson, VT 2020

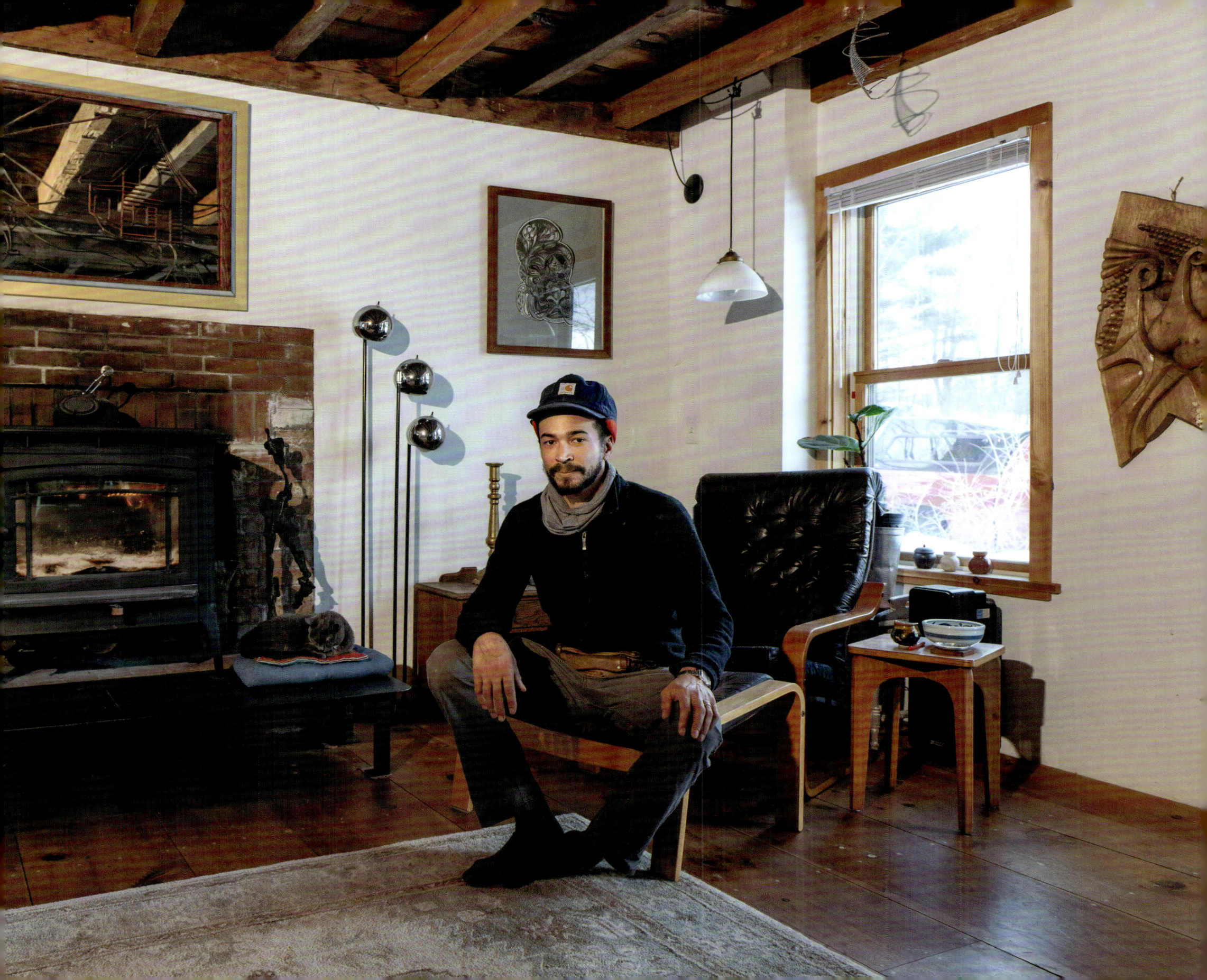

Liz Swindell

$93,000

THE High School Art Teacher.

I worked throughout my 20s and managed
to pay off $20.000+ in undergrad debt. At 30,
I longed for a new career and decided to persue
my MAT Although I was super hesitant about
the cost. I found a program that was perfect
but was terribly misled by an admissions
councelor. The "basically Free" Program
cost me $52,000. Thinking about this
still makes me upset. But the program
led to the opening of all the right doors,
including my dream job. The world works
in mysterious ways.

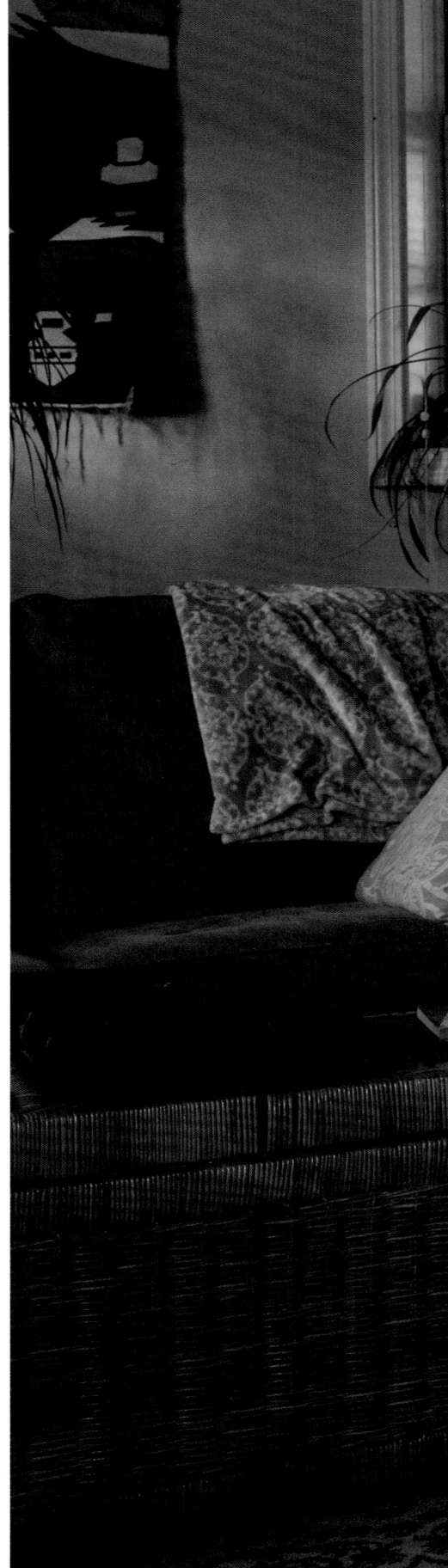

Debt Portrait #97, Waterbury, VT 2020

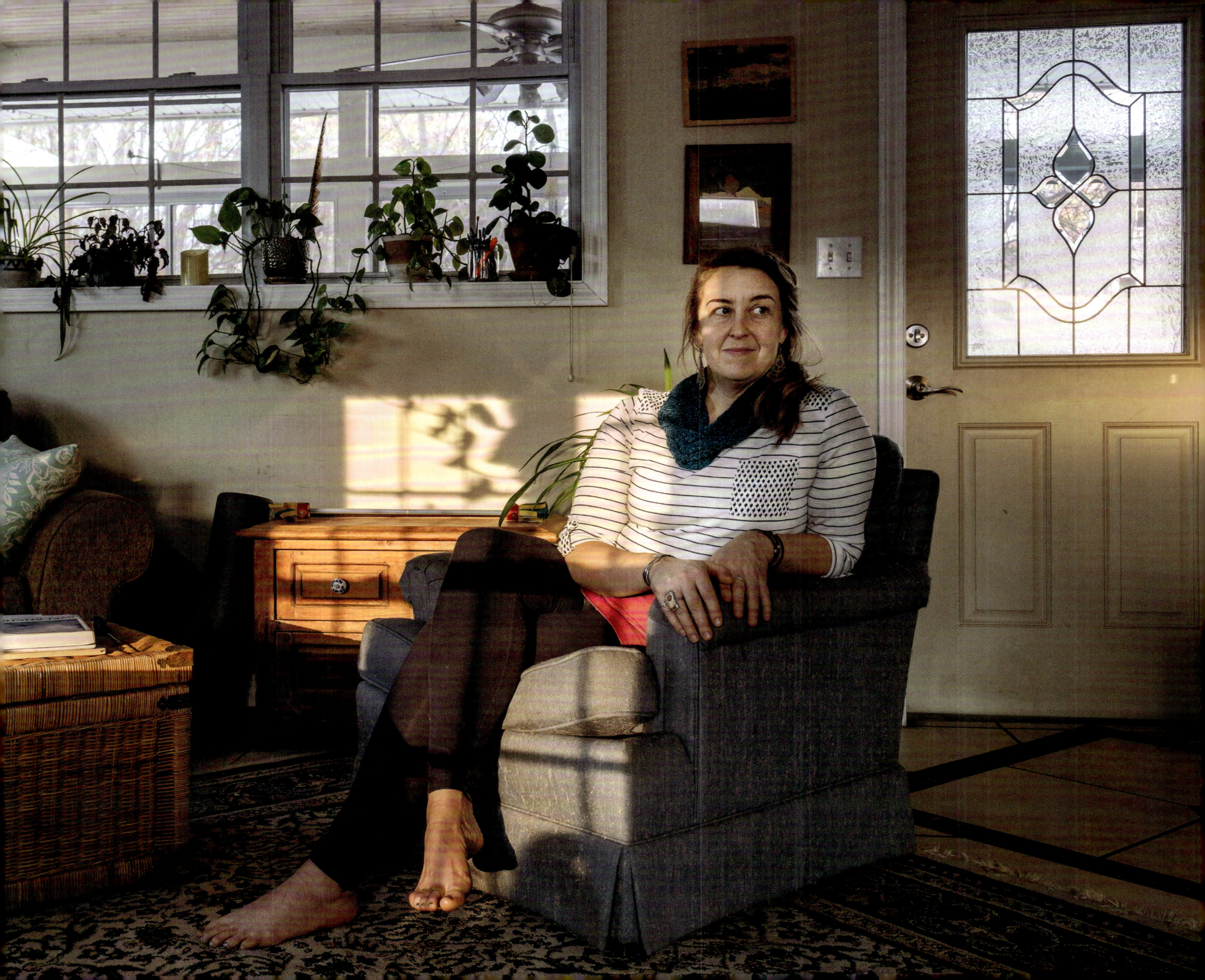

Eric Zuaro
253,000.⁰⁰

My debt consists of a mortgage,
student loans, credit card, and a car
loan. The bulk of it Is the mortgage
on my home. I am ambivalent
towards my debt, this is the
system we use in America and
for most of us if we want to
get an education, own a home,
Run a small buisness, or drive a
Reliable vehicle we will go into
debt for it and thats just how it is.

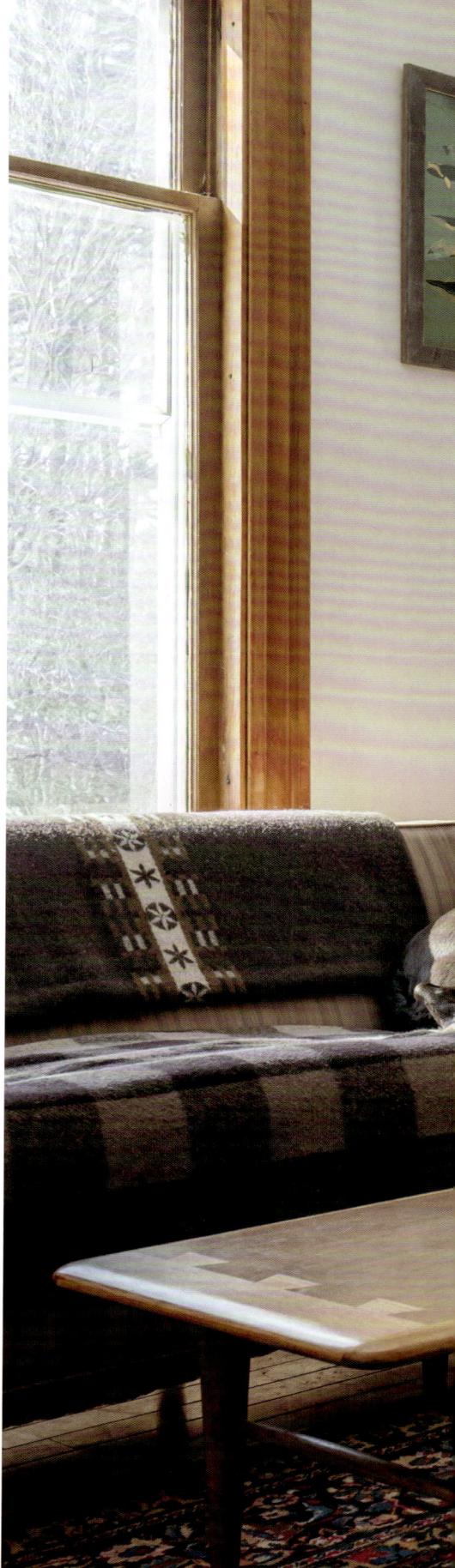

Debt Portrait #98, Middlesex, VT 2020

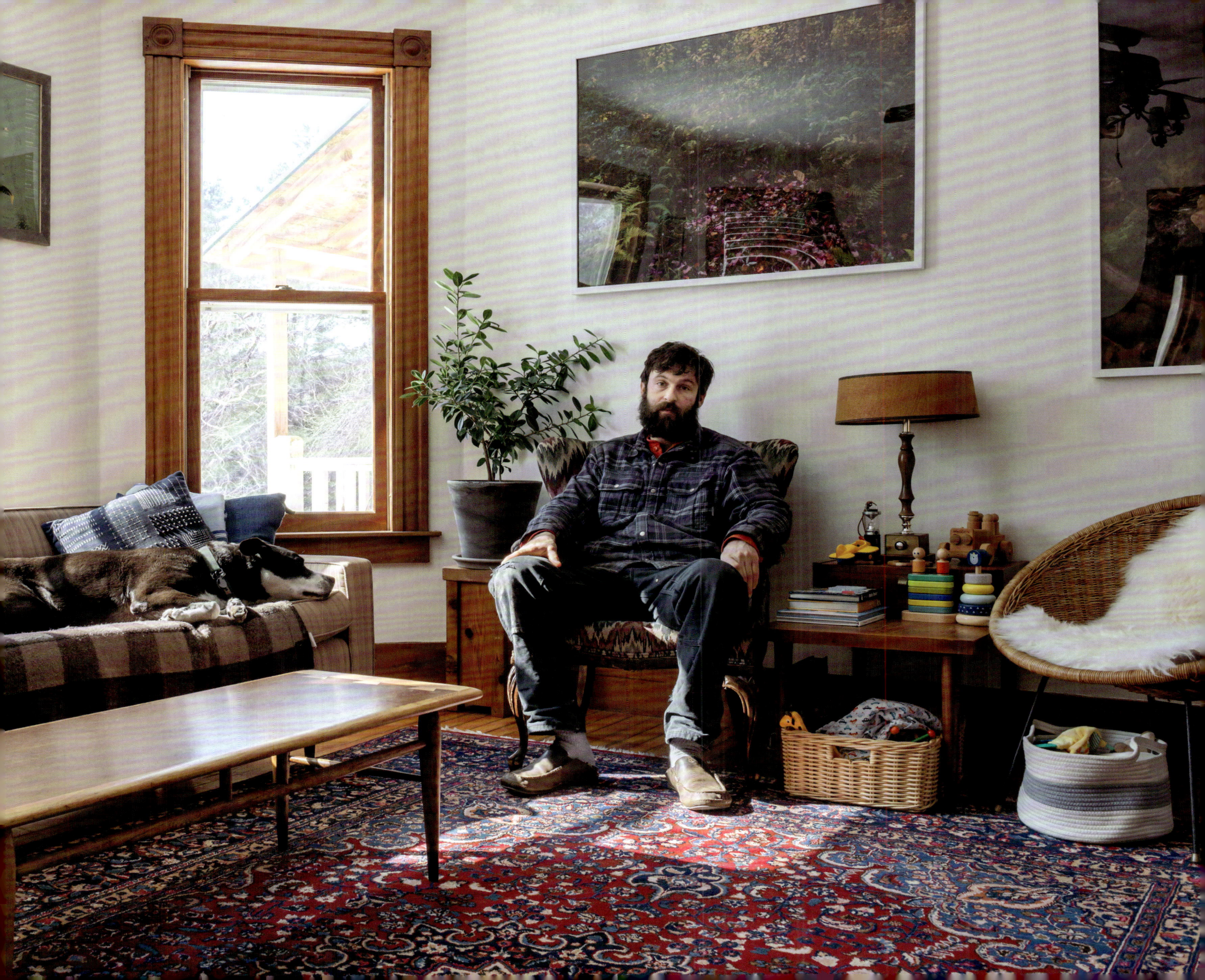

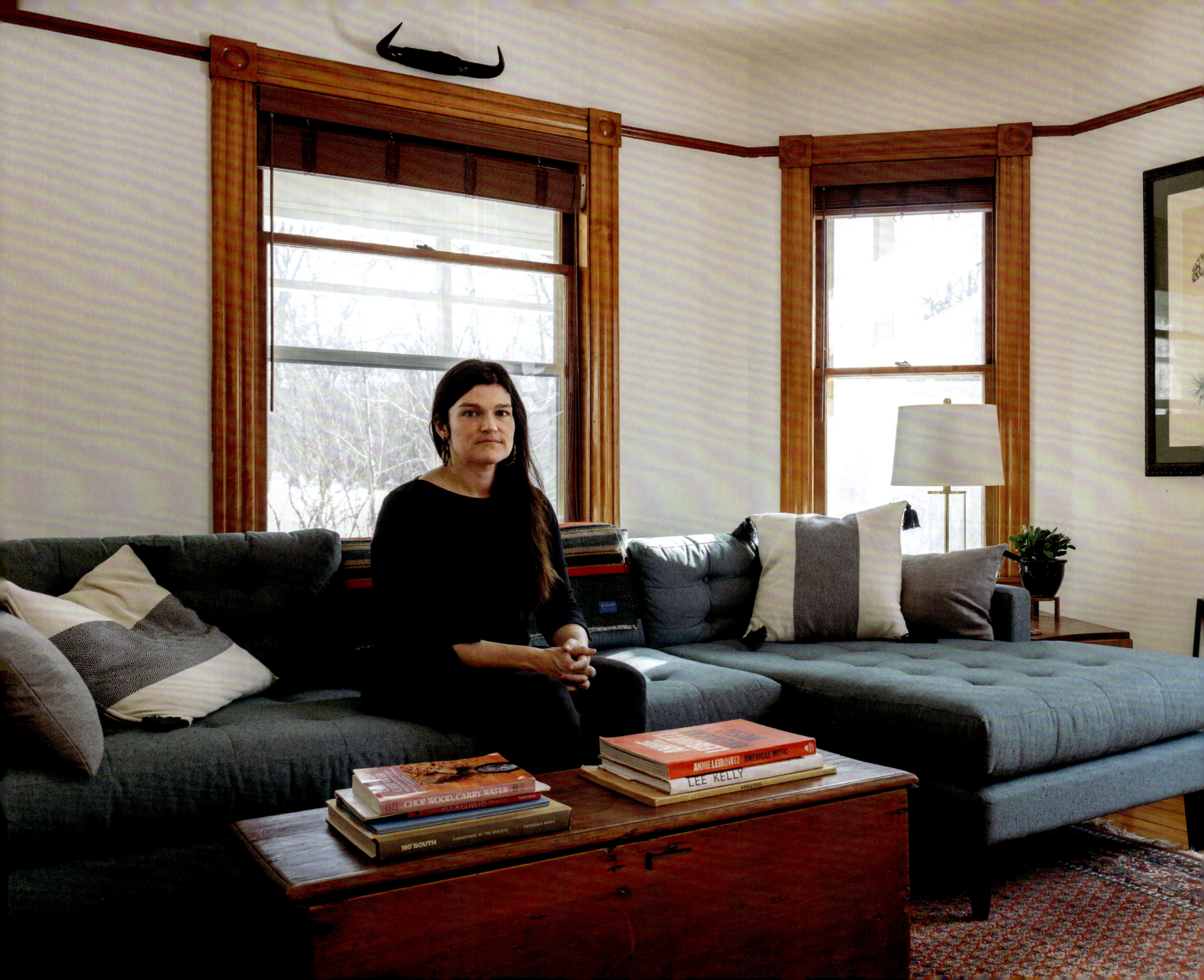

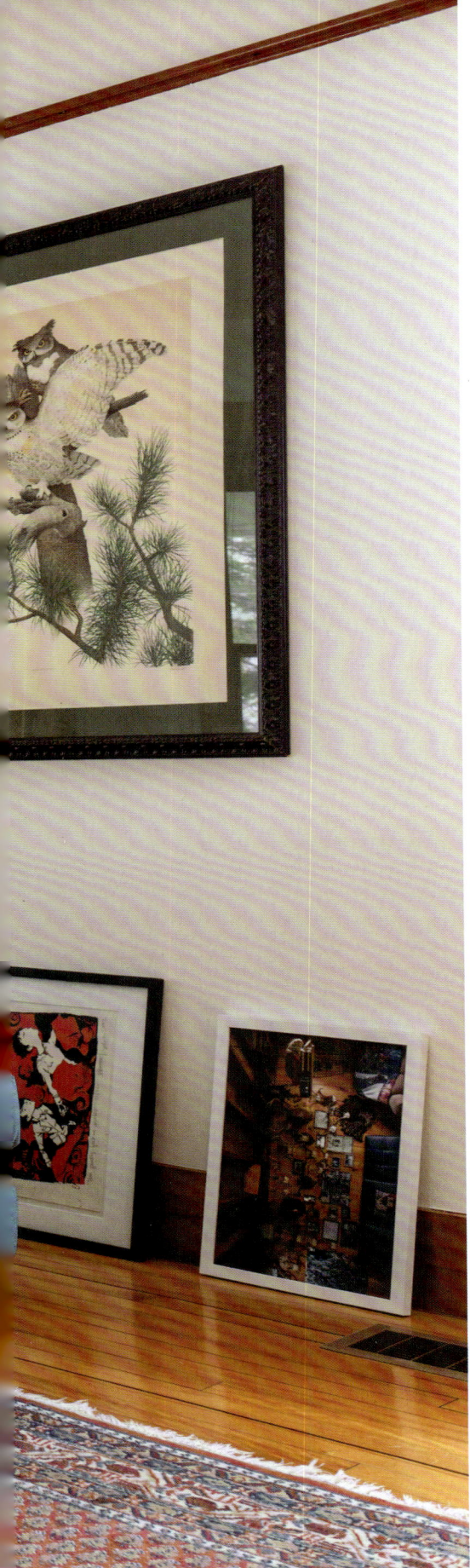

Brittany M. Powell
photographer / college admin / professor

$304,109.92

mortgage / student loan / car / credit card

$227,500.89 $50,912.32 $13,629.76 $2066.95

I started this project after filing bankruptcy in 2013. I spent years with no debt. All of the above was accrued in the last 5 years. After interviewing close to 100 people about their debts, I have a totally different perspective about it. It doesn't keep me up at night; though I realize it's a precarious relationship and things can change in an instant. I wish our economy functioned differently but if you can't beat them, join them I guess.

Debt Portrait #99, Middlesex, VT 2020

RESOURCES

ONLINE RESOURCES

The Debt Collective (debtcollective.org) leverages collective power by offering debtors a shared platform for direct action.

The New Economy Project (www.neweconomynyc.org) works with community groups to build a new economy that works for all, based on principles of cooperation, democracy, equity, racial justice, and ecological sustainability.

Americans for Financial Reform (ourfinancialsecurity.org) is a nonpartisan, nonprofit coalition working to lay the foundation for a strong, stable, and ethical financial system.

Strike Debt (strikedebt.org), no longer active, was a nationwide movement of debt resisters fighting for economic justice and democratic freedom. Resources are still available on its site, including the Debt Resistors Operation Manual.

Rolling Jubilee (rollingjubilee.org) was a Strike Debt project that bought debt for pennies on the dollar, but instead of collecting it, abolished it.

Mapping Student Debt (mappingstudentdebt.org) have maps that show how borrowing for college affects the nation, your city, and even your neighborhood, giving a new perspective on the way in which student debt relates to economic inequality.

BOOKS

Debt: The First 5,000 Years, by David Graeber. New York: Melville House, October 2014.

Payback: Debt and the Shadow Side of Wealth, by Margaret Atwood. Canada: House of Anansi Press, September 2019.

Democracy May Not Exist, But We'll Miss It When It's Gone, by Astra Taylor. New York: Metropolitan Books, May 2019.

The Debt Resisters' Operations Manual, by Strike Debt. PM Press, 2014

Generation Wealth, by Lauren Greenfield. Phaidon Press, May 2017.

Rich and Poor, by Jim Goldberg. Steidl, 2014.

ACKNOWLEDGMENTS

Photographing 99 people across the United States was a much more ambitious goal than I ever realized it would be when I began this project in 2013. The most difficult stretch was the final 27 portraits, which were photographed in the last year, 2019 into 2020. I'd like to thank my husband, Eric Zuaro, for his unwavering support and patience in completing this huge project in the first year of our son's life, while also balancing our full-time (plus) jobs, and an old creaky farmhouse in Vermont that needs a lot of work.

I am lucky to have a family that operates with integrity and support. Thank you to my sister, Bonnie Powell, for her wonderful ideas, endless edits, and insistence that I create the project in the first place. Thank you to my mom, Linda Powell, and my dad, Michael Powell, for raising me to be stubborn and to stand up for what I believe in. Thank you to my in-laws, Joe and Debbie and Carolyn Zuaro, for countless hours of babysitting, enthusiasm, encouragement, and hosting warm family dinners spent together unwinding.

I'm grateful to my dear friend, Sara Newens, who was absolutely integral to completing this project. Thanks to her immeasurable talents as a video editor, and her generosity in sharing this project with so many people who went on to help professionally.

I want to thank my co-workers and friends Thatiana Oliveira and Jennifer Skinder, and my boss, Danielle Dahline, for always being supportive and having my back as I trudged through the difficulties of balancing recent motherhood and a full-time career.

Thank you to the many people who donated to my Kickstarter campaign in 2014—this project could never have grown and been developed into what it is today without your generosity and support.

Thank you to my publishing team at West Margin Press, specifically Jennifer Newens, for taking a chance on my project and being enthusiastic about it from day one.

Most importantly, thank you to the many, many people who volunteered and participated in this project as subjects. Thank you for your bravery and willingness to invite me into your homes and share so many of your personal stories and experiences with me. Without you taking the chance to share publicly about a very stigmatized subject, this book would never been made, and the difficult conversations so necessary to change that narrative wouldn't be possible.

Brittany M. Powell is a photographer, multimedia artist, and educator working in central Vermont. She spent more than a decade as a freelance documentary and editorial photographer in San Francisco, CA, before moving to New England. Her work focuses on income inequality, identity, and class divide across America.

Brittany has exhibited work at the ICP Museum in New York, Aperture Gallery in New York, SF Camerawork, Flux Factory in New York, Smack Mellon, Root Division, SOMArts, Secession Gallery, California College of the Arts, San Francisco State University, the Vermont Studio Center, Vermont College of Fine Arts, Johnson State University, and the Headlands Center for the Arts. Brittany's photographs have been published in *Politico*, the *Washington Post*, *Slate Magazine*, *Fast Company*, *Refinery29*, *Featureshoot*, *Hyperallergic*, *USA Today*, the *Huffington Post*, *Marie Claire*, *National Geographic*, the *San Francisco Chronicle*, *Yoga Journal*, and Chronicle Books, among many others.

In 2015 and 2016, Brittany was a finalist for the Dorothea Lange/Paul Taylor prize in documentary from Duke University, and was awarded fellowships from both the Vermont Studio Center and the Headlands Center for the Arts. In 2019 she was the recipient of a creation grant from the Vermont Arts Council. She is currently an Adjunct Professor of Art at Norwich University and an arts administrator at Vermont College of Fine Arts.

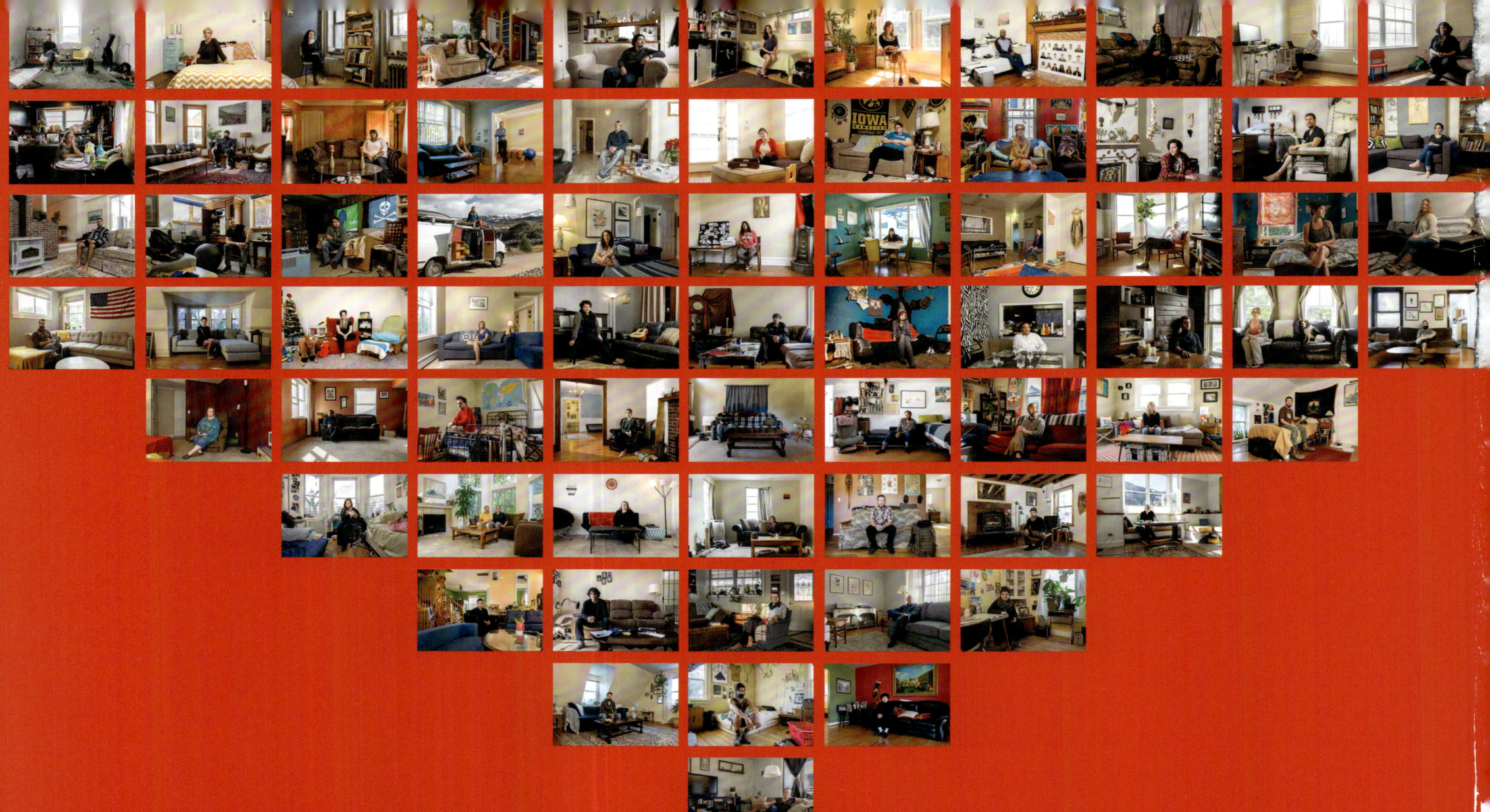